T0314930

THE WINDING ROAD
TO THE WELFARE STATE

The Princeton Economic History of the Western World

Joel Mokyr, Series Editor

A list of titles in this series appears at the back of the book.

The Winding Road to the Welfare State

Economic Insecurity and Social Welfare Policy in Britain

George R. Boyer

PRINCETON UNIVERSITY PRESS

PRINCETON AND OXFORD

Published by Princeton University Press
41 William Street, Princeton, New Jersey 08540
6 Oxford Street, Woodstock, Oxfordshire OX20 1TR

press.princeton.edu

Library of Congress Control Number: 2018937063
ISBN 978-0-691-17873-8

British Library Cataloging-in-Publication Data is available

Editorial: Joe Jackson and Samantha Nader
Production Editorial: Jenny Wolkowicki
Jacket art: L.S. Lowry, "Returning from Work," 1929.
© The Estate of L.S. Lowry. All Rights Reserved, DACS / ARS, 2018
Production: Erin Suydam
Publicity: Tayler Lord and Julia Hall
Copyeditor: Joseph Dahm

This book has been composed in Adobe Text Pro and Gotham

Printed on acid-free paper. ∞

Printed in the United States of America

10 9 8 7 6 5 4 3 2 1

*To Janet
and
In Memory of Mary MacKinnon (1959–2010)*

CONTENTS

Contrasts of economic security, involving, as they do, that, while some groups can organize their lives on a settled plan with a reasonable confidence that the plan will be carried out, others live from year to year, week to week, or even day to day, are even more fundamental than contrasts of income.

—R. H. TAWNEY, *EQUALITY*

ACKNOWLEDGMENTS

This book has been a long time in the making. Its beginnings can be traced back to the summer of 2000, when Roderick Floud and Paul Johnson invited me to contribute a chapter on living standards for volume 2 of *The Cambridge Economic History of Modern Britain*. A few years later the late Frank Lewis kindly gave me the opportunity to contribute a chapter to a volume honoring Stan Engerman. I chose to write on a topic briefly covered in the "Living Standards" paper, economic insecurity, self-help, and social safety nets in nineteenth-century Britain. When I finally sat down several years later to outline a book on Victorian and Edwardian social welfare policy, I based it on the Engerman paper. I planned for the book to end in 1914, but Tim Hatton, among others, suggested that I extend it to cover the interwar period, the Beveridge Report, and the beginning of the welfare state.

I have accumulated many debts in the process of writing the book, and it is my pleasure to thank publicly those who offered assistance. My largest debts are to Peter Lindert, Jeffrey Williamson, Tim Hatton, Stan Engerman, Joel Mokyr, and the late Mary MacKinnon. Peter read the entire manuscript, parts of it several times, and offered detailed comments and suggestions that have significantly improved it. Jeff and Tim provided helpful comments on draft chapters and on drafts of various papers that went into the book. Several years ago Jeff suggested that I write a book on the history of British social policy; without his encouragement this book might never have been written. As noted above, Tim pushed me to extend the book past 1914, and it was his idea that we construct the new estimates of British unemployment from 1870 to 1913 and beyond that appear at various places in the text. Stan Engerman read and made detailed comments on the manuscript. I am grateful for the accident of geography that placed Rochester only 100 miles from Ithaca, making it easy to drive up to see Stan for working lunches, which are always productive learning experiences as well as fun.

Joel Mokyr is all that can be asked for in an editor. He read the entire manuscript and provided detailed and helpful feedback on what should be added, what revised, and what deleted. The attention that he has given the manuscript has substantially improved it.

My dear friend Mary MacKinnon passed away in 2010, before I began writing the book, and yet she had a large impact on it, as anyone who reads the footnotes will see. Mary's D.Phil. thesis was on the Victorian Poor Law, and although over time she moved on from the Poor Laws and concentrated more on Canadian economic history, she continued to read and comment on my papers. Mary was never shy about offering criticism and making suggestions, and her comments always made my papers better. I miss our conversations, and regret that our many discussions never resulted in joint work.

Several other persons commented on drafts of chapters or earlier papers, provided or told me where to find data, answered queries, and helped with sources. They all deserve thanks: the late Charles Feinstein, Stephen Broadberry, Frank Lewis, Humphrey Southall, Paul Johnson, Roderick Floud, Roy Bailey, Chris Hanes, David Mitch, Chris Minns, Ian Keay, Tim Leunig, Michael Huberman, Deirdre McCloskey, Price Fishback, Richard Smith, Susan Wolcott, Jessica Bean, Timothy Schmidle, Andrew Rutten, Robert Hutchens, and Martin Wells. For their helpful comments, I thank the participants at the 2011 Canadian Economic Association meetings, the Sixth World Cliometrics Conference, the All UC Conference on New Comparative Economic History, the 2004 Economic History Association meetings, and the 2004 Conference on Economic History at Queen's University, as well as at seminars at Cornell, Binghamton University, Queen's University, the University of Mississippi, the University of California, Berkeley, the University of Arizona, and the Washington Area Economic History Seminar. I also thank the two anonymous referees who made many helpful comments on the manuscript.

I would like to thank the staffs of Olin and Catherwood Libraries at Cornell, and in particular the staff of Interlibrary Services, for their assistance in securing monographs and government documents that Cornell does not own. I am especially grateful to whoever in the Cornell Library system made the decision several years ago to purchase the online version of the British Parliamentary Papers. I thank Joan MacKinnon, Mary's sister, for lending me her copy of Mary's 1984 Oxford D.Phil. thesis. Thanks to Jessica Bean, Max Kiniria, R. Genevieve Quist, and Gleb Drobkov for their excellent research assistance. Thanks also to Darrie O'Connell and Sophia Harmon for their assistance in preparing the manuscript and in helping me learn how to use various features of Word. I gratefully acknowledge the assistance and encouragement of my editor at Princeton University Press, Joe Jackson, and the production staff, including Jenny Wolkowicki and Joseph Dahm.

Thanks to several cohorts of students in my course, "The Evolution of Social Policy in Britain and America," for putting up with my testing out early versions of some of the ideas in this book before a captive audience. Finally, I want to thank the staff and guests of Loaves and Fishes of Tompkins County, our local community kitchen, for reminding me what is important in life.

Parts of the book have appeared before, in somewhat different form: "Poor Relief, Informal Assistance, and Short Time during the Lancashire Cotton Famine," *Explorations in Economic History* 34 (1997): 56–76; "New Estimates of British Unemployment, 1870–1913," *Journal of Economic History* 62 (2002): 643–75 (with Timothy J. Hatton); "The Evolution of Unemployment Relief in Great Britain," *Journal of Interdisciplinary History* 34 (2004): 393–433; "Poverty among the Elderly in Late Victorian England," *Economic History Review* 62 (2009): 249–78 (with Timothy Schmidle); "'Work for Their Prime, the Workhouse for Their Age': Old Age Pauperism in Victorian England," *Social Science History* 40 (2016): 3–32. I would like to thank the journals for permission to use portions of my earlier work. I also thank Cambridge University Press for allowing me to use portions of the following: "Living Standards, 1860–1939," in Roderick Floud and Paul Johnson, eds., *The Cambridge Economic History of Modern Britain*, vol. 2 (Cambridge: Cambridge University Press, 2004): 280–313; and "Insecurity, Safety Nets, and Self-Help in Victorian and Edwardian Britain," in David Eltis and Frank Lewis, eds., *Human Capital and Institutions: A Long Run View* (Cambridge: Cambridge University Press, 2009): 46–89.

Family and friends have been very supportive throughout this project. My companion Janet Millman has assisted me at all stages of the book, from conception to final product. This book is dedicated to her.

Ithaca, N.Y.
April 2018

THE WINDING ROAD
TO THE WELFARE STATE

1

Economic Insecurity and Social Policy

> However steady a man may be, however good a worker, he is never exempt from the fear of losing his job from ill-health or from other causes which are out of his control. . . . To the insufficiency of a low wage is added the horror that it is never secure.
>
> —PEMBER REEVES, *ROUND ABOUT A POUND A WEEK*

> We forget how terribly near the margin of disaster the man, even the thrifty man, walks, who has, in ordinary normal conditions, but just enough to keep himself on. . . . The possibility of being from one day to the other plunged into actual want is always confronting his family.
>
> —LADY BELL, *AT THE WORKS*

One Saturday afternoon in the spring of 1902, Frank Goss's father arrived home from work early. Giving some coins to his wife, he announced, "That's the last wages you'll get for a bit." He had unexpectedly gotten "the sack." When his wife said that they had always managed when he was out of work in the past, Frank's father replied that things were different this time. Too many people were already without work, some for several months. "Before, there was always a chance of getting in somewhere. . . . But it's not like that now. . . . Once out now, you can't get in anywhere." He then added, "If there's no work in our trade in the winter, Gawd help us." As Goss recalled, "this was the beginning of our second period of dire poverty." With his father unable to find work, "gradually every bit of furniture that would fetch a few coppers went to the pawnshop." Frank's mother took in washing and occasionally did some dressmaking "at the lowest rates that she could possibly accept," and the boys did errands for their better-off neighbors. The family received a bit of help from relatives and friends, and the grocer and milkman allowed them to purchase "small quantities of the bare necessities on tick." They lived on "crusts and scraps"; the rent went unpaid and accumulated into "a formidable sum." Finally, after several weeks without work, Frank's father went on the tramp with another man, but returned home two weeks later penniless. Reminiscing years afterward about that summer, Goss wrote of how the despair of dire poverty "destroys the fibre of a man," and added: "to feel the patterns and habits of living, in which the future has been envisaged as a procession of normalities, destroyed and replaced by a living fear of greater and greater destitution and want becomes an intermidable [*sic*] progress into a greater hopelessness that surely breaks the spirit."[1]

Another example of how a household could fall from relative comfort into poverty in a short time is given by the condition of a Preston family in 1862, during the Lancashire cotton famine. The husband was a middle-aged cotton spinner, and at least one of the five children also worked in a factory. The "thrifty" wife ran a "little provision shop." Sometime before the downturn began, one of the sons lost two fingers in an industrial accident and was temporarily disabled, and four of the children had been sick for several months. All lost their jobs when the factories shut down. After a few months without earnings and with their shop's little stock "oozing away—partly on credit to poor neighbours, and partly to live upon themselves," the family was destitute. They were forced to turn to the Poor Law for assistance; at the time they were interviewed the family was "receiving from all sources, work and relief, about 13s. a week."[2]

Mrs. Hart was a widow in her sixties when she was admitted to the Bromley workhouse in 1882. She had done "canvas work," but had been without work for seven or eight weeks and been forced to sell most of her furniture. She had two grown children, but her son had lost a leg and was receiving poor relief, and her daughter offered her no assistance. After less than a year in the workhouse, she left and moved in with her sister, also a widow. Two years later Mrs. Hart was injured carrying some canvas, and after some time in the Bromley Sick Asylum was readmitted to the workhouse, being no longer able to work. Some years later her sister, then 71, applied for relief. She was destitute; her furniture had been sold and she could not pay her rent.[3]

Frank Goss blamed the industrial revolution for his family's plight. In his words, over the past century and a half "it had come upon an unnumbered host

---

1. Goss autobiographical manuscript, Brunel University Research Archive, 51–67, http://bura.brunel.ac.uk/handle/2438/10909.
2. Waugh (1867: 49–51).
3. Booth (1892c: 67).

like a visitation of a plague destroying their wellbeing, ruining and starving them, and leaving them destitute, crippled and dying in its wake."[4] Goss could have benefited from a course in early modern economic history. Economic insecurity was *not* a new phenomenon in the nineteenth century, nor was it a product of capitalism. Workers in preindustrial Europe were subject "to a myriad of uncertainties and insecurities which could temporarily or permanently undermine the precarious viability of their household economies." Not the least of these was the availability and price of grain, which fluctuated with the state of the harvest. However, the rise of an urban industrial economy in the nineteenth century led to new forms of insecurity and to a decline of the traditional safety net based on church, kin, and neighbors. In the words of R. H. Tawney, "the peasant is insecure, but he curses the weather, not social institutions."[5]

Industrialization also led to a widespread discussion of the problems associated with having an uncertain income. The conclusions reached by Pember Reeves and Lady Bell regarding British workers' income insecurity on the eve of the First World War were based on their investigations of working-class households in south London and Middlesbrough, and they were echoed by other commentators. Seebohm Rowntree, the Webbs, William Beveridge, Arthur Bowley, and Llewellyn Smith, among others, wrote about the problem of economic insecurity and how it could be alleviated, and Robert Tressell brilliantly portrayed the extent of insecurity among building trades workers in turn-of-the-century Hastings (Mugsborough) in his novel *The Ragged Trousered Philanthropists*.[6] Winston Churchill, soon to become President of the Board of Trade, wrote to the editor of the *Westminster Review* in 1907 that "the working classes . . . will not continue to bear, they cannot, the awful uncertainties of their lives." In a speech the following year Churchill called insecurity "that great and hideous evil . . . by which our industrial population are harassed."[7] Insecurity was a major topic examined by the Royal Commission on the Poor Laws and Relief of Distress of 1905–9.

Why is it important to study economic insecurity? The material living standards of British manual workers, as measured by average full-time earnings, nearly doubled from 1850 to 1913—those fully employed in 1913 were far better

4. Goss autobiographical manuscript, 51.

5. Wrightson (2000: 319). Tawney's (1972: 10) quote is from his diary, May 1912. Epstein (1933: 3) asserted that insecurity "has been the bane of mankind" since Adam and Eve were banished from the Garden of Eden.

6. See Rowntree (1901), Rowntree and Lasker (1911), Webb and Webb (1909a; 1909b; 1911), Beveridge (1909), Bowley and Burnett-Hurst (1915), and Smith (1910). Tressell ([1955] 2005) wrote between 1906 and 1910, although his unabridged novel was not published until 1955.

7. Hay (1978: 72); Churchill (1909: 207). Churchill (1969: 759) added that "the main need of the English working classes is Security."

off, in terms of the ability to purchase goods and services, than their fully employed grandfathers.[8] However, long-term trends in full-time earnings tell us nothing about the amount of time lost due to unemployment or illness, or about workers' ability to cope with these periodic losses of income. By focusing on trends in full-time earnings, historians often miss what happened to those in households where the prime-age male breadwinner was unemployed or too sick to work, households headed by female workers due to the death or absence of an adult male, and households where the breadwinner, whether male or female, was too old to work or at least to work full-time.

How did working-class households deal with income insecurity? What role did public and private safety nets play in alleviating insecurity? How did government social policy and workers' coping strategies change from 1834 to 1940? This book addresses these questions, focusing on workers' methods for coping with income insecurity and the evolution of social welfare policy during the nineteenth and early twentieth centuries.

Defining Terms

It is useful to begin with a few definitions. Western et al. define economic insecurity as "the risk of economic loss faced by workers and households as they encounter the unpredictable events of life." Insecurity is associated with income loss caused by "adverse events" such as unemployment and poor health; the negative impact of these shocks on households depends "on the surrounding institutions that regulate risk." Recent attempts to measure insecurity have been undertaken by Osberg and Sharpe and by Hacker et al. Osberg and Sharpe's index of economic security is based on "four key objective economic risks"—income loss associated with unemployment, the "risk of health care costs," and the "prevalence of poverty" among single-parent families and the aged. Hacker et al. construct an economic security index measuring "the share of individuals who experience at least a 25 percent decline in their inflation-adjusted 'available household income' from one year to the next (except when entering retirement) and who lack an adequate financial safety net to replace this lost income until it returns to its original level."[9]

Data constraints preclude the construction of such an index for Victorian Britain. However, the notion of economic insecurity that I use throughout this book is similar to that of Hacker, Osberg, and Western. Insecurity refers to a household's exposure to declines in income of a magnitude large enough

---

8. Feinstein (1995: 263–65) found that real wages of manual workers increased by 98% from 1850 to 1913.

9. Western et al. (2012: 342); Osberg and Sharpe (2002: 305–8; 2014); Hacker et al. (2014: S8–S12).

to create acute financial hardship. The extent of working-class insecurity in Victorian Britain was determined by the interaction of three factors: the probability of large negative income shocks; the ability of households to buffer income shocks with savings or insurance benefits from friendly societies or trade unions, or assistance from kin; and the existence and generosity of government social policies (or charitable institutions) that provided benefits to partially offset income loss.

Any discussion of insecurity has to confront the issue of whether income fluctuations were predictable. Working-class households experienced negative income shocks as a result of unemployment, reductions in wages or work hours, prolonged periods of illness, death, or disability of the chief wage earner, and old age. If most income shocks could be anticipated, why didn't households protect themselves from financial distress by increasing their savings, joining mutual insurance organizations providing unemployment, sickness, old age, and disability benefits, or, at the least, obtaining a stock of pawnable goods that could be used to raise enough cash to live on for a few weeks? Critics of government social welfare programs have raised this issue repeatedly for the past two centuries.

The evidence presented in this book shows that Victorian working-class households *did* save and join friendly societies, but, despite their attempts at income smoothing, many periodically fell into financial distress. Why? First, while the occurrence of income shocks was to some extent predictable, their precise timing and magnitude were not. It is easier to anticipate that a business cycle downturn will occur every six or eight years than to estimate the amount of time one will be out of work during the next downturn. Severe recessions forced many who had not done so during milder downturns to turn to the Poor Law for help. Moreover, the rise of a globalized economy created additional uncertainty that was difficult to predict. The Lancashire cotton famine, which threw thousands of factory workers out of employment for months, was caused by the sharp decline in raw cotton imports during the American Civil War, an event factory workers could not have anticipated. The great expansion in international trade after 1870 led to a corresponding increase in workers' insecurity; in the words of Michael Huberman, "instability rose everywhere as economies became more open."[10] Workers tried to cope with the additional risk, but many, especially among the low-skilled, were fighting a losing battle.

A household's ability to weather income shocks on its own depended on the size of its "financial safety net," determined by how much it saved and whether the head was eligible for insurance benefits from a mutual insurance organization. Some Victorians, such as Samuel Smiles, asserted that virtually

---

10. Huberman (2012: 32).

all working-class households could put aside enough money to provide against income loss due to unemployment or illness, but available evidence suggests otherwise. Households headed by well-paid skilled artisans often were able to protect themselves against all but the most catastrophic income shocks. However, as late as 1901 the poorest third of working-class households had little savings and were not members of societies providing sickness benefits, and only one in eight adult male workers was eligible for unemployment benefits through a trade union. The desire to protect oneself against income loss is not the same as the *ability* to protect oneself. Each of the families described at the beginning of this chapter appeared to be responsible and hardworking, and yet each was plunged into distress by a negative income shock. Low-skilled workers simply did not make enough money to provide against income loss, and many continued to experience acute financial distress at some points in their lives.[11]

While the extent of insecurity in Victorian Britain cannot be precisely measured, rough estimates of the number of insecure households can be constructed. I define a household as economically insecure if it faced a substantial risk of falling temporarily or permanently into poverty in response to negative income shocks. In current terminology, the insecure include both the poor and the "near poor." In turn, I define a household as being in poverty if its total earnings were "insufficient to obtain the minimum necessaries for the maintenance of merely physical efficiency."[12] This is Rowntree's "primary poverty" line. Like all poverty lines, it is to some degree "an arbitrarily defined standard," but it was the basis of nearly all poverty standards constructed from 1899 to 1939, and historians have used modified versions of Rowntree's standard to estimate poverty lines for Victorian towns.[13]

The number of households that were economically insecure at a point in time included not only those with incomes below the poverty line but also those with incomes above the poverty line but at risk of falling below it. This risk was quite real. In Victorian Britain as in present-day America, households were constantly moving into and out of poverty, and many households experienced multiple spells in poverty.[14] Because of the dynamic nature or fluidity of poverty, the number of households experiencing at least one spell in poverty over a period of, say, ten years was far larger than the share living in poverty at any point in time. The town surveys undertaken in early twentieth-century Britain

---

11. Johnson (1985: 3).

12. Rowntree (1901: 86).

13. Anderson (1971); Dupree (1995). According to Bowley (1932: 70–71), all recent poverty estimates had been "based on Rowntree's standard, adapted to the prices and circumstances of other times and places."

14. Bane and Ellwood (1986: 13–20), using U.S. data for 1970–82, found that most households that were ever in poverty experienced short spells.

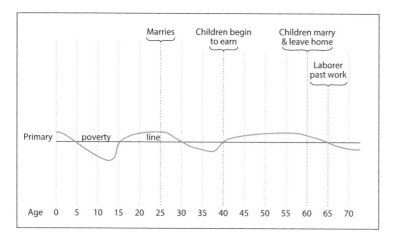

FIGURE 1.1. Rowntree's Diagram of Poverty over the Life Cycle.
Source: Rowntree (1901: 137).

counted the number in poverty at a precise moment and therefore missed poverty's dynamic nature. They greatly understate the extent of temporary spells of financial distress caused by the head or other family members being out of work for more than a few weeks. They also greatly understate the extent of insecurity.

Rowntree understood that "the proportion of the community who at one period or other of their lives suffer from poverty to the point of physical privation" was "much greater . . . than would appear from a consideration of the number who can be shown to be below the poverty line at any given moment." Besides the households that fell into temporary distress as a result of income shocks caused by unemployment or illness, Rowntree also identified life-cycle periods of poverty. The life of a low-skilled worker was "marked by five alternating periods of want and comparative plenty," as shown in Figure 1.1. The laborer typically lived in poverty for part of his childhood, until he or some of his older siblings were able to work and augment the family income. He again lived in poverty during the period from when his second or third child was born until the oldest child reached 14 and began to work, and finally in old age. A laborer who lived to age 70 could expect to spend upward of 25 years in poverty.[15]

Two other terms that occur at various points in the text, destitution and pauperism, should be defined. Victorian commentators used the term "destitution" to denote deep or extreme poverty; destitute households had incomes well below the poverty line. While anyone who was destitute would be in poverty, many of those who were poor would not be considered destitute. A pauper is a person in receipt of Poor Law relief. The number of persons

15. Rowntree (1901: 136–38).

receiving poor relief cannot be used as a proxy for the number in poverty, because the standards used by Poor Law guardians in administering relief varied both across locations and over time, and many of those in poverty did not receive poor relief. Some contemporaries quoted in the text used the term "pauper" in a pejorative sense, to denote someone who was irresponsible and dependent on public welfare. This use of the term often was associated with criticism of public or private assistance—it was claimed that generous poor relief or charity "pauperized" a segment of the population.

The Extent of Income Insecurity

What share of the population of nineteenth- and early twentieth-century England was economically insecure? Put another way, what share was either in poverty or in danger of falling into poverty at any time? This question is easier asked than answered. Rough estimates of the number of economically insecure households can be obtained using occupational data from the census or household income data from town-level poverty surveys. The first approach identifies insecurity by the occupation of the household head. It associates insecurity with occupations characterized by low wages or high employment volatility, and assumes that households headed by low-skilled urban workers, skilled or semiskilled workers in highly cyclical industries, semiskilled workers in the building trades, and agricultural laborers were economically insecure. The second approach assumes that a household was economically insecure if its typical weekly income was no more than a certain amount above the poverty line. In the estimates below, I assume that a household was insecure if its weekly income was below the poverty line or above but within 8s. of the poverty line. A family of five with an income 8s. above the poverty line would be about 40% above the poverty threshold in the 1850s and 33% above the threshold in 1912.[16] This corresponds roughly to the current concept of "near poverty," which typically is defined as having an income above but within 1.5 times the poverty threshold, although some set the top income at 1.25, 1.33, or 2.0 times the poverty threshold.[17]

Table 1.1 presents rough estimates of the share of households or adult males who were economically insecure for several benchmark periods—1688, 1801–3, 1851–67, 1911–14, 1931, and 1951. The data were drawn from differing types of

16. From 1851 to 1912, the poverty line for a family of five was between 20s. and 24.6s.

17. Meyer and Sullivan (2012: 174) and Rank et al. (2014: 206) define "near poverty" as having an annual income above but not more than 150% of the official poverty line. A Census Bureau report by Heggeness and Hokayem (2013) defines the near poor as those with incomes between 100% and 133% of the poverty threshold, but also reports the share with incomes between 100% and 150% of the poverty line.

sources (social tables, town-level poverty surveys, census data on occupational categories), but together they provide a crude index of the changing levels of insecurity over the long run.[18] Where available, the table also reports the share living in poverty, as estimated by the authors. Both the share in poverty and the share insecure declined substantially from the beginning of the nineteenth century to the eve of the First World War. This result is not surprising. What is more surprising is the extent of economic insecurity among the working class throughout the period from 1801 to 1951, and the relationship between the share in poverty and the share insecure. Gregory King's data, as revised by Lindert and Williamson, reveal that one-half of English and Welsh households were economically insecure in 1688.[19] Colquhoun's estimates for 1801–3 indicate that 42% of English households were insecure, and social tables for the 1860s constructed by Baxter and Levi show that the share of adult working-class males who were insecure remained above 40% throughout the first two-thirds of the nineteenth century.[20] The extent of insecurity began to decline thereafter. Census data on occupational categories for 1911 indicate that, on the eve of the First World War, about one-third of adult working-class males were economically insecure. However, town-level survey data for 1912–14 show that the extent of insecurity varied greatly across locations. Some 60% of working-class households in Reading and 37% in Warrington were insecure, as compared to 16% of households in Northampton and 13% in the mining town of Stanley. The major cause of the differences in insecurity across towns was the large variation in manual workers' wages. In Reading, 75% of adult males had a weekly wage below 30s., as compared to 62% of adult males in Warrington, 51% in Northampton, and 25% in Stanley.[21]

The estimates for 1931 and 1951 obtained using census occupational data were calculated precisely the same way as those obtained from the 1911 census. The data indicate that the share of adult male workers who were economically

18. The construction of the insecurity estimates is discussed in Appendix 1.1. Another measure of insecurity is the frequency of mortality crises. National mortality crises declined in both frequency and intensity from the seventeenth century to the mid-nineteenth. See Wrigley and Schofield (1981: 332–36, 645–70).

19. King's unrevised data, found in Lindert and Williamson (1982: 393), suggest that 62.4% of households were economically insecure in 1688, and 29.4% of households were living in poverty.

20. This does not mean, of course, that the share who were insecure was above 40% in all communities. Dupree (1995: 62, 73–74) found that fewer than one-third of households in the Potteries in 1861 were economically insecure. She admits that "the wages of potters were relatively high" compared to the wages of other skilled manual workers. Assuming no professional or middle-class adult males were economically insecure, Baxter's data show that in 1861 about one-third of all gainfully employed adult males were insecure.

21. Wage data from Bowley and Burnett-Hurst (1915: 33). Rowntree (1901: 112) calculated that in 1899, 33.6% of working-class households in York had weekly incomes "below or not more than 6s. above" his estimated "primary poverty" line.

TABLE 1.1. Long-Term Movements in the Share of Households/Workers Economically Insecure, 1688–1951

	Share Insecure (%)	Share in Poverty (%)	Source
1688, England and Wales households	50.8	24.2	Estimated from Gregory King, as revised by Lindert and Williamson (1982; 1983b: 101)
1801–3, England and Wales households	42.3	19.9	Estimated from Colquhoun, as revised by Lindert and Williamson (1982; 1983b: 101)
1851, Preston households	≈47	20.0	Estimated from Anderson (1971: 31)
1861, Potteries households	≈32	9.0	Estimated from Dupree (1995: 74)
1861, England and Wales working-class adult males	41–47		Estimated from Baxter (1868: 50–51, 82–83, 88–93)
All gainfully employed males	31–36		
1867, United Kingdom working-class adult males	42–45		Estimated from Levi (1867: 14–15)
1911, Great Britain adult male manual workers	32–34		Estimated from Routh (1980: 6–7, 28–39)
All gainfully employed males	25–27		
1912, Reading working-class households	60.3	23.2	Estimated from Bowley and Burnett-Hurst (1915: 172)
1912, Warrington working-class households	36.5	12.8	Estimated from Bowley and Burnett-Hurst (1915: 134)
1913, Northampton working-class households	15.5	8.2	Estimated from Bowley and Burnett-Hurst (1915: 88)
1913, Stanley working-class households	13.4	5.4	Estimated from Bowley and Burnett-Hurst (1915: 157)
1914, Bolton working-class households	22.8	7.8	Estimated from Bowley and Burnett-Hurst (1920: 238)
1931, Great Britain adult male manual workers	37–39		Estimated from Routh (1980: 6–7, 28–39)
All gainfully employed males	28–30		
1951, Great Britain adult male manual workers	27–29		Estimated from Routh (1980: 6–7, 28–39)
All gainfully employed males	21–22		

Sources: See Appendix 1.1.

insecure increased slightly from 1911 to 1931, before declining in 1951 to a level below that of 1911. In the early postwar period, slightly more than one in five gainfully employed males was insecure, about half the share who were insecure in 1801-3. It is important to note, however, that the data for 1931 and 1951 overstate the true extent of income insecurity because of the existence in these years of compulsory social insurance policies, which for most households buffered the effects of income loss due to unemployment, sickness, disability, old age, or widowhood.

The other major finding from Table 1.1 is the relationship between the share in poverty and the share economically insecure. For the early social tables constructed by King and Colquhoun, the share insecure was roughly double the share in poverty. In the cotton-producing town of Preston in 1851 there were 2.4 times as many economically insecure households as households in poverty; in the Potteries, the share insecure was 3.6 times the share in poverty. Finally, for the five towns surveyed by Bowley and Burnett-Hurst, the share insecure was 1.9 to 2.9 times the share in poverty. Those who focus on the poverty rate substantially understate the extent of economic hardship among the working class.

Causes of Income Fluctuations

The main causes of negative income shocks for working-class households were unemployment, wage and hours cuts, and prolonged periods of illness of the main breadwinner. To these should be added old age, when individuals were no longer able to work, or at least to work full-time. I will briefly discuss each in turn.

From 1870 to 1913, the industrial unemployment rate averaged 6.6%, and exceeded 8% in 12 years. Unemployment data are less reliable before 1870, but what data exist suggest the unemployment rate was 8% or higher in more than a quarter of the years from 1835 to 1913. Unemployment varied greatly across sectors, being highest in mining, shipbuilding, metals, and unskilled labor, and lowest in clothing and footwear, transport, and printing and bookbinding.[22] Even during prosperous years, large numbers of skilled workers suffered income losses due to unemployment. For example, from 1887 to 1895, the unemployment rate among members of the Amalgamated Engineers trade union

22. Unemployment estimates for 1870–1913 are from Boyer and Hatton (2002) and below, Chapter 4. Estimates of unemployment rates from 1856 onwards were calculated from trade union data by the Board of Trade and revised by Feinstein (1972: T125–26). I adjusted Feinstein's estimates for 1856–69 to make them compatible with Boyer and Hatton's estimates. On the severity of downturns from 1835 to 1850, see Gayer, Rostow, and Schwartz (1953: 342–56) and Lindert and Williamson (1983a: 12–16).

was 6.1%, but on average nearly 30% of engineers were unemployed during a calendar year, for an average of 10.5 weeks. While the majority of workers were fully employed at any point in time even during downturns, a substantial number were unemployed for a month or more every year.[23] Some industries with relatively high average wage rates, such as iron and steel and coal mining, experienced frequent fluctuations in nominal wages as a result of agreements between workers and employers linking wages to product prices.[24] The volatility of wages in these sectors was an additional source of income insecurity.

The extent of year-to-year fluctuations in workers' purchasing power could be quite large. Figure 1.2 presents unemployment-adjusted real wage series for workers in coal mining, shipbuilding, and the building trades for 1870–1913.[25] The figure shows that comparing trends in wage rates masks a great deal of year-to-year volatility in true wage income. Coal miners' expected income increased by nearly 50% during the boom of the early 1870s but then declined sharply in the late 1870s. It did not regain its 1873–74 level until 1890–91, only to fall again before rising in the late 1890s. Movements in shipbuilders' expected income were similar to those for miners. The income series for building trades workers was less volatile. Still, expected income peaked in 1876 and did not regain that level until 1884, after which it increased slowly to a peak in 1896–99, then declined for a decade until in 1908–10 it had returned to its level in the late 1880s. On the eve of the Great War the real income of construction workers was nearly 10% below what it had been in 1896–99. These fluctuations in purchasing power created high levels of insecurity for workers, one of the costs of which was defaulting on debts. Miners' income volatility was matched by large fluctuations in the number of local court cases initiated for the recovery of small debts; their high wages did not protect them from periodic times of economic distress.[26]

Income insecurity was highest for workers in "casual" occupations subject to sudden and irregular fluctuations in the demand for labor. Casual jobs were characterized by "short engagement" and "want of selection." The economic distress suffered by those with fluctuating and uncertain incomes was vividly described by Henry Mayhew in his classic study *London Labour and the London Poor*. Mayhew focused on "the poorest of the poor"—street sellers, sweatshop workers, dock laborers, scavengers, "cleansers," and street entertainers. These were, in the words of J. R. T. Hughes, "unfortunates" pitifully trying "to make a place for themselves" in a labor market that did not want them and

23. Parl. Papers, *British and Foreign Trade and Industrial Conditions* (1905: LXXXIV), p. 101.

24. Wood (1901: 152); Porter (1970); Treble (1987).

25. Wage and cost of living data from Feinstein (1995: 260–65; 1990a: 610–11). Unemployment data from Boyer and Hatton (2002).

26. Johnson (1993).

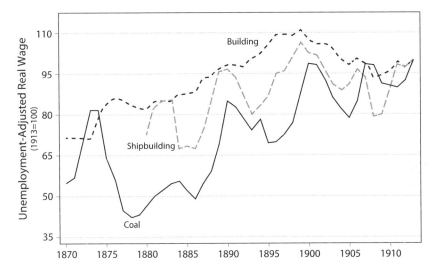

FIGURE 1.2. Unemployment-Adjusted Real Wages, 1870–1913

for which they had little to offer. Mayhew estimated that in the 1840s London street sellers and their families totaled about 50,000 persons (2.5% of London's population), but went on to show that the total number of casual laborers was much larger. Four decades later Booth estimated that casual laborers and their families made up roughly 8.4% of the population of London.[27]

Another major cause of insecurity was loss of employment due to illness or disability of the chief breadwinner. Work time lost due to sickness increased significantly with age. Data obtained from friendly society records indicate that adult males aged 25–35 lost, on average, about a week of work time per year due to sickness, while workers aged 50–59 lost 2–4 weeks per year, and workers aged 60–64 lost 4.6–6.3 weeks per year. These estimates probably understate average work time lost for all manual workers, as sickness rates were higher for unskilled than for skilled workers, and few low-skilled workers were eligible for sickness benefits.[28]

Like unemployment, sickness affected some workers within age groups more than others. Data on the duration of sickness among members of the Steam Engine Makers union in 1852–72 show that 18.9% of workers aged

27. Mayhew (1861: 1:4–6; 2:297–323); Hughes (1969: 531–33); Mokyr (2009: 482–83); Booth (1892b: 2:20–21). Following Jones (1971: 54–56), I assume that Booth's classes A and B provide the best estimate of the share of the population "subject to the dictates of the casual labour market." Beveridge (1909: 77–95) contains an excellent discussion of casual labor markets.

28. Money (1912: 169). On the other hand, friendly society members might have been more likely to miss work when sick, due to the existence of sickness benefits.

50–54 collected sick benefits for at least 10% of a calendar year (about five weeks), and 5.1% collected sick pay for more than six months. Among workers aged 60–64, nearly a quarter collected sick pay for at least five weeks, and 9.1% received sick pay for more than six months.[29]

Throughout the second half of the nineteenth century nearly 5% of the population of England and Wales was aged 65 or older. An individual surviving to 65 could expect to live another 10 to 12 years.[30] Most manual workers continued to work as long as they were physically able, and many made some attempt to plan for old age by saving and joining friendly societies and trade unions offering pension benefits. Still, few low-skilled or semiskilled workers were able to support themselves in old age, and a large share of the aged lived in poverty. The Local Government Board's pauper census for 1891–92 found that 29.3% of all persons 65 and older received poor relief at some point during the 12-month period. The share of aged *working-class* persons assisted by the Poor Law in 1891–92 was even higher, and almost certainly exceeded 40%.[31]

The Changing Role of Social Welfare Policy

The extent to which workers suffered financial distress from income shocks depended in large part on the social safety net—the existing institutions of public and private assistance. For nineteenth-century England and Wales, the main social welfare institution was the Poor Law, a system of public relief administered and financed at the local level. The Old Poor Law of 1795–1834 was "a welfare state in miniature," relieving the elderly, widows, children, the sick, the disabled, and the unemployed and underemployed.[32] While most European countries had systems of public relief, the English Poor Law differed from continental systems in several ways—it was "uniform and comprehensive in its spatial coverage . . . [and] relatively generous and certain in its benefits." The Poor Law was national in scope, although administered at the local level, and the English poor had a well-defined legal right to relief. On the continent, the right to relief was more tenuous, and often "entirely at the discretion of local authorities." Peter Lindert calculated that in the first third of the nineteenth century English poor relief spending was 2.0% or more of national product, compared to less than 1.5% for the Netherlands, France, and Belgium. The

---

29. Southall (1998: 22).

30. Data on the number of persons 65 and older from Mitchell (1988: 9, 15). Life expectancy data from Preston et al. (1972: 224–26, 240–42).

31. The data for 1891–92 are from Parl. Papers, *Return . . . of Paupers over Sixty-Five* (1892: LXVIII), pp. 621–31. The estimate in the text assumes that 70% of persons 65 and older were from the working class.

32. Blaug (1964: 229).

English social safety net, though small by twentieth-century standards, was far larger than those elsewhere in Europe.[33]

After 1830 the Poor Law's role in assisting the needy declined substantially. In 1832, the British government responded to the widespread clamor for Poor Law reform by appointing the Royal Commission to Investigate the Poor Laws, whose 1834 report recommended that able-bodied adults and their families be granted relief only in well-regulated workhouses. The resulting Poor Law Amendment Act ushered in a major shift in social welfare policy. The Poor Law Commission created by the act did not eliminate outdoor relief for the able-bodied, but it succeeded in restricting relief for able-bodied males and in reducing relief spending.

The 1870s saw a further restriction of public assistance, known as the Crusade Against Outrelief. Encouraged by the newly formed Local Government Board (LGB), which issued an 1871 circular stating that generous outdoor relief was destroying self-reliance among the poor, local authorities throughout England and Wales reduced outdoor relief for all types of paupers, and in particular able-bodied males and the elderly.[34] The LGB was aided in convincing the public of the need for reform by the propaganda of the Charity Organisation Society (COS), founded in 1869. The COS maintained that most low-skilled workers earned enough to set aside some income in anticipation of future interruptions in earnings, and that their failure to do so largely was caused by the availability of generous poor relief. Restricting outdoor relief and offering the poor assistance in workhouses would improve workers' moral and economic condition in the long run.

Public opinion regarding social welfare policy shifted once again in the decades leading up to the First World War. Beginning in the 1880s, the British public became increasingly aware that there were holes in the existing public-private safety net. The poverty surveys of London in the 1880s and York in 1899 undertaken by Booth and Rowntree showed that there were large numbers of underemployed, sick, and old people living in poverty, the majority of whom were poor because of economic circumstances rather than personal failure.[35] The growing middle-class understanding of workers' economic insecurity helps to explain why, in the decade before the First World War, Parliament did a major about-face and adopted several pieces of social welfare legislation

33. Solar (1995: 2–7); Greif and Iyigun (2013: 536); Lindert (1998: 108–19). According to Solar (1995), Greif and Iyigun (2012; 2013), and Kelly and Ó Gráda (2011), the generosity and reliability of the English Poor Law from the seventeenth century to 1834 positively affected economic development, fostered risk taking, reduced violence, reduced deaths from famine or epidemic diseases, and in general helped contribute to "the distinctiveness of the English economy on the eve of its industrialization."

34. The circular is reprinted in Rose (1971: 229–30).

35. See Booth (1888; 1892b) and Rowntree (1901).

collectively known as the Liberal Welfare Reforms. The extent to which the Liberal government had moved away from the views on social welfare policy expressed during the Crusade Against Outrelief can be seen in a speech by Winston Churchill, then President of the Board of Trade, in May 1909:

> Unemployment, accident, sickness, and the death of the bread-winner are catastrophes which may reach any household at any moment. Those vultures are always hovering around us. . . . It is our duty to use the strength and the resources of the State to arrest the ghastly waste not merely of human happiness but of national health and strength which follows when a working man's home which has taken him years to get together is broken up and scattered through a long spell of unemployment, or when, through the death, the sickness, or the invalidity of the bread-winner, the frail boat in which the fortunes of the family are embarked founders, and the women and children are left to struggle helplessly on the dark waters of a friendless world. I believe it is well within our power now . . . to establish vast and broad throughout the land a mighty system of national insurance which will . . . embrace in its scope all sorts and conditions of men.[36]

Under the leadership of Churchill and Lloyd George, the Chancellor of the Exchequer, Parliament adopted the Old Age Pension Act in 1908 and the National Insurance Act (which established compulsory sickness and unemployment insurance) in 1911. These acts, along with the other Liberal reforms, greatly extended the social safety net and reduced economic insecurity for workers and their families. Government social transfer spending increased during the interwar years, largely out of necessity, and then greatly expanded with the adoption of the welfare state after the Second World War.

The extent to which the safety net declined from 1834 to 1900 and then grew as a result of the Liberal Welfare Reforms and their extension between the wars is clearly seen in Figures 1.3 and 1.4. Figure 1.3 shows the percentage of the population receiving social benefits from 1829 to 1938, and Figure 1.4 shows social welfare spending as a share of gross domestic product from 1816 to 1960. The only source of public assistance through 1908 was the Poor Law; beginning in 1909 an additional source is included, old age pensions. For the interwar period, the sources of social benefits, in addition to the Poor Law, include old age pensions, unemployment benefits, sickness and disability benefits, and, from 1926 onward, widow, orphan, and old age contributory pensions.

In the five years preceding the adoption of the Poor Law Amendment Act, an average of 15.6% of the population annually was in receipt of public

---

36. The speech, titled "The Budget and National Insurance," is in Churchill (1909: 297–317).

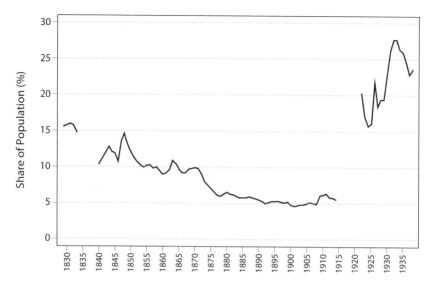

FIGURE 1.3. Share of Population Receiving Social Benefits, 1829–1938

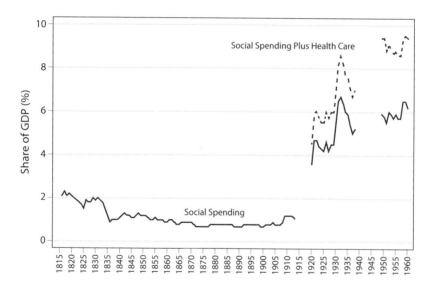

FIGURE 1.4. Social Welfare Spending as a Share of GDP, 1816–1960

assistance. During the "hungry" 1840s, the share receiving relief averaged
12.2%. The peak occurred in 1848, the year of the Communist Manifesto and
revolutions in Europe, when 14.6% of the population and perhaps 20% of
the working class were in receipt of relief. In the 1850s and 1860s the annual
share on relief fluctuated around 10%. It then declined sharply in the 1870s,
largely as a result of the Crusade Against Outrelief, and more slowly thereafter,

until from 1900 to 1908 only 4.9% of the population received public relief. The small increase beginning in 1909 was a result of the implementation of old age pensions.

The situation was completely different between the wars. From 1922 to 1938 an average of 22.1% of the population received public assistance. In 1933, the peak year, nearly 12.9 million persons received some form of social benefit, including 5.1 million recipients of unemployment benefits, 3.4 million recipients of old age, widows, or orphans pensions, and 1.1 million recipients of sickness or disability benefits.[37] This sharp increase in numbers receiving social benefits largely was due to the economic shocks of the interwar period, but also to the safety net put in place by the prewar Liberal reforms and expanded in the 1920s.

Figure 1.4 tells a similar story. From 1816 to 1833, poor relief expenditures for England and Wales averaged 2.0% of GDP. As a result of both economic growth and the increasing stinginess of relief, welfare spending declined to 1.2% of GDP during the hungry 1840s, and 0.8% of GDP from 1871 to 1908. The addition of government old age pensions raised spending to 1.2% of GDP from 1909 to 1913. Two series are reported for the years 1920 to 1960—one contains spending on social insurance and pensions, the other in addition includes spending on health care. Spending as a share of GDP increased sharply in both series after the First World War and again after the adoption of the welfare state legislation in 1946–48. During the interwar years spending on social insurance and pensions averaged 5.1% of GDP; from 1949 to 1960 it averaged 5.9% of GDP. When expenditures on health care are added, social spending as a share of GDP was 6.6% between the wars and 9.0% from 1949 to 1960.[38]

Debating the Proper Role of Social Welfare Policy

The major shifts in government policy between 1830 and 1950 were driven by changing views on the proper role and the effects of social welfare policies. The debate over government's role in protecting the poor has been going on for centuries, and it continues today. It has both economic and moral aspects, which are intertwined in such a way that they are difficult to separate.

The debate heated up in the years around the adoption of the Poor Law Amendment Act. Many commentators opposed public relief on the grounds

37. There were 3.8 million Poor Law recipients in 1933, some of whom also received other benefits. To avoid double counting, in constructing estimates of the total number receiving social benefits I reduced the number of Poor Law recipients by 15%. For details of how the estimated number receiving benefits was constructed, see Appendix 1.2.

38. Expenditures on social insurance and pensions increased to 8.9% of GDP in 1970, 12.7% in 1980, and 17.0% in 1995. See Webb (2000: 572). Appendix 1.3 gives the details on how the estimates of social spending as a share of GDP were constructed.

that the increased security it provided reduced work incentives and thrift among the working class. Tocqueville, in his *Memoir on Pauperism*, claimed that humans have "a natural passion for idleness," and that the English Poor Law, by guaranteeing the poor that their "most pressing needs" will be met, "weakens or destroys their incentive to work" and "creates an idle and lazy class." Over time "the spirit of foresight and saving becomes . . . alien to the poor," and public relief ends up depraving "the population that it wants to help and comfort."[39]

Among the defenders of public assistance was the young Disraeli, who argued that the poor had a right to relief and that the Poor Law Amendment Act, which denied them that right, was based on "a moral error." The act "disgraced the country" by announcing "to the world that in England poverty is a crime." John Stuart Mill admitted that there were negative consequences to relying on public relief, but added that "energy and self-dependence" were "liable to be impaired by the absence of help, as well as by its excess." Indeed, it was "even more fatal to exertion to have no hope of succeeding by it, than to be assured of succeeding without it." For those who were "paralyzed by discouragement, assistance is a tonic, not a sedative."[40]

Mid-Victorian Britain saw the rise of an ethic of respectability and self-help, preached by middle-class reformers such as Edward Denison and Samuel Smiles. Denison, who did philanthropic work in East London in the 1860s, maintained that even the most needy families, "if they had been only moderately frugal and provident," would be able "to tide over the occasional months of want of work or of sickness, which there always must be." Smiles, the author of *Self-Help* and *Thrift*, agreed that working men, so long as they were thrifty, could become "comparatively independent," and added that any self-respecting man "should maintain himself and his family without the help of others." Workers understood the economic risks they faced, and a man with self-respect would take steps to protect his family. In his words, "the uncertainty of life is a strong inducement to provide against the evil day. To do this is a moral and social as well as a religious duty."[41]

Denison, Smiles, and others maintained that the granting of generous assistance in the form of poor relief or private charity demoralized the poor. Canon Barnett called indiscriminate charity one of the "curses of London," which caused the poor never to "learn to work or to save," and asserted that "the poor starve because of the alms they receive." Not all Victorians were convinced. Beatrice Webb noted in her autobiography that "behind all this array of inductive and deductive proof of the disastrous effect on the wage-earning

---

39. Tocqueville ([1835] 1997: 54–62, 70).
40. Monypenny (1910: 374); Mill ([1848] 1909: 967–68).
41. Leighton (1872: 46); Smiles ([1866] 2002: 254; 1876: 33, 35).

class of any kind of subvention, there lay the subconscious bias of 'the Haves' against taxing themselves for 'the Have Nots.'"[42]

Nineteenth-century participants in the social policy debate divided the poor into two groups, "deserving" and "undeserving." All agreed that some of the poor were thrifty and sober and strove to be independent, but had become indigent as a result of unfortunate circumstances. They disagreed on what share of the poor were "deserving," and on the effects of government social policy on the behavior of the working poor. Those who were critical of the Poor Law tended, like Tocqueville, to argue that individuals by nature prefer idleness over work, and that this tendency, combined with generous public assistance, created a large class of "undeserving" poor. Why work hard and save if you were assured a subsistence income? Those who supported public relief viewed the poor as generally hardworking, but with incomes too low and precarious to protect themselves against negative income shocks. In their view, most of the poor were "deserving," and had a right to public relief.

Terms such as "responsibility" continue to be used by modern critics of the welfare state. Peter Bauer, in his maiden speech before the House of Lords in 1983, stated that the "fundamental issue [of the welfare state] is not economic. It is moral. . . . The issue is the responsibility of people to manage their own affairs." When he asserted that "responsible people should normally be able to provide for . . . old age, ill health, the raising of children, interruption of earnings," he was echoing Samuel Smiles.[43]

Many economists, along with Lord Bauer, contend that social welfare programs alter individuals' incentives in a way that reduces work effort, thrift, and self-reliance, and increases unemployment. Martin Feldstein wrote that America's "extensive program of social insurance has important effects on the economy" that "are generally unintended" and "often harmful." Milton and Rose Friedman argued that "paternalistic" welfare programs "weaken the family, reduce the incentive to work, save, and innovate; reduce the accumulation of capital; and limit our freedom. . . . The end result is to rot the moral fabric that holds a decent society together." And Friedrich Hayek maintained that the striving for social justice, which he called a "meaningless conception," will "produce highly undesirable consequences, and in particular lead to the destruction of the indispensable environment in which the traditional moral values alone can flourish, namely personal freedom."[44]

In recent decades some scholars, politicians, and commentators have called for a rolling back of the postwar welfare state and a return to Victorian values (or virtues). Charles Murray maintains that the negative aspects of

---

42. Barnett (1918: 83); Webb (1926: 201).
43. Bauer (1983).
44. Feldstein (1976: 7); Friedman and Friedman (1980: 119, 127); Hayek (1976: 67).

the welfare state extend far beyond its economic consequences. Individuals achieve "deep satisfactions in life" through four institutions—"family, community, vocation, and faith"—and social welfare policies enfeeble each of them. Self-help and private charity are more virtuous than tax-funded social welfare programs: "Throughout history until a few decades ago, the meaning of life for almost everyone was linked to the challenge of simple survival. Staying alive required being a contributing part of a community. Staying alive required forming a family and having children to care for you in your old age. The knowledge that sudden death could happen at any moment required attention to spiritual issues. Doing all those things provided deep satisfactions that went beyond survival. Life in an age of plenty and security requires none of those things."[45] Some of those who want to reduce social welfare spending point to Victorian England as a "golden age." According to Gertrude Himmelfarb, moral principles were a part of all Victorian social policies—poor relief was meant to "promote the moral as well as the material well-being of the poor." Victorian policies were far superior to current social welfare policies: "In recent times we have so completely rejected any kind of moral principle that we have deliberately, systematically divorced poor relief from moral sanctions and incentives. . . . We are now confronting the consequences of this policy of moral neutrality."[46] According to this view, the Victorian virtues of work, thrift, and self-help were held by the working class as well as the middle class. Workers attached a stigma to the acceptance of poor relief and protected themselves against income shocks by joining mutual insurance organizations, depositing money in savings banks, and helping each other, thereby making public assistance largely unnecessary.

The defenders of social policy also present moral as well as economic arguments. R. H. Tawney maintained that true liberty required "securities that the economically weak will not be at the mercy of the economically strong . . . a large measure of equality, so far from being inimical to liberty, is essential to it." Franklin Roosevelt, in his 1944 State of the Union Address, asserted that "true individual freedom cannot exist without economic security and independence. 'Necessitous men are not free men.'" He called for a Second Bill of Rights, providing, among other things, "the right to adequate protection from the economic fears of old age, sickness, accident, and unemployment," and "the right to adequate medical care and the opportunity to achieve and enjoy good health." And T. H. Marshall, in his essay "Citizenship and Social Class," argued that all citizens should have "the right to a modicum of economic welfare and security."[47]

45. Murray (2009: 8; 2006a; 2006b: 2).
46. Himmelfarb (1995a; 1995b).
47. Tawney (1931: 226); Roosevelt (1950: 41); Marshall (1950: 11).

More recently, Amartya Sen has described poverty, lack of economic opportunities, and lack of access to health care as "major sources of unfreedom." Despite unprecedented economic growth, the modern world "denies elementary freedoms to vast numbers." Economic poverty "robs people of the freedom to satisfy hunger, to achieve sufficient nutrition, or to obtain remedies for treatable illnesses, or the opportunity to be adequately clothed or sheltered, or to enjoy clean water or sanitary facilities." Sen accepts the important role played by personal responsibility, but contends that "responsibility *requires* freedom. . . . The argument for social support in expanding people's freedom can, therefore, be seen as an argument *for* individual responsibility, not against it. . . . Without the substantive freedom and capability to do something, a person cannot be responsible for doing it."[48]

Jacob Hacker describes negative economic shocks as being like hurricanes: They "strike powerfully and suddenly. They rip apart what they touch. . . . And although they can be prepared for, they cannot be prevented. . . . What happens in an instant may change a life forever." He rejects the "personal responsibility crusade," the drive to roll back the welfare state and shift economic risk from the government back onto individuals at a time when income volatility is rising and household balance sheets are fragile. In his words, "the old canard that ensuring security always hurts the economy turns out to be cruelly false. Economic security is vital to economic opportunity."[49]

Economists Sen, Robert Haveman, Anthony Atkinson, and Peter Lindert, among others, contend that the economic and social benefits of the welfare state outweigh any negative incentive effects. Haveman contends that "the primary economic gain from the welfare state is the *universal reduction in the uncertainty* faced by individuals. Life in a market economy is a treacherous enterprise." Sen maintains that in postwar Britain severe economic hardship during periods of high unemployment was prevented not by "the high average income or wealth of the British . . . but the guaranteed minimum values of exchange entitlements owing to the social security system." Atkinson argues that economists need to consider the social benefits of the welfare state as well as its economic costs: "There can be little doubt about its importance in providing income support. There are major equity gains." Lindert goes further, and concludes from his study of the evolution of social spending over the past two centuries that economists have greatly overstated the costs of the welfare state, and that it may well be a "free lunch"—there is little evidence that the taxes and transfers associated with social welfare programs reduce productivity or the rate of growth of GDP.[50]

48. Sen (1999: 3–4, 15, 283–84).
49. Hacker (2008: 5–9).
50. Haveman (1985: 449); Sen (1981: 6–7); Atkinson (1999: 183–84); Lindert (2004).

Robert Solow, in *Work and Welfare*, nicely described the social welfare policy debate in both contemporary America and Victorian England: "In a society that places a high value on self-reliance, being the regular beneficiary of altruism may be dangerous to one's moral health. It can lead to unresisted dependency. . . . Unadulterated market outcomes leave some fraction of citizens . . . deeply impoverished; the question is what to do about that collectively. . . . It is important to know whether extreme poverty arises from a failure of the market mechanism or whether the system is working well but with unpromising raw materials." Solow speculated on what would happen if the U.S. welfare system ended and former welfare recipients were forced to work. "The welfare roles will diminish. . . . No one will ask what has happened to the former welfare recipients or to the working poor. . . . They may be living with relatives who cannot afford them, or on the street, or under the bridges of Paris."[51] This applies equally to England in the 1870s, although London should be substituted for Paris.

As the above pages have shown, the arguments for and against government-provided welfare have been remarkably similar over the past two centuries. Recent American campaigns for welfare reform mirror pre-1914 British debates. Let me give two examples. When Lyndon Johnson declared war on poverty in 1964, he was echoing a declaration made by Lloyd George 55 years earlier. In April 1909, Lloyd George concluded his speech introducing the People's Budget to Parliament by declaring, "This is a War Budget. It is for raising money to wage implacable warfare against poverty and squalidness." He hoped "that before this generation has passed away we shall have advanced a great step toward" the elimination of poverty. Three months later, in a speech at Limehouse, he declared it "a shame" that poverty existed in "probably the richest country in the world," and asserted that his budget would protect workers against "the evils and the sufferings" caused by old age, unemployment, sickness, and widowhood. President Johnson, in his 1964 State of the Union message, declared "unconditional war on poverty in America. . . . Our aim is not only to relieve the symptom of poverty, but to cure it and, above all, to prevent it." He added, "It will not be a short or easy struggle . . . but we shall not rest until this war is won. The richest Nation on earth can afford to win it. We cannot afford to lose it."[52]

Second, there are many similarities between the American debate over welfare reform in the 1980s and 1990s and the Victorian debate that led to the Crusade Against Outrelief. Ronald Reagan's "welfare queens" who reputedly collected multiple welfare payments under various names were a modern version of Thomas Wright's "pauper-souled cormorants" who disdained

---

51. Solow (1998: 4, 42–43).
52. Lloyd George (1910, chaps. 6–7); Johnson (1965: 112–18).

work and managed to live well by collecting poor relief and charity at the same time. The debate of the 1990s, like that of the 1870s, focused on the supposed need to restore responsibility and morality among the poor, as is demonstrated by the title of the 1996 welfare reform law—the Personal Responsibility and Work Opportunity Reconciliation Act. Conservative pundit William Bennett praised policies requiring poor people to work for their assistance as making both "common sense and . . . moral sense. . . . It is putting people in a position to hold their heads high and take responsibility for their own lives. This is *true* compassion." On the other hand, historian James Patterson described the continued focus on the morality of relief recipients as "an apparently timeless faith that laws can be crafted that will make better people of the poor."[53]

New Perspectives and Findings

This book rewrites the history of working-class living standards and the growth of government social welfare policies in Britain since 1834. What does it present that is new? The book argues that long-term movements in living standards and the evolution of social welfare policies are intertwined, and that neither can be understood without taking the other into account. Workers' well-being was, and is, strongly affected by the extent of the social safety net under them. Living standards are higher in a society where workers are protected by a tightly woven social safety net than in one where many of those hit by income shocks end up, in Churchill's phrase, "smashing down on the pavement." Moreover, it is not possible to understand the reasons for the major changes in social welfare policies between 1830 and 1950 without understanding what was happening to living standards. Changes in social policy do not occur in a vacuum. By examining movements in living standards and social policy together, this book increases our understanding of both.

The book presents new estimates of the extent of economic insecurity and offers new insights into the ways that working-class households coped with insecurity, and into the changing nature of social welfare policies, from the 1830s to the adoption of the postwar welfare state. The approach adopted in the book and the data presented yield several important findings.

First, the book stresses the important role that economic insecurity played in the lives of working-class households throughout the nineteenth and early twentieth centuries. Nearly one-half of working-class families lived under the constant threat of an income shock large enough to cause acute financial distress. The ever-present possibility of being plunged into want made it

53. Wright (1868: 287–88); Thompson and Bennett (1997: 14–15); Patterson (1998: 253).

imperative that households develop coping strategies for dealing with negative income shocks. Workers dealt with insecurity by saving, joining mutual insurance organizations, relying on relatives and neighbors in times of need, and applying for public and private assistance when necessary. The book shows how the relative importance of these coping strategies changed over time, largely in response to the changing nature of government social welfare programs. The retrenchment of the Poor Law during the long reign of Queen Victoria led those manual workers who could afford it to devote some of their weekly earnings to saving for a rainy day. However, the data presented here show that the self-help option was not feasible for most unskilled and some semiskilled manual workers, who were forced to turn to public and private assistance, no matter how stigmatizing, when hit by negative income shocks.

Second, the book argues that the literature on social welfare policy has not devoted enough attention to the effects of the Crusade Against Outrelief in the 1870s and the Liberal Welfare Reforms of 1906–11, and too much to the effects of the 1834 Poor Law Amendment Act. While the 1834 act did indeed lead to a sharp drop in relief spending, its effect on the actual administration of poor relief, at least in industrial cities, was smaller than the expenditure data suggest. For another three decades, the Poor Law continued to function as a—somewhat stingier—"welfare state in miniature." Despite pressure from the central government to enforce the workhouse test, urban Poor Law unions continued to provide outdoor relief to unemployed and underemployed workers and their families during crisis times. The widespread adoption of the "principles of 1834" did not in fact occur until the Crusade Against Outrelief in the 1870s. The book provides a detailed examination of the causes and consequences of the crusade. The evidence presented offers strong support for Michael Rose's conclusion that "the New Poor Law was a creation of the 1860s and 1870s rather than of the 1830s."[54]

The Liberal Welfare Reforms and their extension in the 1920s were a major watershed in British social welfare policy that marked the end of seven decades of increasing stinginess toward those in need and the beginning of government assistance outside of the Poor Law. Unlike the Poor Law, which was funded by local property taxes, the new social welfare policies were funded either entirely by the central government (old age pensions) or by a combination of worker, employer, and state contributions (unemployment and sickness insurance). The "tripartite scheme of contributions" that began with the 1911 National Insurance Act was adopted by Beveridge in 1942 and by the National Insurance Act of 1946. The Liberal reforms laid the foundations on which the postwar welfare state was constructed.

54. Rose (1981: 52).

Third, the book stresses the important roles played by political voice, public opinion, and information in shaping public policy. The extension of the parliamentary franchise to working-class males in 1867 and 1884 played a major role in Parliament's adoption of the social welfare reforms of 1906–11, as did its further extension to all adult males and females in 1918 and 1928 in the adoption of the postwar welfare state. Public opinion also matters for social policy. If the public believes that poverty largely is a result of laziness, lack of thrift, and drunkenness, they are less likely to support generous tax-funded relief than if they believe that most poor people are poor through no fault of their own. The views of the middle and upper classes toward the poor changed over time. From the 1830s (if not earlier) up to the 1880s, many within the middle class maintained that workers could and should protect themselves against income insecurity rather than rely on the Poor Law or private charity. It was this belief in the "virtue" of self-reliance and the "evils" of generous public and private relief that led to the formation of the COS and to the Crusade Against Outrelief in the 1870s. There was a distinct shift in public opinion in the years leading up to the First World War, driven by the work of Booth, Rowntree, Pember Reeves, and others, which starkly demonstrated the distress suffered by the lower stratum of manual workers and their families. This new information led to a reawakening of the public to the plight of the poor and helped bring about the adoption of the Liberal Welfare Reforms. War also influenced middle-class attitudes toward the poor. During the Second World War, the common sacrifices made by Britons on the battlefield and in the bombed cities led to an increased affinity of the middle for the working class, and to a call for the creation of a postwar New Jerusalem or New Britain.

Finally, the book presents newly constructed estimates of the number of persons aged 65 and older receiving poor relief from 1861 to 1908, the year the Old Age Pension Act was adopted, for England as a whole and for its ten registration divisions. Some historians contend that before the twentieth century most old people were assisted by relatives or private charity and turned to the Poor Law "only in the last resort." According to this view, the "structured dependency" of the elderly is a post-welfare-state phenomenon.[55] The estimates reported here show that this was not in fact the case. In the 1860s about one-half of all working-class persons 65 and older received poor relief, in the form of either a permanent pension or occasional assistance. Old age pauperism rates declined thereafter, but remained high up to the adoption of the Old Age Pension Act. Large-scale government support for the elderly is not a product of the postwar welfare state; it existed at the local level throughout the nineteenth century and earlier.

---

55. Thane (1983: 191); Townsend (1981).

A Brief Road Map

The book is divided into two parts. Part I, "Social Policy and Self-Help in Victorian Britain" (Chapters 2–5), tells the story of the changing roles of self-help, public relief, and private charity in dealing with economic insecurity during the long reign of Queen Victoria, from 1837 to 1901. Part II, "Constructing the Welfare State" (Chapters 6–8), begins with an analysis of the Liberal Welfare Reforms, and then explains the expanding role of government social programs between the wars, the genesis of the Beveridge Plan, and the beginning of the welfare state after the Second World War.

Chapter 2 traces the roles played by the Poor Law, charity, and self-help from 1834 to 1870. Workers responded to the reduced availability of outdoor relief after 1834 by increasing their saving and joining friendly societies, but few were able to save more than a small amount, which was exhausted by spells of unemployment or sickness lasting more than a few weeks. As a result, many households continued to apply for poor relief during downturns, and urban Poor Law unions continued to provide outdoor relief to the unemployed despite pressure not to from the central administration. Unions proved unable to cope financially with the sharp increases in demand for relief during crises, and by the 1860s many were convinced that the system required a "radical restructuring."

Major changes in relief administration were undertaken in the 1870s. After more than three decades of resisting central government pressure to adhere to the "principles of 1834," local authorities, especially in urban districts, adopted some form of the workhouse test and made outdoor relief substantially more difficult to obtain. The reasons for this policy shift, known as the Crusade Against Outrelief, and its effects on working-class behavior, are the subject of Chapter 3. The increased use of the workhouse caused a sharp decline in the share of the population receiving poor relief. The crusade ended the use of the Poor Law to assist those temporarily in need during economic dislocations— after 1870 there is no hint of the trade cycle in aggregate statistics on numbers receiving relief, as there should have been in a modern social insurance regime with its "automatic stabilizers." Working-class self-help increased greatly after 1870, so that by the beginning of the twentieth century most skilled workers had some protection against negative income shocks. The situation was different for the low-skilled, most of whom had little savings and remained quite vulnerable to unexpected income loss.

The extent of economic insecurity caused by unemployment and old age is revealed in the following two chapters. Chapter 4 examines the extent of cyclical, seasonal, and casual unemployment from 1870 to 1914, and shows that reported unemployment rates greatly understate the probability of job loss faced by manual workers. The chapter also reveals the public and private battles over relief for the unemployed. In the 1870s, cities abruptly curtailed granting outdoor relief to able-bodied males, and beginning in 1886 the Local Government Board encouraged municipalities to establish work relief projects during downturns. However, neither municipal relief projects nor the work relief established as a result of the 1905 Unemployed Workmen Act succeeded in assisting the *temporarily* unemployed—most of those employed on relief works were chronically underemployed laborers.

Chapter 5 shows how the aged coped economically and the extent of their reliance on the Poor Law from the 1860s to 1908. New estimates of numbers receiving poor relief reveal that large-scale government support for the aged existed long before the welfare state. The share of working-class persons 65 and older receiving poor relief within a year ranged from about one-half in the 1860s to about one-third in 1908. Some of the late Victorian decline in old age pauperism was a result of improving economic conditions, but a large part resulted from policy changes brought about by the Crusade Against Outrelief. Workers found it difficult to save enough to provide for their old age. Those who were physically able continued to work, albeit at reduced pay, past 65 or even 70, and many received assistance from their children. However, the ability of older workers to support themselves declined with age, and married children with families often were unable to assist aged parents. The combination of little saving, declining earnings, and lack of family support forced many of the aged to turn to the Poor Law.

The remainder of the book tells the story of economic insecurity and social welfare policy from the Edwardian era to the adoption of the postwar welfare state. Chapter 6 argues that the Liberal Welfare Reforms of 1906–11, which created a safety net reducing the economic insecurity associated with industrial capitalism, marked a watershed in the history of British social welfare policy. Their timing is explained by increased middle-class knowledge of workers' insecurity and by the greater willingness of Parliament to act as a result of growing working-class political influence. Chapter 6 also compares British social welfare policies with social policies elsewhere in Western Europe. Britain's welfare reforms did not take place in isolation—several European nations adopted social welfare policies in the decades leading up to 1914. Indeed, Britain was a bit of a latecomer in the adoption of social programs, although it caught up quickly after 1906 and by the eve of the First World War was a leader in social welfare protection.

Chapter 7 describes the interwar expansion of social welfare policies and their role in alleviating economic insecurity in an era of unprecedented unemployment. The social security system established before the war and extended in the 1920s consisted of several independently administered programs— unemployment insurance, sickness and disability insurance, old age pensions, widows' and orphans' insurance, and the Poor Law. This safety net of many colors proved to be quite successful in alleviating poverty and maintaining the well-being of working-class households. The important role played by the safety net is clearly shown in the social surveys undertaken in the 1930s—between one-third and one-half of all working-class families surveyed received social income of some form. While the condition of the working class would have been considerably worse without the safety net, it contained many holes, which led to calls for a restructuring of social policy.

The story of the 1942 Beveridge Report and the beginnings of the welfare state is told in Chapter 8. The policies proposed by Beveridge and the 1945–48 legislation were logical extensions of government's expanding role in social welfare policy beginning with the Liberal Welfare Reforms. This does not mean that the importance of the postwar legislation should be downplayed. Because of the adoption of the National Health Service, universal coverage, and equality of treatment, Britain after 1948 deserves to be called a welfare state, while Edwardian and interwar Britain do not. Unfortunately, despite the enthusiasm with which the public greeted the welfare state, the postwar policies did not eliminate economic insecurity.

The concluding chapter (Chapter 9) sums up the book's major findings and offers some thoughts regarding the reasons for the shifts in social welfare policy from the 1830s to the 1940s.

———

Richard Titmuss began his 1955 Eleanor Rathbone Memorial Lecture by stating that "some students of social policy see the development of the 'Welfare State' in historical perspective as part of a broad, ascending road of social betterment provided for the working classes since the nineteenth century and achieving its goal in our time." He added that such a view suggests that "Britain is approaching the end of the road of social reform." Titmuss rejected this view, as do most recent students of social policy in Victorian Britain. One of the aims of this book is to show that while the social welfare policies of the 1940s may be viewed as an extension of the Liberal Welfare Reforms, the prototype for the Liberal reforms cannot be found in the Victorian Poor Law. Few contemporaries in 1850, or even 1880, could have foreseen the coming of the welfare state. In the words of Michael Rose, "to look for the origins of the welfare state in the nineteenth century Poor Law is to view it through the wrong end of the telescope." There is no "Whig theory of welfare."[56] Britain's road to the welfare state was not a straight and wide thoroughfare. It was a windy road, full of ruts and sharp turns.

56. Titmuss (1958: 34); Rose (1981: 52).

Appendix 1.1: Notes and Sources for Table 1.1

Sources for the estimates of the share of households living in poverty are reported in Table 1.1. The estimates of the share of households or adult males who were economically insecure were calculated as follows:

> **1688:** Calculated using Lindert and Williamson's (1982: 388–89) revisions of King's estimates. I assume that all households whose expenses were greater than their income, according to King, were economically insecure.
>
> **1801–3:** Calculated using Lindert and Williamson's (1982: 400–401) revisions of Colquhoun's estimates. I assume that all households in category F (laborers and the poor) were economically insecure, as well as all households headed by "laboring people in mines, canals, etc." and one-quarter of households headed by "artisans, handicrafts, mechanics, and laborers, employed in manufactures, buildings, and works of every kind." This yields about 926,800 economically insecure households, out of a total of 2,193,114 households.
>
> **1851:** Anderson (1971: 31) calculated that for his 1851 sample of Preston families headed by married couples, 9% had incomes "4s. or more below" the poverty line, 22% had incomes "less than 4s. above or below the" the poverty line, and 32% had incomes 4–12s. above the poverty line. I assumed that all families with incomes less than 8s. above the poverty line were economically insecure, and that half of those with incomes 4–12s. above the poverty line were within 8s. of the poverty line.
>
> **1861:** Dupree (1995: 74) followed Anderson's groupings in reporting her estimates of the extent of poverty for families headed by married couples in the Potteries in 1861. As with Anderson, I assumed that all families with incomes less than 8s. above the poverty line were economically insecure, and that half of those with incomes 4–12s. above the poverty line were within 8s. of the poverty line.
>
> **1861:** Baxter (1868: 88–93) presented estimates of the number of adult male manual laborers employed in various occupations, and average wages for subdivisions of manual workers. I construct two estimates of the number of economically insecure workers. The smaller estimate assumes that workers in the following occupational categories were insecure: unskilled laborers and agricultural laborers (subdivision VI), silk manufacturers (VII), dockworkers and porters, quarry workers, and workers in rural manufactures (V), miners, railway laborers, platelayers, and navies (IV). The larger estimate also includes workers in the following categories: carriers on roads,

coachmen and cabmen, coalheavers, and chimney sweepers (IV), and carriers on canals, bargemen, and watermen, warehousemen, and seamen (III). Neither estimate includes any skilled workers in highly cyclical industries. Estimates for all gainfully employed males include adults in upper- and middle-class occupations in the denominator, from Baxter (1868: 82).

1867: Levi (1867: 14–15, 49–126) presented estimates of the number of adult male manual laborers employed in various occupations in the United Kingdom. I construct two estimates of the number of economically insecure workers. The smaller estimate assumes that workers in the following occupational categories were insecure: agricultural laborers, fishermen, coal miners, other miners, quarry workers, dock laborers, messengers and porters, and silk manufacturers. The larger estimate also includes an approximation of the number of painters and unskilled workers in the building trades. Even the larger percentage reported in the table understates the extent of economic insecurity among manual laborers, as it does not include any skilled workers in highly cyclical industries.

1912–14: Bowley and Burnett-Hurst (1915: 88, 134, 157, 172; 1920: 238) presented data on the relationship between weekly income and the poverty line for each household in their town samples. I assumed that all households with weekly incomes either below the poverty line or above but within 8s. of the poverty line were economically insecure.

1911, 1931, 1951: Routh (1980: 6–7, 28–39) presented occupational data for Great Britain for census years 1911, 1931, and 1951. I constructed two estimates of the number of economically insecure workers. The smaller estimate assumes that workers in the following occupational categories were insecure: unskilled manual workers, agricultural laborers, foresters and fishermen, and workers in mining and quarrying. The larger estimate includes an additional 250,000 workers to take into account semiskilled and skilled manual workers in highly cyclical and seasonal occupations. For each year, the denominator in the top row is the total number of adult male manual workers; the denominator in the second row is the total number of gainfully employed adult males.

Appendix 1.2: Notes and Sources for Figure 1.3

The data in Figure 1.3 represent the share of the population receiving social benefits at some point over the course of the year. The estimates were calculated as follows:

DATA FOR 1829 TO 1914

For 1829–1908, the number of persons receiving social benefits was simply the number receiving poor relief. For 1909–14, the number receiving social benefits includes persons receiving poor relief and persons receiving old age pensions. The data are for England and Wales.

I constructed rough estimates of the number of persons receiving poor relief in 1829–33 using data on the number of relief recipients for 1812–13 through 1814–15 and annual poor relief expenditures for 1812 through 1833. The construction of the estimates is explained in Appendix 2.1. Official estimates of the annual number of persons receiving poor relief for 1840 to 1914 are from Williams (1981: 158–65). Beginning in 1859, the government reported the number of persons receiving relief on two days a year (January 1 and July 1). The average of the two figures provides the day count of paupers. The reported day counts for 1849–59, but not for 1859 onward, include the insane and casuals. I spliced the two series together by reducing the number of paupers for 1849–58 using the ratio of indoor and outdoor paupers to total paupers for 1859, 0.941. For 1840–48, the number reported is the total number of persons who received relief in the first quarter of the year. To make the quarterly estimates comparable with the day counts reported for later years, I spliced the series together using the ratio of the day count of paupers on July 1, 1848, to that of July 1, 1849, reported in the *Second Annual Report of the Poor Law Board*. This yielded a day count pauperism rate for 1848 of 6.5%. The ratio of the quarterly count to the day count for 1848 was 1.662. I divided the reported quarterly pauperism rates for 1840–47 by 1.662, to make them comparable to the day count pauperism rates for 1849 onward.

Pauper censuses undertaken in 1891–92 and 1906–7 show that the day count substantially understated the total number of persons who received relief over the course of a year. To convert the day count to an annual count of numbers receiving relief, for each year from 1840 to 1900 I multiplied the day count by 2.24, the ratio of the 12-month count to the day count for 1891–92. For each year from 1901 to 1914, I multiplied the day count by 2.15, the ratio of the 12-month count to the day count for 1906–7. Figure 1.3 uses the estimated year-counts.

Government old age pensions were paid out beginning in 1909. Data on the number of pensioners for each year from 1909 to 1914 are from the *Eighteenth Abstract of Labour Statistics* (1927: 212).

DATA FOR 1922 TO 1938

The number receiving social benefits for 1922–38 includes those receiving unemployment benefits, sickness and disability benefits, old age pensions, poor relief, and, from 1926 onward, widows', orphans', and old age contributory pensions. The data are for the United Kingdom.

Unemployment Benefits. Data on the number of unemployed insured workers are from Feinstein (1972: T128). Data reported by Thomas (1988: 106) indicate that the share of the labor force unemployed within a year was far larger than the unemployment rate. To take account of workers moving into and out of unemployment, I conservatively estimated that the total number receiving unemployment benefits during a year was double the number unemployed reported by Feinstein.

Government Old Age Pensions. Data on the annual number of pensioners for 1922–36 are from the *Twenty-Second Abstract of Labour Statistics of the United Kingdom* (1937: 173). Data for 1937–38 are from the *Eighty-Third Statistical Abstract for the United Kingdom* (1940: 87).

Sickness Benefits. I calculated the number of recipients of sickness benefits using data on expenditures on sickness benefits from the *Twenty-Second Abstract of Labour Statistics* (1937: 166) and the *Eighty-Third Statistical Abstract* (1940: 85). To convert spending into number of recipients, I assumed that the average duration of benefits was 20 weeks; sickness benefits were 15s. per week throughout the period.

Disability Benefits. I calculated the number of recipients of disability benefits using data on expenditures on disability benefits from the *Twenty-Second Abstract of Labour Statistics* (1937: 166) and the *Eighty-Third Statistical Abstract* (1940: 85). To convert spending into number of recipients, I assumed that the average duration of benefits was 52 weeks; disability benefits were 7.5s. per week.

Widows', Orphans', and Old Age Contributory Pensions. Data on the annual number of pension recipients are from the *Twenty-Second Abstract of Labour Statistics* (1937: 169) and the *Eighty-Third Statistical Abstract* (1940: 89).

Poor Law Benefits. The annual number of poor relief recipients on one day in winter and one in summer for the United Kingdom are reported in the *Twenty-Second Abstract of Labour Statistics* (1937: 193) and the *Eighty-Third Statistical Abstract* (1940: 97). I calculated the annual number relieved (day count) by taking the average of the two days. To convert the day count to an annual count of numbers receiving relief, for each year I multiplied the day count by 2.15, the ratio of the 12-month count to the day count for 1906–7. Some poor relief recipients also received other benefits or pensions. To avoid double counting, in constructing the estimate of the total number of persons receiving social benefits I reduced the estimated number of poor relief recipients by 15%.

Appendix 1.3: Notes and Sources for Figure 1.4

Figure 1.4 presents estimates of social welfare spending as a share of gross domestic product from 1816 to 1960. The estimates were calculated as follows:

The data for 1816–1913 are for England and Wales. Social spending for 1816–1908 consists entirely of spending on poor relief. For 1909–13, social spending includes expenditures on poor relief and old age pensions. Annual poor relief expenditures are from Mitchell (1988: 605) and Williams (1981: 169–71). Expenditures on old age pensions are from the *Seventeenth Abstract of Labour Statistics* (1915: 185). I constructed annual estimates of nominal GDP for England and Wales for 1816–70 by multiplying estimates for Great Britain constructed by Broadberry et al. by .90, the ratio of national income of England and Wales to that of Great Britain in 1861, as estimated by Baxter (1868: 52, 56, 60, 64).[57] For 1870–1913, I constructed estimates of nominal GDP for England and Wales by splicing Thomas and Williamson's (2017) estimates of GDP for the United Kingdom to Broadberry et al.'s adjusted estimates for England and Wales.

The data for 1920–60 are for the United Kingdom. Data on social spending for 1920–38 are from Peacock and Wiseman (1967: 92); data for 1949–60 are from Central Statistical Office, *Annual Abstract of Statistics* (1957: 50; 1962: 43). Data on nominal GDP are from Thomas and Williamson (2017).

---

57. Broadberry et al. (2015). Their nominal GDP data are available on the Bank of England's website: www.bankofengland.co.uk/statistics/research-datasets. The data are contained in the section titled "A Millennium of Macroeconomic Data."

PART I

Social Policy and Self-Help in Victorian Britain

2

Poor Relief, Charity, and Self-Help in Crisis Times, 1834–69

The adoption of the Poor Law Amendment Act in 1834 marked the end of an era of generous public assistance. In the four decades before the act's passage, the Poor Law played the largest role of its 350-year history, assisting the unemployed and underemployed as well as widows, children, the sick, the elderly, and the disabled. Relief expenditures as a share of gross domestic product, real per capita expenditures, and the percentage of the population receiving relief were higher from 1795 to 1834 than at any other time before the twentieth century. The share of relief recipients who were prime-aged males also peaked between 1795 and 1834, and was especially high in the grain-producing South and East, where a large share of relief spending consisted of payments to seasonally unemployed agricultural workers or weekly allowances for poor laborers with large families. For most recipients, poor relief took the form of cash or in-kind payments to the poor in their homes.[1]

The generous nature of the Old Poor Law sparked a wave of criticism from political economists and other commentators. Critics opposed granting outdoor relief to able-bodied males on the grounds that it reduced work incentives and thrift among the working class. Frederic Eden, author of *The State of the Poor* (1797), maintained that public assistance "checks that emulative spirit of exertion, which the want of the necessities . . . gives birth to: for it assures

---

1. Lindert (1998: 114); Boyer (2002: Table 1). On the pre-1834 role of the Poor Law in grain-producing parishes, see Boyer (1990: chaps. 3–5).

a man, that, whether he may have been indolent, improvident, prodigal, or vicious, he shall never suffer want." Thomas Malthus, the most influential participant in the pre-1834 debate, argued that the Poor Laws, by guaranteeing assistance to those in need, "diminish both the power and the will to save among the common people, and thus . . . weaken one of the strongest incentives to sobriety and industry, and consequently to happiness."[2]

Widespread clamor for reform led the government in 1832 to appoint the Royal Commission to Investigate the Poor Laws. The commission's 1834 report called for the grouping of parishes into Poor Law unions and the appointment of a centralized Poor Law Commission to direct the administration of relief. The report focused largely on the granting of outdoor relief to able-bodied males, concluding that it tended to "diminish, we might almost say to destroy, all . . . qualities in the labourer." It recommended that relief be granted to able-bodied adults and their families only in well-regulated workhouses, and confidently predicted that the use of workhouses would restore the industry and "frugal habits" of the poor, and improve their "moral and social condition."[3]

Critics of the Old Poor Law believed that the substitution of workhouses for outdoor relief would lead workers to protect themselves against income loss by saving more and joining friendly societies. The number of able-bodied male applicants for relief would greatly decline, and the Poor Law's main job would be to assist widows and orphans, the non-able-bodied, and the elderly. The New Poor Law would usher in an era of financially independent workers and lower taxes.

The relief system initiated in 1834 was subjected to a major test within a decade of its creation by the downturns of the hungry 1840s, and to additional tests in the 1860s by the Lancashire cotton famine and the Poor Law crisis in London. These shocks revealed serious flaws in the new system. While the New Poor Law led to increased savings by working-class households, the amount that the typical household was able to save was small, and any spell of unemployment lasting more than a few weeks exhausted most workers' savings. Second, the Poor Law was not set up to deal with the sharp increases in need that occurred during business-cycle downturns. The downturns of the 1840s led to widespread unemployment, and many of the unemployed, once their savings were depleted, were forced to apply for poor relief. Both the working class and local relief officials believed that the cyclically unemployed, who lost their jobs through no fault of their own, should be eligible for outdoor relief. Moreover, the number of able-bodied relief applicants far exceeded the available workhouse space. Poor Law unions in manufacturing districts found it physically impossible and morally unacceptable to relieve the cyclically unemployed

2. Eden (1797: 1:447–48); Malthus ([1798] 2008: 40–41).
3. Royal Commission to Investigate the Poor Laws, *Report on the Administration and Practical Operation of the Poor Laws* (1834: 261–63).

and their families in workhouses. Finally, the system of taxation used to fund the Poor Law proved unable to raise enough money to assist all those in need. These flaws led to the rise of short-term charitable movements to fill the gap between the demand for relief and its supply during both the 1840s and 1860s.

This chapter explores the roles of the Poor Law, private charity, and self-help in urban areas during the hungry 1840s, the Lancashire cotton famine of 1862–65, and the London crisis of the 1860s. I set the stage with a brief summary of the effects of the Poor Law Amendment Act on public relief and on the rise of working-class self-help.

I. The Decline in Relief Spending and the Rise of Self-Help

Soon after the Royal Commission's report was published in 1834 Parliament adopted the Poor Law Amendment Act, which implemented some of the report's recommendations and left others, like the regulation of outdoor relief, to the newly appointed Poor Law Commissioners. By 1839 the vast majority of rural parishes had been grouped into Poor Law unions, and most unions in southern and eastern England either had constructed or were constructing workhouses. By contrast, the commission met with strong opposition when it attempted in 1837 to set up unions in the industrial North, and the implementation of the New Poor Law in several industrial cities was delayed.[4]

The change in the administration of relief led to a sharp fall in poor relief expenditures. From 1812 to 1832, relief expenditures for England and Wales as a whole averaged 1.9% of GDP, peaking at 2.2% during the post-Waterloo downturn of 1816–20. For 1835–50, relief spending averaged only 1.1% of GDP, peaking at 1.3% during the downturns of 1842 and 1848.[5]

Data on the number of poor relief recipients in the first four decades of the nineteenth century are available only for 1802–3 and for 1812–13 to 1814–15. However, it is possible to use these data, along with annual expenditure data, to construct rough estimates of the number of relief recipients in the years leading up to the Poor Law Amendment Act. These new estimates of the share of the population receiving poor relief for the years 1812–32 are presented in Figure 2.1, along with estimates for 1840–50. The construction of the estimates is explained in Appendix 2.1. It must be stressed that these estimates are rough and are meant to yield only a general idea of the extent of the decline in numbers

4. Driver (1989). On northern opposition to implementing the New Poor Law, see Edsall (1971) and Knott (1986). On the opposition in southern rural districts, see Digby (1975; 1978).

5. Annual estimates of Poor Law expenditures as a share of GDP for 1812–50 are reported in Appendix 2.1. My estimates differ slightly from those by Lindert (1998: 113–15) because I use more recent GDP estimates.

FIGURE 2.1. Share of Population Receiving Poor Relief, 1812–50

on relief after 1834. That said, Figure 2.1 shows that on average 15.1% of the population was in receipt of relief in the two decades leading up to the Poor Law Amendment Act. The peak occurred in 1817–20, when the share relieved averaged 16.7%. In 1830–32, on the eve of the appointment of the Royal Poor Law Commission, nearly 16% of the population received public assistance. The size of the "pauper host" declined after 1834. During the "hungry 1840s," an average of 12.2% of the population received poor relief at some point in a year. The share receiving relief averaged 10.4% in the 1850s, and continued to decline thereafter.

The magnitude of the decline in relief spending varied across regions, being largest in rural southern England, where Poor Law unions were first organized and workhouse construction began (see Table 2.1). From 1834 to 1837, per capita relief expenditures declined by 48% in the South and 42% in the East, as compared to 32% in the industrial North West and 27% in the North. The sharp downward trajectory in spending lasted only three years. In all regions per capita expenditures were higher during the hungry 1840s than in 1837. In the North West, per capita relief spending during the downturns of 1841–43 and 1847–48 was higher than it had been the year before the Poor Law Amendment Act was adopted, suggesting that the Poor Law's role in industrial cities was not altered substantially by the act.

The group most affected by the New Poor Law was adult able-bodied males and their families, in particular those in the rural South and East where the new system initially was enforced. Outside of this region, the Poor Law Commission and its 1847 replacement, the Poor Law Board, issued several orders to selected Poor Law unions in an attempt to regulate the granting of relief to

TABLE 2.1. Regional Poor Relief Expenditures, 1834–52

	PER CAPITA POOR RELIEF EXPENDITURES (SHILLINGS)						
Region	1834	1837	1840	1843	1846	1848	1852
London	8.3	4.9	5.3	6.2	5.8	6.9	5.4
South	13.6	7.2	7.8	8.3	7.8	9.0	6.9
East	15.2	8.8	9.2	9.1	9.2	10.4	8.1
South West	9.1	6.2	7.5	7.7	7.2	8.9	6.7
Midlands	7.8	4.9	5.1	5.8	5.2	6.3	4.8
North West	4.3	2.9	3.4	4.9	3.6	5.5	3.6
North	6.8	5.0	5.1	5.5	4.9	5.4	4.6

	PER CAPITA POOR RELIEF EXPENDITURES (RATIO)						
Region	1834	1837	1840	1843	1846	1848	1852
London	100.0	59.2	64.0	74.9	70.1	83.1	65.2
South	100.0	52.3	57.0	60.5	56.5	66.2	50.3
East	100.0	57.8	60.8	60.2	60.8	68.8	53.2
South West	100.0	68.7	82.0	84.4	79.6	97.9	74.3
Midlands	100.0	63.4	65.9	74.2	67.2	81.1	61.5
North West	100.0	67.9	79.3	113.1	84.1	127.4	83.4
North	100.0	73.0	75.5	81.0	72.3	79.4	67.3

Source: Constructed by author from poor relief expenditure data in the Annual Reports of the Poor Law Commission and the Poor Law Board.

able-bodied males. The Outdoor Labour Test Order of 1842, sent to unions without workhouses or where the workhouse test was deemed unenforceable, stated that able-bodied males could be given outdoor relief only if they were set to work by the union. The Outdoor Relief Prohibitory Order of 1844 prohibited outdoor relief for both able-bodied males and females except on account of sickness or "sudden and urgent necessity," and the Outdoor Relief Regulation Order of 1852 extended the labor test for those relieved outside of workhouses. However, as will be made clear in the next section, these orders were evaded by urban Poor Law unions throughout England, especially during cyclical downturns. Urban workers viewed the right to outdoor relief when unemployed as part of an "unwritten social contract" with employers, and most local relief administrators in manufacturing cities agreed.[6]

6. See Hunt (1981: 215), Rose (1966: 612–13), and Rose (1970: 121–43). Lees (1998: chap. 6) found that in three London parishes and six provincial towns in the years around 1850 large numbers of prime-age males continued to apply for relief, and that a majority of those assisted were granted outdoor relief. Digby (1975) presents evidence that restrictions on granting outdoor relief to able-bodied males also were evaded by rural Poor Law unions in the grain-producing East.

SELF-HELP

Working-class self-help was relatively small before 1834, largely because of the low level of wage rates, but perhaps also because of the generous nature of poor relief. Pre-1834 data exist for two forms of working-class thrift—membership in mutual insurance organizations known as friendly societies and deposits in savings banks. Returns from local Poor Law overseers indicated that in 1815 there were 925,400 members of friendly societies in England, representing 29% of males aged 15 and over. All of these societies were local organizations, and some were little more than burial clubs. Many were financially unstable and provided only "short-term benefits."[7] Probably no more than 50–60% of members were in societies that paid sickness benefits.

The share of the population belonging to friendly societies in 1815 varied substantially across regions. It was largest in Lancashire and other northern and Midlands industrial counties, where one-third to one-half of males 15 and older were members of societies, and lowest in southern and eastern rural counties, where fewer than one-in-five adult males were members. A House of Lords Select Committee reported county-level estimates for 1821 of friendly society membership as a share of total population. The ranking of counties is similar to that in 1815—the incidence of membership was highest in Lancashire (17%) followed by Staffordshire (14%), and lowest in Sussex (2.5%).[8] Membership was highest in counties where per capita poor relief spending was low, and lowest in counties where per capita spending was high. There are several possible but conflicting explanations for this finding. Perhaps, because wages were higher in the North and Midlands than in the South, northern workers had "surplus earnings" to devote to mutual insurance. Another explanation, put forward by many contemporaries, was that the generosity of the Poor Law in the rural South and East reduced insecurity for working-class households by enough that most found it unnecessary to purchase mutual insurance.[9] Proponents of this explanation maintained that restricting outdoor relief would lead southern workers to join friendly societies even if their wage rates did not increase.

Membership in local societies stagnated from 1815 to the early 1830s. However, this same period witnessed the rise of the national affiliated orders. The largest of these, the Independent Order of Oddfellows, Manchester Unity (IOOMU), was founded in Manchester in 1810 and by 1831 claimed to have 31,000 members. The Ancient Order of Foresters (AOF) was founded in Leeds

---

7. Gorsky (1998: 493); King and Tomkins (2003: 267).

8. Data for 1815 from Gorsky (1998: 493–97); data for 1821 from Gosden (1961: 22–24).

9. Gorsky (1998) discusses various explanations for the regional nature of friendly society membership in the first third of the nineteenth century. See also King and Tomkins (2003: 266–68).

in 1813 and claimed 16,510 members in 1835.[10] Adding together local societies and affiliated orders, membership in friendly societies in the early 1830s probably totaled slightly less than a million. Perhaps 600,000 members (16% of adult males) were in societies paying sickness benefits.

Parliament established the Trustee Savings Banks in 1817 in an attempt to encourage working-class saving. These banks had about 425,000 depositors in 1830, with deposits totaling £14.6 million (see Table 2.2). In order to determine the extent of working-class saving, it is necessary to separate deposits of manual workers from those of the middle class. Few if any workers had deposits greater than £50, and many deposits under £50 "belonged to children of prosperous parents."[11] In 1830, 79% of depositors had balances less than £50, and 51% had balances less than £20. The upper limit of the number of working-class depositors therefore was 340,000; the actual number probably was about 280,000. Depositors with balances less than £50 held 38% of the £14.6 million in deposits in 1830, or £5.5 million. Total working-class deposits almost certainly were less than this; a rough estimate suggests that workers' balances totaled £3.2 million, or 22% of deposits.[12] This represented about 57% of spending on indoor and outdoor poor relief in 1830.[13] In sum, before 1834 only a small minority of working-class households either belonged to friendly societies offering sickness benefits or had deposits in a savings bank.

THE EFFECT OF POOR LAW REFORM ON SELF-HELP

The relative importance of self-help and public relief began to change after 1834. The Poor Law Commission did not eliminate outdoor relief to the able-bodied, but it succeeded in restricting relief for able-bodied males and in

---

10. Neave (1996: 46–47); Gosden (1973: 27–30).

11. The quote is from Fishlow (1961: 32). Johnson (1985: 103) considered £50 to be "an upper limit for most working-class savings bank deposits" in 1911–13. Given the large increase in wages from 1830 to 1911, the upper limit for working-class savings must have been far below £50 in 1830; using this number as a cutoff provides an upper-bound estimate of the importance of working-class saving.

12. Fishlow (1961: 32). Johnson (1985) presents evidence that about 30% of savings bank deposits were held by workers in the decades leading up to World War I. Assuming that 30% of deposits were held by workers in 1830 gives an unreasonably large average account balance. My estimate of £3.2 million assumes that manual workers held all deposits under £20 and half of the deposits between £20 and £50, and that the average working-class balance for this larger category of deposits was £25.

13. Poor relief expenditures in England and Wales totaled £6.8 million in 1830, but some of this was for administration. In 1840, spending on indoor and outdoor relief represented 82% of total relief spending. Applying this same ratio to 1830 yields an expenditure level of about £5.6 million.

TABLE 2.2. Friendly Society Membership and Working-Class Savings Accounts, 1830–70

	Adult Males Aged 20+	Estimated Friendly Society Members	Four Affiliated Friendly Societies Members	Friendly Society Members with Sickness Benefits	% Males with Friendly Society Sickness Benefits	Working-Class Savings Accounts	Savings Bank Deposits (£ million)	Estimated Working-Class Savings Deposits (£ million)
1830	3,684,500	1,000,000	45,000	600,000	16	280,000	14.6	3.20
1840							23.5	5.88
1845			368,801				30.7	7.68
1850	4,717,000	2,000,000	328,663	1,350,000	29	750,000	28.9	7.23
1860			524,417				41.3	10.33
1870	5,866,000	3,500,000	859,040	2,400,000	41	1,900,000	53.1	15.93

Sources: Column 1: Mitchell (1988: 11, 15). Number for 1830 estimated by author assuming that the ratio of adult males to all males was the same as in 1851. Column 2: Estimate for 1830 from Hopkins (1995: 24). Estimates for 1850 and 1870 (1872) by author. See text. Column 3: Numbers for 1846 to 1870 from Neave (1996: 49). Number for 1830 estimated by author. See text. Column 4: Estimated by author. See text. Column 5: Calculated as column 4 divided by column 1. Column 6: Estimated by author from data in Fishlow (1961) and Johnson (1985: 91–93). Column 7: Mitchell (1988: 671–2). Column 8: Estimate for 1870 calculated by assuming that 30% of savings bank deposits belonged to working-class accounts. See Johnson (1985: 100–105). Estimates for 1840–60 assume that 25% of deposits belonged to working-class accounts. I chose lower estimates for the percentage of deposits held by members of the working class in 1830–60 because using 30% yielded unreasonably large average deposits per working-class account. For a discussion of how the estimate for 1830 was calculated, see text. The estimates for 1830–60 are based on a substantial amount of guesswork.

reducing relief expenditures.[14] At the same time, there was a sharp increase in friendly society membership and private saving. Membership in the Manchester Unity Oddfellows increased from 31,000 in 1832 to 90,000 in 1838 and 259,000 in 1846, while membership in the Foresters increased from 16,500 in 1835 to nearly 77,000 in 1846. Of the 3,074 English lodges of the IOOMU in 1875, 1,470 (48%) were established between 1835 and 1845, more than three times as many as were founded in any other decade. Other, but smaller affiliated orders also were established during these years, including the Independent Order of Rechabites and the Loyal Order of Ancient Shepherds, who between them had 32,000 members in 1846.[15] Table 2.2 shows that membership in the four affiliated orders, taken together, increased from under 50,000 in 1830 to nearly 370,000 in 1846, before declining to about 329,000 in 1850. There are no data on the membership of local societies in the 1830s and 1840s, but it probably increased as well, albeit more slowly than the affiliated orders. I estimate that total friendly society membership in 1850 was roughly 2 million, about 40% of adult males (Table 2.2).[16] Membership in societies paying sickness benefits probably was between 1.2 and 1.35 million.[17] Thus, from 1830 to 1850, the share of adult males insured against income loss due to sickness increased from roughly 16% to 25–29%.

Private saving also increased greatly after 1834, as shown in Table 2.2. The number of working-class depositors grew from about 280,000 in the early 1830s to 750,000 in 1850, at which time between one-fifth and one-quarter of adult working-class males had a savings bank account.[18] It should be stressed, however,

14. Williams (1981: 68–75) claimed that the New Poor Law succeeded in abolishing outdoor relief for the able-bodied by 1850. However, as noted above, Rose (1966; 1970), Digby (1975), and Lees (1998) have shown that orders regulating outdoor relief largely were evaded by both urban and rural unions.

15. Neave (1996: 47–49); Gosden (1961: 34). There were 569 IOOMU lodges in 1835.

16. Hopkins (1995: 30) contends that "the leading affiliated orders clearly proved more attractive to many working men than the small local club with its often inadequate financial resources and uncertain future." My estimate of friendly society membership in 1850 is lower than previous estimates by Supple and Perkin. Supple (1974: 215) estimates that about one-half of adult males were members of friendly societies in 1850, which suggests that membership at midcentury exceeded 2.35 million. This number almost certainly is too high, in that it assumes that membership in local societies more than doubled from 1830 to 1850, so that in the latter year there were roughly 2 million local society members. Perkin (1969: 381) gives an estimate for total friendly society membership in 1849 of 3 million, but he gives no citation for this figure, which must be a substantial overestimate.

17. Johnson (1985: 57) estimated that 75.7% of the members of ordinary and affiliated friendly societies in 1901 were in societies paying sickness benefits. The share of local society members eligible for sickness benefits in 1850 probably was substantially below 75%. I assume that 60–67% of all members in 1850 were in societies paying sickness benefits.

18. The average number of accounts in Trustee Savings Banks in 1842–46 was 999,000 (Fishlow 1961: 39). I assume that workers held 75% of these accounts.

that even with the impressive growth in private saving and friendly society membership, before 1850 the majority of working-class households neither had a savings account nor belonged to a friendly society paying sickness benefits.

What caused the increase in self-help after 1834? It was not caused by a sharp increase in wage income; from 1830–32 to 1844–46, manual workers' real earnings increased on average by only 10%.[19] The Assistant Poor Law Commissioners for the rural South East reported examples of wages and employment increasing as a result of the abolition of outdoor relief for able-bodied males, but these increases were not large enough to explain the change in workers' behavior.

The Poor Law Commission attributed much of the growth in friendly society membership and working-class saving to the reform of the Poor Law. Assistant Poor Law Commissioners reported in 1835 that "medical clubs are starting up in all directions" in districts where the New Poor Law had been implemented.[20] One wrote in 1842 that Kent and Sussex had witnessed a "vast increase" in friendly society members and a substantial increase in deposits in savings banks since 1834.[21] Tidd Pratt, the barrister appointed to certify the rules of savings banks and friendly societies, reported in 1838 that there had been a sharp increase in the number of benefit-society lodges since the passage of the Poor Law Amendment Act, and that from November 1833 to November 1836 the amount of money deposited in savings banks by individuals had increased by 22%. Pratt stated that the founders of new lodges wrote to him that "now is the time that parties must look to themselves, as they could not receive out-door relief under the new law." He attributed the increasing number of depositors in savings banks to the reform of the Poor Law.[22]

In sum, while the effect of the New Poor Law on working-class self-help cannot be determined precisely, it seems probable that some part of the increase in friendly society membership and savings bank deposits after 1834 represented a working-class response to the declining availability of outdoor relief, and that working-class households, on average, devoted a larger share of their income to self-help in the 1840s than they did before 1834. It is important not to misinterpret this conclusion. It should not be viewed as support for the Royal Poor Law Commission's assertion that large numbers of workers abused the Poor Law before 1834. Workers sought to minimize their economic insecurity, and they responded to the shrinking public sector safety net by protecting themselves against income loss.

---

19. Feinstein (1998: 653).

20. *First Annual Report of the Poor Law Commissioners* (1835: 54–56). The best discussion of the relationship between friendly societies and the Poor Law is Gosden (1961: 198–210).

21. *Eighth Annual Report of the Poor Law Commissioners* (1842: 247).

22. *Fourth Annual Report of the Poor Law Commissioners* (1838: 84–87).

II. Poor Relief, Charity, and Self-Help during the Hungry 1840s

THE FUNDING OF POOR RELIEF

The Poor Law was administered at the local level. Before 1865, each parish within a Poor Law union was responsible for relieving its own poor, within the legal and fiscal constraints imposed from above. Poor relief was financed by a property tax, known as the poor rate, assessed on "land, houses, and buildings of every description" within the parish, but not on firms' profits or stock in trade. Machinery typically was not taken into account in estimating the rateable value of factory buildings.[23] Under this system of assessment, a large share of the poor rate was levied on occupiers of dwelling houses. An 1842 report concerning Stockport classified all assessments of £8 or less as working-class dwellings, and assessments of £8–20 as dwellings of foremen, clerks, small shopkeepers, and "persons of small independent means." Assessments of more than £20 included the "higher classes of private residences," large shopkeepers, and publicans, as well as factories.[24] In 1848–49 the majority of collected poor-rate assessments in each of three Lancashire cities—Ashton-under-Lyne, Manchester, and Preston—were valued at less than £8, and more than 80% were valued at less than £20. I estimate that assessments on working-class dwellings contributed 14–28% of the poor rate in these cities, and that all assessments valued at less than £20 contributed 32–45% of the poor rate.[25]

The assessment system had important implications regarding who paid for poor relief. Ratepayers in industrial cities can be divided into three groups—manufacturers and other major employers of labor, working-class households, and the remaining ratepayers (merchants, shopkeepers, landlords, tradesmen, etc.). If manufacturers in Ashton-under-Lyne, Manchester, and Preston paid between one-half and two-thirds of the rate collected from assessments of £20 or more, then they contributed 27–46% of the poor rate, "a distinctly modest contribution to local expenditure."[26] Because rates were levied on occupiers of dwelling houses rather than owners, workers, most of whom

23. Rose (1965: 348–59).

24. Parl. Papers, *Report of the Assistant Poor Law Commissioners . . . on the State of the Population of Stockport* (1842, XXXV), p. 6.

25. "Collected" assessments refer to assessments that were paid, rather than defaulted on. Parl. Papers, *Returns Relating to Rating of Tenements in Lancashire, Suffolk, Hampshire, and Gloucestershire* (1849, XLVII), pp. 10–15; Parl. Papers, *Return of Amount Levied for Poor and County Rates, etc.* (1847–48, LIII), p. 166.

26. The quote is from Eastwood (1997: 79). A detailed poor rate assessment for Sheffield in 1834 indicates that dwelling houses paid 74.1% of the poor rate and factories paid only 16.6% of the rate. See Rose (1965: 349). Factories' contributions to the poor rate surely were greater than this in the cotton-textile district of south Lancashire in the 1840s.

rented their tenements, paid part of the tax, though poor workers often were excused from paying "on account of poverty." Moreover, some of the tax levied on occupiers would have been shifted to their landlords.[27] Non-labor-hiring middle-class taxpayers paid a quarter or more of the poor rate. The more successful working-class occupiers were in shifting the rates on dwelling houses to their landlords, the larger the share of the poor rate paid by middle-class taxpayers.[28]

The Poor Law generally was capable of handling relief costs. However, during the "hungry" 1840s it proved unable to meet the increased demand for assistance in many cities, due to both the high number of unemployed workers and the decline in the effective tax base resulting from sharp increases in the default rate of taxpayers. The problem faced by parishes during downturns can be seen from some basic accounting. A parish's supply of poor-relief funds at a point in time t can be written as $r_t(1 - d)_t V_t$, where r is the poor (tax) rate, d is the share of the tax bill that was not paid (the default rate), and V is the total value of rateable property in the parish. Relief expenditures at time t are equal to $g_t s_t P_t$, where g is the generosity of relief per recipient, s is the share of the local population being granted relief, and P is the population of the parish. Setting tax revenue equal to relief expenditures yields the equation $r_t(1 - d)_t V_t = g_t s_t P_t$. Rearranging terms, the poor rate at time t is determined as $r_t = g_t s_t P_t / (1 - d)_t V_t$. In recession years, the share of the population granted relief increased, the parish's value of rateable property often declined, and the default rate increased. In order to assist everyone who applied for relief, parishes were forced to increase the poor rate, reduce the generosity of relief, or deny relief to some who should have qualified for it. Increases in the poor rate tended to cause further increases in the default rate, so that there was a maximum beyond which parishes refused to raise rates. The inability of the Poor Law to meet the increased demand for relief during downturns was made clear within a decade of the passage of the Poor Law Amendment Act, when the sharp increase in relief spending in 1841–42 caused a financial crisis for Lancashire Poor Law unions and forced many to cut benefits and appeal to private charities for help in assisting the needy.

27. In 1869 Parliament adopted the Poor Rate Assessment and Collection Act, which empowered parish vestries to assess the owners of dwelling houses "which do not exceed a certain prescribed limit of rateable value," rather than occupiers. See Blunden (1895: 27–28). The fact that Parliament felt it necessary to pass such an act suggests that before 1869 working-class occupiers of dwelling houses paid a share of the poor rate.

28. There is little information on landlords in industrial cities. Some employers built and owned cottages in which their workers lived. However, this appears to have been prevalent in smaller industrial towns, where housing was particularly scarce. I assume that, in large cities, employers owned only a small share of working-class housing and that the majority of housing was owned by other middle-class taxpayers.

DISTRESS IN THE MANUFACTURING DISTRICTS
DURING THE HUNGRY 1840S

After the boom of 1835–36, the economy slumped badly in 1837. There was a weak recovery in 1838–39, followed by the severe depression of 1841–42. The recovery that began in 1843 culminated in the prosperous years 1845–46, but another serious downturn followed in 1847–48. The downturns of 1841–42 and 1847–48 were particularly severe in the Lancashire cotton industry. Profit rates were low from 1837 to 1840, largely because of overinvestment in plant and equipment, and when demand declined in 1841–42 firms had few reserves and many went bankrupt and stopped production. In 1847 the cotton industry experienced a shortage and high price of raw cotton as a result of poor harvests in the United States in 1845 and 1846. At the same time, domestic demand for cotton goods declined, possibly due to declining real wages caused by rising food prices.[29]

The unemployment data for the cotton industry in Manchester and surrounding towns in 1841–42 are not complete and historians do not agree on how to interpret the existing data. Leonard Horner, the inspector of factories, reported data on employment in 1,164 cotton mills in the fall of 1841, and found an unemployment rate at the time of inspection of about 15%. An additional 14% of factory workers were employed for a reduced number of hours per week. Horner admitted that because the information was collected over a 15-week period, the figures did not "strictly apply to . . . any one day for the whole district," and Huberman contends that the reported data substantially understate the importance of short-time employment.[30]

The bottom of the downturn occurred in the spring of 1842. In his April report, Horner wrote that wage reductions of 10–12.5% were "becoming very general" and that short time probably was increasing. Three months later, he reported that "the great and general depression of trade continues unabated. . . . Many mills have stopped, many are working only four days in the week, and several only three days. This working short time, together with the reduction of wages, which has been very general, must press very severely upon the workpeople."[31] On July 9, 1842, the *Manchester Times* wrote that "any man passing through the district and observing the condition of the people, will at once perceive the deep and ravaging distress that prevails. . . . The picture which the manufacturing districts now present is absolutely frightful."

29. Matthews (1954: 137–43); Boot (1984: 34–35).

30. Parl. Papers, *Reports of the Inspectors of Factories for the half year ending the 31st December 1841* (1842, XXII), pp. 20–21; Huberman (1996: 113–20).

31. Parl. Papers, *Reports of the Inspectors of Factories . . . for the Half Year Ending June 30, 1842* (1842, XXII), pp. 6, 26.

The economy was just beginning to recover when a young Friedrich Engels arrived in Manchester for the first time in November 1842. He later wrote that "there were crowds of unemployed working men at every street corner, and many mills were still standing idle."[32]

Detailed studies of the magnitude of employment loss in 1841–42 are available for the cotton manufacturing towns of Bolton and Stockport. A director of Manchester's Chamber of Commerce estimated that in the spring of 1842 some 62% of Bolton's cotton workers were either unemployed or working short time, and that the extent of lost income for all Bolton workers resulting from unemployment, short time, and wage cuts was nearly £3,900 per week. Two Assistant Poor Law Commissioners sent in January 1842 to enquire into the state of the population in Stockport reported that "a considerable number of [cotton] mills" had completely stopped production, that many of the mills in operation had gone to short time, and that the wages of those employed had been reduced by 10% to 30%. They estimated that the loss of income for workers in the town's cotton mills amounted to £5,483 per week.[33]

Unemployment rates in Manchester area mills were as high or higher in 1847–48. Data collected by the Manchester police and reported in the *Economist* indicate that during the week ending November 16, 1847, near the trough of the downturn, 19 of 91 cotton mills had stopped production and another 34 were working short time. Fewer than half of the area's cotton operatives were working full-time—some 26% were unemployed, and an additional 26% were working reduced hours. Conditions improved somewhat from December to February. Nevertheless, during the second quarter of 1848, 18.3% of the workforce in Manchester area cotton mills was unemployed, while another 13.6% was working short time.[34]

SELF-HELP, POOR RELIEF, AND PRIVATE CHARITY

Working-class households suffered substantial income shocks during the downturns in 1841–42 and 1847–48. The initial response of most households to employment loss was to reduce spending, withdraw money from savings accounts, and pawn unnecessary items. However, this was a short-term strategy for all but the most highly paid manual workers, as few had the resources to subsist for more than one or two months before applying to the Poor Law or organized charities for assistance.

32. The quote from the *Manchester Times* is in Read (1959: 53); Engels ([1845] 1987: 121–22).
33. Ashworth (1842: 75–76); Parl. Papers, *State of the Population of Stockport* (1842, XXXV), pp. 43–45.
34. Data from the *Economist*, weekly issues from November 27, 1847, through July 1, 1848. The data were originally published in the *Manchester Guardian*. Boot (1990: 218–22).

The ability to save varied greatly across households, being determined by the household head's wage, family size, and the number of household members working. It was difficult for any but highly paid manual workers to accumulate more than a few pounds in savings.[35] Anderson concluded that "few even in good times could afford to save anything very significant to meet temporary losses in income . . . so that even short or comparatively minor crises caused severe destitution." The unemployed often turned to locally residing relatives for help, although the amount of aid they could expect from kin was "definitely limited," especially during serious downturns. Some moved in with relatives or neighbors in order to save money on rent and fuel.[36] Many households pawned furniture, clothing, bedding, and other items, but the amount of money (loans) obtained from pawnbrokers typically was quite small, and the rates of interest charged were often 20–25% per annum. Still, for many low-skilled workers the pawnshop was "their one financial recourse. . . . In times of sudden and overwhelming distress there is no doubt of its utility."[37]

Once savings were exhausted, workers turned to the Poor Law or charity. For most workers, the lag between becoming unemployed and applying for poor relief was short. Boot found that in Manchester during the 1847–48 downturn "the average lag between becoming unemployed and receiving [poor] relief" was about six weeks. Many low-skilled workers did not have the resources to hold out for six weeks, while some highly paid skilled artisans might have held out for much longer.[38]

Despite attempts by the Poor Law Commissioners to abolish its use, Poor Law unions in industrial areas continued to provide outdoor relief to unemployed and underemployed factory workers. As Rose stated, "the workhouse test was largely irrelevant to the problems of cyclical unemployment." When the Poor Law Commission issued the Outdoor Labour Test Order of 1842, stating that able-bodied males could be given outdoor relief only if they were set to task work, urban Boards of Guardians objected, arguing that "it was degrading for those unemployed through no fault of their own to be set to work with idle and dissolute paupers." Guardians in several unions also

35. In 1899, 83% of accounts in Post Office Savings Banks had a balance of under £25; the average balance in these accounts was £4 (Johnson 1985: 100–102). Given the increase in real wages during the second half of the nineteenth century, the median balance of working-class households' savings accounts must have been smaller than this in the 1840s.

36. Anderson (1971: 32, 149–51). The ability of working-class households to assist needy kin was limited by their own, typically low, incomes.

37. Bosanquet (1896: 98–99). On the role played by pawnbroking in Victorian working-class households, see Johnson (1985: 165–88).

38. Boot (1990: 225–26). MacKinnon (1986: 301–2) concluded that for most workers a lack of assets meant that the lag between the onset of unemployment and applying for relief "was likely to be fairly short." See also Kiesling (1996) and Boyer (1997).

FIGURE 2.2. Per Capita Poor Relief Expenditures, 1840–52

provided small payments to those whose hours of work were reduced during downturns.[39]

The share of the population of England and Wales receiving poor relief exceeded 10% throughout the decade, peaking at 14.6% in 1848 (Figure 2.1). The cyclical nature of relief spending is more pronounced at the city level. Figure 2.2 shows per capita relief spending for fiscal years (ending March 25) 1840–52 in three northern industrial cities: Manchester and Preston, which specialized in cotton textiles, and Sheffield, which specialized in steel production. Spending increased sharply in each city in 1841–42 and 1847–48. Table 2.3 shows the number of persons receiving poor relief during the "quarters ended Lady-Day" (March 25) in 1841–43 for 12 urban industrial Poor Law unions, and the number receiving relief in the "six months ended Lady-Day" in 1846–48 for eight urban unions. The number relieved increased substantially during both downturns. In Stockport it doubled from 1841 to 1842 and more than quadrupled from 1846 to 1848, while in Manchester it increased by 58% from 1841 to 1843 and more than tripled from 1846 to 1848.

Increases in relief spending during downturns created serious financial problems for industrial cities. The size of the poor rate levied each year by a Poor Law union was determined by the expected demand for relief. When demand increased unexpectedly unions often were forced to levy two or more assessments per year. Stockport's relief spending increased from £1,331 for

39. Rose (1970: 121, 133); Edsall (1971: 248–49); Rose (1966).

TABLE 2.3. Numbers in Receipt of Relief in Industrial Cities, 1841–48

(A) 1841–43	POPULATION	PAUPERS RELIEVED QUARTER ENDING MARCH 25			% INCREASE
	1841	1841	1842	1843	1843/1841
Blackburn	75,091	5,057	8,604	10,307	103.8
Bolton	97,519	8,016	10,378	11,934	48.9
Bradford	132,164	7,340	9,514	9,572	30.4
Halifax	109,175	7,436	8,992	9,474	27.4
Huddersfield	107,140	6,880	9,431	13,092	90.3
Liverpool	223,054	15,045	20,652	22,727	51.1
Manchester	192,408	12,978	15,994	20,449	57.6
Preston	77,189	8,672	13,237	11,822	36.3
Sheffield	85,076	6,113	6,555	15,402	52.0
Stockport	85,672	3,918	8,153	6,895	76.0
Leicester	50,932	5,306	7,057	8,293	56.3
Nottingham	53,080	4,589	7,938	5,751	25.3

(B) 1846–48		PAUPERS RELIEVED HALF YEAR ENDING MARCH 25			% INCREASE
		1846	1847	1848	1848/1846
Bolton		9,033	15,527	16,004	77.2
Bradford		20,070	24,055	39,759	98.1
Halifax		13,758	19,512	17,950	30.5
Liverpool		15,887	24,597	27,982	76.1
Manchester		27,503	50,737	94,702	244.3
Stockport		5,512	11,699	25,563	363.8
Leicester		6,431	11,792	19,642	205.4
Nottingham		5,581	8,648	9,232	65.4

Sources: Data for 1841–43 from Parl. Papers, *Return of Average Annual Expenditure of Parishes in Each Union in England and Wales* (1844, XL), pp. 5, 13, 17, 25. Data for 1846–48 from Parl. Papers, *Return of the Comparative Expenditure for Relief of the Poor . . . in the Six Months Ending Lady-Day in 1846, 1847 and 1848* (1847–48, LIII), p. 1.

the fourth quarter of 1838 to £2,329 for the same quarter in 1840 and £3,537 for the quarter in 1841.[40] Table 2.4 gives the particulars of each of Stockport's poor-rate assessments from October 1836 to June 1841. There were three assessments in 1841 totaling 4s. in the pound.[41] The 2s. assessment in November was

40. Parl. Papers, *State of the Population of Stockport* (1842, XXXV), pp. 4–5.

41. Details are not available for the November 1841 assessment. The precise timing of assessments is difficult to explain, being determined in part by unforeseen increases in spending. Boards of guardians also might have felt that during downturns it was less of a burden on taxpayers to collect two or three small assessments over the course of a year than one large assessment.

necessary because the number of relief recipients increased by 63% from June to December 1841. Default rates increased sharply during the downturn. In October 1836, a time of prosperity, 92% of the assessed poor rate was actually collected. However, as a result of the large number of defaulters, only 63% of the rates levied in February and June 1841 were collected. When Stockport collected its poor rate in November 1841, it was found that 1,632 of 6,180 working-class dwelling houses were unoccupied, as were 85 shops and 11 public houses. In addition, the occupiers of nearly 3,000 other dwelling houses did not pay the poor rate; upon examining 1,950 of the defaulters, the guardians excused 58% of them on the grounds of poverty. Most seriously, 12 of the town's 40 factories had shut down, and could not pay their assessment.[42] Under the circumstances, local officials surmised that another increase in the poor rate would cause more ratepayers to default and would yield little additional tax revenue.

Boards of guardians tried to set the generosity of relief benefits at a level high enough to ensure that unemployed or underemployed workers and their families were able to subsist in good health, but low enough so as not to interfere with work incentives. Benefit levels were remarkably similar across towns; guardians typically granted 2–3s. per week to a single adult male, and 1s. 6d.–2s. 6d. per week for each additional family member. Benefits were smaller if the applicant was working short time or if the family had other sources of income. In 1841 Bolton guardians granted applicants enough relief to make up their income "to 2s. 3d. per head per week . . . where we clearly ascertain the amount [the family] earned."[43]

When downturns became severe, as in 1841–42, lack of funds often forced guardians to reduce relief generosity and to give relief in kind rather than cash. After the stoppage of several mills in August 1841 the Stockport guardians shifted to relieving the able-bodied entirely in kind. Bacon and butter were included in the provisions dispersed in August and September, but thereafter relief was entirely made up of bread, meal, and potatoes. Those in need also were provided with clothes, bedding, and clogs. The unemployed and local shopkeepers objected to the shift, but the guardians maintained that in-kind relief reduced the cost of relieving the unemployed by 20%.[44]

The relief distributed by the guardians did not come close to making up the income loss of Stockport's mill workers. During the fourth quarter of 1841, spending on poor relief totaled £3,537, which was less than the estimated income loss of mill workers in one week (£5,483). The Assistant Poor Law Commissioners reporting on the state of the Stockport union defended the guardians' actions,

---

42. Parl. Papers, *State of the Population of Stockport* (1842, XXXV), pp. 21–24.

43. Rose (1965: 195–96); Parl. Papers, *A Copy of Reports Received by the Poor-Law Commissioners in 1841, on the State of the Macclesfield and Bolton Unions* (1846, XXXVI), pp. 12–13.

44. Parl. Papers, *State of the Population of Stockport* (1842, XXXV), pp. 37–38.

TABLE 2.4. Poor Rate Returns for Stockport, October 1836–June 1841

Date When Administered	Amount in the Pound	Rateable Value	Rate	Arrears Due	Amount to Be Collected	Amount Actually Collected	Share of Poor Rate Collected	Present Arrears	Amount Not Recoverable or Excused
October 1836	1s. 3d.	65,375.3	4,086.0	811.0	4,896.9	3,745.1	0.917	494.3	657.5
July 1837	1s. 9d.	66,015.3	5,776.3	494.3	6,270.6	4,745.6	0.822	648.2	876.8
May 1838	0s. 6d.	66,067.8	1,651.7	648.2	2,299.9	1,310.1	0.793	700.3	289.5
October 1838	2s. 0d.	66,098.3	6,609.6	700.3	7,309.9	4,787.3	0.724	772.7	1,749.9
November 1839	1s. 6d.	65,950.8	4,946.3	772.7	5,719.0	3,245.4	0.656	1,239.1	1,234.5
July 1840	2s. 0d.	65,515.0	6,551.5	1,239.1	7,790.6	4,446.8	0.679	1,848.4	1,495.4
February 1841	1s. 0d.	64,527.3	3,226.4	1,848.4	5,074.8	1,837.3	0.569	2,646.2	591.3
June 1841	1s. 0d.	63,184.0	3,159.2	2,646.2	5,805.4	2,195.4	0.695	2,494.5	1,115.5

Source: Parl. Papers, *State of the Population of Stockport* (1842, XXXV), p. 87.

stating that "the certain exhaustion of the relief-fund at no distant period . . . [justified] the guardians in dispensing with the utmost care and economy the funds now supplied by a greatly-reduced number of rate-payers, whose number and whose resources are still continually on the decrease."[45]

The inability of the Poor Law to support all who needed assistance led to large-scale charitable efforts to relieve the poor. In Manchester in 1841–42, local charitable organizations set up soup kitchens and provided the poor with bedding, clothing, and coal. More than 8,000 families were supplied with articles of bedding, and at the peak of the depression soup was supplied daily to 2–3,000 persons.[46]

In Stockport in October 1841, a committee composed of the mayor, clergymen, magistrates, and "leading manufacturers" was appointed to "inquire into the state of the poor and unemployed . . . and to suggest means for their relief." The committee reported in December that while the poor rate had doubled, "it is impossible to collect sufficient [funds] to meet the current expenditure, and as small as the relief afforded is, . . . it is more than the resources of the rate-payers, if unaided, will continue to afford." It appealed to the public for donations, and in December 1841 and January 1842 the committee raised nearly £3,000 from private contributions. From the last week of December through the end of February, it relieved on average 3,350 families at a cost of £340 per week. By comparison, during the two-year period from Lady Day 1841 to Lady Day 1843, the Stockport union spent £40,670 on poor relief, or about £390 per week. Most of the money raised by the Stockport relief committee was donated by "the wealthier inhabitants of the borough and those resident in the neighbourhood."[47]

Stockport's need to appeal for private charity to assist the unemployed reveals the inadequate nature of the poor-rate assessment system, which did not effectively tap the new wealth created by industrialization. The three poor rates levied in 1841 were both inadequate to relieve the large number of unemployed workers and at the same time large enough to be "a serious drain upon the diminished resources of the comparatively few [individuals and firms] who are able to pay them."[48] Rather than levy another poor rate, which would have resulted in even more defaults, Stockport set up a relief committee to raise funds privately. A large share of the charitable contributions must have been

45. Parl. Papers, *State of the Population of Stockport* (1842, XXXV), pp. 4–5, 37–38, 45.

46. Adshead (1842: 40–41).

47. Parl. Papers, *State of the Population of Stockport* (1842, XXXV), pp. 41–42, 91; Parl. Papers, *Return of Average Annual Expenditure of Parishes in Each Union in England and Wales* (1844, XL), p. 4.

48. Rose (1965: 348–50); Parl. Papers, *State of the Population of Stockport* (1842, XXXV), p. 93.

made by mill owners and merchants, two groups whose wealth was relatively lightly taxed under the assessment system. This was an inefficient way to tap the resources of the industrial elite; cities had no authority to compel manufacturers or merchants to make large contributions to the relief funds. Yet cities were forced to proceed in this manner because of the nature of the poor rate.

Not all charitable relief was raised locally. In its 1841 report, the Stockport relief committee stated that because of the great amount of distress among the unemployed, it was "fully convinced that all the efforts that can possibly be made in the town and neighbourhood will be utterly inadequate to meet the pressing necessities of the case." It therefore appealed for assistance "to those individuals and classes of society who feel little of the pressure of the times."[49] In response to similar appeals from several cities, the Home Secretary instituted the London Manufacturers' Relief Committee in the spring of 1842 "to co-ordinate and regulate the distribution to the provinces of charitable funds raised in England . . . to relieve industrial distress." The committee contained 60 members, including the Archbishops of Canterbury and York. It received slightly more than £100,000 in donations. Three-quarters of the funds raised were in response to a letter from Queen Victoria read in English churches, appealing for aid for the unemployed. The rest was raised by subscription. By far the largest individual contribution came from Rev. J. H. Fisk, who made "the magnificent donation of £1,000." Queen Victoria contributed £500, Prince Albert £200, and the Queen Dowager £300. The Bank of England and the Corporation of the City of London each contributed £500. Contributions of £200 or more were received from three London livery companies, three insurance companies, and eight individuals, including Prime Minister Peel.[50]

The committee granted relief to localities requesting it, provided they had already organized a local committee consisting of "magistrates, clergy and principal inhabitants," and that local subscriptions had been raised for relief of the poor. It required that the major part of the relief be granted to able-bodied men and their families, that at least one-half of the relief be given in kind, and that work be required from able-bodied men in return for relief.[51] From May 1842 until April 1843 the committee made a total of 734 grants—some cities received several grants. The recipients of the largest grants were Stockport, which received £8,100, Burnley, which received £12,300, and Paisley, which received over £15,000. More than 80% of the money distributed by the committee went to towns in Lancashire, Yorkshire, Cheshire, and Scotland.[52]

49. Parl. Papers, *State of the Population of Stockport* (1842, XXXV), p. 93.

50. Manufacturers Relief Committee (1844: vi–vii, 5, 71–80, 171).

51. Parl. Papers, *Report from the Select Committee on Distress (Paisley)* (1843, VII), pp. 2–3.

52. Manufacturers Relief Committee (1844: iv–v, 58, 61, 80); Parl. Papers, *Report from the Select Committee on Distress (Paisley)* (1843, VII), p. 5.

Paisley's large grant was a result of the severity of its depression and the fact that under the Scottish Poor Law able-bodied males were not eligible for poor relief even when unemployed. At the beginning of the depression Paisley formed a General Relief Committee to raise money for the unemployed and their families. When the local fund proved insufficient, subscriptions were started in the county of Renfrew, in Edinburgh and Glasgow, and in London, where merchants connected with Paisley contributed to relieve the unemployed. Together, these funds raised £28,233 from June 1841 to May 1842. From December 1841 to May 1842, the committee assisted an average of 12,188 persons per week, or 20% of the population. Given the severity of the depression—a large share of Paisley's businesses and merchants had gone bankrupt—the local community was unable to contribute more to the relief fund, and in spring 1842 the committee asked Parliament for help. From May 1842 to February 1843, 79% of the money spent to assist the Paisley unemployed was contributed by the London committee.[53]

The extent of charitable assistance for the unemployed during the 1847–48 downturn is more difficult to measure. Manchester charities raised approximately £19,000 in 1848 from subscriptions, donations, and collections, but it is not clear how much of this money went to aid the unemployed. In Leeds the unemployed were assisted by the Benevolent or Strangers' Friend Society and by an ad hoc relief fund. The role played by private charity in 1847–49 was much smaller than it had been in 1842—the relief funds collected in 1847 and 1849 combined totaled £3,500, half of the amount collected in 1842.[54]

In sum, during the two major downturns of the 1840s the unemployed and their families were assisted by a combination of public and private sources. The Poor Law proved incapable of relieving the unemployed, so local voluntary organizations mobilized to help meet the increased demand for assistance. When this proved inadequate, localities appealed to Parliament for help. The government did nothing to fix the defects of the poor-rate assessment system, and the problems associated with the Poor Law came to a head in Lancashire in 1862.

III. Poor Relief and Charity during the Lancashire Cotton Famine

There were no severe economic downturns during the 1850s. The 1858 recession was shorter than either of the 1840s downturns, and is barely perceptible in the Poor Law statistics. The relatively low unemployment of the 1850s

---

53. Smout (1979: 226–28); Parl. Papers, *Report from the Select Committee on Distress (Paisley)* (1843, VII), p. 135. See also Cage (1981: 10–15).

54. Shapely (2000: 38) gives sources of income for nine Manchester charities in 1848. Kidd (1984: 47–48) contends that the activities of Manchester charities declined in the 1840s and 1850s. Morris (1990: 302–3); Harrison (1988: 57).

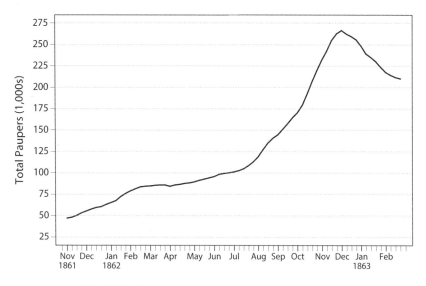

FIGURE 2.3. Number of Relief Recipients in 23 Lancashire Poor Law Unions, 1861–63

ended, at least in the industrial North West, shortly after the beginning of the American Civil War in 1861, when the Union blockade of southern ports led to the so-called Lancashire cotton famine. Raw cotton imports declined sharply, forcing Lancashire cotton factories to severely curtail production or shut down.

Weekly consumption of raw cotton began to decline in the fall of 1861, plummeting to 38% of its prefamine level in the last six weeks of the year. After rebounding in the first half of 1862 to two-thirds of its prefamine level, it fell sharply in the summer of 1862. In September consumption declined even further, to its lowest point during the famine. From August 29 to October 16 average weekly consumption was less than average *daily* consumption during the previous boom. Consumption increased slightly in late October and November, but remained less than a third of its prefamine level.[55]

Figure 2.3 shows the number of persons receiving poor relief in 23 "distressed" unions and townships in Lancashire and Cheshire for each week from November 1861 through February 1863.[56] From the beginning of November 1861 to the third week in February 1862, the number receiving relief increased by 78%, from 47,039 to 83,550. The growth in numbers relieved then slowed considerably until early July, after which it increased at a rapid and accelerating

55. Data on raw cotton consumption from the *Economist*, weekly issues, January 1861–December 1862. See Boyer (1997: 59–60, 74).

56. Parl. Papers, *Return of Number of Paupers in receipt of Relief, January–August 1858, 1862 and 1863* (1863, LII), pp. 182–92. I excluded Liverpool because it contained few cotton workers and because the number of relief recipients there was determined largely by conditions at the port.

pace until December. At the peak of the famine, in December 1862, there were 266,500 persons in receipt of poor relief in the 23 unions, out of a population of 1,870,600.

The extent of distress varied substantially across Poor Law unions, as a result of differences "in their dependence on the cotton industry [and] on the supply of American cotton," and in the types of cotton cloth produced.[57] Table 2.5 shows the percentage of the population receiving poor relief at six points of time for 11 large distressed unions and townships. From September 1861 to February 1862 the number of persons in receipt of poor relief more than tripled in Blackburn, Preston, and Stockport, increased by 162% in Ashton-under-Lyne, but rose by only 64% in Salford and 37% in Bolton. By June numbers on relief were five times greater than in the previous September in Ashton, four times greater in Blackburn and Stockport, and 3.75 times greater in Preston, and the relief roles continued to grow throughout the summer and fall. In September more than 10% of the population was receiving relief in five towns, and in November over 20% of the population was in receipt of public relief in four towns. An additional 200,000–236,000 persons were receiving relief from charitable funds at the peak of the famine. In total, 25–27% of the population of the distressed region was assisted by either public or private sources; in several Poor Law unions more than a third of the population must have received some form of assistance at the peak of the famine. Some of those receiving poor relief were assisted from charitable funds at the same time; the total number of persons receiving charitable relief in the winter of 1862–63 was almost certainly over 300,000, and might have exceeded 350,000.[58]

Most contemporaries agreed that demand for poor relief during the cotton famine was unprecedented. Arnold wrote that "the incidence of the poor-rate was never so oppressive over an equal extent of the kingdom as in the cotton districts during the months which included the crisis of the famine."[59] As had occurred in 1842, the increased demand for relief and the large number of defaults on poor-rate assessments caused Poor Law unions to run into serious financial problems. Wigan, Blackburn, Rochdale, Preston, and Ashton formed private relief committees early in 1862, and most of the other towns in the distressed area soon followed suit. By May 1862 the Blackburn committee had collected £5,234, the Preston committee £7,500, and the Rochdale committee

<hr/>

57. Farnie (1979: 158); Purdy (1862: 377).

58. Watts ([1866] 1968: 120); Arnold (1865: 191). The central relief committee of Manchester estimated that in January 1863, 235,741 persons were relieved by private relief committees only, and an additional 138,889 were relieved both by the poor law guardians and local committees; the total number of persons receiving private relief therefore was 374,630 (*Journal of the Statistical Society of London* 1864: 600).

59. Arnold (1865: 208). MacKay (1899: 258) maintained that the cotton famine was "the most serious crisis with which the English Poor Law has ever been called on to grapple."

TABLE 2.5. Numbers Receiving Poor Relief in 11 Distressed Districts, September 1861–February 1863

Poor Law Union	PERCENTAGE OF POPULATION RECEIVING POOR RELIEF						
	September 1861	February 1862	June 1862	September 1862	November 1862	February 1863
Ashton-under-Lyne	1.3	3.4	7.1	15.2	25.6	19.9
Blackburn	2.3	7.7	9.6	14.7	20.0	9.4
Bolton	2.4	3.3	3.4	4.2	6.7	6.5
Burnley	1.8	3.3	4.5	8.8	11.2	6.0
Bury	1.9	3.7	3.8	7.6	11.7	8.5
Manchester	3.4	6.4	7.7	11.7	21.1	20.0
Oldham	1.6	2.6	2.8	6.5	14.2	8.8
Preston	2.9	10.5	11.0	15.3	21.0	20.0
Rochdale	2.2	4.5	4.8	9.8	15.2	12.7
Salford	2.5	4.1	4.4	6.4	10.9	9.1
Stockport	1.6	4.8	6.4	10.2	13.0	7.3

Sources: Data for September 1861 through November 1862 from Parl. Papers, *Return of Number of Paupers in Receipt of Relief (in Cotton Manufacturing Districts), 1858, 1861 and 1862* (1862, XLIX, pt. 1). Data for February 1863 from Parl. Papers, *Return of Number of Paupers in Receipt of Relief, January–August 1858, 1862 and 1863* (1863, LII), p. 33.

Notes: Data are for the last week of the month. Data for Manchester refer to the township rather than the Poor Law union.

£3,300. In order to induce wealthy individuals to contribute generously to the local relief committees, newspapers published the names of donors each week, often "listing the names in decreasing order of amount given."[60]

In the spring of 1862 Lancashire officials began appealing to the rest of Britain for help. In April a group of London merchants associated with the cotton industry convinced the Lord Mayor of London to form the Lancashire and Cheshire Operatives Relief Fund (or Mansion House Fund). From May 1862 to June 1865, the fund contributed £528,336 to the distressed cotton districts. Another relief fund, the Bridgewater Fund, emerged in London, eventually raising £52,000 for the relief of Lancashire.[61] Soon after the initiation of the Mansion House Fund the (Manchester) Central Relief Committee was formally established; it included the mayors and ex-mayors of the principal towns of the cotton district and a number of gentlemen associated with the commercial interests of Manchester. One of its first acts was the drafting of a resolution directed at city and county officials throughout Britain, requesting aid for families of distressed workers connected with the cotton trade. The money raised by the London relief committees went to either the Central Relief Committee in Manchester or the individual local committees to distribute.[62]

The total amount expended by public and private sources for relief of the Lancashire poor from March 1861 to March 1864 was about £3,530,400. Poor-relief expenditures equaled £1,937,900, or 55% of the total; charity accounted for the remaining 45%. Of the charitable funds raised, £786,400 (22%) came from the cotton districts; the remaining £806,000 came from elsewhere in Britain or overseas. Altogether, slightly more than three-quarters of expenditures came from local sources.[63]

There was some friction between authorities in the cotton districts and the London relief committees, as well as between the central executive committee in Manchester and the local boards of guardians and relief committees. The administrators of the London committees, anxious that the funds they raised should "relieve the destitute and not the ratepayers," complained that local boards of guardians were not spending enough on poor relief. The guardians replied that there had already been an "oppressive increase in the rates," and that any attempt to further raise rates "would have the effect of pauperizing those who are now solvent, and to augment rather than diminish the distress of the district."[64] Before making a grant to a local relief committee, the central

60. Henderson (1934: 74–75); Kiesling (1997: 222–23).
61. Watts ([1866] 1968: 160–61); Henderson (1934: 79).
62. Arnold (1865: 82–83).
63. MacKay (1899: 416).
64. Arnold (1865: 150–52); Watts ([1866] 1968: 190).

executive committee required information about the locality's expenditures on poor relief, the amount of charitable funds collected by the local committee, the number of unemployed operatives in the town, the number relieved by the guardians and the local committee, and the generosity of public and private relief. In this way the central committee was able to monitor the actions of the local committees.[65]

It also was suggested by many, in Lancashire and elsewhere, that wealthy cotton manufacturers were not contributing their fair share to the relief funds. The manufacturers replied that the famine had caused them serious financial difficulties, but that even so, they contributed to relieve the destitute in several ways. Some continued to run their factories even when it was not profitable for them to do so. Others "gave their 'hands' daily meals and established soup kitchens," and those manufacturers who owned the cottages in which their workers lived generally did not collect rent during the famine.[66] If manufacturers and other large employers paid 40% of the poor rate, and contributed half of the charitable funds raised within the distressed area, they would have paid one-third of the amount spent on public and private relief during the famine. Counting the value of rents excused and meals given to workers, manufacturers paid, at most, 40% of the cost of relieving the unemployed.

In the summer of 1862, when the resources of both the local boards of guardians and the relief committees began to be strained, Parliament intervened to ease the financial burdens of the distressed areas. The Union Relief Aid Act, adopted in August 1862, had three major provisions. First, if the poor rate of any parish in the distressed area exceeded 3s. in the pound, the excess should be charged to the other parishes in the Poor Law union. Second, if the aggregate rate for a union exceeded 3s. in the pound, it could apply to the Poor Law Board to borrow the excess, to be repaid within seven years. Third, if the aggregate poor rate for a union exceeded 5s. in the pound, the Poor Law Board could order other unions in the county to contribute money to meet the excess. The first provision effectively shifted part of the cost of relieving the unemployed from working-class parishes to wealthier parishes in the same Poor Law unions. The extent of this cost shift was quite large in some unions. For the half year ended Lady Day 1863, 82.9% of relief expenditures in Ashton-under-Lyne were charged to the union common fund, and only 17.1% to the individual parishes. In Stockport, Rochdale, Preston, and Blackburn, two-thirds or more of relief expenditures were charged to the union. The major beneficiaries of the second and third provisions appear to have been Ashton-under-Lyne and Preston—from August 1862 to July 1864 Ashton borrowed

65. Henderson (1934: 76–77).
66. Arnold (1865: 111).

£31,300 and received £7,000 from other Lancashire unions, while Preston borrowed £28,900 and received £10,800 from other unions.[67]

In July 1863 Parliament adopted the Public Works (Manufacturing Districts) Act, which allowed local boards of guardians to borrow money from the national government for 30 years at an interest rate of 3.5%. The money was to be used for public works projects using the labor of unemployed cotton operatives, who were to be hired to do unskilled manual labor and paid the going wage for unskilled workers. From 1863 to 1865, 90 local authorities borrowed £1.85 million to construct public works. Although many beneficial projects were undertaken, the act was a failure as an employment project. Rather than create so many as 30,000 jobs for unemployed operatives, as its sponsors expected, peak employment on public works was 6,424 in October 1864; only 4,990 of those employed were cotton operatives.[68]

During the cotton famine, officials who typically tried to maintain relief benefits at about 2s. per person per week were forced to reduce benefits to less than 1s. 6d. per person. Guardians realized that the relief they were granting was inadequate and "assumed that this meagre sum would be augmented from other sources." Their assumption appears to have been correct. A January 1863 estimate suggests that over 60% of individuals receiving outdoor relief from the guardians also received assistance from the local committees.[69] In combination, poor relief and private charity were able to maintain the generosity of relief at about its prefamine level. George Buchanan reported at the peak of distress in 1862 that "taking the great mass of the cotton workers with their families as a whole, their average income . . . from all sources is nearly 2s. per head per week. This is exclusive of clothing, bedding and firing which are now usually supplied in addition."[70]

Modern studies of relief generosity often focus on the relationship between benefits and wages. During the cotton famine, the central executive committee in Manchester strove to maintain an average benefit/wage ratio of about one-third. However, because an unemployed individual's benefits were tied

67. Watts ([1866] 1968: 291–93); Henderson (1934: 58). Parl. Papers, *Sixteenth Annual Report of the Poor Law Board* (1864, XXV), p. 330. The principle of shifting responsibility for paupers from the parish to the Poor Law union was made permanent by the Union Chargeability Act of 1865, discussed in Chapter 3. The third provision created some controversy in Lancashire, since it was believed by many to penalize those unions that had kept their poor rates down.

68. MacKay (1899: 398–404); Henderson (1934: 61–63).

69. Kiesling (1996: 83); Rose (1977: 189); *Journal of the Statistical Society of London* (1864: 600).

70. Henderson (1934: 99). The *Manual for the Guidance of Local Relief Committees in the Cotton Districts Arising Out of the Experience of 1862–63* stated that "the Scale of Relief which has obtained the approval of the Central Executive Committee is one which provides, on the average, two shillings per head for the whole mass of recipients; to which may be added, in winter, supply of fuel and clothing, if the family have been long out of work" (quoted in Henderson 1934: 100).

to the size of his family rather than his wage, the benefit/wage ratio varied across relief recipients. If unemployed cotton operatives received 2s. per family member per week in public and private relief, an unemployed class 3 spinner from a family of four would have had a replacement rate of 37% in 1862–63; for a class 1 spinner the replacement rate was 20%.[71]

IV. The Crisis of the 1860s in London

The Lancashire cotton famine was not the only Poor Law crisis of the 1860s. During the decade "the English poor relief system was subjected to an almost continual series of shocks which exposed its basic weakness."[72] London was especially hard hit. By the 1850s the metropolis contained 30 separate Poor Law unions, each responsible for its own poor. Population shifting within London led to increasing divergences in financial resources across unions. Middle-class taxpayers moved from central London to outlying districts, while the working class became ever more concentrated in certain unions, especially in the East End. As a result, districts where the demand for poor relief tended to be high were also those where the tax base was low.[73]

The extent to which poor rates varied across London Poor Law unions is shown in Table 2.6, which presents information on rateable value and poor rates for 12 unions in the 1860s. Rateable value per capita, a rough measure of wealth, varied substantially across unions, exceeding £7 in St. George Hanover Square, Paddington, and Kensington, and being less than £2.5 in the East End unions of Shoreditch and Bethnal Green. As discussed in Section II, a union's poor rate in any year was determined both by the value of its rateable property and by the demand for relief. In 1860 the poor rate varied from 0.35s. in the pound in Paddington to 2.71s. in the pound in St. George in the East—taxpayers in the East End paid rates more than four times higher those of taxpayers in the wealthier West End.[74]

The Thames froze in the winter of 1860–61, causing a decline in all outdoor work and the complete cessation of riverside employment for several weeks. The resulting flood of applications for relief created severe problems in East London Poor Law unions. During five weeks of severe frost in December and January, the number of relief recipients increased by nearly 40%.[75] As in northern industrial cities, the increased demand for assistance led to a large

---

71. Rose (1977: 191). In 1861 the average weekly wage of cotton spinners was 24s. 4d.; wages ranged from 39s. 6d. for a class 1 spinner to 21s. 6d. for a class 3 spinner. Wood (1910: 28).

72. Rose (1981: 54).

73. Green (1995: 226–35); Green (2010: chaps. 6–7).

74. In percentage terms, the poor rate in 1860 was below 3% in Paddington, St. George Hanover Square, and Kensington, and over 12% in Shoreditch and St. George in the East.

75. Green (2010: 203–6); Parl. Papers, *Report from the Select Committee on Poor Relief* (1864: IX), p. 3. Hollingshead (1861: 39–97) provides a description of East London in January 1861.

TABLE 2.6. Poor Rates in Metropolitan Unions, 1860–68

Poor Law Union	Population 1861	Rateable Value 1866	Rateable Value per Capita	Rate in the Pound for Poor Relief (Shillings) Year Ending March 25						Net Amount (£) from MCPF 1867–69
				1860	1862	1864	1866	1868(A)	1868(B)	
Kensington	70,108	503,891	7.20	0.54	0.60	0.71	0.75	1.02	0.92	-10,220
Paddington	75,784	646,256	8.53	0.35	0.40	0.44	0.50	0.69	0.58	-15,657
St. Geo Hanover Sq.	87,771	820,448	9.35	0.48	0.48	0.52	0.54	0.75	0.67	-16,431
St. Marylebone	161,680	974,273	6.03	1.04	1.19	1.10	1.15	1.58	1.58	-2,198
St. Pancras	198,788	956,039	4.81	1.02	1.33	1.15	1.25	1.54	1.54	5,479
Clerkenwell	65,681	207,486	3.16	1.48	1.56	1.63	1.77	2.23	2.15	2,536
Shoreditch	129,364	298,300	2.31	2.44	2.10	1.94	2.69	2.75	2.81	9,447
Bethnal Green	105,101	191,372	1.82	1.63	2.21	2.21	2.98	3.48	3.92	15,675
Whitechapel	78,187	266,553	3.41	1.90	2.17	2.02	2.42	2.98	3.33	11,446
St. Geo in the East	48,891	166,373	3.40	2.71	2.92	2.88	3.19	3.19	3.48	6,953
Stepney	56,572	230,695	4.08	2.04	2.02	2.46	2.73	3.29	3.58	9,376
Lambeth	162,044	596,174	3.68	1.50	1.48	1.44	1.60	1.67	1.69	6,840
Metropolitan unions	2,802,367	14,730,232	5.26	1.08	1.19	1.19	1.33	1.56	1.56	

Sources: Data for columns 2–7 from Parl. Papers, *Return Relating to Poor Relief, etc. (Metropolis)* (1867, LX), pp. 2–3. Data for columns 1, 8–10 from Parl. Papers, *Returns Relating to Pauperism and Relief, etc. (Metropolis)* (1870, LVIII), pp. 2–3, 7.

increase in private charitable expenditures. One witness testifying before the Select Committee on Poor Law Relief, appointed to examine the distress in London in 1860–61, estimated that between £28,000 and £40,000 was raised by various charities to assist the poor.[76] Much of this money was distributed at the local Police Courts. The magistrates in charge of distributing relief "had no knowledge ourselves whether [applicants] were in distress or not," and admitted that, due to the large number applying for assistance, money was distributed quickly and rather indiscriminately. The Select Committee concluded that "a large proportion of the charitable funds was wasted upon undeserving objects."[77]

Witnesses appearing before the committee disagreed as to whether Poor Law unions could have met the demand for assistance without the help of charitable relief. The chairman of the Shoreditch Board of Guardians testified that he was "certain" that the guardians could have relieved all persons in his district who needed assistance, including those who turned instead to charity. On the other hand, Rev. McGill of St. George in the East testified that "it was too much to ask the local guardians of a distressed district like St. George's-in-the-East, or like Bethnal Green . . . [to relieve] the distress which existed during those five weeks of frost." The assistant overseer of St. George Southwark testified that the increased demand for relief made it increasingly difficult to collect the poor rate, and that each quarter between 1,200 and 1,500 persons had to be summoned before the magistrates because they did not pay their rate.[78] The committee concluded that "the Guardians could have raised the funds which would have been required, if the relief of the whole of the distress had been cast upon them, but it must be borne in mind that the chief portion of the destitution was confined to those districts of the Metropolis which are always most heavily burthened with the poor. . . . It is obvious, therefore, that the additional charge upon the pauperized parishes would have sensibly increased the difficulties of the ratepayers."[79]

The London Poor Law suffered an even larger shock from 1866 to 1869, when the combination of a business-cycle downturn, the decline of the London shipbuilding industry, and severe winter weather greatly increased the

76. Parl. Papers, *First Report from the Select Committee on Poor Relief (England)* (1861: IX), qq. 4,311, 4,415, pp. 184, 189.

77. Parl. Papers, *First Report from the Select Committee on Poor Relief (England)* (1861: IX), qq. 2,193–97, 2841–43, pp. 81, 104–5; Parl. Papers, *Report from the Select Committee on Poor Relief* (1864: IX), p. 9.

78. Parl. Papers, *First Report from the Select Committee on Poor Relief (England)* (1861: IX), qq. 994–95, 3297–99, pp. 36, 130; Parl. Papers, *Third Report from the Select Committee on Poor Relief* (1862: X), qq. 7580–81, 7586–92, pp. 107–8.

79. Parl. Papers, *Report from the Select Committee on Poor Relief* (1864: IX), p. 9.

demand for poor relief. Once again, the East End was hardest hit.[80] Panel (a) of Table 2.7 shows the number of persons in receipt of poor relief in the last week of the Christmas quarter for East London Poor Law unions from 1859 to 1870. In East London as a whole, the number of relief recipients nearly doubled from late December 1864 to the same time in 1867. In Poplar, numbers on relief more than tripled over these three years. Expenditures on poor relief for years ended on Lady Day are shown in panel (b). From 1865 to 1868 spending increased by 70% in the eight unions. It rose by 144% in Poplar, 99% in Hackney, and 95% in Bethnal Green.[81]

The resulting strain on East End Poor Law unions was enormous. Poor rates increased sharply in response to the increased demand for relief (Table 2.6). For the year ending March 25, 1868, poor rates in the East End ranged from 2.75s. in the pound in Shoreditch to 3.48s. in Bethnal Green. The increase was not felt equally throughout London—the poor rate averaged only 1.56s. in the pound in the metropolis as a whole, and remained below 1s. in some wealthy West End unions.

The increase in poor rates led to a sharp rise in defaults—thousands of taxpayers in East End districts were unable to pay their rates. The Select Committee on Metropolitan Local Government reported in 1866 that "so heavy has the charge of local taxation become in the less wealthy districts, that the Metropolitan Board [of Works] is of opinion that direct taxation on the occupiers of property there has reached its utmost limits," and the Poor Law Board admitted that others had reached a similar conclusion.[82] In 1866–67 boards of guardians throughout the East End turned to the Poor Law Board and the West End for assistance. London's wealthier districts responded generously but in an uncoordinated fashion. A Mansion House Relief Fund was established and distributed over £15,000 to the poor in eastern districts, and many additional relief agencies were established. J. R. Green, a vicar in Stepney, wrote in December 1867 that "a hundred different agencies for the relief of distress are at work over the same ground, without concert or co-operation, or the slightest information as to each other's exertions." He added: "What is now being done is to restore the doles of the Middle Ages. The greater number of the East-end clergy have converted themselves into relieving officers. Sums of enormous magnitude are annually collected and dispensed by them either personally or through district visitors."[83]

---

80. Green (2010: 206) contends that "in January 1867 as much as a half of the male labour force in eastern districts was without work."

81. For the metropolis as a whole, relief expenditures increased by 45% from 1865 to 1868.

82. Green (1903: 131); Jones (1971: 249–51); Green (1995: 235); Parl. Papers, *First Report from the Select Committee on Metropolitan Local Government* (1866: XIII), p. xi; Parl. Papers, *Nineteenth Annual Report of the Poor Law Board, 1866–67* (1867: XXXIV), pp. 17–18.

83. Green (1903: 133).

TABLE 2.7. Number of Paupers Relieved and Relief Expenditures in East London Unions, 1859–68

(A) NUMBER IN RECEIPT OF POOR RELIEF, LAST WEEK OF CHRISTMAS QUARTER

	1859	1860	1861	1862	1863	1864	1865	1866	1867	1868	1867/1864
East	18,114	19,324	18,337	18,628	18,174	18,735	19,988	27,508	36,407	32,008	1.943
Poplar	2,624	2,771	2,782	2,743	2,781	3,066	3,462	6,954	9,612	7,333	3.135
St. George	2,791	2,976	2,838	3,089	3,122	3,130	3,230	3,567	4,028	3,951	1.287
Whitechapel	2,596	2,696	2,642	2,685	2,705	2,780	2,912	3,898	4,323	4,176	1.555
Shoreditch	4,081	4,176	3,411	3,561	3,540	3,366	3,470	3,925	5,371	5,306	1.596
Bethnal Green	1,407	2,119	2,453	2,096	1,956	2,340	2,537	3,389	4,921	4,305	2.103
Stepney	2,776	2,555	2,386	2,525	2,407	2,432	2,470	3,356	5,032	4,103	2.069
Mile End Old Town	1,839	2,031	1,825	1,929	1,663	1,621	1,907	2,419	3,120	2,834	1.925
Hackney	2,478	2,986	2,577	2,489	2,358	2,698	2,803	4,476	6,168	6,026	2.286
East + Hackney	20,592	22,310	20,914	21,117	20,532	21,433	22,791	31,984	42,575	38,034	1.986

(B) EXPENDITURES FOR RELIEF OF THE POOR, YEAR ENDED LADY-DAY (£)

	1859	1860	1861	1862	1863	1864	1865	1866	1867	1868	1868/1865
East	165,514	161,136	170,067	171,026	171,301	170,618	178,594	204,241	254,754	298,137	1.669
Poplar	22,097	21,512	22,823	23,789	22,656	23,189	24,120	27,285	48,067	58,949	2.444
St. George	23,857	22,580	25,957	24,188	23,195	23,987	25,028	26,467	31,422	31,463	1.257
Whitechapel	27,031	25,282	27,544	28,989	29,790	26,865	28,777	32,330	36,090	44,492	1.546
Shoreditch	37,422	36,289	28,711	31,347	30,730	28,918	31,320	40,020	44,819	51,589	1.647
Bethnal Green	16,748	15,492	19,178	21,051	21,270	21,200	22,262	28,538	36,802	43,356	1.948
Stepney	23,679	23,614	23,214	23,330	25,667	28,351	29,279	31,424	36,028	44,223	1.510
Mile End Old Town	14,680	16,367	22,640	18,332	17,993	18,108	17,808	18,177	21,526	24,065	1.351
Hackney	15,767	15,875	17,301	17,945	17,896	16,464	17,453	19,654	26,604	34,661	1.986
East + Hackney	181,281	177,011	187,368	188,971	189,197	187,082	196,047	223,895	281,358	332,798	1.698

Sources: Numbers in receipt of poor relief from appendices to the Twelfth to the Twenty-First Annual Reports to the Poor Law Board. Data on expenditures for relief of the poor from Parl. Papers, *Return Relating to Poor Relief, etc.* (*Metropolis*) (1867, LX), pp. 2–3, and from appendices to the Twentieth and Twenty-First Annual Reports to the Poor Law Board.

The indiscriminate nature of charitable relief appalled many middle-class observers. Sir Charles Trevelyan lamented the effects of "the wholesale, indiscriminate action of competing [charitable] societies" in an 1870 letter to the *Times*. In his view, "the pauperized, demoralised state of London is the scandal of our age." The effect of indiscriminate charity was "to destroy, in large classes of our people, the natural motives to self-respect and independence of character, and their kindred virtues of industry, frugality, and temperance." In late December 1867 Green wrote, "It is not so much poverty that is increasing in the East as pauperism, the want of industry, of thrift, of self-reliance . . . what is really being effected by all this West-end liberality is the paralysis of all local self-help." Two weeks later, Green maintained that "some half a million of people in the East-end of London have been flung into the crucible of public benevolence, and have come out of it simply paupers. . . . The very clergy who were foremost in the work of relief last year stand aghast at the pauper Frankenstein they have created."[84]

Some contemporaries blamed the boards of guardians in East End unions for creating much of the distress of 1866–68. The guardians' objective, according to this view, was to assist the poor at the lowest possible cost to local taxpayers. Since it cost more to relieve the poor in workhouses than in their homes, guardians offered outdoor relief to the able-bodied. This was a "shortsighted economy," since the abandonment of the workhouse test made it difficult to discriminate between the "worthy" and "unworthy" poor, and led to a sharp increase in demand for relief. Given the fiscal constraint they faced, guardians' only possible response to the high demand was to lower the benefits offered to applicants to an amount too small to live on. According to Edward Denison, the low level of benefits led to the rise of private charity.[85]

Others defended the guardians' actions, contending that the number of able-bodied adults driven by unemployment to apply for poor relief was far larger than the capacity of East End workhouses, making the workhouse test impossible to administer. According to this view, guardians dealt with the enormous demand for relief as best they could, by giving applicants small amounts of outdoor relief. Some contemporaries maintained that the problem lay not with the guardians but with the actions of local charities. Green wrote that "there are, in fact, considerable local resources, but they can only be obtained by a large system of charity . . . dispensed by local agencies." This was unfortunate, because the administrators of charitable funds were less able than the guardians to discriminate "between real poverty and confirmed mendicancy." Green concluded that it would have been far better had the "public

84. Trevelyan (1870: 3, 6); Green (1903: 127, 133, 137, 139).
85. Leighton (1872: 64–65).

benevolence" been used to supplement "the funds which the Boards of Guardians now devote to out-door relief," rather than distributed separately from poor relief.[86]

A third group maintained that the crises of 1860–61 and 1866–68 largely were due to the method used to fund poor relief. Several who testified before the Select Committee on Poor Relief noted the large differences in poor rates across London unions and argued that if rates were equalized within the metropolis the increased demand for relief could have been handled by the Poor Law alone, without need for the flood of indiscriminate charity. The vice-chairman of the City of London union, Robert Warwick, stated in 1861 that "the poor of London are the poor of the whole metropolitan community, and not of the particular parish" in which they live. The East End dockworker or the Bethnal Green weaver labored "more for the benefit of the city merchant, or the west-end resident, than for his own neighbours; . . . those who have benefit of his labour ought to bear a fair share of the relief required in the time of his distress." He added that "the equalization of the poor rate throughout London would be an immense benefit to all classes of the community, and one of justice both to the poor and ratepayer."[87]

Warwick also was Secretary of the Society for the Equalization of the Poor Rates, founded in 1857 to promote the sharing of the cost of poor relief across London unions. Six members of the society's Executive Committee testified before the Select Committee on Poor Relief, and their statements helped persuade the committee to "recommend the general question of extending the area of rating to the further consideration of the House."[88] In response to the crises in 1860–61 and 1866–67, the lobbying of the Society for the Equalization of the Poor Rates, and appeals from various ratepayers' associations, Parliament adopted the Metropolitan Poor Act in March 1867. The act created the Metropolitan Common Poor Fund (MCPF), to which all London unions contributed according to the value of their rateable income. Not all relief expenditures were transferred from the union to the MCPF. The act stipulated that some medical expenses, the cost of maintaining lunatics in asylums and pauper children in schools, and the relief of the casual poor were to be paid out of the common fund. An amendment in 1870 added a subsidy of 5d. per

86. Green added that East End employers, who reaped "enormous fortunes from these very masses of the poor whom they employ," should have been responsible for relieving their workers' distress. This was made unnecessary by the flood of "money from the West." Green (1903: 133–34).

87. Parl. Papers, *Second Report from the Select Committee on Poor Relief (England)* (1861: IX), pp. 198–200. See also Parl. Papers, *Report from the Select Committee on Poor Relief* (1864: IX), pp. 41–44.

88. Parl. Papers, *Report from the Select Committee on Poor Relief* (1864: IX), p. 44. Ashbridge (1997) examines the role played by the Society for the Equalization of the Poor Rates.

person per day for adult paupers in workhouses; no subsidy was provided for adults receiving outdoor relief.

The MCPF, which came into operation in September 1867, led to a redistribution of income from wealthy metropolitan districts to working-class districts, although it did not equalize poor rates across unions.[89] The effects of the MCPF on poor rates for fiscal year 1868 can be seen by comparing the columns labeled 1868(a) and 1868(b) in Table 2.6. The poor rate for Bethnal Green in 1867–68 was 3.48s. in the pound; in the absence of the transfer from the MCPF, the same expenditure on relief would have required a poor rate of 3.92s. in the pound. On the other hand, the poor rate for Kensington increased from 0.92s. to 1.02s. in the pound as a result of its contribution to the MCPF. The final column of Table 2.6 shows the net amount received from (or contributed to) the MCPF during the 18 months from September 1867 to March 1869. The wealthy unions of Kensington, Paddington, and St. George Hanover Square contributed over £42,000 to the MCPF during this period, while the East End unions of Shoreditch, Bethnal Green, Whitechapel, St. George in the East, and Stepney received nearly £53,000. Despite this substantial redistribution of income, there remained large differences in poor rates across unions, and rates remained very high in working-class districts. The adoption of the MCPF ameliorated the crisis of 1866–69 in East London, but it did not solve the problem inherent in the system.

V. Conclusion

The New Poor Law was supposed to usher in an era of self-help, in which manual workers protected themselves against income loss by increasing their saving and joining friendly societies. Its supporters assumed that, as a result of the increase in self-help, demand for poor relief by working-class households would greatly decline, even during downturns, and the Poor Law's main job would be to assist widows and orphans, the non-able-bodied, and the elderly. This assumption proved to be wide of the mark. Working-class self-help did indeed increase after 1834, but few households were able to save more than a small amount, and spells of unemployment lasting more than a few weeks exhausted most workers' savings. Large numbers of workers continued to turn to the Poor Law during economic crises, and Poor Law unions continued to provide outdoor relief to the unemployed and their families.

The Poor Law's inability to cope financially with the increased demand for relief during crises led to the rise of short-term large-scale charitable movements to assist those in need. These charities invariably were a mixed blessing—they were able to raise large amounts of money quickly, but they

---

89. For a detailed discussion of the effects of the MCPF, see Green (2010: 235–46).

proved to be less successful at distributing it, often handing out relief in an indiscriminate manner to all comers.

The breakdown of the Poor Law in the 1860s, together with the unsystematic nature of charitable aid, convinced many that the system of poor relief required a "radical restructuring," and that the way to restore self-help among the poor was to greatly restrict the provision of outdoor relief and strictly regulate the provision of private charity. In the decade that followed, major changes in the Poor Law were undertaken that significantly altered the form of public assistance for working-class households.

Appendix 2.1

For the first 40 years of the nineteenth century data on the number of poor relief recipients exist only for 1802–3 and 1812–13 through 1814–15. The data reported for 1802–3 include children permanently relieved outdoors, but those for 1812–15 do not. For reasons that are not given, the questionnaire sent to parishes at the later date specifically stated that children whose parents were permanently relieved outdoors should not be reported, although children of persons permanently relieved in workhouses are included in the returns for 1812–15. It is not clear whether children of persons relieved occasionally are included in either the 1802–3 or 1812–15 returns. For each year 1812–13 to 1814–15, I estimated the number of children permanently relieved outdoors, by assuming that the ratio of children to adults permanently relieved outdoors was equal to that for 1802–3. I then added the estimated number of children relieved to the reported number receiving relief for each year 1812–13 to 1814–15. This increases the average share of the population relieved for the three years from 8.9% to 12.6%.

Annual relief expenditure data are available from 1812–13 onward. The average annual expenditure per relief recipient for 1812–13 through 1814–15, calculated by dividing real expenditures for England and Wales by the number receiving relief, was £4.714. Assuming that this ratio held until 1834, I calculated crude estimates of the annual number of persons receiving poor relief from 1815–16 to 1833–34 by dividing annual real relief expenditures by 4.714. I used the estimated numbers on relief to calculate the annual share of the population receiving poor relief, reported in Table 2.A.1 and Figure 2.1.[90] The share receiving relief averaged 15.1% for 1812–33; it varied from a low of 11.8% in 1814 to a high of 17.1% in 1817.

Table 2.A.1 also presents annual estimates of relief expenditures for England and Wales as a share of gross domestic product for 1812–50. The construction of these estimates is explained in Appendix 1.3.

90. Poor Law expenditure data are reported for the year ending on March 25. That is, the expenditures reported for 1813 are for March 26, 1812, to March 25, 1813. Following Blaug (1963: 180), I consider the spending data reported for 1813 as in fact referring to 1812.

TABLE 2.A.1. Estimated Share of Population Receiving Poor Relief, 1812–50

	Estimated % Receiving Poor Relief	Poor Law Expenditures as % of GDP
1812	13.2	1.9
1813	12.7	1.7
1814	11.8	1.5
1815	14.3	1.6
1816	15.4	2.1
1817	17.1	2.3
1818	16.5	2.1
1819	16.6	2.2
1820	16.7	2.1
1821	16.1	2.0
1822	15.6	1.9
1823	14.7	1.8
1824	14.1	1.7
1825	13.5	1.5
1826	15.1	1.9
1827	15.3	1.8
1828	15.0	1.8
1829	15.6	2.0
1830	15.8	1.9
1831	16.0	2.0
1832	15.8	1.9
1833	14.9	1.8
1834	—	1.5
1835	—	1.2
1836	—	0.9
1837	—	1.0
1838	—	1.0
1839	—	1.0
1840	10.4	1.1
1841	11.1	1.2
1842	12.0	1.3
1843	12.8	1.2
1844	12.1	1.2
1845	11.9	1.1
1846	10.7	1.1
1847	13.6	1.2
1848	14.6	1.3
1849	13.2	1.2
1850	12.1	1.2

Source: Annual Reports of the Poor Law Board and the Local Government Board.

3

Social Welfare Policy, Living Standards, and Self-Help, 1861–1908

To middle-class observers inside and outside the government, there were definite lessons to be learned from the crises of the 1840s and, especially, the 1860s. First, the system used to finance the Poor Law was not able to handle sharp increases in demand for relief. Second, while it was possible to raise large amounts of charitable assistance quickly, that aid, when administered in an indiscriminate manner, often did more harm than good. Third, and perhaps most important, the "principles of 1834" clearly were not being enforced in northern industrial cities or working-class districts of London. Not only were large numbers of able-bodied males still receiving outdoor relief, the 1860s had witnessed an upward trend in numbers on relief and relief spending, which suggested to many that the administration of the Poor Law was becoming more lax. Contemporaries argued that manual workers' wage rates had been increasing since 1850 or earlier, and that by the 1860s most workers earned enough to protect themselves against income insecurity by saving and joining mutual insurance societies. The fact that numbers on relief had not declined, and appeared to be increasing, was seen as evidence that workers were not saving as much as they should and that self-reliance among the working class might be decreasing. Many believed that there was a simple explanation for workers' behavior—the generous nature of poor relief and private charity made it unnecessary for workers to protect themselves against insecurity.

During the 1860s and 1870s these issues were addressed by both the central and local governments and by middle-class reformers. Parliament altered the system for financing the Poor Law in a series of measures, culminating with the Union Chargeability Act in 1865 and the Metropolitan Poor Act in 1867, which shifted the cost of relief from parishes to Poor Law unions and in the case of London from individual unions to the Metropolitan Common Poor Fund. The problems of lax relief administration and workers' lack of self-reliance were addressed by the Crusade Against Outrelief, initiated by the Local Government Board in the early 1870s with the full support of the Charity Organisation Society. The leaders of the crusade asserted that substituting the workhouse test for outdoor relief would both improve the behavior of the poor and reduce local ratepayers' tax bills.

Section I of this chapter examines the beginnings of the Crusade Against Outrelief and its effects on the administration of poor relief. The crusade was brought about by the combination of the supposed failure of Poor Law administration, in particular the London Poor Law crisis of the 1860s, the rise of a self-help ethic in mid-Victorian England and a resulting hardening of middle-class attitudes toward the poor, and the reaction of middle-class taxpayers to the increase in their poor rates brought about by the Union Chargeability Act. Section II examines trends in living standards and working-class self-help from 1870 to 1910. Membership in mutual insurance organizations and deposits in savings banks increased substantially in the second half of the nineteenth century, but largely remained out of reach of low-skilled workers. The bottom one-third of the working class remained quite vulnerable to unexpected income loss at the beginning of the twentieth century.

I. The Crusade Against Outrelief and the Changing Role of the Poor Law

The early 1870s represent a watershed in the history of the Poor Law. Poor Law unions throughout England and Wales sharply restricted the use of outdoor relief for all types of paupers, and in particular able-bodied males and the elderly. This change in policy, known as the Crusade Against Outrelief, was not driven by legislation—the newly formed Local Government Board strongly encouraged but did not compel unions to restrict outdoor relief. After more than three decades of resisting central government pressure to adhere to the "principles of 1834," local authorities, especially in urban districts, adopted some form of the workhouse test and made outdoor relief substantially more difficult to obtain. This increase in stinginess had the blessing of local middle-class taxpayers.

In November 1869, in the aftermath of the Poor Law crisis in East London, George Goschen, President of the Poor Law Board, issued a Minute to Poor Law officials in the metropolis criticizing local guardians for granting relief not only to the "actually destitute," whom they had a legal obligation to assist, but also to "those in receipt of insufficient wages." The consequence of such policies was to "supplant, in a further portion of the population, the full recognition of the necessity for self-reliance and thrift." He also criticized local charities for granting food or money to those destitute individuals whom the Poor Law guardians were legally bound to assist. Goschen concluded that "it appears to be a matter of essential importance that an attempt should be made to bring the authorities administering the Poor Laws and those who administer charitable funds to as clear an understanding as possible, so as to avoid the double distribution of relief to the same persons."[1]

Two years later, in December 1871, the newly formed Local Government Board issued a circular to all Poor Law inspectors stating that the increase in expenditures on outdoor relief during the 1860s was "so great, as to excite apprehension," and that generous outdoor relief was destroying self-reliance among the poor. The circular blamed this increase in spending largely on local boards of guardians, contending that many granted outdoor relief "too readily and without sufficient inquiry," and in particular "in numerous circumstances in which it would be more judicious to apply the workhouse test." In doing so, guardians often disregarded "the advantages which result not only to the ratepayers but to the poor themselves from the offer of in-door in preference to out-door relief." The circular concluded that "a certainty of obtaining outdoor relief in his own home whenever he may ask for it extinguishes in the mind of the labourer all motive for husbanding his resources, and induces him to rely exclusively upon the rates instead of upon his own savings for such relief as he may require. It removes every incentive to self-reliance and prudent forethought on his part."[2]

The government was not alone in condemning generous poor relief. Beatrice Webb wrote that in the 1860s and 1870s the upper classes became obsessed that "the mass-misery of great cities arose mainly, if not entirely, from spasmodic, indiscriminate and unconditional doles, whether in the form of alms or in that of Poor Law relief." For example, Thomas Hawksley, in an influential pamphlet on *The Charities of London, and Some Errors of Their Administration*, calculated that from 1858 to 1868 the London pauperism rate increased from 2.9% to 5.1%. The failure of rapid economic growth to sweep away pauperism, he argued, was a result of the maladministration of the Poor Law, which had created "an abject, miserable race, who now feel it to be no humiliation to be dependent," and the "want of organization, or the absence of any system in the administration of the charities of London."[3]

1. The text of Goschen's minute is in Parl. Papers, *Twenty-Second Annual Report of the Poor Law Board* (1870, XXXV), pp. 9–12.

2. The text of the 1871 Circular is in Parl. Papers, *First Annual Report of the Local Government Board* (1872, XXVIII), pp. 63–68.

3. Webb (1926: 200); Hawksley (1869: 7–14).

Contemporaries did not just blame the bad administration of public relief and private charity—they placed much of the blame for the crisis of the 1860s on the behavior of the poor. Mid-Victorian Britain saw the rise of an ethic of respectability and self-help, preached by middle-class reformers who argued that improvements in workers' living standards had greatly reduced the need for public social welfare policies. An early leader of this movement was Samuel Smiles, who in his book *Self-Help* argued that "simple industry and thrift will go far towards making any person of ordinary working faculty comparatively independent in his means. Even a working man may be so, provided he will carefully husband his resources." It was "the duty of the prudent man" to set aside money to provide against income loss due to unemployment and sickness. In a later book, *Thrift* (1876), Smiles wrote that workers could "economize" by drinking less. In his words, "a glass of beer a day is equal to forty-five shillings a year. This sum will insure a man's life for a hundred and thirty pounds payable at death. Or, placed in a savings bank, it would amount to a hundred pounds in twenty years." He added, "The uncertainty of life is a strong inducement to provide against the evil day. To do this is a moral and social as well as a religious duty."[4]

Thomas Wright, the so-called journeyman engineer, went even further in criticizing those who "habitually prey upon charity." He wrote, "To these pauper-souled cormorants the bread of charity has no bitterness. . . . It is these self-degraded dwellers on the threshold of mendicancy who in times of special distress among the working classes chiefly profit by the funds which at such times a British public never fails to subscribe."[5]

The views of Hawksley, Smiles, and Wright were echoed by the Charity Organisation Society, founded in London in 1869, partly in response to the supposed indiscriminate nature of charitable giving by Londoners in 1866-69.[6] Its early leaders—including Octavia Hill, Canon Samuel Barnett, and C. S. Loch—blamed workers' failure to save on the easy availability of generous outdoor relief and unregulated private charity. Loch, longtime Secretary of the COS, maintained that "the State shares with indiscriminate charity the distinction of being a mighty engine for evil" and that "to foster independence is true charity." Canon Barnett wrote that "indiscriminate charity is one of the curses of London. . . . The effect of this charity is that . . . the people never learn to work or to save." In his view, charity's essential role should be "to create a sturdy self-helpful independence" among its recipients. Hill believed that "it was impertinent to the poor and injurious to their character to offer them

---

4. Smiles ([1866] 2002: 254); Smiles (1876: 33, 35).

5. Wright (1868: 287–88).

6. On the beginnings of the COS, see Mowat (1961), Owen (1964: 215–39), Jones (1971: 256–80), Himmelfarb (1991: 185–206), and Humphreys (1995: 50–63; 2001: 1–59).

doles. They should be lifted out of pauperism by being expected to be self-dependent."[7] The goals of the COS were to systematize "the benevolence of the public," to put an end to indiscriminate charity and the lax administration of poor relief, to separate the "deserving" poor from the "undeserving" poor, and to reach "an understanding with the Poor Law authorities which would mark off from each other the respective spheres of public relief and private charity." COS officials argued that a return to the "principles of 1834" would improve both the moral and economic conditions of the poor in the long run.[8]

Government and COS officials asserted that the number of poor relief recipients increased sharply in the 1860s, and that most working-class households earned enough income to protect themselves against economic insecurity. Were these assertions correct? Consider first the earnings of manual workers. Table 3.1 presents estimates of adult male manual workers' weekly wages and annual income in 1867, calculated by Dudley Baxter. Baxter divides manual workers into three classifications, and further divides each classification into two categories. The highest skilled workers, in category 1, include instrument makers, watchmakers, persons working with gold and silver, and engine drivers. Category 2 includes printers, skilled ironworkers, shipbuilders, and skilled workers in the building trades. The lower-skilled workers include manufacturers of machines and implements, brass and mixed metal workers, copper, tin, zinc, and lead workers (category 3), and skilled workers in cotton and wool, boot and shoe workers, railway workers, and coal miners (category 4). Category 5 includes messengers and porters, policemen, maltsters and brewers, workers in stone and slate quarries, and dock laborers, while category 6 includes agricultural and general laborers.[9]

The average weekly wage of a "higher skilled" worker in full work was 29.3s., while that of an unskilled laborer was 14.6s. In estimating workers' average annual income, Baxter deducted 20% from full-time wages of workers in categories 1–5, and 10% from wages of agricultural laborers, to take account of "loss of work from every cause."[10] His calculation takes into account paupers and "non-effectives," and therefore overadjusts for lost time for those regularly in work. Column 4 presents revised estimates of annual income, in which full-time earnings are reduced by 10% for all categories of manual workers, and column 5 presents revised average weekly wages, calculated by dividing

7. The quotes relating to Loch are from Webb (1926: 196); those for Barnett and Hill are from Barnett (1918: 35, 83, 86). Canon Barnett and his wife left the COS in the mid-1880s and turned to socialism. According to Webb (1926: 207), their 12-year residence in London's East End led them to discover "that there was a deeper and more continuous evil than unrestricted and unregulated charity, namely, unrestricted and unregulated capitalism and landlordism."

8. See Owen (1964: 221–22) and MacKinnon (1987: 605–8).

9. Baxter (1868: 88–93).

10. Baxter (1868: 47–49).

TABLE 3.1. Manual Workers' Wages and Earnings: England and Wales, 1867

	Number of Adult Men	Full Work Average Weekly Wage (s.)	Baxter Average Annual Earnings (£)	Revised Average Annual Earnings (£)	Revised Average Weekly Wage (s.)
Higher skilled labor					
Category 1	42,200	35.0	73.0	81.9	31.50
Category 2	798,600	29.0	60.0	67.9	26.10
Lower skilled labor					
Category 3	582,000	25.0	52.0	58.5	22.50
Category 4	1,028,000	22.0	46.0	51.5	19.80
Unskilled labor					
Category 5	260,360	17.5	36.8	41.0	15.75
Category 6	1,148,500	14.0	33.0	32.8	12.60
Total	3,859,660	21.4	45.6	50.0	19.22

Source: Baxter (1868: 94–95).

Note: See text for an explanation of how Baxter calculated annual earnings (column 3) and how I calculated revised annual earnings and revised average weekly wages.

revised earnings by 52. The adjusted average weekly wage for lower-skilled workers was 20.8s., while that for unskilled laborers was 13.2s.

How do these wage estimates compare with estimates of the poverty line? In the 1870s, school boards in many English boroughs and Poor Law unions set rudimentary poverty lines—families with incomes below these lines were considered to be in poverty and exempted from paying school fees. These poverty lines varied substantially across locations, in part, one suspects, because school boards did not agree on how to define poverty. The Salford school board in 1871 set the poverty line at 17s. per week for a family of four and 20s. for a family of five; in the same year the Manchester, Jarrow, and Stalybridge school boards set the poverty line at 14s. (after allowing for rent) for a family of four and 15s. for a family of five. Assuming an average weekly rent of 2.5s., the Manchester poverty line was 16.5s. for a family of four and 17.5s. for a family of five. Other boards adopted far less generous poverty lines. The Exeter and Derby school boards set the poverty line at 10.25s. for a family of four and 11.5s. for a family of five.[11]

Historian Marguerite Dupree calculated that the poverty line for the Potteries in 1861 was 17.2s. per week for a family with two children and 20s. for a family with three children; it increased by 2.8s. for each additional child. G. J. Barnsby estimated that the weekly earnings necessary to maintain a Black

11. Gillie (2008) provides a detailed discussion of the poverty lines estimated by school boards throughout England and Wales. The examples in the text are from Gillie (2008: 307–9).

Country household consisting of a husband, wife, and two small children in "a minimum standard of comfort" was 28s. in 1860 and 26.75s. in 1870 and 1880. Subtracting expenditures on shoes, clothing, drink, tobacco, durables, and services yields an estimate of weekly "subsistence" expenditures on food, rent, and fuel of 14s. in 1860 and 13.4s. in 1870 and 1880. Barnsby admits that his "food budget is very Spartan" and that his estimate for rent "would provide for an inferior three-roomed house."[12]

A comparison of the wage data in Table 3.1 with the estimated poverty scales shows that most unskilled workers in the late 1860s were paid wages that were close to, and often below, the poverty line, and that many lower-skilled workers in category 4 earned only slightly more than a subsistence income. To the extent that wives and older children living at home also worked for pay, family earnings exceeded the wage rates reported in Table 3.1.[13] Still, the data suggest that in the 1860s few unskilled workers, and probably no more than half of lower-skilled workers in category 4, would have been able to become "comparatively independent in their means" through "simple industry and thrift."

Was the fear of rapidly increasing numbers receiving poor relief justified? Hawksley reached his conclusion about the alarming growth of London pauperism by comparing growth in population and number of paupers for London from 1858 to 1868. His data are somewhat misleading because pauperism rates were relatively low in 1858 and because 1868 was at the peak of the crisis of 1866–69. The London pauperism rate was roughly constant from 1861 to 1866 (between 3.3% and 3.5%), then increased to 5.0% in 1868 before declining to 4.6% in 1869 and 4.8% in 1871.[14] Pauperism was increasing in the metropolis, but at a slower rate than Hawksley suggested.

The growth in London pauperism was not mirrored in other parts of England. Table 3.2 shows pauperism rates for England's ten registration divisions for 1861 and 1871. For England as a whole, the pauperism rate increased little over the decade, from 4.2% to 4.5%. By far the largest increase occurred in London, where the pauperism rate rose from 3.5% to 4.8%. It declined slightly in the East and North Midlands, remained constant in the North, and increased by only 0.1% in the South East, South Midlands, and West Midlands. The problem of rapidly increasing numbers on relief identified by the Local Government Board (LGB) occurred only in London.

12. Dupree (1995: 356–58); Barnsby (1971: 228–29). Dupree's poverty scale is based on a revision of Rowntree's (1901) primary poverty scale for York. Barnsby's estimate of subsistence income, which includes no spending on clothing, is almost certainly below Rowntree's poverty scale.

13. The labor force participation rate of married women was slightly below 25% in the 1860s. Burnette (2008: 306–7).

14. One-day pauperism rates were calculated using data from the Annual Reports of the Local Government Board.

TABLE 3.2. Share of Population Receiving Poor Relief on January 1 by Registration Division, 1861–71

Registration Division	Ratio of Paupers 1871/1861	PAUPERISM RATE (%)	
		1861	1871
London	1.603	3.5	4.8
South East	1.179	5.3	5.4
South Midlands	1.135	6.2	6.3
East	1.055	7.0	6.9
South West	1.146	5.6	6.2
West Midlands	1.148	3.9	4.0
North Midlands	1.062	4.1	4.0
North West	1.248	2.7	3.0
Yorkshire	1.293	2.7	2.9
North	1.225	3.6	3.6
England	1.217	4.2	4.5

Source: Annual Reports of the Poor Law Board and the Local Government Board.

Government officials and middle-class reformers were overly optimistic about the ability of low-skilled workers to protect themselves against income loss, and at the same time overly pessimistic regarding the trend in numbers receiving poor relief. One-third or more of manual workers in 1867 had earnings close to or below the poverty line, and outside of the metropolis pauperism rates increased slowly if at all during the 1860s. But perceptions often matter more than facts, and many contemporaries *believed* that pauperism was increasing rapidly due to the maladministration of public and private relief and workers' lack of thrift.

THE UNION CHARGEABILITY ACT

The second catalyst of the Crusade Against Outrelief was Parliament's adoption of the Union Chargeability Act in 1865 and the Metropolitan Poor Act in 1867. The Union Chargeability Act placed the entire cost of poor relief on the Poor Law union rather than the parish, and directed that each parish's contribution to the union common fund be based on its value of taxable property. The adoption of union rating shifted a large share of the cost of relief from working-class to middle-class parishes. The Metropolitan Poor Act, discussed in Chapter 2, shifted some of the costs of poor relief from individual London unions to the Metropolitan Common Poor Fund.

To understand the reasons for the 1865 act's adoption, it is necessary to examine briefly the issues of Poor Law financing and settlement. The 1834 Poor Law Amendment Act led to the grouping of parishes into Poor Law unions, but each parish within a union remained responsible for relieving its own poor. Unions were directed to set up a union common fund to be used to construct or maintain workhouses and for other "establishment charges." Each parish's contribution to the common fund was based on its average expenditure for the relief of its own paupers over the previous three years, and not on its rateable value of property. In other words, poor working-class parishes contributed more to the common fund than did wealthier middle-class parishes.

The Poor Law Amendment Act did not alter the law of settlement. Individuals were guaranteed poor relief only in their parish of settlement (typically their parish of birth), and nonsettled persons who applied for relief could be removed from a parish. By the 1830s, migrants made up one-third to one-half, and in some cases more, of the populations of English industrial cities. Urban relief officials used the power of removal to reduce relief expenditures. Those who appeared before the 1847 and 1855 Select Committees on Poor Removal testified that the mere threat of removal was enough to keep large numbers of nonsettled migrants from applying for poor relief.[15]

The Poor Removal Act of 1846 amended the Settlement Law to make irremovable persons who had continuously resided in a parish for five years, widows whose husbands had been dead for less than a year, and persons "who applied for temporary relief on account of sickness or accident." The creation of a category of nonsettled but irremovable poor caused relief expenditures of industrial cities to increase. Bradford's relief spending rose by "perhaps £5,000 annually" as a result of the act, while Leeds's annual relief spending increased by £3–4,000. Virtually all of the increase was borne by working-class parishes; "the parishes which had a large number of settled poor to relieve had a still larger amount to pay for the relief of the irremovable poor."[16]

To help ease the financial burden on urban parishes caused by the Poor Removal Act, Parliament in 1847 adopted Bodkin's Act, which shifted the cost of relieving irremovable paupers from their parish of residence to the union common fund. However, Bodkin's Act, which was extended in 1848, did little to aid working-class parishes because contributions to the common fund still were determined by relief expenditures rather than by rateable value of property. In 1854 the President of the Poor Law Board introduced a bill in Parliament to abolish the power of removal, replace the existing parish/union system of finance with complete union rating, and have each parish's contribution to the common fund be based on its rateable value of property. The bill met

---

15. Parl. Papers, *Report from the Select Committee on Settlement and Poor Removal* (1847, XI); Parl. Papers, *Report from the Select Committee on Poor Removal* (1854–55, XIII). Urban guardians were selective in the threat of removal—nonsettled temporarily unemployed able-bodied males often were granted short-term relief. Boyer (1990: 255–57).

16. Rose (1976: 29, 41); Ashforth (1985: 79); Green (2010: 224–29); Glen (1866: 12).

with opposition in the House of Commons and was withdrawn. Seven years later, Parliament adopted the Irremovable Poor Act (1861), which reduced the time of continuous residence necessary to become irremovable from five to three years, and directed that parishes contribute to the union common fund according to the value of their rateable property.[17]

Parliament's adoption of the Union Chargeability Act in 1865 marked the end of a two-decade-long debate over settlement, removal, and the local financing of poor relief. The act made the Poor Law union the unit of settlement and reduced the period of residence to become irremovable to one year. Most importantly, it "made the union rather than the parish the basic unit for all purposes relating to rating and poor law expenditure," and, by making all parish contributions to the common fund based on the value of rateable property, it equalized tax rates across parishes within unions.[18] The act finalized the shift in the source of funding for relief spending from the individual parishes to the Poor Law unions that began with the creation of union common funds after 1834. Before the adoption of the Irremovable Poor Act in 1861, the vast majority of relief spending was paid for by individual parishes, and poor rates varied substantially across parishes within unions. After the adoption of the 1861 act the share of relief expenditures charged to the union common fund increased to about 50%, on average.[19] The Union Chargeability Act, by making all relief spending the responsibility of the union common fund, increased poor rates in middle-class parishes and reduced rates in working-class parishes.

The infusion of money generated by union rateability eased the financial burdens that had plagued the Poor Law, and enabled unions to construct new, and larger, workhouses.[20] The increase in tax rates in wealthier parishes also sparked a middle-class reconsideration of the proper role of poor relief. Poor Law unions' boards of guardians typically were dominated by members from the wealthier parishes, who responded to the increase in their taxes by looking for ways to reduce relief costs.[21] The propaganda campaign of the Local Government Board and the Charity Organisation Society therefore fell on ready ears. Both the LGB and the COS claimed that the substitution of relief in workhouses for outdoor relief would reduce relief spending and therefore tax rates, even though the cost per pauper of workhouse relief was substantially higher than the cost of outdoor relief. Overall costs would decline because of

---

17. For more on the debate over settlement, removal, and union rateability, see Webb and Webb (1929: 419–31), Rose (1976), and Caplan (1978).

18. Green (2010: 232–33); Caplan (1978: 290–96); MacKinnon (1987: 613–14); Webb and Webb (1929: 430–31).

19. Caplan (1978: 290).

20. Expenditures on workhouse construction increased sharply after the adoption of the Union Chargeability Act. Williams (1981: 218–19).

21. MacKinnon (1987: 607–8).

the deterrent effect of the workhouse—the vast majority of applicants would refuse to enter workhouses, so that a shift from outdoor relief to workhouse relief would greatly reduce the number of paupers. Edmond Wodehouse, a Poor Law inspector for the LGB, gave the following example in his 1871 report on outdoor relief:

> A family applies for relief; if they are given out-relief to the amount of four shillings a week, they will be satisfied; if they come into the workhouse, their maintenance will cost ten shillings a week. The economists therefore argue, that by giving out-relief they will save six shillings a week. Now the very same guardians, who have used this argument, have frequently acknowledged to me, that when the workhouse test is offered, it is not accepted in more than one case out of ten. By offering the workhouse then in ten such cases the Guardians would indeed lose six shillings a week in the one case in which it was accepted, but in each of the remaining nine cases they would save four shillings, so that their total gain upon the ten cases would amount to thirty shillings a week.[22]

Wodehouse's assertion that nine out of ten persons offered workhouse relief would refuse it was an exaggeration, but it was accepted by many COS members and boards of guardians.

In the first half of the 1870s boards of guardians throughout England adopted some form of the workhouse test, enticed by the notion that restricting outdoor relief would both improve the morality of the poor and reduce the cost of poor relief. In the words of MacKinnon, "Whether or not guardians and ratepayers agreed with . . . the COS philosophy, it is easy to understand why they accepted many of the Local Government Board's recommendations."[23] Some contemporaries were blunter in commenting on guardians' motives. Beatrice Webb wrote that "it is not surprising that the . . . tenets of the originators of the idea of charity organisation found ready acceptance among the enlightened members of the propertied class." Behind the COS's "array of inductive and deductive proof of the disastrous effect on the wage-earning class of any kind of subvention, there lay the subconscious bias of 'the Haves' against taxing themselves for 'the Have Nots.'" Charles Marson, a leader of the Christian Social Union, similarly concluded, "Theories which, on the lips of Canon Barnett, are spiritual, if mistaken; and from the pen of Mr. Loch are able, though fallacious, become in the practice of meaner men merely the gospel of the buttoned pocket."[24]

---

22. Parl. Papers, *First Annual Report of the Local Government Board* (1872: XXVIII), pp. 88–103. The quote is on p. 97.

23. MacKinnon (1987: 625).

24. Webb (1926: 201); Marson quote cited in Owen (1964: 215).

EFFECTS OF THE CRUSADE AGAINST OUTRELIEF

The effect of the Crusade Against Outrelief on pauperism rates is shown in Table 3.3, which presents annual data for England and Wales from 1861 to 1901. Columns 1–3 report "official" estimates of the number of paupers, calculated as the average of the number relieved on January 1 and July 1; column 4 gives the pauperism rate estimated using the numbers in column 3. The day count substantially understates the number of persons receiving poor relief at some point during a year—the LGB calculated in 1892 that the number relieved over a 12-month period was 2.24 times the number recorded in the day counts. Column 5 gives the annual number receiving relief, estimated by multiplying each year's day count by 2.24. From 1861 to 1871 the share of the population receiving poor relief sometime during the year ranged from 9.2% to 10.9% during the cotton famine.

The short-run effects of the crusade are evident in the pauperism data for the 1870s. From 1871 to 1877, the official number of persons receiving poor relief declined by one-third, from 983,000 to 660,000, while the share of the population receiving relief (year count) declined from 9.8% to 6.1%. After 1875 the pauperism rate never again exceeded 6.5%. The crusade put an end to the use of the Poor Law to assist those temporarily in need during economic dislocations. From the 1840s through the 1860s, numbers on relief varied with the trade cycle, increasing during downturns and declining during booms. The Lancashire cotton famine, which affected only a small part of England and Wales, is clearly discernible in Table 3.3. After 1870 there is no hint of the trade cycle in the aggregate pauperism statistics. The unemployment rate increased from an average of 3.1% in 1871–75 to 9.5% in 1878 and 11.1% in 1879, and yet the share receiving relief declined from 1871 to 1878–79.[25]

The sharp drop in numbers relieved largely was caused by the policy change associated with the crusade, and in particular with the increased use of the workhouse test. In the 1860s, 12–15% of paupers were relieved in workhouses (column 7); by 1878 the share relieved indoors had increased to 21%, and it continued to rise thereafter, until by 1901 nearly 30% of paupers were relieved indoors. The strong deterrent effect associated with the workhouse test is revealed by comparing changes in numbers receiving indoor and outdoor relief. From 1871 to 1881, the number of persons receiving outdoor relief fell by 282,000 (a decline of 33%), while the number relieved in workhouses increased by only 21,000. Many of those offered indoor relief removed themselves from the relief roles rather than enter a workhouse, and others simply chose not to apply for relief.

25. The unemployment data are from Table 4.1.

TABLE 3.3. Numbers in Receipt of Poor Relief: England and Wales, 1861–1901

	DAY COUNT (MEAN OF JANUARY 1 AND JULY 1)				12-MONTH COUNT		
	Indoor Relief (1,000s)	Outdoor Relief (1,000s)	Total on Relief (1,000s)	Percentage Receiving Relief	Total on Relief (1,000s)	Percentage Receiving Relief	Percentage Relieved Indoors
1861	108	709	817	4.1	1,830	9.2	13.2
1862	119	743	862	4.3	1,931	9.6	13.8
1863	123	872	995	4.9	2,229	10.9	12.4
1864	120	844	964	4.7	2,159	10.5	12.4
1865	118	783	901	4.3	2,018	9.7	13.1
1866	118	746	864	4.1	1,935	9.2	13.7
1867	122	755	877	4.1	1,964	9.2	13.9
1868	134	801	935	4.3	2,094	9.7	14.3
1869	140	817	957	4.4	2,144	9.8	14.6
1870	141	838	979	4.4	2,193	9.9	14.4
1871	140	843	983	4.4	2,202	9.8	14.2
1872	133	791	924	4.1	2,070	9.1	14.4
1873	128	702	830	3.6	1,859	8.0	15.4
1874	127	646	773	3.3	1,732	7.4	16.4
1875	129	616	745	3.1	1,669	7.0	17.3
1876	125	567	692	2.9	1,550	6.5	18.1
1877	130	530	660	2.7	1,478	6.1	19.7
1878	139	527	666	2.7	1,492	6.0	20.9
1879	147	555	702	2.8	1,572	6.3	20.9
1880	159	582	741	2.9	1,660	6.5	21.5
1881	161	561	722	2.8	1,617	6.3	22.3
1882	161	557	718	2.8	1,608	6.2	22.4
1883	162	551	713	2.7	1,597	6.0	22.7
1884	160	534	694	2.6	1,555	5.8	23.1
1885	162	533	695	2.6	1,557	5.8	23.3
1886	164	542	706	2.6	1,581	5.8	23.2
1887	167	555	722	2.6	1,617	5.9	23.1
1888	170	554	724	2.6	1,622	5.8	23.5
1889	168	548	716	2.6	1,604	5.7	23.5
1890	166	530	696	2.5	1,559	5.5	23.9
1891	163	515	678	2.4	1,519	5.3	24.0
1892	163	499	662	2.2	1,483	5.0	24.6
1893	169	505	674	2.3	1,510	5.1	25.1
1894	180	519	699	2.4	1,566	5.3	25.8
1895	184	523	707	2.4	1,584	5.3	26.0
1896	187	535	722	2.4	1,617	5.3	25.9
1897	186	530	716	2.3	1,604	5.2	26.0
1898	188	525	713	2.3	1,597	5.1	26.4
1899	190	538	728	2.3	1,631	5.2	26.1
1900	188	500	688	2.2	1,541	4.8	27.3
1901	204	494	698	2.2	1,564	4.8	29.2

Source: Data on numbers receiving relief (day count) from the Annual Reports of the Poor Law Board (through 1870) and the Local Government Board. The data are reported in Williams (1981: 159–61).

Note: In column 5, the adjusted number of relief recipients was calculated by multiplying the official number by 2.24. See Lees (1998: 180).

TABLE 3.4. Poor Relief Expenditures, England and Wales, 1871–81

(A) NOMINAL EXPENDITURES (£ 1,000S)

	Indoor	Outdoor	Indoor + Outdoor	Other	Total
1871	1,525	3,664	5,189	1,951	7,140
1872	1,516	3,584	5,100	2,166	7,266
1873	1,549	3,279	4,828	2,083	6,911
1874	1,649	3,111	4,760	2,074	6,834
1875	1,578	2,959	4,537	2,093	6,630
1876	1,534	2,761	4,295	2,158	6,453
1877	1,614	2,616	4,230	2,258	6,488
1878	1,727	2,622	4,349	2,382	6,731
1879	1,721	2,642	4,363	2,482	6,845
1880	1,758	2,711	4,469	2,552	7,021
1881	1,839	2,660	4,499	2,569	7,068
1881/1871	1.206	0.726	0.867	1.317	0.990

(B) REAL EXPENDITURES (£ 1,000S)

	Indoor	Outdoor	Indoor + Outdoor	Other	Total
1871	1,483	3,563	5,047	1,897	6,944
1872	1,414	3,343	4,758	2,021	6,778
1873	1,435	3,037	4,471	1,929	6,400
1874	1,599	3,017	4,616	2,011	6,628
1875	1,554	2,914	4,467	2,061	6,528
1876	1,508	2,713	4,221	2,121	6,342
1877	1,588	2,573	4,161	2,221	6,382
1878	1,751	2,658	4,409	2,415	6,824
1879	1,828	2,806	4,633	2,636	7,269
1880	1,829	2,821	4,650	2,655	7,305
1881	1,939	2,805	4,744	2,709	7,452
1881/1871	1.307	0.787	0.940	1.428	1.073

Sources: Data on nominal relief spending from Williams (1981: 170). Cost of living estimates from Feinstein (1995: 264).

The effect of the Crusade on Poor Law expenditures is not as straightforward. Table 3.4 shows that from 1871 to 1881 nominal spending on outdoor relief declined by just over £1 million, while spending on workhouse relief increased by £314,000. However, "other" costs, a combination of "bricks and mortar" costs and administrative costs, increased by 31.7% due to the increased costs associated with workhouse relief. As a result, total expenditures declined by only £72,000 (1.0%) from 1871 to 1881, despite the fact that the number of persons in receipt of poor relief (day count) declined by 261,000, and the share of the population receiving relief fell by 27%. Panel (b) shows that real expenditures on indoor plus outdoor relief declined by 6% from 1871 to 1881, while "other" costs increased by 42.8%. Real total expenditures increased by 7.3%; real per capita spending declined, but only by 2.6%. In sum, while the crusade led to a sharp reduction in numbers on relief, as the COS and LGB predicted, their assertion that the workhouse test would reduce local poor rates was not correct, at least not in the short run.[26]

Table 3.5 shows the number of able-bodied and non-able-bodied persons receiving poor relief in each English registration division on January 1, 1871 and 1881. Non-able-bodied paupers consisted mainly of old people and the disabled. The data show that the crusade was aimed at all paupers, not just the able-bodied—the number of able-bodied and non-able-bodied paupers receiving outdoor relief declined in all ten divisions over the decade. For England as a whole, the number of able-bodied adults and their children in receipt of outdoor relief declined by 42% from 1871 to 1881, while the number of non-able-bodied persons relieved outdoors declined by 31%. The number of non-able-bodied paupers relieved in workhouses increased in eight divisions and declined slightly in two rural southern divisions, while the number of able-bodied paupers relieved indoors declined throughout the South and in the rural North Midlands, and increased in the three northern divisions and the more industrial West Midlands. That is, one effect of the crusade was to change the demographic makeup of workhouse inmates. The deterrent effect of the workhouse test was stronger for the able-bodied than for the elderly, many of whom had few alternatives to accepting whatever form of poor relief they were offered.

The final two columns of Table 3.5 give the overall pauperism rate and the share relieved in workhouses in 1871 and 1881 for each division. The pauperism rate declined everywhere over the decade, but the extent of decline was much larger in London and the South than in the Midlands or the North. As a result, the North-South differential in pauperism rates, which had existed since at least the late eighteenth century, declined in the 1870s.[27] The use of the workhouse increased in every division, although the data indicate that the crusade was centered more in urban than rural districts. By far the largest increase occurred in London, where the share relieved indoors increased from 22.8% in 1871 to 52.2% in 1881. The fact that the COS was based in London and

26. The extent of workhouses' deterrent effects and the high administrative costs of indoor relief are discussed in MacKinnon (1987), Kiniria (2016), and Lindert (2004: 51–55). Kiniria (2016: 30), who has done the most detailed empirical study of the cost-effectiveness of the welfare reforms of the 1870s, concluded that the costs associated with building and maintaining workhouses and administering indoor relief "precluded the Crusade Against Outrelief from achieving the savings that it anticipated. In this sense, the Crusade can be seen as an ideological success and a financial failure."

27. Regional differences in pauperism rates are discussed in more detail in Chapter 5.

TABLE 3.5. Able-Bodied and Non-Able-Bodied Persons in Receipt of Poor Relief by Registration Division

Registration Division		Indoor AB	Outdoor AB	Indoor NAB	Outdoor NAB	Total Paupers	Pauperism Rate (%)	% Relieved Indoors
		NUMBER OF PERSONS IN RECEIPT OF RELIEF ON JANUARY 1						
London	1871	10,073	82,344	25,731	39,023	157,171	4.8	22.8
	1881	8,611	23,281	38,275	19,729	89,896	2.4	52.2
South East	1871	8,040	48,455	12,847	46,788	116,130	5.4	18.0
	1881	5,008	25,120	13,687	29,042	72,857	2.9	25.7
South Midlands	1871	4,517	38,789	7,029	40,846	91,181	6.3	12.7
	1881	2,646	18,486	7,791	27,379	56,302	3.5	18.5
East	1871	5,013	35,438	6,247	37,632	84,330	6.9	13.4
	1881	2,902	16,762	6,059	23,197	48,920	3.6	18.3
South West	1871	4,151	40,231	8,112	64,786	117,280	6.2	10.5
	1881	3,407	22,752	7,827	48,491	82,477	4.4	13.6
West Midlands	1871	4,922	42,462	10,354	50,275	108,013	4.0	14.1
	1881	6,087	34,411	13,401	39,375	93,274	3.1	20.9
North Midlands	1871	2,322	20,000	4,601	29,545	56,468	4.0	12.3
	1881	2,272	13,823	5,031	20,428	41,554	2.5	17.6
North West	1871	4,536	48,168	15,666	32,248	100,618	3.0	20.1
	1881	6,736	36,015	18,073	21,872	82,696	2.0	30.0
Yorkshire	1871	2,560	32,484	5,941	29,674	70,659	2.9	12.0
	1881	3,935	31,697	7,920	25,090	68,642	2.4	17.3
North	1871	1,530	25,313	3,966	19,721	50,530	3.6	10.9
	1881	1,913	17,637	5,065	14,255	38,870	2.4	18.0
England	1871	47,664	413,684	100,494	390,538	952,380	4.5	15.6
	1881	43,517	239,984	123,129	268,858	675,488	2.8	24.7

Source: Annual Reports of the Local Government Board.

that one of the major catalysts of the crusade was the London poor relief crisis of the 1860s explains why the crusade was particularly strong in the metropolis.

After declining sharply from 1871 to 1877, the pauperism rate continued to fall, but at a much slower pace, thereafter. The share of the population receiving relief during a year fell from 6.3% in 1881 to 5.3% in 1891 and 4.8% in 1901.[28] The post-1881 decline was caused in part by improvements in material living standards and an increase in working-class self-help, as will be shown in Section II. Some part of the decline, however, was a result of changes in working-class attitudes toward the Poor Law. One of the crusade's aims was to make reliance on the Poor Law during times of "personal distress" a less palatable option for workers, and in this regard it was very successful. Prior to 1870, the working class regarded access to public relief as a legal right, although they rejected the workhouse as a form of relief. In the words of Lees, it is necessary "to distinguish between the rejection by the poor of specific welfare institutions and their adamant insistence upon their own entitlement to parish relief."[29] Opinions changed after 1870, however, and by the end of the century many within the working class viewed poor relief as stigmatizing. This change in perceptions led many poor people to go to great lengths to avoid applying for relief. According to Thompson, working-class resolve "not to touch poor relief at all except in sickness, had become a matter of avoiding social disgrace . . . above all avoiding disparagement and humiliation in front of friends and neighbors. . . . Resort to poor relief, in other words, came to be equated with the loss of respectability, a concept nourished and enforced by local communities and peer groups."[30] MacKinnon provides a more nuanced view of late Victorian working-class perceptions of the Poor Law. Friends and neighbors strongly disparaged the acceptance of poor relief by healthy able-bodied adults, but there was "little or no stigma attached" to outdoor relief for the old, which was widespread—"it was considered normal for the elderly to live on a combination of charity and poor relief." She also gives another reason why working-class households strived to remain off the Poor Law. The ability to obtain credit was "vitally important to the very poor," and shopkeepers and landlords viewed the application for poor relief as "a clear signal of increased risk of default."[31]

28. While the number of paupers in all categories declined, the largest rate of decline was among prime-age adults. On March 31, 1906, only 0.97% of persons aged 16–60 were in receipt of poor relief. Parl. Papers, *Royal Commission on the Poor Laws and Relief of Distress, Appendix Vol. XXV* (1910: LIII), p. 50.

29. Lees (1998: 162–65); Hunt (1981: 215).

30. Thompson (1988: 352–53). See also Lees (1998: 294–301).

31. MacKinnon (1984: 172–73). On the important role played by credit in working-class life, see Johnson (1985: chap. 6).

In sum, there were economic, institutional, and cultural reasons for the decline in pauperism from 1871 to 1901. The sharp drop in numbers relieved in the 1870s was driven by the Crusade Against Outrelief and the widespread adoption of the workhouse test. The impact of this institutional change was reinforced by a change in working-class attitudes toward poor relief. Finally, some share of the decline was a result of improvements in working-class living standards and a rise in self-help. Victorian reformers, and in particular COS officials, maintained that improving living standards played the most important role in causing the fall in pauperism. However, evidence presented in Section II indicates that the living standards of the bottom one-third or so of the working class improved little in the last three decades of the nineteenth century.

II. Trends in Manual Workers' Earnings and Self-Help, 1860–1913

Officials of the LGB and the COS predicted that working-class self-help would increase over time as a result of increases in earnings and improvements in morals and thriftiness brought about by changes in the administration of poor relief. Were these predictions correct? How much did manual workers' purchasing power improve in late Victorian England? What share of working-class households took steps to protect themselves against income insecurity, through depositing money in savings banks and joining mutual insurance organizations? This section addresses these questions.

British economic growth in the second half of the nineteenth century typically is divided into two periods, the Victorian boom from 1850 until roughly 1873, followed by a period of slower growth, sometimes known as the Great Depression, from the mid-1870s to the late 1890s. By most measures the economy remained sluggish from 1899 to 1913. Real disposable income per head increased at an annual rate of 1.7% from 1856 to 1873 and 1.0% from 1873 to 1913.[32]

The late nineteenth-century slowdown in economic growth was reflected in a slowdown in earnings growth. Table 3.6 presents estimates of the average rate of growth of manual workers' nominal and real earnings for 1855–1913 and for three subperiods.[33] For the period as a whole, real earnings grew at an annual rate of 1.27%. There were significant differences in rates of earnings growth across subperiods. Real (and nominal) earnings grew much faster

32. Matthews, Feinstein, and Odling-Smee (1982: 498); Feinstein (1990b: 339). The data are for the United Kingdom as a whole.

33. The wage data series were constructed by Feinstein (1995: 259–65). The estimated rates of growth are for weekly earnings.

TABLE 3.6. Trends in Weekly Earnings of Manual Workers, 1855–1913

	1855–1913	1855–74	1874–99	1899–1913
(A) ALL MANUAL WORKERS (ANNUAL PERCENTAGE GROWTH RATES)				
Money earnings	1.09	1.84	0.42	1.27
Cost of living	−0.17	−0.22	−0.77	0.97
Real earnings	1.27	2.07	1.20	0.30
(B) REAL EARNINGS BY SECTOR (ANNUAL PERCENTAGE GROWTH RATES)				
Agriculture	0.95	1.54	1.01	0.05
Building	1.04	1.75	1.40	−0.55
Coal	1.16	2.29	0.53	0.77
Cotton	1.49	2.65	1.38	0.12
Engineering, etc.	0.91	0.96	1.52	−0.23

Source: Calculated from data in Feinstein (1995).

during the Victorian boom from the 1850s to the early 1870s than during the last quarter of the century, and real earnings growth was even slower from 1899 to 1913. Panel (b) presents estimates of real earnings growth for five sectors—agriculture, building, coal mining, cotton textiles, and engineering, shipbuilding, and vehicles. For all sectors except engineering, the growth rate of real earnings was greater from 1855 to 1874 than from 1874 to 1913. Real earnings in the building trades and engineering declined from 1899 to 1913, and earnings in agriculture and cotton textiles were virtually constant. What effect did the late Victorian slowdown in the rate of growth in purchasing power have on the growth in working-class self-help?

GROWTH IN SELF-HELP, 1850–1913

A major assumption of the Crusade Against Outrelief was that the workhouse test would lead workers to protect themselves against unexpected income loss. To determine if workers responded to changes in policy as middle-class reformers assumed they would, it is useful to begin by examining the growth in self-help in the decades leading up to the crusade.

Deposits in savings banks and membership in friendly societies grew rapidly from 1850 to 1870 (see Tables 3.7 through 3.9). The combined membership of the Manchester Unity Oddfellows and the Foresters was nearly 811,000 in 1870, a 140% increase over 1846. By 1872, membership in registered friendly societies was about 1.86 million, and the Royal Commission on Friendly Societies (1870–74) estimated that overall friendly society membership was about 4 million (Table 3.8). This last figure is likely an overestimate; total

TABLE 3.7. Working-Class Saving and Poor Relief Spending, 1850–1910

	Trustee Savings Bank Deposits (£ million)	Post Office Savings Bank Deposits (£ million)	Total Savings Bank Deposits (£ million)	Estimated Working-Class Bank Deposits (£ million)	Indoor + Outdoor Poor Relief Spending (£ million)	Working-Class Deposits/Poor Relief Spending	Real Per Capita Poor Relief Spending (1830 = 100)
1850	28.9		28.9	7.23	4.069	1.78	62.8
1855	34.3		34.3	8.58	4.287	2.00	50.0
1860	41.3		41.3	10.33	3.775	2.74	44.2
1865	38.7	6.5	45.2	13.56	4.370	3.10	49.8
1870	38.0	15.1	53.1	15.93	5.136	3.10	53.9
1875	42.4	25.2	67.6	20.28	4.537	4.47	43.9
1880	44.0	33.7	77.7	23.31	4.469	5.22	42.7
1885	46.4	47.7	94.1	28.23	4.392	6.43	43.0
1890	43.6	67.6	111.2	33.36	4.354	7.66	41.1
1895	45.3	97.9	143.2	42.96	4.747	9.05	44.4
1900	51.5	135.5	187.0	56.10	5.246	10.69	43.4
1905	52.7	152.1	204.8	61.44	6.211	9.89	48.4
1910	52.3	168.9	221.2	66.36	6.701	9.90	47.1

Sources: Columns 1 and 2: Mitchell (1988: 671–72). Column 3: Calculated as column 1 plus column 2. Column 4: Estimates for 1870–1910 calculated by assuming that 30% of savings bank deposits belonged to working-class accounts. See Johnson (1985: 100–105). Estimates for 1850–65 assume that 25% of deposits belonged to working-class accounts. I chose lower estimates for the percentage of deposits held by members of the working class in 1850–65 because using 30% yielded unreasonably large average deposits per working-class account. The estimates for 1850–65 are based on a substantial amount of guesswork. Column 5: Williams (1981: 169–71). Column 6: Calculated as column 4 divided by column 5. Column 7: Constructed by the author, using expenditure data from column 5, cost of living estimates from Feinstein (1995), and population data from Mitchell (1988: 11–13).

TABLE 3.8. Friendly Society Membership, 1850–1911

	Adult Males Aged 20+	Estimated Friendly Society Members	Author Est. Friendly Society Members	Registered Friendly Society Members	OFS + AFS Members	OFS + AFS Sick Benefit Members	Nine Major Friendly Societies Members	Four Affiliated Friendly Societies Members
1850	4,717,000	3,000,000	2,000,000					328,663
1860								524,417
1870	5,866,000						1,039,940	859,040
1872		4,000,000	3,500,000	1,857,896				
1875								1,075,864
1877				2,750,000				
1885								1,280,313
1886					3,760,000	2,845,000	1,630,972	
1887				3,600,000				
1889		4,395,160						
1891	7,516,000		4,500,000		4,110,000	3,110,000		1,464,791
1892		6,000,000		3,860,000				
1896							2,004,092	1,563,466
1899				5,466,000			2,143,845	
1901	8,856,000				5,470,000	4,140,000		1,678,601
1905				6,164,000				
1910				6,623,000			2,444,632	1,688,379
1911	10,260,000				6,420,000	4,430,000		

Sources: Column 1: Mitchell (1988: 11, 15). Column 2: Estimate for 1850 (1849) from Perkin (1969: 381). Estimate for 1872 from the Royal Commission on Friendly Societies, 1874, reported in Gosden (1961: 7). Estimate for 1889 from Wilkinson (1891: 191). Estimate for 1892 from Brabrook, reported in Neave (1996: 49). Column 3: Estimated by author. See text. Column 4: Number for 1872 from Royal Commission on Friendly Societies, 1874, reported in Gosden (1961: 7). Numbers for 1877–1910, with the exception of 1892, from Neave (1996: 61). Number for 1892 from Gosden (1973: 91). Column 5: Johnson (1985: 50, 57). Column 6: Johnson (1985: 57). Estimates for 1886 and 1891 were calculated by author assuming that the share of OFS + AFS members who were eligible for sickness benefits was roughly the same as in 1901. Column 7: Numbers for 1872 and 1886 from Beveridge (1948: 31). Number for 1896 from *Fifteenth Abstract of Labour Statistics* (1912: 256–57). Numbers for 1899 and 1910 from *Seventeenth Abstract of Labour Statistics* (1915: 258–59). Column 8: Numbers for 1850 to 1885 from Neave (1996: 49). Numbers for 1891 and 1896 from *Eleventh Abstract of Labour Statistics* (1907: 180). Numbers for 1901 and 1910 from *Seventeenth Abstract of Labour Statistics* (1915: 258).

Notes: OFS refers to ordinary friendly societies; AFS refers to affiliated friendly societies.

TABLE 3.9. Working-Class Savings Accounts and Membership in Friendly Societies
with Sickness Benefits

	Adult Males Aged 20+ (1,000s)	Working-Class Savings Deposits (1,000s)	FS Memb. with Sickness Benefits (1,000s)	% Males with Sickness Benefits (FS)	FS + TU with Sickness Benefits (1,000s)	% Males with Sickness Benefits (FS + TU)	Adjusted % with Sickness Benefits (FS + TU)
1850	4,717	750	1,350	29			
1871	5,866	1,900	2,400	41	2,525	43	39
1891	7,516	4,640	3,370	45	3,950	53	47
1911	10,260	7,211	4,780	47	5,509	54	48

Sources: Column 1: From census data reported in Mitchell (1988: 15). Column 2: Estimated by author from data
in Fishlow (1961) and Johnson (1985: 91–93). Column 3: Estimated by author. See text. Column 4: Calculated as
column 3 divided by column 1. Column 5: Calculated as column 3 plus number of trade union members with sickness
benefits. See text. Column 6: Calculated as column 5 divided by column 1. Column 7: Estimated by author, by reducing
numbers in column 5 by 10% to account for duplication of policies. The adjusted estimates of individuals with sickness
benefits were then divided by column 1.
Notes: FS refers to friendly societies; TU refers to trade unions.

membership was closer to 3.0–3.5 million. The number in societies that paid
sickness benefits was smaller, perhaps 2.1–2.4 million, or 36–41% of the adult
male population.[34]

Total friendly society expenditures are not known. Expenditure data
are available for the Manchester Oddfellows and the Foresters, the two
largest affiliated societies; in 1870 they paid out £653,000 in sickness and
funeral benefits.[35] Slightly more than one-third of friendly society members
eligible for sickness benefits were in one of these two affiliated societies. If the Manchester Oddfellows and Foresters accounted for one-third
of expenditures by those societies offering sickness benefits, then total

34. These estimates are based on the assumption that 75% of registered friendly society
members were in societies that paid sickness benefits, and that 60% of members of nonregistered or local societies were eligible for sickness benefits. If 75% of all members were in societies
paying sickness benefits, then the total number eligible for sickness benefits in 1872 was 2.25–
2.63 million. If, on the other hand, we assume that there were 4 million total members, and that
50% of members of nonregistered or local societies were in societies paying sickness benefits,
then the total number eligible for sickness benefits was 2.46 million.

35. Neison (1877: 74–75). The expenditure per member on sickness and funeral benefits in
1870 was 16.1s.

friendly society spending in 1870 was £1.96 million, or 38% of poor relief expenditures.[36]

The weekly benefits paid by friendly societies and the Poor Law were similar from 1850 to 1870. The level of poor relief benefits given to an unemployed or sick worker was determined by the size of the worker's family and the income earned by other family members. Benefit levels were similar across towns and over time, typically 2–3s. for a single adult male per week, and 1s. 6d.–2s. per week for each additional family member. An unemployed man with a wife and two (three) children would receive about 8s. (10s.) per week if the family had no other sources of income, less if other family members were working. Friendly society sickness benefits varied across societies, but were on average 8–10s. per week in the 1850s and 1860s. The median weekly wage for manual workers was about 18s. in 1860, and the upper quartile averaged 22.5s.[37] Since most friendly society members would have been from the upper half of the income distribution, the sickness benefit likely replaced between a third and a half of their wages.

Table 3.9 shows that, from 1850 to 1871, the number of working-class deposits in the Trustee Savings Banks and the newly formed Post Office Savings Bank increased from about 750,000 to 1.9 million, an increase of more than 150%.[38] The real value of workers' savings bank deposits roughly doubled from 1850 to 1870. To put the extent of workers' savings in some perspective, in 1870 the value of working-class savings deposits was more than three times the annual expenditures on poor relief (Table 3.7).

In sum, working-class self-help increased substantially in the two decades leading up to the Crusade Against Outrelief; indeed it was increasing at the very time that, according to the LGB, the growth in poor relief spending was "so great, as to excite apprehension." Relief spending and self-help increased at the same time because they were associated with different parts of the working class. In 1870 less than one-half of working-class households had savings

36. The above calculations are based on the assumption that the total number of members of friendly societies paying sickness benefits was 2.4 million. To calculate an upper-bound estimate of friendly society spending, suppose that membership in societies paying sickness benefits was 3 million. Then the Manchester Oddfellows and Foresters made up 27% of total membership. If they also accounted for 27% of expenditures, then total friendly society spending in 1870 was about £2.42 million, 47% of poor relief expenditures.

37. Average Poor Law benefit levels from Rose (1965: 195–96). Riley (1997: 281) maintains that the average friendly society benefit was 8s. per week in 1860. Hopkins (1995: 34) states that the typical weekly benefit was 8–10s.; Neave (1996: 55) maintains that the typical benefit was 10s. Median wage estimates from Bowley (1937: 46).

38. In 1871 there were 2.7 million total depositors in savings banks. I estimate that 1.8–2.0 million were from the working class.

accounts or were members of friendly societies paying sickness benefits. "Friendly society membership was the badge of the skilled worker," and the same can be said about having a bank account. Few low-skilled workers were able to save, nor could they afford the premiums charged by friendly societies offering sickness benefits.[39] When they lost any significant amount of work time, they were forced to turn to the Poor Law, private charity, or family and friends for assistance.

By 1870, then, there were distinct differences in the methods used by skilled and unskilled workers to cope with income insecurity. Skilled workers largely had accepted the Victorian ethic of respectability and self-help, and protected themselves against income loss by saving and joining friendly societies. Few skilled workers ever used the Poor Law, although some applied for relief during prolonged periods of unemployment or when they were elderly. For a large share of low-skilled workers, however, the Poor Law provided an important safety net that they turned to periodically. Most laborers would have preferred the strategy of self-help, but their wages were too low to make this a viable option. Behavior that the LGB and the COS attributed to character flaws largely was a result of low incomes.

The last third of the nineteenth century saw a continuation of the self-help movement, spurred on by the Crusade Against Outrelief. The number of accounts in the Post Office Savings Bank and Trustee Savings Banks nearly quadrupled from 1871 to 1911, by which date there were about 7.2 million working-class depositors (see Table 3.9).[40] In real terms, deposits in workers' savings accounts increased by 141% from 1870 to 1890, and by another 94% from 1890 to 1913.

Membership in registered friendly societies increased from 1.86 million in 1872 to 3.6 million in 1887 (Table 3.8), although some of this increase likely represented a greater registration of existing societies. Total membership in ordinary and affiliated societies increased from 3.76 million in 1886 to 5.47 million in 1901, and 6.42 million in 1911 (Table 3.8, column 5).[41] Following Neave,

---

39. Gilbert (1966a: 166–67); Johnson (1985: 57–63). The conclusion that few low-skilled workers were members of friendly societies has been challenged by Riley (1997: 31–34), who contends that the records of individual clubs show that many poorly paid workers joined friendly societies. By the mid-1860s, membership in the IOOMU and the AOF was spreading into agricultural counties (Gosden 1961: 44–45). However, there seems little doubt that in 1870 the share of low-skilled workers who were members of friendly societies offering sickness benefits was small.

40. There were 10.3 million savings accounts in 1911. Johnson estimates that 70% of the accounts were held by members of the working class. See Johnson (1985: 91–92, 104–5).

41. I have not been able to determine what accounts for the discrepancies between the number of registered friendly society members in column 4 and Johnson's estimates in column 5. Johnson's figures are for registered affiliated and ordinary—those with only one office—societies. Not all friendly societies were registered. The number of unregistered members probably was

I estimate that the total number of friendly society members in 1891 was 4.5 million, and that the membership of societies paying sickness benefits prob-ably was about 3.37 million.[42] This represented 45% of the adult male popula-tion in 1891. Johnson estimates that the number of friendly society members eligible for sickness benefits was 4.14 million in 1901 and 4.43 million in 1911. If we multiply his numbers by 1.08 to take account of those (relatively few) nonregistered members in societies with sickness benefits, we get estimates of friendly society members eligible for sickness benefits of 4.47 million in 1901 and 4.78 million in 1911 (Table 3.9).[43] The 1911 figure represented 47% of adult males, up from 41% in 1871 and 29% in 1850. If three-quarters of adult males were members of the working class, then in 1911 62% of adult working-class males were members of friendly societies that provided sickness benefits, up from 55% in 1871 and 38% in 1850.

Annual expenditure data on benefits are available for 14 large societies from 1886 onward, and rough estimates can be made of total friendly society ex-penditures (see Table 3.10). Edward Brabrook, the Chief Registrar of Friendly Societies, estimated that in 1891 total friendly society expenditures on benefits was £4,277,000.[44] The 14 societies for which data are available accounted for 52% of this total. If this ratio held throughout the period, then friendly society expenditures increased from £3.48 million in 1886 to £8.20 million in 1913. Friendly society spending was 81% of poor relief expenditures in 1886; it rose to 104% by 1908.

TRADE UNIONS AND MUTUAL INSURANCE

Adding to this was mutual-insurance spending by trade unions. The last three decades of the nineteenth century witnessed a rapid growth in union mem-bership. The Trades Union Congress claimed to have 289,000 members in

---

relatively small; Wilkinson's (1891: 191) estimate for 1889 put total membership at 4.4 million, 7% greater than the number of registered members in 1891.

42. Neave (1996: 49–50). I assume that the share of OFS + AFS members eligible for sick-ness benefits in 1891 was the same as in 1901, and that two-thirds of the 390,000 friendly society members not included in ordinary or affiliated friendly societies (4.5 million – 4.11 million) were in societies paying sickness benefits. There are two very different estimates of the total number of friendly society members in 1889–92: Wilkinson's estimate of 4.4 million members in 1889 and Brabrook's estimate of 6 million in 1892. Neave (1996: 49–50) contends that Wilkinson's estimate is much closer to the actual number, and gives his own estimate of 4.5 million for 1891.

43. Johnson (1985: 57). My estimates for 1891 suggest that the total number of friendly so-ciety members with sickness benefits was about 8% greater than the number of OFS + AFS members with sickness benefits.

44. Brabrook's estimates are in Parl. Papers, *Royal Commission on Labour, Fourth Report, Minutes of Evidence* (1893–94, XXXIX, Pt. 1), q. 1321.

TABLE 3.10. Friendly Society, Trade Union, and Poor Relief Expenditures, 1870–1913

	14 Friendly Societies Expenditure (£s)	Estimated Total Friendly Society Expenditure (£s)	Trade Union Benefit Expenditure (£s)	Friendly Society + Trade Union Expenditure (£s)	Indoor + Outdoor Relief Expenditure (£s)	Friendly Society + Trade Union/Poor Relief
1870		1,960,000	250,000	2,210,000	5,136,000	0.430
1886	1,827,002	3,484,286	555,855	4,040,141	4,328,000	0.933
1892	2,310,661	4,406,675	805,969	5,212,644	4,418,000	1.180
1900	2,871,354	5,475,976	1,019,192	6,495,168	5,246,000	1.238
1908	3,531,054	6,734,094	2,339,275	9,073,369	6,467,000	1.403
1910	3,605,171	6,875,443	1,772,841	8,648,284	6,701,000	1.291
1913	4,301,896	8,204,172	1,879,971	10,084,143	5,979,000	1.687

Sources: Column 1: Data for 1886 from Sixth Abstract of Labour Statistics (1900: 50–77). Data for 1892 from Eleventh Abstract of Labour Statistics (1907: 184–85). Data for 1900 through 1913 from Seventeenth Abstract of Labour Statistics (1915: 260–61). Column 2: Estimated by author. The estimates for 1886–1913 assume (following Brabrook) that the expenditures of the 14 largest friendly societies accounted for 52% of total friendly society expenditures on benefits. The estimate for 1870 assumes that total friendly society expenditures were equal to three times the expenditures of the two largest friendly societies, the Manchester Unity Oddfellows and the Foresters. See text. Column 3: Estimated by author from various Board of Trade reports on trade unions. Column 4: Calculated as column 2 plus column 3. Column 5: Seventeenth Abstract of Labour Statistics (1915: 185). Column 6: Calculated as column 4 divided by column 5.

1871. Union membership increased sharply in the following three years, then declined during the downturn of the late 1870s, although at its lowest point in 1881 membership was about 460,000, more than 50% above its 1871 level. By 1888 there were about 750,000 adult male trade union members, increasing to 1.5 million in 1898 and 2.1 million in 1908. Union density was 15.2% in 1898 and 19.0% in 1908.[45]

The rapid union growth after 1870 was accompanied by the spread of mutual insurance benefits to a broad range of occupations. Craft unions provided their members with insurance against unemployment, sickness, and accidents, pensions for retired members, and death benefits to ensure workers and their wives a proper funeral. The importance attached by workers to unions' insurance function can be seen in the objectives listed in union rules. The Boilermakers and Iron and Steel Shipbuilders, for example, sought "to provide against a train of evils of the most serious magnitude, which evils, when they arise from any cause except sickness, are not provided for by any of the ordinary 'Benefit Societies.'" Similarly, the rules of the Friendly Society of Iron Founders stated that "the objects of this society are the establishment of a fund for the relief of its members out of work, and for the mutual support of its members in case of sickness, accident, or superannuation," as well as "the promotion of their trade interests and general welfare."[46]

The number of workers with trade union benefits was relatively small compared to the membership of friendly societies. In 1892, 728,000 trade union members (8% of the adult male workforce) were eligible for unemployment benefits, 580,000 for sickness benefits, and 429,000 for old age (superannuation) benefits. By 1908, 1,474,000 workers (12% of the male workforce) were eligible for unemployment benefits, and 729,000 were eligible for sickness benefits.[47] Unemployment insurance was the most important of the union-provided benefits because it was not offered by friendly societies.[48] The relatively small number of union members eligible for sickness and old age benefits was due largely to their being provided by friendly societies and the fact that many union members also were members of friendly societies.

45. Trade union membership data for 1870 and 1881 from Pollard (1965: 102). Data for 1888 from Clegg, Fox, and Thompson (1964: 1). Data for 1898 and 1908 from Bain and Price (1980: 39).

46. Board of Trade, *Statistical Tables and Report on Trade Unions* (1887: 7). On the important role played by unions' mutual insurance benefits, see Webb and Webb (1897: pt. 2, chap. 1) and Boyer (1988).

47. Data for 1892 from Board of Trade, *Seventh Annual Report on Trade Unions* (1895: 5). Data for 1908 from Board of Trade, *Report on Trade Unions in 1908–10* (1912: xxxv). Data on the adult male workforce and total union membership in 1892 and 1908 from Bain and Price (1980: 37).

48. The reason why friendly societies did not offer unemployment benefits is discussed in Chapter 4.

The benefit packages offered by unions differed markedly across occupations. In metals, engineering, shipbuilding, and the building trades, most unions provided unemployment, sickness, accident, old age, and death benefits. Most mining and textile unions provided death benefits, and several provided unemployment benefits under certain conditions (when a mine or factory was shut down). Few, however, provided sickness or old age benefits. Unions of low-skilled workers typically provided only death and accident benefits. Only a third of low-skilled union members were eligible for sickness or old age benefits, and fewer than 10% were eligible for unemployment benefits.[49]

Table 3.10 (column 3) presents data on insurance benefits paid out by trade unions for selected years from 1870 to 1913. Before 1890 union expenditures were small, and concentrated among a few unions of skilled workers. The number of unions offering insurance benefits expanded in the 1890s; still, as late as 1908, seven large unions accounted for 51% of total spending.[50] Annual expenditures on insurance benefits increased sharply after 1892 and peaked at nearly £2.34 million during the downturn of 1908. Spending on unemployment benefits typically exceeded spending on every other type of benefit, and in cyclical downturns, such as 1886 and 1908, unemployment benefits accounted for most of union benefit expenditures.

BENEFIT LEVELS AND TOTAL SPENDING
ON MUTUAL INSURANCE

The benefits paid by friendly societies and trade unions to sick or unemployed members grew over time, but at a slower rate than wages. The average weekly sickness benefit paid by friendly societies increased from 10s. in the 1870s to 12s. by 1900, and remained at that level until 1914.[51] The typical trade union sickness or unemployment benefit was 9–10s. per week in 1892. Benefits increased little if at all in the next two decades; in 1908 the median union sickness or unemployment benefit was 9.25–10s. per week.[52] The median weekly wage for adult male workers was 24.17s. in 1886 and 29.33s. in 1906. Thus, the

---

49. Boyer (1988: 326–28).

50. These unions were the Amalgamated Engineers, Amalgamated Carpenters and Joiners, Operative Bricklayers, Iron and Steel Shipbuilders, Friendly Society of Ironfounders, Durham Miners, and Amalgamated Cotton Spinners. Their combined membership was 434,000. Expenditure data for 1908 from Board of Trade, *Report on Trade Unions in 1908–10* (1912: 80–113).

51. The estimates of average sickness benefits from Riley (1997: 280–81), who states that some societies paid as much as 15s. per week. Johnson (1985: 61) reckons that the average benefit might have been as high as 14s. in the decade before 1914.

52. Union benefit levels in 1892 from Parl. Papers, *Royal Commission on Labour: Rules of Associations of Employers and of Employed* (1892, XXXVI). Benefit levels in 1908 from Board of Trade, *Report on Trade Unions in 1908–10* (1912: xxxv).

average friendly society benefit replaced about 45% of lost wages in 1886 and 40% of lost wages in 1906, while the typical union benefit replaced somewhat less. Benefit payments were enough to feed a moderate-sized family in 1900, but not high enough to also cover rent, fuel, clothing, and sundries.[53] They needed to be supplemented by other sources of income, but they served "as a nucleus" and kept their recipients from having to apply for public relief.[54]

Some workers obtained additional sickness insurance by joining more than one friendly society, or by belonging to both a friendly society and a trade union paying sickness benefits. William Allen, the Secretary of the Amalgamated Society of Engineers, commented in 1867 that a "great many" members of the union "join other benefit societies . . . in order to have a sufficient amount during illness." As part of his 1899 analysis of poverty in York, Rowntree surveyed 400 men with sickness insurance through either a trade union or a friendly society and found that 185 (46%) belonged either to more than one friendly society or to a union and one or more friendly societies.[55]

The combined expenditures of friendly societies and trade unions on insurance benefits increased from £2.2 million in 1870 to £5.2 million in 1892, and £10.1 million in 1913 (Table 3.10). In 1870 spending by friendly societies and trade unions was less than half of poor relief expenditures. From 1870 to 1886, poor relief spending declined by £808,000, while spending by friendly societies increased by £1,524,000, and benefit payments by trade unions increased by slightly more than £300,000. In 1886 spending by friendly societies and trade unions was 93% of poor relief expenditures, and 40% greater than poor relief expenditures in 1908. In real terms, the expenditure of friendly societies and trade unions in 1908 was 4.5 times greater than in 1870.

The data in Tables 3.7–3.10 suggest that the Victorian self-help movement was a resounding success in terms of its own objectives. Workers responded to the Crusade Against Outrelief by protecting themselves against financial insecurity, as COS officials had predicted, and the increase in benefit payments made by mutual insurance organizations from 1870 to 1900 was greater than the decline in Poor Law expenditures. The real value of working-class savings deposits, another form of insurance, increased by nearly 450% from 1870 to 1908. These data and the fact that the day count pauperism rate was below 2.5% from 1891 onward led many observers to conclude that by the turn of the century poverty had been virtually eliminated.

53. Wage data from Bowley (1937: 42). Rowntree (1901: 110) estimated that minimum necessary food expenditure for a family consisting of a husband, wife, and two children was 10.5s. per week in 1899. Minimum expenditure on rent, fuel, clothing, and sundries was 8.33s. Minimum weekly food expenditure for a family with three children was 12.75s.

54. Beveridge (1909: 225).

55. The Allen quote is cited in Boyer (1988: 330). Rowntree (1901: 356–58).

But the aggregate data tell only part of the story. Self-help worked well for those who could afford to save or join mutual insurance organizations, but it remained largely outside the sphere of the bottom third of the income distribution. As late as 1911, only two-thirds of adult working-class males were members of friendly societies or trade unions offering sickness benefits. Fewer were eligible for old age benefits, and only 12% of the adult male workforce was eligible for trade union unemployment benefits. Most working-class households had savings accounts by 1901, but the balances in those accounts typically were quite small. In 1899, 83% of all Post Office Savings Bank accounts had balances of £25 or less. The average balance in these accounts was £4, and the median balance was smaller; £4 was the equivalent of less than 2.5 weeks' pay for a machinist or a skilled worker in the building trades, and less than four weeks' pay for a police constable or a bricklayer's laborer.[56]

The fact that many manual workers had little savings and were not members of friendly societies frustrated some turn-of-the-century observers, who criticized the low-skilled for their "thoughtlessness," "self-indulgence," or "ignorance." For example, Helen Bosanquet, a leader of the COS, wrote in 1904 that the "mental horizon" of the poor "tends to be limited to a stretch of seven days, and many feel that they have amply satisfied the claims of providence if they can see their way clear to next Saturday. . . . The habit of short views seems to make it impossible for him (or his wife) to save for the weeks out of work."[57] However, the low wages of unskilled workers made saving difficult. As noted above, the average *full-time* earnings of adult male unskilled laborers in 1906 was 21.7s. per week. This was close enough to the poverty line that only those with incredible willpower could set aside money each week to deposit in a savings account or pay friendly society dues.[58]

Despite the increasing earnings of manual workers and the rise of a culture of self-help, the bottom one-third of the working class remained vulnerable to unexpected income loss at the beginning of the twentieth century. The workhouse test and the propaganda of the Crusade Against Outrelief were successful at convincing the working class to attach a stigma to the acceptance of poor relief. Indeed the propaganda campaign was too successful, for it led many poor working-class households unable to protect themselves to refuse to

---

56. Data on savings account balances from Johnson (1985: 101). Wage data from Board of Trade, *Eighth Abstract of Labour Statistics* (1902: 34–45).

57. Bosanquet (1904: 136–37). See also the quotes of middle-class observers in Johnson (1985: 217–19).

58. Rowntree (1901: 110) calculated that in York the minimum necessary expenditure for a family of five in 1899 was 21.67s. per week. In 1906 prices, the poverty line for a family of five was 22.7s.

turn to the Poor Law for assistance. As a result, the Poor Law data significantly understate the true level of poverty. For example, Rowntree concluded that in 1899 some 7,230 persons in York (9.9% of the population) were living in primary poverty, while the "total number of different persons who received relief" in 1900 was 3,571, or 4.6% of the population.[59] The number of persons living in poverty was more than twice the number who received poor relief at some point over the course of the year.

III. Conclusion

The period from the mid-1870s to 1901 was the nadir of English social welfare policy. Convinced that overly generous public relief and private charity were reducing the thriftiness, self-respect, and morality of the working class, and encouraged by the LGB and the Charity Organisation Society, local Poor Law guardians throughout England and Wales adopted the "principles of 1834" and restricted the granting of outdoor relief to the poor. The pauperism rate declined sharply in the early 1870s and continued to creep downward for the next three decades. As numbers on relief declined, working-class attitudes toward the Poor Law changed, so that by the turn of the century many of the poor went to great lengths to avoid applying for relief.

The last three decades of the nineteenth century saw a continued rise in working-class self-help, as a larger share of households joined friendly societies and deposited money in savings banks. To some observers, the increase in self-help and the decline in pauperism were evidence that the ideology of respectability preached by COS officials had become well entrenched in working-class culture. However, self-help remained largely outside the sphere of the bottom third of the income distribution. The assertion of Smiles, Hill, and others that almost all workers, assuming they were thrifty, could protect themselves against income loss due to sickness, unemployment, and old age was incorrect in the 1870s and remained incorrect at the turn of the twentieth century.

In the decade before the First World War, Parliament adopted several pieces of social welfare legislation collectively known as the Liberal Welfare Reforms, which created government programs to provide benefits that large numbers of workers already obtained privately through friendly societies and trade unions. I argue in Chapter 6 that the continued economic insecurity among the lower third of the income distribution and its political ramifications were the reasons for this about-face in government policy.

59. Rowntree (1901: 143–51, 365–67). Persons living in households with incomes below the poverty line were deemed to be in primary poverty. Rowntree's survey is discussed in detail in Chapter 6.

4

Unemployment and Unemployment Relief

The existence of unemployed workers was not a new phenomenon, nor was the unemployment rate necessarily higher, on average, after the onset of industrialization than before. But the nineteenth century witnessed the rise of the business cycle and cyclical downturns, and contemporaries viewed large-scale involuntary unemployment as "the characteristic disease of the modern industrial system." The second half of the century saw the rise of another "modern evil"—a growth in the number of chronically underemployed low-skilled laborers in London and urban industrial centers. By the beginning of the twentieth century, contemporary observers concluded that in many large towns the supply of low-skilled workers was larger than the demand for labor "even in times of brisk trade." The threat of income loss due to unemployment was a major cause of economic insecurity for manual workers. In the words of Beveridge, "society is built up on labour; it lays upon its members responsibilities which in the vast majority of cases can be met only from the reward of labour. . . . Reasonable security of employment for the bread-winner is the basis for all private duties and all sound social action."[1]

Most urban boards of guardians continued to assist cyclically unemployed workers through the late 1860s, despite Parliament's attempt in 1834 to restrict the granting of outdoor relief to able-bodied males. However, the Crusade Against Outrelief led to a major change in public policy toward the unemployed—after the early 1870s most urban Poor Law unions offered unemployed workers relief

---

1. Webb and Webb (1929: 633); Webb and Webb (1909b: 243); Beveridge (1909: 1).

only in workhouses. During major downturns local governments and charities adopted ad hoc methods for relieving the unemployed, and many skilled workers received unemployment benefits from trade unions. The new solution proved no better at relieving the nonunionized unemployed, or preventing unemployment, than the Poor Law had been. The amount of assistance offered to individual workers typically was quite small, and only a minority of the unemployed—mostly unskilled laborers—applied for and received relief. The problems associated with relying on ad hoc emergency relief funds became apparent during the downturn of 1885–86, and the Local Government Board responded by encouraging municipalities to set up work relief projects to aid the unemployed. However, the downturns of 1893–96 and 1904–5 revealed the inability of municipal work-relief programs to adequately assist temporarily unemployed workers. From 1886 onward, each business-cycle downturn put additional pressure on Parliament to adopt a national system of unemployment relief.

For most of the century, middle-class observers believed that, except during severe downturns, the majority of those out of work were voluntarily unemployed. A shift in public attitudes occurred in the decades leading up to the First World War; the extent of this shift can be seen in the title of Beveridge's influential 1909 book, *Unemployment: A Problem of Industry*. Beveridge rejected the view that any able-bodied adult who wanted work could readily find a job. Unemployment was caused by cyclical and seasonal fluctuations in the economy and maladjustments of supply and demand for labor, not by the deficiencies of individual workers. The shift in public opinion, along with the failure of local relief policies, paved the way for the adoption of national unemployment insurance.

The chapter proceeds as follows. Section I examines the extent of cyclical, seasonal, and casual unemployment from 1870 to 1913. Section II describes trade unions' unemployment benefit policies, and the shift in measures used by local authorities and private charities to assist the unemployed from the Crusade Against Outrelief until the adoption of national unemployment insurance in 1911.

I. The Extent of Unemployment, 1870–1913

In 1905 the Board of Trade constructed an unemployment index back to 1860 using information supplied to it by trade unions, and Feinstein incorporated the series into his estimates of unemployment for 1855–1913. The Board of Trade index has serious shortcomings, as Feinstein and others have noted.[2]

---

2. See Parl. Papers, *British and Foreign Trade and Industrial Conditions* (1905, LXXXIV), pp. 79–98 and Feinstein (1972: 225–26). For a detailed discussion of the Board of Trade series and its shortcomings, see Boyer and Hatton (2002: 644–48).

In 2002 Boyer and Hatton constructed new estimates of the industrial unemployment rate from 1870 to 1913, relying chiefly on trade union records but incorporating other information where possible in order to include sectors for which union unemployment data are not available. They combined unemployment series for 13 broad industrial sectors to form an aggregate series using labor force weights based on Lee's reworked census totals for males employed in industry.[3]

Table 4.1 and Figure 4.1 report two versions of the aggregate Boyer and Hatton index, including and excluding employment loss from short-time work, which was common in mining and textiles. The average unemployment rate for 1870 to 1913 was 6.6% when employment loss from short time is included and 5.4% when it is excluded. The effect of including short time is large because mining and textiles were large sectors—in 1901 they account for a quarter of the workforce included in the index—in which the number of "wholly unemployed" workers "substantially under-stated the true volume of unemployment."[4] When employment loss from short-time work is included, the unemployment rate exceeded 8% in 1878–79, 1885–87, 1893–95, 1904–5, and 1908–9, more than a quarter of the years from 1870 to 1913.

Unemployment varied substantially across sectors. For 1870–1913, it was highest in mining (11.3%), shipbuilding (8.7%), metals (6.7%), textiles (7.0%), and general unskilled labor (9.5%), and lowest in woodworking (3.1%), printing and bookbinding (3.7%), clothing and footwear (3.8%), and carriage and wagon (3.8%).[5] It is useful to examine a few sectors in more detail. Figure 4.2 presents the unemployment series for two large sectors—metals and the building trades. While the two series move in a similar pattern, at least through 1903, the average unemployment rate was higher and the severity of cyclical fluctuations larger in metals than in construction. The other major difference between the two series is their trends over time. From 1870 to 1898, the average unemployment rate was much higher in metals (6.7%) than in the building trades (3.9%). Unemployment in construction increased sharply thereafter, while that for metals remained roughly constant, so that for 1899–1913 the average unemployment rate in the two sectors was nearly identical—6.8% in metals and 6.7% in construction.

Mining was an important and growing sector during this period, employing over one million workers in 1911. Figure 4.3 presents unemployment series for mining both including and excluding employment loss from short-time working. Wide fluctuations in the demand for labor were accommodated largely by short-time rather than layoffs. According to the *Labour Gazette*, the "state of employment" in coal mining was "best gauged, not by the proportion of

3. Boyer and Hatton (2002: 648–57); Lee (1979).
4. Beveridge (1944: 332).
5. Boyer and Hatton (2002: 661).

TABLE 4.1. Unemployment Rates, 1870–1913: Two Variants and the Board of Trade Index

Year	Excluding Short Time	Including Short Time	Board of Trade
1870	4.4	4.6	3.7
1871	3.1	3.6	1.6
1872	2.1	2.3	0.9
1873	2.3	2.5	1.1
1874	2.8	3.2	1.6
1875	3.3	4.1	2.2
1876	4.1	5.2	3.4
1877	5.4	7.7	4.4
1878	7.0	9.5	6.2
1879	9.1	11.1	10.7
1880	6.3	7.7	5.2
1881	5.4	6.5	3.5
1882	4.7	5.6	2.3
1883	4.6	5.4	2.6
1884	5.9	7.3	8.1
1885	7.5	9.5	9.3
1886	7.8	9.4	10.2
1887	6.9	8.4	7.6
1888	5.6	6.7	4.9
1889	3.8	4.5	2.1
1890	3.3	4.2	2.1
1891	3.8	5.3	3.5
1892	5.2	7.0	6.3
1893	6.8	8.6	7.5
1894	6.6	8.2	6.9
1895	6.5	8.6	5.8
1896	5.3	7.0	3.3
1897	5.3	6.7	3.3
1898	4.6	5.4	2.8
1899	4.0	4.5	2.0
1900	4.0	4.5	2.5
1901	5.0	6.5	3.3
1902	5.6	6.8	4.0
1903	6.0	7.6	4.7
1904	7.8	9.6	6.0
1905	7.4	8.9	5.0
1906	6.0	6.9	3.6
1907	5.5	5.7	3.7
1908	8.7	9.9	7.8
1909	9.1	10.6	7.7
1910	6.6	7.9	4.7
1911	5.2	6.2	3.0
1912	4.8	5.0	3.3
1913	4.1	4.4	2.1

Source: Boyer and Hatton (2002: 662).

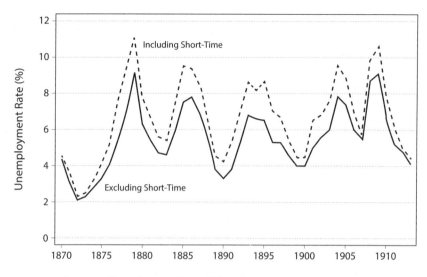

FIGURE 4.1. Aggregate Unemployment Rates, 1870–1913

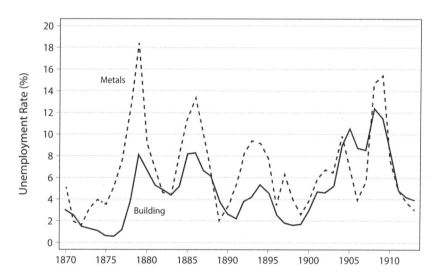

FIGURE 4.2. Unemployment in Metals and Building Trades, 1870–1913

workpeople entirely unemployed, but by the average number of days per week on which work is available. . . . Except in times of great depression or expansion of trade, fluctuations in demand are met rather by working more or fewer days per week, than by the engagement of more or fewer men." From 1870 to 1913, the average number of days worked per week was 5.2, varying from a maximum of 5.87 in 1873 to a minimum of 4.63 in 1877–78. The average unemployment

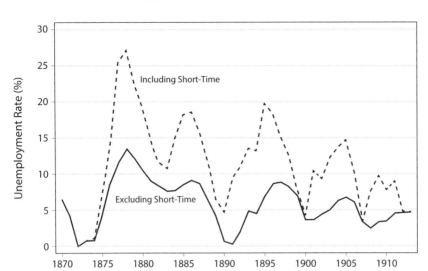

FIGURE 4.3. Unemployment in Mining, 1870–1913

rate for 1870–1913, including short time, was 11.3%, nearly twice the unemployment rate excluding short time (5.9%).[6]

Unemployment data for unskilled workers do not exist. Following Mac-Kinnon, Boyer and Hatton constructed an unemployment series for general unskilled laborers using time-series data for male able-bodied indoor paupers as a share of the male population aged 15–64.[7] The estimated unemployment series for general unskilled laborers is presented in Figure 4.4. The series follows the same cyclical pattern as the other sectoral series, except that unemployment among unskilled laborers increased sharply over time—the unemployment rate was below 10% in every year from 1870 to 1892, then above 10% in all but four years from 1893 to 1913. Figure 4.4 also presents an unemployment series constructed using vagrancy data.[8] Vagrants were typically adult males under age 60. While not all vagrants were in search of work, their numbers increased during downturns and declined during booms, suggesting that a substantial share were in fact unemployed men "forced to

6. Board of Trade, *Labour Gazette*, October 1895, p. 308; Boyer and Hatton (2002: 661).

7. MacKinnon (1986: 306–7, 330–34); Boyer and Hatton (2002: 654–56, 659–60). The unemployment rate was benchmarked at 5.0% in 1875.

8. Data on the number of vagrants on January 1 and July 1 of each year are from MacKinnon (1984: 118, 337), and from the Board of Trade, *Seventeenth Abstract of Labour Statistics* (1915: 332–33). For the construction of the vagrancy series, see Boyer and Hatton (2002: 655, 659). To turn the vagrancy series into an unemployment series, the unemployment rate was benchmarked at 5.0% in 1875.

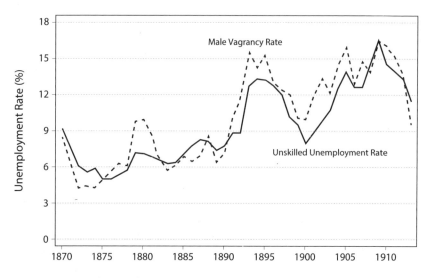

FIGURE 4.4. Unemployment for Unskilled Laborers, 1870–1913

migrate in search of work."[9] The unemployment series constructed using vagrancy data is quite similar to that constructed using data for male indoor paupers. These series indicate that employment opportunities for casual and general laborers deteriorated—both absolutely and relative to those of skilled workers—during the last two decades before the First World War.[10]

Contemporary observers agreed that unemployment rates were higher for the unskilled than for skilled workers. The Boyer and Hatton estimates show that the average unemployment rate for unskilled workers in 1870–1913 was 50% greater than that for skilled and semiskilled workers. The aggregate unemployment rate is a poor measure of the extent of economic insecurity among the unskilled.[11]

Annual unemployment rates give an idea of the average level of distress among manual workers in a given year, but they greatly understate the share of workers who were unemployed *at some point* during a year. Table 4.2 presents

9. MacKinnon (1984: 117). Beveridge (1909: 48–49) and Crowther (1981: 254) also concluded that unemployment was a cause of vagrancy.

10. The Majority Report of the Royal Poor Law Commission concluded in 1909 that while the "material condition" of most workers improved "during the last few decades," that of "the lower grades of unskilled labourers . . . was worse than formerly." Parl. Papers, *Report of the Royal Commission on the Poor Laws and Relief of Distress* (1909, XXXVII), p. 361.

11. The average unemployment rate, including short time but excluding the unskilled, was 6.3%. See Boyer and Hatton (2002: 663). Thomas (1988: 123) calculated that in 1931 the unemployment rate for skilled and semiskilled manual workers was 12.0%, while that for unskilled manual workers was 21.5%, nearly 80% greater.

TABLE 4.2. Distribution of Unemployment in Four Trade Unions

	Amalgamated Engineers (Manchester and Leeds)			Carpenters and Joiners		London Compositors		Woodcutting Machinists	
	1887–95	1899	1904	1898–99	1904–5	1898	1905	1898	1904
Unemployment rate	6.1	3.0	7.6	1.1	6.0	2.8	5.0	1.4	4.3
% unemployed at some time in year	29.7	18.6	35.0	19.7	43.1	17.9	22.4	22.1	33.7
Days lost per member	18.7	9.1	23.3	3.4	18.8	8.9	15.7	4.5	13.4
Days lost per unemployed member	63.1	49.1	66.5	17.4	43.6	49.5	70.3	20.5	39.8
% unemployed for 4 weeks or more	16.7	9.1	21.1	4.3	24.3	11.5	16.0	5.7	16.6
% unemployed for 8 weeks or more	12.0	5.6	15.0	1.7	15.9	7.3	11.5	2.9	10.6
% unemployed for 12 weeks or more	9.3	3.8	11.0	0.7	9.5	4.7	8.3	1.4	7.2

Sources: Parl. Papers, *British and Foreign Trade and Industrial Conditions* (1905, LXXXIV), p. 101; Parl. Papers, *Royal Commission on the Poor Laws and Relief of Distress. Statistics Relating to England and Wales* (1910, LIII), pp. 870–76.

data on the distribution of unemployment among skilled workers in four trade unions. For each union, data are given for a year of low unemployment and a year of high unemployment; for the Amalgamated Engineers, data also are given for the average of nine years from 1887 to 1895. Even during prosperous years, nearly one in five skilled workers experienced some income loss due to unemployment. The average unemployment rate among engineers for 1887–95 was 6.1%, but nearly 30% were unemployed during a calendar year. Some 12.0% of union members were unemployed for at least eight weeks during a year, and 9.3% were unemployed for twelve or more weeks. The data for the Carpenters and Joiners, London Compositors, and Woodcutting Machinists yield similar results. The unemployment rate for the Carpenters and Joiners was 6.0% in 1904–5, but 43.1% of members were unemployed at some point in the year, and 15.9% were unemployed for at least eight weeks.

For each of the unions, the share of workers unemployed for at least eight weeks a year was roughly double the annual unemployment rate. The distribution of unemployment for the four unions probably overstates the share of workers who experienced income loss due to unemployment in stable industries such as the railways; on the other hand, it understates the share who experienced income loss in metals and shipbuilding, and among general unskilled laborers. If the data are reasonably representative of the incidence of unemployment among all manual workers in late Victorian England, then during bad years on average nearly 15% of manual workers were unemployed for eight or more weeks, and nearly one in ten were unemployed for at least twelve weeks. The threat of being unemployed for two months or longer within a calendar year was far higher than the annual unemployment estimates suggest.

Seasonal unemployment differed from cyclical unemployment in that it was to a large degree predictable. Economists since Adam Smith have argued that workers in seasonal occupations were paid higher daily or hourly wages than similarly skilled workers to compensate for their periodic spells of unemployment. Even if seasonal industries paid compensating wage differentials, however, seasonal unemployment still created insecurity, especially among low-skilled workers who found it difficult to save enough from their peak-season earnings to carry them through slack seasons.

The extent of nonagricultural seasonal unemployment is difficult to measure precisely. Table 4.3 presents evidence from the early twentieth century on the extent of seasonal fluctuations in employment for five industrial sectors. The first two columns present indices of monthly employment in the building trades in 1907–10. Column 3 presents an index of the total amount of wages paid to building workers in each month. The magnitude of the seasonal fluctuation in wage income is larger than in employment because the workweek was slightly shorter in winter. The wage income of construction workers was, on average, 17–24% lower from November to February than it was in May.

TABLE 4.3. Seasonality of Employment in Five Sectors

| | BUILDING TRADES | | | COAL MINERS | GAS WORKERS | FURNISHING TRADES | TOBACCO WORKERS |
| | Skilled Men | Laborers | All Men | | | | |
	Number Employed 1907–10	Number Employed 1907–10	Wage Income 1906	Days Worked per Week 1897–1911	Number Employed 1906	Unemployment Rate 1897–1906	Unemployment Rate 1897–1906
January	84.4	84.0	76.2	5.20	97.2	7.9	5.8
February	89.0	87.7	82.7	5.43	93.9	6.5	6.5
March	94.5	92.5	92.6	5.39	89.1	3.3	7.4
April	96.3	95.3	97.6	5.03	85.5	2.4	7.8
May	96.3	96.2	100.0	5.23	84.2	2.5	8.3
June	94.5	95.3	96.5	4.92	83.0	3.2	8.6
July	96.3	98.1	96.6	4.98	83.6	4.1	9.3
August	100.0	100.0	98.7	4.99	84.4	4.1	9.4
September	95.4	96.2	96.3	5.35	87.8	4.2	7.3
October	89.0	90.6	91.3	5.41	92.3	4.5	5.1
November	86.2	87.7	82.6	5.39	97.2	4.9	3.2
December	80.7	82.1	78.7	5.47	100.0	7.1	4.7

Sources: Columns 1 and 2: Webb (1912: 334). Column 3: Board of Trade, *Earnings and Hours of Labour . . . Building and Woodworking Trades* (1910: 13). Column 4: Data for 1897–1901 from Board of Trade, *Eleventh Abstract of Labour Statistics* (1907: 5). Data for 1902–11 from Board of Trade, *Fifteenth Abstract of Labour Statistics* (1912: 9). Column 5: Popplewell (1912: 196). Columns 6 and 7: Poyntz (1912: 23–24).

Notes: The series in columns 1, 2, and 5 are indices; the index numbers show each month's employment as a percentage of the peak month's employment. The series in column 3 is an index; the index numbers show each month's wage income as a percentage of the peak month's wage income.

The extent of seasonal fluctuations in labor demand varied across sections of the building trade, being relatively low for plumbers and especially high for bricklayers and painters.[12]

Seasonality in mining typically was handled by reducing the number of shifts worked per week in slack seasons rather than by laying off workers. From 1897 to 1911, the average number of days worked per week varied from 5.47 in December to 4.92 in June. Employment at gas works was highly seasonal, with 11–17% fewer workers employed from March to September than in December. In the furnishing trades, unemployment varied from a low of 2.5% in April and May to over 7% in December and January; in tobacco, unemployment exceeded 9% in July and August, but was 3.2% in November. Other trades experienced less pronounced seasonal fluctuations in labor demand; a 1909 Board of Trade memorandum concluded that "seasonal fluctuation is found to a more or less marked degree in nearly every industry."[13]

Systems of temporary or casual employment developed in some low-skilled occupations that were subject to sudden and irregular fluctuations in labor demand. Casual employment existed to some degree among painters and un-skilled laborers in the building trades, and among workers in land transport, menial services, and certain declining manufacturing trades.[14] It was especially pronounced among dockworkers, due to the irregularity in the arrival and departure of ships. Dockworkers were hired by the day or half day, chosen by foremen each morning and afternoon from groups of workers at calling-on stands. As a result employment was extremely intermittent, and apart from a minority who were regularly employed, most dockworkers spent a substantial proportion of the year unemployed. Booth found that in 1891–92 approximately 22,000 men regularly competed for work at the London docks, and that the average number employed per day was 15,175.[15] Thus, on an average day upward of 6,800 London dockers were without work. A 1908 Charity Organisation Society Report on Unskilled Labour concluded that "the independent action of the separate employing agencies, each seeking to retain a following of labour as nearly as possible equal to its own maximum demand" led to "the maintenance of a floating reserve of labour far larger than is required to meet the maximum demands of employers . . . [and] a mass of men chronically

---

12. Dearle (1908: 66–81).

13. The Board of Trade memorandum was published in Parl. Papers, *Royal Commission on the Poor Laws, Appendix Vol. IX, Unemployment* (1910, XLIX), pp. 638–55. See also Poyntz (1912). On seasonality in U.S. labor markets, see Engerman and Goldin (1994).

14. Jones (1971: 52–66) estimated that in London in 1891 casual workers and their families totaled about 400,000 persons, or one-tenth of the population.

15. Booth (1892a: 532–33). Howarth and Wilson (1907: 185–254) give a detailed discussion of the labor market at the Victoria and Albert Docks. See also Beveridge (1909: 77–95).

under-employed."[16] A large share of dockworkers suffered chronic distress as a result of their irregularity of employment.

The method of hiring painters and low-skilled laborers in the building trades was similar to that of the docks, except that there were no fixed calling-on stands and workers were hired by the job rather than the day. Hiring was done by foremen at job sites. A foreman would start a new job with a few "permanent" employees and hire more workers as they arrived at the job site, "guided by recommendations from their mates or stray hints in public houses . . . [or] tramping without guidance about likely districts." Hiring typically was done on a first-come first-served basis—workers who proved unsatisfactory were fired after a few days or weeks and replaced by newcomers. This system led to the creation of "a floating mass of labour . . . drifting perpetually about the streets" in search of work. Robert Tressell, in *The Ragged Trousered Philanthropists*, described the process as follows: "It is usual for [casual hands] to put in a month with one firm, then a fortnight with another, then perhaps six weeks somewhere else, and often between there are two or three days or even weeks of enforced idleness." Beveridge concluded that, while distress among dockworkers was chronic, among building laborers it was "recurrent, with bad weather or the end of a job."[17]

In sum, the possibility of employment loss faced by manual workers was far greater than the aggregate unemployment estimates suggest. A majority of workers lost no time due to unemployment within a calendar year, but a substantial minority lost several weeks of work even during years of low unemployment. Low-skilled workers were the most likely to suffer income loss due to unemployment, and before 1870 they also had relied most heavily on the Poor Law for assistance when unemployed. Section II examines the major changes in the forms of income assistance for the unemployed brought about by the Crusade Against Outrelief.

II. Unemployment Relief, 1870–1911

After 1870 trade unions became a major source of unemployment benefits for skilled workers, who became less and less likely to turn to local authorities or charitable institutions for assistance. On the other hand, low-skilled workers continued to rely on public and private assistance until the First World War. The restriction of poor relief that occurred as a result of the Crusade Against Outrelief did not signal the end of local government involvement in assisting the unemployed. Beginning in 1886 the Local Government Board encouraged cities to set up work relief projects during cyclical downturns, and the idea of temporary

---

16. Charity Organisation Society (1908: 34).
17. Beveridge (1909: 96–98); Dearle (1908: 82–102); Tressell ([1955] 2005: 385).

work relief was given statutory recognition by the Unemployed Workmen Act of 1905. When examining unemployment relief during this period, it therefore is necessary to examine skilled and unskilled workers separately.

TRADE UNION UNEMPLOYMENT BENEFITS

Although certain craft unions began providing their members with "friendly benefits" early in the nineteenth century, the adoption of mutual insurance policies increased sharply in the third quarter of the century. A strong emphasis on mutual insurance was a characteristic of the "New Model" unionism, which began in the 1850s and by 1870 included several unions in the building trades, iron and steel, engineering, shipbuilding, printing, and elsewhere. Unemployment benefits were the most important of the union-provided insurance benefits because they typically were not offered by friendly societies. Workers anxious to insure themselves against unemployment could do so only through a trade union.[18]

Why didn't friendly societies provide benefits to unemployed members? There were moral hazard issues associated with the provision of unemployment benefits. An insuring organization had to determine whether a member who applied for relief was in fact eligible for benefits, and whether benefit recipients were actively searching for work. Most craft unions eliminated this moral hazard by forcing applicants to make their claims for benefits at branch meetings in front of fellow workmen, and those deemed eligible had to sign their branch's "vacant book" every day. Branch secretaries directed unemployed members to local firms in need of labor, and members who did not apply for a job when informed of a vacancy or refused a job offer forfeited their unemployment benefits. The cost of monitoring members' eligibility for benefits and search activity, and of finding work for unemployed members, was far higher for friendly societies than for trade unions because their membership typically belonged to several occupations. Contemporaries recognized the unique ability of trade unions to reduce moral hazard. The Webbs maintained, "Out of Work pay cannot be properly administered except by bodies of men belonging to the same trade and working in the same establishments." Similarly, Beveridge concluded that unions "come nearer than any other bodies to possessing a direct test of unemployment by which to protect their funds against abuse. . . . They are better able, therefore, than anyone else at the present time to assist the unemployed on honourable terms without imminent risk of encouraging unemployment."[19]

---

18. Webb and Webb (1897: 160–61); Harris (1972: 295).

19. Webb and Webb (1897: 160–61); Beveridge (1909: 227). A similar conclusion was reached by the *Minority Report of the Royal Commission on Trades Unions*. See Parl. Papers (1868–69, XXXI), p. xliii.

In 1893, 744,000 trade union members (59% of union members) were eligible for unemployment benefits. Table 4.4 shows that by 1906 more than 1,456,000 workers were eligible for unemployment benefits, representing nearly 73% of union members, but only 12% of the adult male workforce.[20] The benefits took various forms. Many unions provided weekly benefits to unemployed members. Others provided "payments to members travelling in search of work, . . . payments on account of cessations of work due to fires, failures of firms, temporary stoppages and breakdowns of machinery, emigration grants (in a few instances), and special grants in times of excessive slackness."[21]

The availability of unemployment benefits differed markedly across occupations. Virtually all union members in engineering, shipbuilding, cotton weaving, printing, woodworking, and glass trades were entitled to unemployment benefits, compared with 89% in the building trades, 44% in mining, and 40% in iron and steel unions. Among low-skilled workers, 29% of unionized laborers in the building trades, 20% of carmen and dock laborers, and 62% of general laborers were eligible for unemployment benefits of some sort. One must be careful in interpreting these numbers, however, because the types of unemployment benefits differed across occupations. This can be seen by examining expenditures per union member—spending was far greater in unions providing unemployed members with weekly benefits than in unions that provided only traveling benefits or occasional grants. Column 4 shows that spending per union member varied substantially across occupations. It exceeded 10s. per member for carpenters, iron founders, engineers and shipbuilders, printers, woodworkers, and glass workers. On the other hand, it was less than 3s. per member in mining and textiles, and less than 1s. per member for railway servants, building laborers, carmen and dockworkers, and general laborers. The benefits offered to low-skilled workers were quite meager.

Why didn't all unions offer their unemployed members weekly benefits? In coal mining, textiles, and some other industries, the widespread use of short time and sliding wage scales meant that there were few layoffs except at times of "excessive slackness." Unions of low-skilled workers did not provide unemployment benefits because the irregularity of employment in most low-skilled occupations and the typical oversupply of labor raised the cost of insurance substantially above the weekly premium paid by skilled workers and above what the unskilled could afford to pay.[22]

20. Data for 1893 are from the Board of Trade's *Seventh Annual Report on Trade Unions* (1895). Data for 1906 are from Parl. Papers, *Royal Commission on the Poor Laws, Appendix Vol. IX, Unemployment* (1910, XLIX), pp. 614, 620–21. Data on total union membership and the adult male workforce in 1906 are from Bain and Price (1980: 37).

21. Parl. Papers, *Royal Commission on the Poor Laws, Appendix Vol. IX, Unemployment* (1910, XLIX), p. 613.

22. Boyer (1988: 324–28); Beveridge (1909: 220–21); Porter (1970).

TABLE 4.4. Trade Unions Paying Unemployment Benefits of Some Form, 1906

Sector	UNIONS WITH UNEMPLOYMENT BENEFITS				UNIONS WITHOUT UNEMPLOYMENT BENEFITS		% Eligible for Benefits
	Number of Unions	Membership	Expenditure (£s)	Expenditure per Member (s.)	Number of Unions	Membership	
Building trades	53	175,434	127,909	14.6	43	20,902	89.4
Masons	6	16,310	5,043	6.2	4	3,932	80.6
Carpenters	4	78,434	84,701	21.6	0	0	100.0
Laborers	18	4,684	37	0.2	23	11,248	29.4
Mining	40	251,858	36,566	2.9	29	319,262	44.1
Metals, etc.	164	314,396	181,480	11.5	58	46,570	87.1
Iron and steel	3	18,379	7,370	8.0	6	27,101	40.4
Iron founding	7	33,800	25,246	14.9	2	4,380	88.5
Engineering/shipbuilding	82	237,580	139,918	11.8	24	8,749	96.4
Textiles	204	280,586	37,365	2.7	55	20,299	93.3
Cotton weaving	120	150,271	13,350	1.8	6	1,381	99.1
Clothing	20	55,095	5,277	1.9	17	4,419	92.6
Transport	9	115,391	4,533	0.8	49	73,570	61.1
Railway servants	4	98,165	4,401	0.9	2	3,410	96.6
Carmen, dock laborers	5	17,226	132	0.2	47	70,151	19.7
Printing	36	63,472	50,789	16.0	5	979	98.5
Woodworking	90	41,849	29,586	14.1	8	480	98.9
Misc. trades	123	89,045	38,000	8.5	70	34,501	72.1
Glass trades	18	8,620	13,701	31.8	1	40	99.5
General labor	6	68,991	2,223	0.6	12	42,843	61.7
Total	745	1,456,117	513,728	7.1	346	563,825	72.1

Source: Parl. Papers, *Royal Commission on the Poor Laws, Appendix Vol. IX, Unemployment* (1910, XLIX), pp. 620–21.

Union-provided unemployment benefits were financed by members' weekly contributions. The typical union member paid 6d. to 1s. per week in dues. No unions maintained separate unemployment insurance funds, but it is possible to estimate the cost of unemployment insurance by calculating individual unions' average annual expenditure per member on unemployment benefits. Such a calculation for three major unions—the Amalgamated Society of Engineers, the Amalgamated Carpenters and Joiners, and the London Compositors—for 1870–96 yields average annual expenditures on unemployment benefits per member of 22.3s., 15.3s., and 16.4s., respectively, or 3.5–5.1d. per member per week. Adding a small amount for administrative costs brings the cost to insure a skilled worker against unemployment to 4–6d. per week, which was 1–2% of his weekly income.[23]

The Board of Trade reported total expenditures on unemployment benefits of 100 principal trade unions for the years 1892–1910. Spending varied from a low of £184,600 in 1899 to a high of £1,004,685 in 1908; the average annual expenditure was £468,500. The Labour Department estimated that all British trade unions spent a total of £1,257,913 on unemployment benefits in 1908—the 100 principal unions accounted for 80% of total expenditure.[24] If that ratio held throughout 1892–1910, then the average annual expenditure on unemployment benefits by all trade unions was £585,600.

The generosity and maximum duration of benefits differed substantially across unions. In 1892, the average weekly benefit was about 10s., at least for the first 12–14 weeks of unemployment. The benefit plans of the following four unions provide an idea of the range in generosity and duration. The Amalgamated Engineers paid an unemployed member 10s. per week for the first 14 weeks of unemployment, then 7s. per week for the next 30 weeks, and 6s. per week for another 60 weeks. An unemployed member could collect benefits for 104 consecutive weeks. The Amalgamated Carpenters and Joiners paid 10s. a week for the first 12 weeks of unemployment, then 6s. a week for the next 12 weeks. The maximum duration of benefits was 24 weeks. The London Society of Compositors paid an unemployed member 12s. per week for a maximum of 16 weeks in one calendar year. The Amalgamated Smiths and Strikers paid 6s. per week for a maximum of 8 weeks.[25]

Table 4.5 presents data on generosity and duration of unemployment benefits in 1908 for all trade unions and for unions in building, mining, metals,

23. Data on unions' annual expenditures on unemployment benefits are from Wood (1900: 83–86).

24. In 1908 the 100 principal trade unions contained 61% of the total membership of all 1,058 trade unions. See Board of Trade, *Report on Trade Unions in 1908–10* (1912: xxxviii, lxxv).

25. Parl. Papers, *Royal Commission on Labour: Rules of Associations of Employers and of Employed* (1892, XXXVI), pp. 31–32, 45–46, 84–85, 157–58.

TABLE 4.5. Unemployment Benefits Paid by Trade Unions, 1908

(A) MAXIMUM WEEKLY BENEFITS (PERCENTAGE DISTRIBUTION OF UNION MEMBERS)

Weekly Benefits	Building Trades (21 Unions)	Mining and Quarrying (46 Unions)	Metals, Engineering, and Shipbuilding (166 Unions)	Textile Trades (212 Unions)	All Trades (699 Unions)
12s. 3d. and over	0.0	0.3	0.9	13.2	11.4
10s. 3d. to 12s.	0.1	9.4	2.3	4.5	8.7
9s. 3d. to 10s.	70.8	60.5	50.4	17.9	41.2
8s. 3d. to 9s.	25.6	20.2	9.3	14.0	13.6
7s. 3d. to 8s.	0.1	0.7	5.8	10.3	4.5
5s. 3d. to 7s.	0.7	0.3	1.2	20.3	6.2
5s. and under	0.4	2.0	27.8	17.2	10.1
Not ascertainable	2.2	7.0	2.3	2.6	4.2
Total Union Members	95,077	392,542	293,666	310,499	1,473,593

(B) MAXIMUM DURATION OF BENEFITS (PERCENTAGE DISTRIBUTION OF UNION MEMBERS)

Duration	Building	Mining	Metals	Textiles	All Trades
52 weeks or more	0.0	41.0	48.4	1.2	21.9
39–51 weeks	0.0	0.4	2.6	4.3	1.9
27–38 weeks	0.0	9.0	7.9	3.4	4.8
26 weeks	0.1	0.9	8.1	9.9	11.9
19–25 weeks	57.7	3.1	7.8	9.3	12.1
14–18 weeks	0.0	0.2	17.4	17.7	9.0
12–13 weeks	3.0	8.9	3.0	16.3	11.9
7–11 weeks	36.4	23.5	1.8	2.8	13.3
6 weeks or under	0.7	6.1	1.2	33.3	9.6
Not ascertainable	2.2	7.0	2.0	1.8	3.8
Total Union Members	95,077	392,542	293,666	310,499	1,473,593

Source: Board of Trade, *Report on Trade Unions in 1908–10* (1912), pp. lxxvi–lxxxi.

engineering and shipbuilding, and textiles. For all unions, the maximum weekly benefit was between 9s. 3d. and 10s. for 41% of workers, and 10s. 3d. or above for 20% of workers. On average, benefits in 1908 were about equal to their level in 1892. The maximum duration of benefits varied widely—it was 52 weeks or longer for 48% of workers in metals and 41% of miners, but only 19–25 weeks for the majority of workers in the building trades, and 13 weeks or less for the majority of textile workers. For trade unions as a whole, the median duration of benefits was 19–25 weeks.

How did benefits compare to wage rates? The average weekly wage for carpenters in 29 large cities was 34.2s. in 1892 and 38.6s. in 1908. The maximum replacement rate for carpenters was, on average, 29% in 1892 and 26% in 1908. For fitters, the maximum replacement rate was, on average, 30% in 1892 and 28% in 1908.[26] These replacement rates were relatively small, and they declined over time. A member of the Amalgamated Engineers unemployed for more than 14 weeks in 1892 would see his replacement rate fall to 21%; if unemployed for more than 44 weeks, his replacement rate fell to 18%. Similarly, a member of the Amalgamated Carpenters and Joiners unemployed for more than 12 weeks would see his replacement rate fall to 18%; if unemployed for more than 24 weeks, his benefit fell to zero.

The weekly benefit was supposed to be enough to enable unemployed members to subsist without turning to charity or the Poor Law. In this, most trade unions appear to have been successful. Beveridge maintained that union members receiving unemployment benefits hardly ever applied to local distress committees. He added, however, that by itself the typical benefit was too small to provide subsistence for a worker and his family, and had "to be supplemented . . . by the earnings of wife and children, by private saving, by assistance from fellow-workmen and neighbours, by running into debt, by pawning and in other ways." Nevertheless, union benefits prolonged "almost indefinitely the resisting power of the unemployed."[27]

UNEMPLOYMENT RELIEF FOR LOW-SKILLED WORKERS

The Crusade Against Outrelief strove greatly to reduce, if not eliminate, the payment of outdoor relief to unemployed workers. It faced its first real test during the downturn of 1878–79. The Local Government Board and the Charity Organisation Society pressured local boards of guardians not to grant outdoor relief to the unemployed, and the COS also tried to block the indiscriminate

---

26. Wage data for carpenters and fitters in 1892 are from an unpublished Board of Trade report on *Rates of Wages and Hours of Labour in Various Industries* (1908). Wage data for 1908 are from Board of Trade, *Twelfth Abstract of Labour Statistics* (1908: 40–42).

27. Beveridge (1909: 225).

use of charity. Their policies were especially successful in East London, where outdoor relief for the unemployed was virtually eliminated by the mid-1870s. Those who applied for poor relief during the downturn of the late 1870s were offered a place in the Poplar "test workhouse." The COS also succeeded in keeping the Lord Mayor from starting a Mansion House Relief Fund, as had occurred in 1860–61 and 1866–67, although local unorganized charity must have increased.[28]

Outside of London, the policies of the LGB and the COS were less successful. Some Poor Law unions that had begun to shift to workhouse relief in the early 1870s felt compelled to provide outdoor relief to the unemployed in 1878–79.[29] In those unions that resisted the temptation to provide outdoor relief, local governments and voluntary agencies adopted ad hoc measures for relieving the unemployed. The typical procedure was for a city's mayor to set up an emergency fund whenever distress reached a certain level: "[The mayor] issued an appeal in the Press or by letter, the response to which in the form of donations was of course very uncertain, varying with his personal popularity as well as with the general opinion of the wealthier classes as to the existence of exceptional distress. . . . The distribution was usually undertaken by a committee formed either from a few people selected by the Mayor, or from the borough councilors, or from a public meeting to which representatives of charitable agencies and others were specifically invited."[30] During the winters of 1878–79 and 1885–86 emergency funds were initiated in several large cities. In 1878–79 the Manchester and Salford District Provident Society, a philanthropic organization "dominated by the elite of Manchester's commercial and industrial bourgeoisie," raised £26,000 for the "temporary relief of distressed operatives." In the same year the Glasgow Unemployed Relief Fund raised over £33,000 to assist the unemployed, and relief funds were established in Liverpool, Leeds, and elsewhere.[31] These emergence funds typically provided the type of indiscriminate relief that the COS strenuously opposed.

The provision of emergency funds for the unemployed was even more pronounced during the 1885–86 downturn. The largest, and most notorious, of these was London's Mansion House Fund of 1886, established by the Lord Mayor in response to unemployed workers' demands for assistance, despite the opposition of the COS. A "riot" in London's West End shortly thereafter by 20,000 workers—mostly unemployed dockworkers and building laborers—led

28. Ryan (1985: 145–50); Jones (1971: 278).

29. On the use of outdoor relief in 1878–79, see, for example, Trainor (1993: 305–9).

30. Parl. Papers, *Royal Commission on the Poor Laws and Relief of Distress, Report . . . on the Effects of Employment or Assistance given to the "Unemployed" since 1886* (1909, XLIV), pp. 72–73.

31. Kidd (1984: 52, 54); Beveridge (1909: 66); Cage (1987: 92–95); Webb and Webb (1929: 640–41).

to a rapid influx of money, eventually reaching £78,600. The central committee administering the fund attempted at the outset to ensure that relief was given only to "respectable" workers who were temporarily unemployed, but most districts relaxed these rules almost instantly, granting assistance to applicants indiscriminately. R. Roberts, who distributed relief in Islington, testified before a Special Committee of the COS that "the tendency of the fund was to drift to the relief of the permanent poor. Do what we would to avoid it, we could not help the drifting." When asked if any investigation was made into the character of applicants, he replied, "Yes . . . all were in distress, and that was considered sufficient ground" for relief. The result was an "orgie of relief" in which most of the assistance went to the chronically unemployed. The 1886 Mansion House Fund caused a "widespread revulsion" among the middle class against "indiscriminate almsgiving to the unemployed."[32]

The story of the Mansion House Fund reveals a serious unintended consequence of the Crusade Against Outrelief—the decline of options for assistance available to unemployed low-skilled workers. Most workers felt a strong stigma against entering a workhouse, and the COS was unable, and unwilling, to relieve more than a small share of the unemployed. When levels of distress increased during downturns, the unemployed pressured local governments for aid. Feelings of compassion, guilt, and fear among the middle and upper classes led to the launching of emergency funds and the granting of indiscriminate relief. To many, the consequences of the Mansion House Fund's lax administration were far worse than the consequences of outdoor poor relief had been. The crusade had succeeded in reducing the relief roles, but the downturn of 1885–86 showed that it was unable to cope with unemployment during cyclical downturns.

The experiences of 1878–79 and 1885–86 convinced many observers that government involvement was necessary to relieve the cyclically unemployed, and officials searched for a method that local governments could administer and finance without the stigma of the Poor Law. In March 1886 Joseph Chamberlain, President of the Local Government Board, issued a circular to boards of guardians stating that "there is evidence of much and increasing privation . . . in the ranks of those who do not ordinarily seek poor law relief," and advising municipal authorities in districts where "exceptional distress prevailed" to set up work relief projects to employ workers who were "temporarily deprived of employment." The work provided should "not involve the stigma of pauperism"; it should "not compete with that of other labourers at present in employment"; and it should "not [be] likely to interfere with resumption of regular employment in their own trades by those who seek it." To ensure the

---

32. Charity Organisation Society (1886: 91); Beveridge (1909: 158–59); Jones (1971: 291–94, 298–300); Harris (1972: 111).

employment of respectable workers, all "men employed should be engaged on the recommendation of the guardians as persons whom . . . it is undesirable to send to the workhouse, or to treat as subjects for pauper relief." Finally, in order not to compete with private employment, "the wages paid should be something less than the wages ordinarily paid for similar work."[33]

The LGB reissued the Chamberlain Circular in 1887, 1891, 1892, 1893, and 1895. An 1893 Board of Trade inquiry found that 96 local authorities had initiated some form of public employment in the winter of 1892–93 in response to the issuance of the circular; 33 of them were in London. The forms of work relief included road repairing, road sweeping, sewerage work, stone-breaking, snow removal, leveling land, and planting trees.[34] Few local authorities offered full-time work to those who applied; rather, they dispersed the available work among all of the applicants. Each person typically was employed two or three days per week.

For example, from December 1892 through April 1893, the corporation of Leeds employed 1,103 men to excavate and level ground for new parks. Each person was employed three days a week; the average man was given about 60 days' work. Wages were 5d. an hour for a 9-hour day, so that each worker was paid about 11.25s. per week. Similar projects were initiated in other years. In the winters of 1903–4 and 1904–5, the corporation of Leeds employed 2,644 and 2,384 men to work on parks and roads, paint, and lay out a cemetery. As before, each worker was employed three days a week, and paid 5d. per hour for a 9-hour day.[35]

The borough of West Ham, just east of London, initiated relief works during six of the ten winters from 1895–96 to 1904–5. From November 1904 to May 1905, the borough council employed 5,271 men to lay out and pave streets and to paint and clean buildings. In order to distribute the available work fairly, every applicant was offered two or three days' work until all had been employed, at which point the first applicants were offered another two days' work. The rate of pay was 7d. per hour, for an 8-hour day.[36]

Sometimes charities worked together with local authorities. In the winter of 1895 the lord provost of Glasgow initiated relief works breaking stones; an average of 1,036 men were employed per day for 36 days. The total cost of the project was £4,854. When the weather grew more severe, the lord provost,

33. Parl. Papers, *Sixteenth Annual Report of the Local Government Board, 1886–87* (1887, XXXVI), pp. 5–7.

34. Parl. Papers, *Agencies and Methods for Dealing with the Unemployed* (1893–94, LXXXII), p. 212.

35. Parl. Papers, *Agencies and Methods for Dealing with the Unemployed* (1893–94, LXXXII), pp. 222–28; Parl. Papers, *Report . . . on the Effects of Employment or Assistance* (1909, XLIV), p. 359.

36. Parl. Papers, *Report . . . on the Effects of Employment or Assistance* (1909, XLIV), pp. 541, 551.

unwilling to raise taxes any further to provide work, set up a relief fund and appealed to the local newspapers for contributions to enable local authorities to "give food, fuel, and clothing to those who were suffering terribly." Within eight days, the Citizens' Relief Fund had received £9,586 in cash and £1,362 "worth of food, provisions, coals, and clothing." Eleven soup kitchens were set up; coal, boots, and clothing were distributed to those in need; 22,669 grocery tickets were allocated; and rent arrears were paid.[37]

Similarly, in the winter of 1904–5 several London newspapers raised relief funds for West Ham. The *Daily News* raised £11,800, £7,000 of which was spent on work relief; the rest was used to purchase bread, groceries, and coal, which was distributed to the poor. The *Daily Telegraph* raised £14,835, much of which they gave to local clergy and the Salvation Army to distribute to the poor. Altogether, newspaper funds raised £27,900 for relief of the unemployed, slightly more than the amount spent on work relief by the borough council.[38]

In view of the fact that the relief works outlined in the Chamberlain Circular were supposed to employ workers "temporarily deprived of employment," almost all of the projects undertaken between 1886 and 1905 must be deemed failures. The 1893 Board of Trade inquiry noted above reported data on the occupations of men registered for work relief in nine London districts and six provincial cities in 1892–93. In London three-quarters of those on the registers were general or "chronically irregular" laborers, while in Liverpool 62% of those registered were general laborers, carmen, stablemen, porters, or messengers and another 26% were unskilled laborers in the building trades. Finally, in Leeds, where work relief was set up in response to an "acute depression of the iron trades," 23% of those registered were from the engineering and metal trades, whereas nearly 50% were general laborers.[39]

Relief work was meant to avoid the problems associated, in the minds of the middle class, with the granting of outdoor poor relief or indiscriminate charity to able-bodied males, but the work relief of 1886–1905 turned out to be similar in many ways to pre-1870 Poor Law relief. Both were financed out of local taxation. Despite the LGB's urging that municipal relief works hire only the temporarily unemployed, they ended up employing mostly the low-skilled and those employed in seasonal and casual trades, the same type of workers who had previously turned to the Poor Law for assistance. Jackson and Pringle concluded from their study of work relief programs that "the best

---

37. Parl. Papers, *Third Report from the Select Committee on Distress from Want of Employment* (1895, IX), pp. 232–33, 515, 519–20.

38. Parl. Papers, *Report . . . on the Effects of Employment or Assistance* (1909, XLIV), pp. 108–9; Howarth and Wilson (1907: 346–48).

39. Parl. Papers, *Agencies and Methods for Dealing with the Unemployed* (1893–94, LXXXII), pp. 210–11.

that the relief works have accomplished is to provide another—generally in-considerable—odd job to honest men who have to live by odd jobs, because of the irregularity of so much of our industry. The man for whom they were designed is not known to have had work from them yet."[40]

THE UNEMPLOYED WORKMEN ACT OF 1905

Public awareness of unemployment as a problem increased during the late 1880s. The reason for the change in public perception is not entirely clear, but the publication of Charles Booth's study of poverty in London—the first volume of which appeared in 1889—and the increased agitation by the un-employed were probably instrumental. Socialist groups such as the Social Democratic Federation began to organize protest marches at times of high unemployment during the mid-1880s.[41] Pressure for new government poli-cies to deal with the unemployed declined during the prosperity of the late 1880s, but reappeared during the downturn of 1893–95. In response to the high level of distress in the winter of 1894–95, the government established the Select Committee on Distress from Want of Employment. Nothing of practi-cal importance came from it, but it bought time for the government until the pressure for reform died down when the economy returned to normal in the late 1890s. When unemployment rates increased sharply in 1904–5, demand that the government intervene returned. Demonstrators in London, Liver-pool, Manchester, and other major cities "demanded that great works should be carried out by the municipalities on which they should be employed."[42]

In response to this pressure, Parliament in 1905 adopted the Unemployed Workmen Act, which established distress committees in all 29 metropolitan boroughs and in municipal boroughs and urban districts with populations exceeding 50,000.[43] The act also provided for the formation of a Central (Un-employed) Body in London, to administer relief and coordinate the work of the metropolitan distress committees. The committees—comprising nominees chosen by the local boards of guardians, borough councils, and charitable orga-nizations—were empowered to register applicants for relief and provide tem-porary employment to those "deserving" applicants who previously had been regularly employed, had resided in the locality for the previous 12 months,

40. Parl. Papers, *Report . . . on the Effects of Employment or Assistance* (1909, XLIV), p. 39.

41. Harris (1972: 6–101); Himmelfarb (1991: 40–53); Brown (1971).

42. The quotation is from the testimony of Walter Long, President of the Local Government Board, before the Royal Commission on the Poor Laws: Parl. Papers, *Minutes of Evidence . . . of Witnesses Relating Chiefly to the Subject of Unemployment* (1910, XLVIII), p. 59.

43. Boroughs and urban districts with populations between 10,000 and 50,000 could apply to the Local Government Board for permission to establish a distress committee. By 1909, 14 such districts had established committees.

were "well-conducted and thrifty," and had dependents. The work projects were to be of "actual and substantial utility," and workers' total remuneration was to be less than would be earned by unskilled laborers.[44]

The act enabled localities to levy a rate of 0.5d. in the pound for administrative expenses, which could be increased to 1d. with consent of the LGB. Money from the rates was not to be used for work relief—relief projects were to be funded exclusively from voluntary contributions. The act's framers apparently believed that, once distress committees and the machinery for administering relief were in place, the charitable public would contribute generously to relief funds during times of distress. This system of financing relief worked smoothly at first. In November 1905, Queen Alexandra's appeal to the public for funds drew nearly £154,000, of which £125,000 was distributed to distress committees throughout Britain and Ireland.[45]

Despite the success of the queen's appeal in raising money, few in the government believed that such appeals could be repeated annually. In 1906 Parliament made a grant of £200,000 to local distress committees; similar grants were made in the four following years. The parliamentary grant was meant to supplement voluntary contributions, but instead it led to a sharp reduction in contributions. According to Harris, "the charitable public declined to subscribe voluntarily to a scheme for which they were being compulsorily taxed."[46] The grants also led many local authorities to stop levying the 0.5d. rate for administrative expenses. Evidence of the changing nature of relief-project funding is given in Table 4.6, which compares the sources for the receipts of distress committees in 1906–7, the first year of the parliamentary grant, and 1909–10. In 1909–10, the distress committees received £146,835 from the parliamentary grant, or £41,415 more than they had received in 1906–7. During the same period, income from local rates and voluntary contributions declined by £46,774. By 1909–10 the majority of funding for local work relief projects came from the Treasury rather than from local contributions and taxes, as the Unemployed Workmen Act had envisaged.

The act stated that distress committees were to investigate applicants for relief and to provide work for those "deserving" workers who were temporarily unemployed because of a dislocation of trade. However, the distress committees proved no better than previous relief committees at separating

---

44. The best discussions of the Unemployed Workmen Act are found in Beveridge (1909: 162–91) and Harris (1972: 157–210).

45. Slightly more than half of the money distributed, £65,900, went to the London and West Ham distress committees. The fund also gave £9,450 to assist migrants to Canada, and made grants to the Salvation Army, the Church Army, and other charitable agencies. Parl. Papers, *Report . . . on the Effects of Employment or Assistance* (1909, XLIV), pp. 82–83.

46. Harris (1972: 179).

TABLE 4.6. Sources of Funds for Distress Committees, 1906–7 and 1909–10

	1906–7		1909–10	
Source of Funds	£	%	£	%
Parliamentary grant	105,420	40.2	146,835	57.2
Local rates	90,088	34.3	68,069	26.5
Voluntary contributions	36,202	13.8	11,447	4.5
Other sources (including repayments for work done)	30,759	11.7	30,463	11.9
Total receipts	262,469		256,814	

Sources: Board of Trade, *Labour Gazette*, vols. 15 and 18 (1907: 327; 1910: 370).
Note: For 1906–7, voluntary contributions include donations from the Queen's Unemployed Fund.

the temporarily unemployed from the chronically underemployed. In 1907–8 general or casual laborers composed 53.3% of all applicants for relief; another 19.4% of applicants were employed in the building trades. A large share of these men were unskilled laborers who were more or less casually employed.[47]

Reports of individual distress committees give a better idea of the composition of the applicants for relief. In 1905–6 the Manchester distress committee registered 1,532 applicants for work relief. Of these, 52% were general laborers, 13% were laborers in the building trades, and 11% were carmen, stablemen, porters, and messengers. Altogether, three-quarters of the applicants could be classified as general or casual laborers.[48] The COS, analyzing the registration papers of 2,000 applicants in West Ham in 1905–6, determined that 55% were casual laborers, 12% were laborers in the building trades, and 3% were carmen. Only 12% of applicants were classified as skilled workers, and half of these were in the building trades and subject to irregular employment. In 1906–7, 64% of the applicants for work relief in West Ham were classified as casual laborers, and an additional 14% were classified as "chronically bad—industrially, privately, or both," or physically or mentally incapable of regular work. Less than 2% of applicants were skilled and regular artisans.[49] In sum, only a small share of those given work relief were in fact temporarily unemployed.

Like all previous attempts to assist the unemployed, the Unemployed Workmen Act accepted the principle of less eligibility; that is, workers on relief projects should earn less than regularly employed unskilled workers in order to

47. Beveridge (1909: 168–69).
48. Data on the occupations of Manchester applicants for work relief were obtained from the Webb Local Government Collection in the British Library of Political and Economic Science, Part 2: The Poor Law, vol. 307.
49. Howarth and Wilson (1907: 370–72, 376).

preserve work incentives. Some distress committees achieved this objective by paying workers on relief projects hourly wages below those of unskilled workers. Others chose to pay "full trade union wage rates per hour" but employ workers for a reduced number of hours per day or for two to four days per week.[50]

The London Central (Unemployed) Body employed men on relief works for 43 hours per week at 6d. an hour, for a weekly income of 21.5s. For comparison, in 1907 building laborers in London were paid 7d. per hour for a 50 hour week in summer.[51] Weekly hours typically were shorter in winter, when relief works were in operation. If the workweek was six hours shorter in winter than in summer—one hour shorter per day—a man employed on a relief project would earn 84% as much per week as a fully employed laborer in the building trades. In 1905 "preference men" and casual laborers at the London docks were paid 6d. per hour for an uncertain number of hours per week. The average weekly earnings of this group of dockworkers, who made up nearly a quarter of the workforce at the docks, was almost certainly less than that of men employed on relief works.[52]

Outside of central London, employment on relief projects was less continuous. The reports of local distress committees to the Board of Trade for February 1907 show that the average number of days worked by men employed on relief works varied from 21 in Leicester and Glasgow and 17 in Norwich to 11 in Bristol and 6.8 in Brighton. The average earnings for the month varied from 83.8s. in Leicester to 44.3s. in Bristol, 42.5s. in Glasgow, 34.1s. in Norwich, and 21.6s. in Brighton. The average daily wage of men on work relief projects was slightly higher than the estimated wage of unskilled laborers in the building trades in Bristol, and was 80% or more of building laborers' wages in Brighton and Leicester, but less than 60% of laborers' wages in Glasgow and Norwich. Despite the high daily wage rates for work relief jobs in some cities, the low number of days worked per week meant that such jobs clearly were not a substitute for full-time employment in the building trade. However, many building laborers did not work full-time in the winter months, and many other casual labor markets also experienced "seasonal slackness" in winter. Because laborers in these markets could alternate work relief with private sector employment, it is not surprising that the majority of applicants for work relief were general or casual laborers, or that the same men tended to reapply for work relief year after year.[53]

50. Beveridge (1909: 187).

51. Webb and Webb (1909b: 138). Wage date are from the Board of Trade, *Eleventh Abstract of Labour Statistics of the United Kingdom, 1905–06* (1907: 38–39).

52. Beveridge (1909: 89–94).

53. Work relief data from Board of Trade, *Labour Gazette*, vol. 15, March 1907, p. 67. Wage data from Board of Trade, *Eleventh Abstract of Labour Statistics of the United Kingdom, 1905–06* (1907), pp. 38–39. Webb (1912: 312–93); Jones (1971); Howarth and Wilson (1907: 378).

Contemporaries also maintained that local charity and work relief affected employers' hiring practices, encouraging the system of hiring and firing workers at will that was adopted by employers of dock labor at the port of London. Many dockworkers were underemployed even in relatively prosperous times, and often were forced to apply for work relief or private charity during slack periods. Beveridge concluded that the municipal work relief "doled out winter after winter" and the "perennial stream of charity descending upon the riverside labourer" was "a great convenience to the industry which needs his occasional services and frequent attendance. It amounts to nothing more or less than a subsidy to a system of careless and demoralising employment."[54]

Some historians maintain that the Unemployed Workmen Act "marked a decisive turning-point in national policy" because it accepted "a measure of national responsibility" for relieving the unemployed.[55] Most contemporaries, however, viewed the act not as the beginning of state intervention in the labor market, but rather as the last in a long line of failed attempts to use municipal relief works to solve the unemployment problem. According to Beveridge, "The Act started as a carefully guarded experiment in dealing with a specific emergency—exceptional trade depression—by assistance outside the Poor Law. One by one all the guards and restrictions have been swept away, or have become forgotten. The assistance, for the most part, has been given neither out of the resources contemplated by the Act (voluntary subscriptions), nor to the persons contemplated by the Act (workmen temporarily and exceptionally distressed), nor in substantial accordance with the principles of the Act as interpreted by the Local Government Board (that assistance should be less eligible than independence)."[56]

For many, the Unemployed Workmen Act was merely a stopgap measure. The same pressure that led to its adoption led the Conservative Government in December 1905 to appoint the Royal Commission on the Poor Laws and Relief of Distress. Virtually everyone who testified before the Royal Commission was impressed with the existing trade union unemployment insurance schemes and was in favor of extending insurance to a larger share of the workforce, although many opposed the adoption of a state-administered program. Despite the opposition to an increased role for the state, Parliament in 1911 established a compulsory, state-run system of unemployment insurance in a limited number of industries. The findings of the Royal Commission and Parliament's reasons for adopting compulsory unemployment insurance are discussed in detail in Chapter 6.

54. Beveridge (1909: 109).
55. Bruce (1968: 188).
56. Beveridge (1909: 189).

III. Conclusion

Unemployment was a major cause of economic insecurity for British workers throughout the nineteenth century. Industrialization led to periodic business cycle downturns, and the second half of the century witnessed an alarming growth in the number of chronically underemployed urban low-skilled laborers. For manual workers not eligible for unemployment benefits from a trade union, spells of unemployment longer than a few weeks led to financial distress, and forced many to turn to other sources—typically local government or charities—for income assistance.

The forms of public and private assistance for the unemployed changed substantially from the 1860s to 1911. The Crusade Against Outrelief of the 1870s led to a sharp decline in the role played by the Poor Law in assisting the unemployed. However, the policies favored by the crusade—a combination of self-help and private charity—broke down during the 1885–86 downturn, leading the LGB to encourage municipalities to set up work relief projects when unemployment was high to assist those temporarily out of work. Neither the voluntary municipal relief works nor the work relief projects undertaken as a result of the 1905 Unemployed Workmen Act were successful in assisting the temporarily unemployed—most of those employed on relief works were chronically underemployed laborers.

The public assistance for the unemployed provided under the various policies adopted after 1870 was less certain, and less generous, than that available before 1870. Parliament's adoption in 1909–11 of a national system of labor exchanges and compulsory unemployment insurance was more of a repudiation of late nineteenth-century policies toward the unemployed than an extension of them.

5

Old Age Poverty and Pauperism

Old age was a major cause of economic insecurity in Victorian England. Working-class individuals who survived past age 65 found it difficult to earn enough to meet their needs. How did the aged cope with declining income? Some historians contend that before the twentieth century most old people who were unable to support themselves were helped by relatives or private charity rather than public assistance. Peter Townsend asserted that the "structured dependency" of the elderly largely is a post-welfare-state phenomenon, while Pat Thane maintained that in Victorian England the aged turned to the Poor Law "only in the last resort" when they had no family to assist them or access to private charity. Other historians contend that a large share of the aged received communal assistance throughout the nineteenth century and even earlier. David Thomson concluded that "during much of the nineteenth century a clear majority of all women aged 70 or more in England and Wales, married, widowed, or single, were regular pensioners of the Poor Law," as were "slightly less than one-half of all men aged 70 or more, together with substantial minorities of both men and women in their sixties."[1]

The debate over the Poor Law's role in assisting the aged has been fueled by a lack of data. Government officials throughout the nineteenth century were

1. Townsend (1981: 5–28); Thane (1983); Thomson (1986: 355–78). Thomson's estimates are based on a limited number of (mainly southern rural) parishes, and Hunt (1989) claimed they overestimate the share of the aged receiving weekly pensions in England as a whole. However, several historians found old age pauperism rates similar to those reported by Thomson in the late seventeenth and eighteenth centuries. Smith (1998: 88) concluded from an analysis of parish records from 1670 to 1740 that "a significant minority, and, in some communities, a noteworthy majority, of elderly persons [were] in receipt of parish support."

more concerned with "the far more controversial nature of male able-bodied pauperism" than with the elderly. The Poor Law Board (PLB) and its successor the Local Government Board (LGB) did not collect statistics on the number of aged paupers until the 1890s, when interest in the aged poor increased.[2]

This chapter examines how the aged poor coped economically and the extent to which they relied on the Poor Law. Section I uses data on the number of aged paupers for 1890 to 1906, along with published statistics on adult non-able-bodied paupers, to construct annual estimates of the number of persons 65 and older receiving poor relief from 1861 to the adoption of the Old Age Pension Act in 1908. The estimates show that the share of aged persons receiving poor relief was larger than many contemporaries and historians believed.

Section II examines how households dealt with the economic insecurity of old age. Many workers, especially the low-skilled, were unable to provide adequately for old age through savings or membership in friendly societies or trade unions offering pensions. Those who were able continued to work, albeit at reduced pay, past age 65 or even 70, and some received assistance from children or neighbors. However, the ability of older workers to support themselves declined with age. The combination of declining earnings, little saving, and lack of support from children forced a large share of the elderly to apply for poor relief.

The extent to which the aged turned to the Poor Law for assistance varied substantially across Poor Law unions. Section III examines the reasons for these variations in pauperism rates using data for all 585 English Poor Law unions in 1891–92. Regressions are estimated to test several conjectures made by contemporaries, and repeated by historians, regarding the deterrent effect of workhouse relief, the effects of wages and the industrial character of unions on pauperism rates, and possible regional differences in welfare culture. Section IV briefly discusses why old age pauperism rates, after declining from 1871 to 1891, remained roughly constant from 1891 to the adoption of the Old Age Pension Act.

I. The Extent of Pauperism among the Aged, 1861–1908

How many people survived to old age in Victorian England? In 1861, there were 932,000 persons aged 65 and older in England and Wales, representing 4.6% of the population. The number of aged persons increased to more than 1.5 million in 1901, but the share of the population 65 and older remained nearly constant over the four decades, at 4.6–4.7%. The share of the population 70 and older was 2.8% in 1861 and 2.7% in 1901. The life expectancy of the aged

2. MacKinnon (1988: 9; 1984: 103).

TABLE 5.1. Old Age Pauperism, August 1, 1890 (Burt's Return): England and Wales

Ages	Population	Total Paupers	Pauperism Rate	% Relieved Indoors
60–65	772,879	41,180	5.3	32.5
65–70	571,948	62,240	10.9	25.4
70–75	417,914	77,708	18.6	21.6
75–80	233,333	60,879	26.1	20.3
80 and older	149,407	44,860	30.0	21.7
60 and older	2,145,481	286,867	13.4	23.7
65 and older	1,372,602	245,687	17.9	22.3
70 and older	800,654	183,447	22.9	21.2

Source: Parl. Papers, *Return . . . of Paupers over Sixty* (1890–91, LXVIII), pp. 566–67.

changed little during this period. A 65-year-old male in 1861 had, on average, an additional 10.7 years to live, while a 65-year-old female had an additional 11.6 years to live. Forty years later, in 1901, life expectancy for a 65-year-old male was 10.6 years, while that for a female was 11.8 years.[3]

Official statistics on the number of old persons receiving poor relief were collected by pauper censuses in 1890, 1891–92, and 1906. The first official estimate, "Burt's return," gives the number of paupers and pauperism rate for five-year groupings from age 60 onward on August 1, 1890 (see Table 5.1). Pauperism increased sharply with age, rising from 5.3% for persons aged 60–65 to 10.9% for those 65–70, and 30.0% for those 80 and older. Overall, 17.9% of persons 65 and older and 22.9% of persons 70 and older received poor relief.

The data in Table 5.1, based on a one-day count of paupers, substantially understates the number of old people who received poor relief at some point over a 12-month period. The LGB constructed a 12-month count of the number of paupers from March 1891 to March 1892 for three age groups: those under 16, 16–64, and 65 and older. Table 5.2a shows a summary of "Ritchie's return," and compares pauperism rates on January 1, 1892, with rates constructed from the 12-month count. Two results stand out. First, the pauperism rate for persons 65 and older was far greater than the overall pauperism rate or the rate for children or prime age adults. Second, the share of persons 65 and older who received relief during the 12-month period was 29.3%, an amount 50% greater than the share relieved on January 1. Many aged persons required assistance for only part of the year.

3. Data on the age distribution of the population from Mitchell (1988: 15). The life expectancy of a 50-year-old male was 19.8 years in 1861 and 19.3 years in 1901, while that of a 50-year-old female was 21.1 years in 1861 and 22.4 years in 1901. Preston et al. (1972: 224, 226, 240, 242).

TABLE 5.2A. Ritchie's Return for 1891–92: England and Wales

| | PAUPERISM RATE (%) | | | |
Ages	January 1, 1892	Year Count	Year Count/ Day Count	% Relieved Indoors
Under 16	2.1	5.1	2.416	22.5
16–64	1.2	3.7	3.040	38.1
65 and older	19.6	29.3	1.497	23.6
Total	2.4	5.4	2.245	27.5

Source: Parl. Papers, *Return . . . of Paupers over Sixty-Five* (1892, LXVIII), pp. 621–31.

TABLE 5.2B. Ritchie's Return for 1891–92: English Registration Divisions

| | PAUPERISM RATE 65+ (%) | | | |
Registration Division	January 1, 1892	Year Count	Year Count/ Day Count	% Relieved Indoors
London	19.5	35.3	1.810	58.1
South East	18.5	25.3	1.367	27.1
South Midlands	21.1	28.1	1.334	16.8
East	23.4	30.8	1.319	16.1
South West	23.8	30.0	1.259	10.8
West Midlands	19.0	27.3	1.436	21.5
North Midlands	20.0	26.8	1.339	14.0
North West	13.6	21.6	1.591	33.8
Yorkshire	15.6	22.7	1.451	18.7
North	15.0	20.4	1.362	20.2

Source: Parl. Papers, *Return . . . of Paupers over Sixty-Five* (1892, LXVIII), pp. 621–31.

Table 5.2b reports old age pauperism rates in 1891–92 for each English registration division.[4] The three northern divisions—North West, Yorkshire, and North—had the lowest pauperism rates by either the one-day or 12-month measure, while the highest rates were in the South West, East, South Midlands, and London. Table 5.2b also reports the share of paupers 65 and older relieved in workhouses. The use of the workhouse varied greatly across registration divisions and was closely related to the extent of urbanization. It was far higher in London than elsewhere, followed by the industrial North

4. The PLB and the LGB reported data on the number of relief recipients at the Poor Law union, county, and registration division level of aggregation. Each division (except London) included multiple counties and both rural and urban areas, although the extent of urbanization varied substantially across divisions.

West, and was lowest in the more rural South West, North Midlands, East, and South Midlands.

Some of those included in the 12-month count received relief only for short periods of time.[5] Whether or not they should be counted when constructing pauperism rates depends on the question one is addressing. The day count gives a good idea of the number of "permanent" paupers—those who received relief week in and week out. The 12-month count includes those old persons who were living right at the margin. They were able to subsist on their own much of the time, but needed to apply for relief now and then, for instance in winter when they were less likely to find employment. C. S. Loch and members of the Charity Organisation Society maintained that the 12-month count, by giving equal weight to permanent and temporary paupers, exaggerated the extent of pauperism among the aged. Other contemporaries disagreed. Charles Booth argued that the day count "disguises the *extent of pauperisation*," and added that the "wide margin" between the two counts "gives some . . . idea of the mass of poverty which lies continually on the verge of pauperism." More recently MacKinnon concluded that "occasional relief could play as important a part in assisting the destitute in a time of crisis as did permanent relief."[6]

Another pauper census was conducted on March 31, 1906, the eve of the adoption of the Old Age Pension Act. Table 5.3 shows pauperism rates for persons 65 and older for each English registration division on that date. The pauperism rate for England and Wales was 19.9%, virtually identical to that for January 1, 1892. Pauperism rates were lowest in the three northern divisions, and highest in the East and London. However, the size of the North-South differential declined from 1892 to 1906, as pauperism fell in all southern divisions outside of London, and increased in the Midlands and the three northern divisions.

From 1859 to 1912, the PLB/LGB annually reported statistics on the number of persons receiving poor relief on two days a year, January 1 and July 1. The categories included in the annual returns are, for both indoor and outdoor paupers, adult able-bodied males and females and their children, and non-able-bodied adult males, females, and children, including orphans. Statistics on the number of aged paupers were not reported. However, Booth determined that it was possible to construct estimates of the number of aged paupers from the published statistics on non-able-bodied paupers. Using data from Burt's and Ritchie's returns, he calculated that in 1890–92, 75% of adult non-able-bodied paupers were aged 65 or older. He constructed three estimates of the number of paupers 65 and older from 1851 to 1891. The first assumed that the ratio of

5. The data reported in Tables 5.2a and 5.2b exclude approximately 25,000 persons 65 and older who received only outdoor medical relief in 1891–92. This represents 6.7% of the total number of persons 65 and older relieved during the 12-month period.

6. Loch (1894: 472); Booth (1899b: 213–14); MacKinnon (1984: 122).

TABLE 5.3. Pauper Census of March 31, 1906

	PAUPERISM RATE BY AGE			
Registration Division	60–65	65–70	65 and Up	70 and Up
London	9.4	17.3	22.3	26.1
South East	5.1	9.8	16.4	20.8
South Midlands	5.2	11.1	19.3	25.0
East	7.1	13.0	22.7	29.1
South West	5.7	10.7	19.3	24.6
West Midlands	6.0	12.6	19.4	24.3
North Midlands	6.8	13.1	21.5	27.5
North West	6.4	11.7	15.0	17.9
Yorkshire	5.2	11.0	15.8	19.7
North	6.1	12.2	16.3	19.6
England	6.4	12.3	18.6	23.3

Source: Parl. Papers, *Royal Commission on the Poor Laws and Relief of Distress, Appendix Vol. XXV, Statistical Memoranda* (1910, LIII), pp. 176–93.

aged paupers to non-able-bodied paupers remained constant at the ratio for 1890–92 from the 1850s to 1891. The second estimate assumed that the number of non-able-bodied paupers aged 16–65 decreased "proportionately to the able-bodied of same ages." Finally, the third estimate calculated the number of paupers 65 and older as the mean of the numbers obtained from the first and second estimates. Booth's second estimate yielded a ratio of paupers 65 and older to non-able-bodied paupers that declined from 0.75 in 1891 to 0.64 in 1861; the third or "mean" estimate yielded a ratio that declined from 0.75 in 1891 to 0.69 in 1861.[7]

More recently, MacKinnon also maintained that it was possible to estimate the number of old age paupers using data on non-able-bodied paupers. After comparing the number of aged persons receiving relief with the number of non-able-bodied paupers in 1890, 1899, 1900, and 1906, she concluded that "not-able-bodied and old-age pauperism can be used as interchangeable terms. . . . The ratio of paupers over sixty, sixty-five, or seventy to [all] not-able-bodied paupers . . . was nearly constant between 1890 and 1906." Moreover, "unless there was a substantial (unrecorded) shift in the way the aged were classified before 1906, it seems reasonable" to assume that these ratios held back to 1860.[8]

7. Booth (1899b: 218–19). In a slightly earlier paper, Loch (1894: 483–85) estimated pauperism rates for persons aged 60 and above for the census years 1851 to 1891 by assuming that the ratio of aged paupers to non-able-bodied paupers remained constant over the four decades.

8. MacKinnon (1984: 103, 105; 1988: 9).

TABLE 5.4. Pauperism Rates for Persons 65 and Older, Day Count

Registration Division	PERCENTAGE OF AGED PAUPERS RECEIVING RELIEF					
	1861	1871	1881	1891	1901	1908
London	22.5	27.9	23.1	21.5	21.6	23.1
South East	27.6	27.8	19.6	17.7	15.7	15.3
South Midlands	33.8	32.9	24.4	20.3	18.4	17.7
East	32.2	30.1	21.8	20.5	21.4	21.3
South West	31.7	32.1	27.3	22.7	21.1	18.2
West Midlands	25.2	25.0	21.9	19.8	18.3	18.3
North Midlands	24.3	24.2	18.9	18.7	20.1	20.2
North West	21.8	22.5	17.8	15.8	15.4	15.5
Yorkshire	19.4	20.6	18.2	15.8	15.6	14.9
North	22.9	22.9	18.0	15.0	15.2	16.8

Sources: Data on the annual number of non-able-bodied paupers for each registration division from the annual Reports of the Poor Law Board (for 1861) and the Local Government Board (for 1871–1908).
Note: See text for the method used to construct the estimates.

I use the technique employed by Booth and MacKinnon to estimate the annual number of paupers 65 and older from 1861 to 1908. The ratio of paupers aged 65 and older to adult non-able-bodied paupers in England and Wales for 1890, 1892, 1900, and 1906 ranged from 0.700 in 1890 to 0.754 in 1892. I use these ratios to construct two estimates of the number of paupers 65 and older from 1861 to 1908. The first is obtained by multiplying the number of non-able-bodied paupers on January 1 of each year by 0.725. The second estimate assumes that the ratio of 0.725 holds for 1881–1908, then declines by 0.0075 each year from 1881 to 1871, when it is equal to 0.65, and then remains equal to 0.65 for 1861–71. This estimate represents a compromise between the methods suggested by Booth and MacKinnon. It takes account of the changes that occurred in the makeup of the pauper host in the 1870s as a result of the Crusade Against Outrelief, but assumes that the ratio of aged paupers to non-able-bodied paupers remained constant after the crusade and in the decade preceding it. I prefer this estimate, and report the results obtained from it in Tables 5.4 and 5.6.

Table 5.4 shows the estimated pauperism rates for persons 65 and older for each English registration division for the census years 1861 to 1901 and 1908 based on the January day counts of non-able-bodied paupers. In 1861, the one-day pauperism rate for England as a whole was 25.4%. It exceeded 30% in three southern divisions and was below 25% in the three northern divisions. After remaining roughly constant from 1861 to 1871, the pauperism rate declined over the following two decades in all divisions. From 1891 to 1908, pauperism declined slightly in some divisions and increased slightly in others. Over the entire period from 1861 to 1908, old age pauperism declined in all divisions except London.

TABLE 5.5. Share of Paupers 65 and Older Relieved in Workhouses

Registration Division	PERCENTAGE OF AGED PAUPERS RELIEVED IN WORKHOUSES					
	1861	1871	1881	1891	1901	1908
London	41.8	34.5	59.8	63.3	61.8	61.9
South East	16.5	16.8	26.7	28.3	28.6	31.9
South Midlands	10.6	11.3	17.5	18.7	19.8	22.2
East	10.2	11.1	16.7	17.3	19.8	20.4
South West	7.0	8.2	11.1	11.4	13.0	17.2
West Midlands	10.9	13.7	21.6	23.2	25.9	28.9
North Midlands	9.2	10.1	16.2	14.7	15.4	18.1
North West	18.6	26.8	40.7	42.0	40.1	42.8
Yorkshire	9.7	12.5	19.4	22.0	23.8	26.2
North	9.5	12.2	20.7	21.5	23.4	25.1

Sources: Data on the percentage of non-able-bodied paupers relieved in workhouses for each registration division from the annual Reports of the Poor Law Board (1861) and the Local Government Board (1871–1908).

The largest decadal decline in pauperism, for all divisions except Yorkshire, occurred during the 1870s. The divisions most affected were the South Midlands, East, and South East, which witnessed declines in old age pauperism of 8.2–8.5 percentage points. The decline in pauperism during the 1870s becomes even larger if one assumes that the ratio of old age paupers to non-able-bodied paupers remained constant at 0.725 throughout the decade.[9] Some of the decline in old age pauperism was a result of increases in workers' wages, and thus in their ability to provide for old age, but a large part was caused by major changes in the administration of the Poor Law as a result of the Crusade Against Outrelief. As discussed in Chapter 3, in the early 1870s Poor Law unions throughout England, encouraged by the LGB and the newly formed COS, curtailed outdoor relief for all types of paupers, including the elderly. The effect of the crusade on the relief of the aged can be seen in Table 5.5, which shows the share of paupers 65 and older who were relieved in workhouses. This increased in all registration divisions during the 1870s, although the increase was especially pronounced in the more urban divisions, London and the North West.

Table 5.6 presents estimates of the share of persons 65 and older who received poor relief at some point during a year, calculated by multiplying the day count by the ratio of the 12-month count to the day count for 1891–92 for each registration division (see Table 5.2b). In constructing these estimates, I

9. Under this assumption, the old age pauperism rate declined by between 12.3 percentage points in the South Midlands and 4.7 percentage points in Yorkshire.

TABLE 5.6. Pauperism Rates for Persons 65 and Older, Year Count

Registration Division	PERCENTAGE OF AGED PAUPERS RECEIVING RELIEF					
	1861	1871	1881	1891	1901	1908
London	35.9	44.4	36.8	34.2	34.4	36.8
South East	37.7	37.9	26.7	24.1	21.5	20.9
South Midlands	45.1	43.9	32.5	27.0	24.6	23.6
East	42.5	39.7	28.8	27.0	28.3	28.1
South West	39.9	40.4	34.4	28.6	26.6	23.0
West Midlands	36.2	35.9	31.5	28.5	26.3	26.3
North Midlands	32.6	32.4	25.3	25.1	26.9	27.0
North West	34.8	35.8	28.3	25.1	24.5	24.6
Yorkshire	28.1	29.9	26.4	22.9	22.7	21.7
North	31.2	31.2	24.5	20.4	20.7	22.9

Sources: Data on the number of non-able-bodied paupers for each registration division from the annual Reports of the Poor Law Board (1861) and the Local Government Board (1871–1908).
Note: See text for the method used to construct 12-month pauperism estimates.

have assumed that the ratio remained constant from 1861 to 1908.[10] In 1871, on the eve of the crusade, more than one-third of persons 65 and older were in receipt of poor relief at some point during the year in seven registration divisions. In 1908, the share in receipt of relief exceeded one-third only in London. For England as a whole, 37.6% of persons 65 and older received poor relief in 1871, falling to 25.7% in 1908.

As noted above, much of the decline in old age pauperism after 1871 was a result of changes in policy rather than improving economic conditions. Mac-Kinnon constructed "policy constant" estimates of the number of poor relief recipients after 1871, and concluded that if the Crusade Against Outrelief had not occurred as many as "200,000 more old people would have been on outdoor relief in 1900."[11] This is an upper-bound estimate of the impact of the crusade; adding 100,000 to the number of relief recipients 65 and older in 1908 yields an old age pauperism rate of 31.7%, only 6 percentage points lower than the pauperism rate in 1871. Late Victorian economic growth did not lead to a sharp reduction in poverty among the aged.

10. The ratio of the 12-month count to the day count of aged paupers for London in 1891–92 is far larger than that for any other division, and Loch (1894) and others argued that it overestimated the extent of London pauperism. In calculating 12-month pauperism rates for London in Table 5.6, I set the ratio for London equal to that for the North West. My assumption that the ratio of the 12-month count to the day count remained constant during the second half of the nineteenth century follows Lees (1998: 180–81).

11. MacKinnon (1984: 327–28).

The Poor Law was an institution meant exclusively for the working class—few if any members of the middle class applied for poor relief. If one assumes, following MacKinnon, that 70% of persons 65 and older were from the working class, in 1871 a majority of aged working-class individuals in southern England received poor relief, in the form of either a permanent pension or occasional assistance.[12] Working-class pauperism rates were somewhat lower in the northern divisions, but exceeded 40% throughout England. Pauperism rates declined thereafter, but remained surprisingly high up to the adoption of the Old Age Pension Act, when more than one-third of working-class persons 65 and older were in receipt of poor relief in six of the ten registration divisions. These results are for a 12-month period; the share of persons who received poor relief at some point after their 65th birthday was even larger.

The estimates of old age pauperism rates presented here are high, but they are supported by other evidence. Booth concluded from a study of Paddington Poor Law union in London that the number of persons 65 and older who received poor relief at some point in the two years beginning on January 1, 1890, was more than twice the number relieved on January 1, 1892. In his testimony before the Royal Commission on the Aged Poor, Booth argued that the bulk of England's paupers came from the bottom 40% of the income distribution, and concluded that of this class of workers, "not less than two out of three of those who survive do at some time in their old age receive aid from the rates." Canon Blackley examined the burial registers of 26 rural parishes in the 1870s and 1880s, and found that 42% of old persons had received poor relief "during the closing years of their lives."[13]

The Poor Law continued to play a major role in the lives of the aged in late Victorian England despite its increasing stinginess and the increase in workers' real wages over time. Moreover, "policy constant" estimates of the number of aged paupers show that the official pauperism statistics substantially overstate the improvement in living standards for the aged poor in the late nineteenth century—the data suggest that "the very poor were little better off in 1910 than in 1860."[14] Large-scale government assistance for the elderly is not a product of the welfare state; it existed at the local level throughout the nineteenth century and earlier.

---

12. MacKinnon (1984: 328) concluded that "70% of the population over 65 were potentially recipients of outdoor relief." Booth (1894b: 243) maintained that "a considerable section—perhaps one-third—of the population is lifted so far above parish relief as to yield a very small percentage of pauperism in old age."

13. Booth's comments are in minutes of evidence taken before the *Royal Commission on the Aged Poor*, Parl. Papers, vol. 3 (1895, XV), qq. 10,854–59. Blackley's calculation is reported in Booth (1892c: 165).

14. MacKinnon (1984: 269).

II. Coping with the Economic Insecurity of Old Age

Why were old age pauperism rates so high in Victorian England? Why didn't workers provide for their old age through savings or membership in pension-providing friendly societies or trade unions? Some of the witnesses who testified before the Royal Commission on the Aged Poor in 1893–94 attributed the high rate of old age pauperism to the moral deficiencies of the working class, and in particular to drunkenness, thoughtlessness, and lack of thrift and energy. Canon Blackley and others maintained that the generosity of the Poor Law was a major cause of pauperism because the certainty of support in old age discouraged "the thrift instinct in the young."[15]

Other witnesses attributed the majority of old age pauperism to economic causes, and maintained that it was difficult for all but the highest paid skilled workers to save enough to be self-sufficient in old age. Rev. J. Frome Wilkinson stated that "the bulk of unskilled labour, both urban and rural, have never been, and are not now, in a sufficiently good economic position to provide for their old age."[16] Joseph Chamberlain, a member of the commission, maintained that "the great bulk of the working classes, during their working lives . . . are fairly provident, fairly thrifty, fairly industrious, and fairly temperate. . . . [The poor] have less opportunities of thrift than the well-to-do classes, and it is a little too much to expect from them . . . the extremely penurious lives which would be necessary if they were to make, by their own efforts alone, a sufficient provision for old age."[17] Seven years later, the report from the Select Committee on the Aged Deserving Poor (1899) concluded that, despite "the remarkable development of habits of thrift . . . among the working classes in recent times," large numbers of poor elderly persons "whose conduct and whose whole career has been blameless, industrious, and deserving, find themselves from no fault of their own . . . with nothing but the workhouse or inadequate out-door relief, as the refuge for their declining years."[18]

As was discussed in Chapter 3, working-class saving and membership in insurance-providing friendly societies and trade unions increased greatly in late Victorian England. Despite the increase in self-help, many workers remained unable to support themselves in old age. To determine the adequacy of workers' savings, it is necessary to estimate the living expenses of the aged.

15. Drage (1895: 18–25); Johnson (1985: 217–19); Parl. Papers, *Royal Commission on the Aged Poor*, vol. 3 (1895, XV), q. 12,819. See also the testimony of Robert Hedley, Inspector of the Local Government Board for the Metropolis: Parl. Papers, *Royal Commission on the Aged Poor*, vol. 2 (1895, XIV), qq. 1376–77.

16. Drage (1895: 25–26). Parl. Papers, *Royal Commission on the Aged Poor*, vol. 2 (1895, XIV), qq. 5,840–43.

17. Parl. Papers, *Royal Commission on the Aged Poor*, vol. 3 (1895, XV), qq. 12,174, 12,182.

18. Parl. Papers, *Report from the Select Committee on the Aged Deserving Poor* (1899, VIII), p. iv.

Rowntree estimated that in 1899 the minimum necessary weekly expenditure for a man or woman was 7s. For a couple, the minimum necessary expenditure was 11s. 8d.: 6s. for food, 2s. 6d. for rent, and 3s. 2d. for sundries. Assuming that the aged ate less and spent less on sundries than prime-age adults, I estimate that the minimum necessary weekly expenditure for a person 65 or older was 6s., and for an aged couple 10s.[19]

While most working-class households had savings accounts by the late nineteenth century, the average size of their account balances was small. In 1894 and 1899 the average balance in working-class accounts was £4–6.[20] Of course, a large share of the aged had other sources of income. Still, a couple needing to draw on only 1s. in savings per week would exhaust a balance of £4 in just over 18 months and a balance of £6 in less than two and a half years.

The typical pension benefit paid by friendly societies to their members was equal to one-quarter of sickness benefits—between 2s. 6d. and 3s. per week. These benefits, by themselves, were not sufficient to maintain an aged person. However, combined with savings, part-time work, or help from relatives or friends, they often were enough to keep aged friendly society members from having to apply for poor relief.[21] Trade union superannuation benefits were more generous. In 1892 the Amalgamated Society of Engineers paid a weekly benefit of 7s. to those unable to work who had been members for 25 years; benefits increased by 1s. for each five-year interval up to 40, so that an elderly worker who had been a member for 40 or more years received 10s. per week. The Boilermakers and Iron and Steel Shipbuilders paid 4–7s. per week, the Operative Bricklayers 5–9s., and the London Compositors 4–5s., depending on length of membership. These benefits often were large enough to support a retired worker, but not large enough to support an aged couple. Neither friendly society nor union benefits passed on to a widow upon her husband's death. The absence of survivors' benefits was "one of the greatest defects of the modern thrift system."[22]

19. Rowntree (1901: 110). Spender (1892: 7) concluded that 10s. per week was "about the minimum on which it is possible to support two people in a town, and prevent the break-up of the home." My estimated necessary weekly expenditures for an aged couple are as follows: food, 5s.; rent, 2s. 6d.; sundries, 2s. 6d.

20. See Chapter 3 and Johnson (1985: 101).

21. Brabrook (1898: 112–13). Several witnesses who testified before the Royal Commission on the Aged Poor maintained that few members of friendly societies ever applied for poor relief. See Parl. Papers, *Royal Commission on the Aged Poor*, vols. 2–3, *Minutes of Evidence* (1895, XIV; 1895, XV), qq. 983–84, q. 1,453, q. 2,829, q. 3,244, q. 3,683, q. 4,116, q. 5,445, qq. 11,051–53, q. 11,613, q. 17,699.

22. Altogether, 94 of the 376 trade unions for which information is available in 1892 offered some form of old age benefit to their members. Parl. Papers, *Royal Commission on Labour: Rules of Associations of Employers and of Employed* (1892, XXXVI); Spender (1892: 44).

Few aged working-class persons were able to live entirely on savings or insurance benefits. A majority of men continued to work past age 65—the labor force participation rate for men 65 and older was 73.4% in 1881 and 60.6% in 1901—but many of those employed worked less than full-time, and the share employed, and hours worked, decreased as age increased. Moreover, census occupational data suggest that large numbers of older workers experienced "life-cycle deskilling," shifting to low-skilled and poorly paid jobs as they aged.[23]

Those who were unable to support themselves through earnings or savings often turned to relatives, friends, the Poor Law, or private charity for assistance. Working-class "mutual self-help"—gifts of food or cash from neighbors to old people in need—was especially prevalent in rural areas, but also existed in towns. Rowntree found that in York persons "in particularly hard straits, are often helped by those in circumstances but little better than their own." In Poor Law unions where generous private charity existed, some needy old people received charity rather than poor relief. Charitable help took many forms: free coal or blankets in winter, subsidized (or free) housing, medical assistance, or small weekly doles. It is not possible to measure the extent of charitable assistance for the aged at the local or national level, but it clearly was substantial.[24]

Some idea of how the aged coped financially is given by two surveys undertaken in the 1890s, one by a governmental committee and the other by Booth. In 1899 the Departmental Committee on the Aged Deserving Poor conducted a "test census" of 12,400 persons aged 65 and older in 28 "representative" Poor Law unions.[25] Table 5.7 presents the results of the test census. Overall, 46% of aged males and 74% of females had weekly incomes from all sources (including assistance from children and others) of 10s. or less.[26] Some 35% of these low-income individuals were in receipt of poor relief. A detailed study was carried out on the sources of income for those reporting weekly incomes

---

23. In the 1881 to 1911 censuses, men 65 and older were highly overrepresented in agriculture, clothing, and laboring (all low-wage sectors) and underrepresented in high-wage sectors. Johnson (1994: 116, 118). The term "life-cycle deskilling" was coined by Ransom and Sutch (1986: 19), who found strong evidence of "downward occupational mobility" in late nineteenth-century America. Spender (1892: 23–46) provides evidence of downward occupational mobility in Victorian England.

24. See Booth (1894a: 47), Rowntree (1901: 43), Digby (2000: 1442–44), McCord (1976), Goose and Basten (2009), and Goose (2014).

25. The unions were distributed as follows: 5 metropolitan (London) unions, 6 urban unions (large towns), 3 mining unions, and 14 rural unions. Parl. Papers, *Report of the Departmental Committee on the Aged Deserving Poor* (1900, X), pp. 10–15.

26. The report assumed that those whose income was not stated but who were maintained by relatives and friends had weekly incomes less than 10s.

TABLE 5.7. Pauper Test Census of 1899

PERSONS 65 AND OLDER WITH WEEKLY INCOMES OF 10S. OR LESS

Poor Law Unions	Income of 10s. or Less (%)	Receiving Poor Relief (%)	Sources of Income for Those Not in Receipt of Poor Relief			
			Earnings (%)	Help from Children (%)	Friendly Society/ Union Benefits (%)	Savings (%)
All 28 unions						
Male	45.7	32.6	58.5	27.9	16.2	12.8
Female	73.7	36.3	25.8	70.3	1.7	9.9
Total	61.3	35.1	37.1	55.6	6.7	10.9
London						
Male	36.3	30.3	54.5	40.4	9.1	4.0
Female	75.5	34.8	26.9	78.1	3.1	5.4
Total	59.5	33.6	34.5	67.7	4.7	5.0
Large towns						
Male	41.3	30.8	60.1	38.5	8.6	5.3
Female	74.4	35.4	31.9	71.6	0.6	5.9
Total	60.5	34.1	40.4	61.6	3.0	5.7
Mining unions						
Male	49.3	31.8	24.8	42.0	35.0	15.3
Female	73.8	35.6	10.6	81.6	2.8	9.5
Total	62.6	34.2	15.9	66.8	14.8	11.7
Rural unions						
Male	48.6	33.8	68.3	18.0	14.7	16.1
Female	72.9	37.3	27.2	63.9	1.4	13.2
Total	61.8	35.1	42.6	46.7	6.4	14.3

Source: Parl. Papers, Report of the Departmental Committee on the Aged Deserving Poor (1900, X), pp. 10–15.

TABLE 5.8. Sources of Maintenance for Persons 65 and Older in Rural Districts, 1892–93

Sources of Maintenance	England (%)	North (%)	Midlands (%)	East (%)	West (%)	South (%)
Parish only	5.0	2.0	4.4	5.7	6.0	6.5
Parish and charity	5.1	4.0	5.5	6.4	6.5	4.0
Parish and relatives	5.1	1.7	5.9	8.2	3.4	5.1
Parish, charity, and relatives	3.2	2.8	4.5	3.3	2.7	2.5
Parish and earnings	3.6	2.9	3.1	5.0	3.7	3.4
Charity and relatives	4.0	4.2	5.3	2.8	3.0	4.2
Charity, relatives, and earnings	5.9	5.4	8.4	6.5	3.1	4.9
Relatives only	5.3	4.8	4.7	5.1	7.5	5.3
Relatives and earnings	4.0	3.2	4.7	4.5	3.5	3.9
Relatives, earnings, and means	3.4	5.7	3.0	3.0	2.9	2.9
Earnings only	24.4	23.2	23.1	26.3	24.1	25.1
Earnings and means	7.6	12.8	5.7	5.6	7.6	7.4
Means only	23.4	27.3	21.8	17.5	25.9	25.0

Source: Booth (1894a: 344).

Note: There is no overlap in the above categories. Some of the percentages reported have been corrected from errors in the original data.

of 10s. or less and not receiving poor relief. Nearly 60% of males and slightly more than one-quarter of females in this category reported having earnings, including pension payments, from their current (or former) employer. The share of old people with income from savings was quite low; the share with income from benefit societies was low everywhere except in mining unions, and was especially low for women. Two-thirds of aged females, but only 28% of males, received assistance from children.

As part of his study on *The Aged Poor*, Booth surveyed 9,125 persons aged 65 and older (4,450 men and 4,675 women) living in 262 rural parishes throughout England and Wales. Table 5.8 shows the sources of maintenance for those surveyed. For England and Wales as a whole, 22% of those 65 and older received outdoor relief, although only 5% relied entirely on the Poor Law.[27] Nearly half had some (often quite meager) wage earnings, and slightly more than a third had savings ("means"); 55% maintained themselves entirely through earnings and savings. Only one-quarter of those surveyed received assistance from relatives. The importance of the various sources of maintenance differed across regions. The two extremes were, not surprisingly, the high-wage North and the low-wage East. In the North, 46% of the aged had some savings,

---

27. Booth (1894a: 335–52). Booth does not include those relieved in workhouses, and therefore understates the number of aged persons receiving poor relief and the share who relied entirely on the Poor Law.

and only 13% received outdoor relief. By contrast, in the East only 26% of the aged had savings, and 29% received outdoor relief.

The sources of maintenance varied with age and sex; 53% of those aged 65–70 were able to "earn their own living," as compared to 18.5% of those 75–80. The share receiving poor relief, charity, or help from relatives increased with age. Of those aged 65–70, 11% received poor relief and 21% charity or help from relatives; of those 80 and older, 35% received poor relief and 34% charity or help from relatives. Females were much less likely than males to have earnings, and more likely to receive poor relief, charity, or assistance from relatives.[28] In sum, most aged persons had income from one or more sources, including wages, savings, friendly society or trade union benefits, or help from relatives or friends. For many, however, income from these sources was less than they needed to subsist, forcing them to turn to the Poor Law for help. The vast majority of the aged poor in receipt of outdoor relief did not require full maintenance, but only enough, in combination with other sources, to achieve a subsistence income.

The Royal Commission on the Aged Poor provides detailed information on the role of the Poor Law in assisting the aged in the early 1890s. The testimony of Poor Law officials before the commission indicates that the outdoor relief given to aged paupers seldom was enough to provide them with full maintenance. Sir Hugh Owen, Permanent Secretary of the Local Government Board, stated that "in a great proportion of cases" the outdoor relief granted was not adequate. Local relief officials admitted that outdoor relief benefits were intended to provide the aged with only partial support, and that they relied "upon the relief being supplemented in some way or another, either by charity or small earnings from occasional work, odd jobs of one kind or another, or assistance from relatives."[29]

The typical weekly benefit was between 2s. 6d. and 3s. 6d. for single persons, and between 4s. and 7s. for married couples.[30] The amount of relief given often depended on a person's other sources of income.[31] Several officials stated

28. Some 18% of aged males and 3% of females were members of friendly societies or other benefit clubs. Booth (1894a: 346–49). These numbers understate the importance of poor relief at various ages because the share receiving relief was lower for those whose precise age was known (20.5%) than for those whose age was not stated (30.5%). Booth obtained the precise ages of 7,624 of those surveyed.

29. Parl. Papers, *Royal Commission on the Aged Poor, Minutes of Evidence* (1895, XIV), q. 206, qq. 585–99.

30. For information on weekly benefit levels, see Parl. Papers, *Royal Commission on the Aged Poor, Minutes of Evidence* (1895, XIV; 1895, XV), q. 574, q. 2039, q. 2803, qq. 3302–3, q. 5790, q. 7935, qq. 13,777–80, and Booth (1894a: 341).

31. For instance, a Brighton guardian stated that weekly benefits varied from 2s. 6d. to 4s. for a single person and from 5s. to 8s. for a married couple "according to circumstances." Parl. Papers, *Royal Commission on the Aged Poor, Minutes of Evidence* (1895, XIV), qq. 3302–3.

that outdoor relief was given in aid of wages, although in some unions no assistance was given to old people who worked, and in others relief recipients were allowed to take odd jobs but not to have regular employment.[32]

Some unions refused to grant outdoor relief to virtually all paupers, while others gave outdoor relief to all aged persons able to maintain themselves at home. Between these two extremes there was a continuum of policies. Many unions attempted to determine the character of relief applicants, and offered outdoor relief to those deemed to be "deserving" and workhouse relief to those deemed "undeserving." Those who testified before the Royal Commission disagreed on the merits of outdoor versus indoor relief, but all agreed that the aged attached a stigma to relief in workhouses. On the other hand, there was little if any stigma associated with outdoor relief, and many paupers viewed it as an entitlement.[33]

Witnesses testified that the stricter administration of relief after 1870 in several London unions, Birmingham, Manchester, and rural Bradfield and Brixworth led to sharp reductions in pauperism rates, as persons willing to accept outdoor relief refused to enter workhouses.[34] While some praised the restriction of outdoor relief for improving thrift and morality among the poor, others maintained that the decline in pauperism rates associated with the workhouse test came at a high price, in the form of increased hardship for the aged.[35]

III. Gender Differences in Old Age Pauperism

There were substantial differences in male and female pauperism rates and in the methods used to relieve male and female paupers in Victorian England. The day count and 12-month estimated pauperism rates for men and women 65 and older in each registration division from 1871 to 1908 are presented in Table 5.9. The one-day pauperism rates were higher for old women than men

32. For evidence that relief was given in aid of wages, see Parl. Papers, *Royal Commission on the Aged Poor, Minutes of Evidence* (1895, XIV; 1895, XV), qq. 2,243–45, q. 2,929, qq. 7,518–22, q. 13,788, qq. 15,346–47. For evidence that in some unions outdoor relief was not given to persons working, see qq. 14,215–19.

33. Sir Hugh Owen stated that a pauper's relatives "often will not move a finger to help as long as the person can get outdoor relief, but if he has to go into the workhouse it is regarded as a reflection upon themselves, and assistance which would never be given under other circumstances is given, when the alternative is the workhouse." On the views of paupers, and their relatives, toward indoor and outdoor relief, see Parl. Papers, *Royal Commission on the Aged Poor, Minutes of Evidence* (1895, XIV; 1895, XV), q. 211, q. 1,926, q. 2,814, q. 5,791, qq. 6,041–42, q. 6,720, qq. 7,919–20, q. 8,710, qq. 11,024–25.

34. On the effects of stricter administration of poor relief, see Parl. Papers, *Royal Commission on the Aged Poor, Minutes of Evidence* (1895, XIV), q. 236, q. 2,493, qq. 2,851–55, qq. 4,156–73, qq. 5,088–89, qq. 9,774–78.

35. See, for example, Parl. Papers, *Royal Commission on the Aged Poor, Minutes of Evidence* (1895, XIV), q. 4,908, qq. 6,086–91, qq. 6,574–75.

TABLE 5.9. Pauperism Rates for Men and Women 65 and Older, Day and Year Counts

Registration Division	Year/Day Count	1871		1881		1891		1908	
		Day	Year	Day	Year	Day	Year	Day	Year
London									
Male	1.849	23.1	42.7	21.8	40.4	22.3	41.2	25.6	47.3
Female	1.448	31.0	44.9	23.9	34.7	21.0	30.4	21.5	31.1
South East									
Male	1.516	23.0	34.9	16.5	25.1	15.8	23.9	14.1	21.3
Female	1.271	32.1	40.7	22.1	28.1	19.2	24.4	16.2	20.6
South Midlands									
Male	1.432	26.5	37.9	19.7	28.3	17.4	24.9	16.0	22.9
Female	1.273	38.7	49.2	28.4	36.2	22.6	28.8	19.0	24.2
East									
Male	1.423	24.0	34.1	17.2	24.5	16.9	24.1	18.2	25.9
Female	1.256	35.6	44.8	26.0	32.6	23.6	29.6	23.8	29.8
South West									
Male	1.362	25.1	34.2	21.1	28.7	17.6	24.0	14.7	20.0
Female	1.207	37.9	45.7	32.3	38.9	26.6	32.1	20.8	25.1
West Midlands									
Male	1.619	20.0	32.3	18.9	30.6	17.4	28.2	17.2	27.8
Female	1.322	29.4	38.9	24.4	32.3	21.8	28.8	19.2	25.4
North Midlands									
Male	1.463	18.5	27.1	14.8	21.6	15.3	22.4	17.3	25.3
Female	1.264	29.6	37.5	22.7	28.6	21.8	27.5	22.5	28.5
North West									
Male	1.849	17.0	31.4	15.4	28.6	14.0	25.9	14.8	27.4
Female	1.448	27.1	39.2	19.6	28.4	17.2	24.8	16.0	23.1
Yorkshire									
Male	1.625	15.0	24.3	14.4	23.3	12.9	21.0	13.6	22.0
Female	1.352	25.5	34.5	21.5	29.1	18.1	24.5	16.0	21.7
North									
Male	1.557	15.6	24.4	13.5	21.0	11.5	17.8	14.5	22.5
Female	1.264	28.8	36.5	21.8	27.6	18.0	22.8	18.9	23.8

Source: Data on the annual number of non-able-bodied paupers for each registration division from the annual Reports of the Poor Law Board (1861) and the Local Government Board (1871–1908).

Notes: The ratio of the year count to the day count of aged paupers for London in 1891–92 is far larger than that for any other division, and almost certainly overstates the extent of London pauperism. In column 1, I set the ratio for London equal to that for the North West.

in all registration divisions except London throughout the period. The gender differences were largest in the more rural regions—the East, South West, and North. The relationship between the 12-month male and female pauperism rates is less clear cut. Column 1 shows that the ratio of the number of paupers who received relief at some point over the 12-month period ending on March 25, 1892, to the day count for January 1, 1892, was larger for old men than women in all ten divisions. Old women were more likely to be "permanent" paupers who received relief week in and week out, while old men were more likely to receive relief for only part of each year.[36] As a result, the differences in male and female 12-month pauperism rates are smaller than the day count differences, and after 1881 male pauperism rates were higher than female rates in London and the industrial North West. Table 5.9 also shows the changes in male and female pauperism rates over time. From 1871 to 1908, the female pauperism rate (both one-day and 12-month) declined by more than the male rate for all ten registration divisions.[37] The decline in both male and female pauperism was especially pronounced during the 1870s.

The form of relief offered to the aged differed markedly between men and women. Table 5.10 shows that far more old men than women were relieved in workhouses in each registration division throughout the late nineteenth century. The male-female differential became more pronounced following the Crusade Against Outrelief. Despite changes over time in the use of the workhouse, those registration divisions that relieved a relatively large (small) share of males in workhouses also relieved a relatively large (small) share of females in workhouses throughout the period from 1861 to 1908.

There were several economic reasons for the male-female differential in pauperism rates. Old women were far less likely to be employed than men and were paid lower wages. The 1899 test census (Table 5.7) found that nearly three-quarters of women 65 and older had weekly incomes from all sources of 10s. or less, as compared to 46% of men. Old women also were less likely to have any savings or benefits from friendly societies. Booth's 1892–93 survey found that 32% of widows and single women 65 and older were able to live off of earnings and savings, less than half the share of men (or married women) who supported themselves.[38]

Old women were far more likely to obtain assistance from relatives or friends than old men. The 1899 test census found that 70% of women 65 and older with income less than 10s. and not in receipt of poor relief received help from children, other relatives, or friends, as compared to 28% of old men. These large differentials occurred in urban, rural, and mining districts. Booth's survey found

36. The annual day counts of paupers on January 1 and July 1 reveal substantial seasonal fluctuations in the number of old men in workhouses. There typically were 20–25% more old men relieved in workhouses in January than in July, whereas the increase in the number of old women relieved in workhouses in winter was only 5–10%. The seasonality in male indoor pauperism suggests that many old men were able to get enough work to maintain themselves in the summer. See MacKinnon (1984: 111).

37. For London, both the one-day and 12-month male pauperism rates increased from 1871 to 1908, while the female one-day and 12-month rates declined.

38. Booth (1894a: 346–52) found that most of the widows who were able to subsist off of savings "had an independence left them by their husbands."

TABLE 5.10. Percentage of Male and Female Paupers 65 and Older Relieved in Workhouses

Registration Division	1861	1871	1881	1891	1901	1908
London						
Male	54.6	50.9	79.8	82.3	81.7	80.5
Female	35.8	26.7	48.0	50.1	48.4	47.0
South East						
Male	28.2	29.4	45.4	46.7	47.8	51.8
Female	9.2	8.6	14.7	15.9	17.1	18.7
South Midlands						
Male	20.7	21.8	32.4	33.1	34.3	37.1
Female	4.9	4.8	8.6	9.6	11.3	12.8
East						
Male	19.5	20.8	31.4	31.5	34.0	34.9
Female	4.9	5.1	7.9	8.5	11.7	11.5
South West						
Male	12.2	14.5	20.1	20.9	23.8	30.8
Female	4.4	4.8	6.4	6.6	7.9	10.3
West Midlands						
Male	19.5	25.0	36.8	38.5	42.8	46.4
Female	6.1	7.1	11.7	13.4	15.3	16.8
North Midlands						
Male	17.2	19.6	30.9	27.2	28.9	31.7
Female	4.6	4.4	7.3	6.9	7.2	9.3
North West						
Male	30.4	42.4	59.3	61.3	62.2	65.5
Female	12.6	18.9	29.1	29.9	27.0	27.5
Yorkshire						
Male	19.3	25.5	36.7	38.8	41.6	44.2
Female	5.2	5.8	9.5	12.1	13.4	14.2
North						
Male	18.9	24.4	39.2	39.9	40.7	42.8
Female	5.5	6.7	11.0	11.4	12.9	13.0

Source: Data on the percentage of non-able-bodied paupers relieved in workhouses for each registration division from the annual Reports of the Poor Law Board (1861) and the Local Government Board (1871–1908).

that 27% of women and 18% of men 65 and older received help from relatives or charity, although the male-female differential declined with age.

Why were aged male paupers more likely to be relieved in workhouses than aged female paupers? Local officials denied treating old men differently than old women, and in particular "denied that old men were systematically refused outdoor relief." Some unions claimed to make indoor/outdoor relief decisions based on the character of the applicant, and there is evidence that women were more likely than men to be judged of "good character." In his testimony before the Royal Commission on the Aged Poor, Booth stated that one reason why so many more old women than men were granted outdoor relief was because "a very large number of [women] are decent respectable people."[39]

Old people who lived with relatives were able to get by on a small amount of outdoor relief, and there is some evidence that children were more willing to have their aged mothers live with them than their fathers. Anderson maintained that "old people who were able to make some contribution to the family with whom they lived were most likely to be welcomed, while those who imposed a particular strain on the family were most likely to be rejected." Old women typically were better able to perform useful domestic functions, such as child minding, cooking, and cleaning, than were old men. Crowther suggested that children often were willing to assist their mothers but not their fathers because "affectionate ties with the mother were likely to be stronger." Some contemporaries maintained that old men were more willing to enter workhouses than old women.[40] In sum, the male-female differential in workhouse relief was the result of a combination of administrative, economic, and social causes.

During the Crusade Against Outrelief, the female pauperism rate declined by more than that for males, while the share of men relieved in workhouses increased far more than that for women. How can these two results be reconciled? Is this evidence that local Poor Law authorities treated old men and women differently? Suppose that the same share of men and women were offered workhouse relief during the crusade. If old men were more likely to accept indoor relief while women were more likely to refuse relief altogether rather than enter a workhouse, we would observe both a greater decline in the share of old women on relief and a greater increase in the share of old men relieved in workhouses. The same result would be observed if children were willing to assist their mothers, but not their fathers, rather than have them enter a workhouse. It seems reasonable to conclude, along with Thane, that "the change of policy [initiated by the crusade] hit women especially hard since they had greatly outnumbered men as recipients of outdoor relief."[41] This was one of the (presumably) unintended consequences of the crusade, the sort of effect that economists love to point out.

IV. Cross-Sectional Analysis of Pauperism in 1891–92

In *The Aged Poor in England and Wales*, Booth presented data on pauperism rates among those aged 65 and older, as well as other demographic and economic information, for every Poor Law union in England and Wales in

---

39. MacKinnon (1984: 110). Parl. Papers, *Royal Commission on the Aged Poor, Minutes of Evidence* (1895, XV), q. 10,865.

40. Anderson (1977: 51); Crowther (1981: 234); MacKinnon (1984: 110–11).

41. Thane (1996: 34).

1891–92, obtained from Ritchie's return of pauperism, the 1891 census, and various LGB reports. These data present the best available snapshot of the Poor Law's role in assisting the elderly in late Victorian England.

The data include information for 585 English Poor Law unions on the number of persons who received poor relief during the 12-month period ending in March 1892, for three age groups—those younger than 16, "prime-age" adults (aged 16–64), and those 65 and over.[42] For each age group, the data provide the number (and share) who received relief in workhouses, outdoor relief, and medical relief during the year. In two-thirds of Poor Law unions, the share of persons 65 and older who received poor relief during the 12-month period was between 20% and 40%; in about one in five unions it was less than 20%, and in one in eight unions it exceeded 40%.

CONTEMPORARIES' EXPLANATIONS FOR DIFFERENCES IN PAUPERISM RATES ACROSS UNIONS

How did contemporaries explain these large differences across unions in elderly pauperism rates? Most focused on the local administration of relief. Unions in which guardians readily gave outdoor relief, without enquiring into the character of applicants or pressuring children to assist their parents, had high pauperism rates, while unions that strictly administered relief, and offered the workhouse to persons of bad character and those whose children refused to assist them, had low pauperism rates. All agreed that the aged attached a stigma to indoor relief and that, other things equal, the offer of the workhouse lowered pauperism rates. The poor's objections to the workhouse were not necessarily those portrayed by early and mid-Victorian writers such as Charles Dickens—by the 1860s workhouses had "ceased to threaten cold, hunger, and mistreatment."[43] Sir Hugh Owen testified that "the great majority" of aged paupers in workhouses were "better fed, better housed, and better provided for than they ever were before." The poor objected to the discipline of the workhouse and to their loss of freedom—a witness before the Royal Commission on the Aged Poor stated that the poor "look upon the workhouse as a kind of prison." Moreover, the acceptance of workhouse relief threatened "social disgrace" both for the pauper who accepted it and for his or her family.[44]

---

42. The data set includes all but one English Poor Law Union. The excluded union is the City of London, the financial district, for which some data are not available.

43. Crowther (1981: 246). See Dickens's description of workhouse life in chapter 2 of *Oliver Twist* ([1838] 2002).

44. Parl. Papers, *Royal Commission on the Aged Poor, Minutes of Evidence* (1895, XIV), q. 211, q. 5,791, q. 6,720. See also q. 1,926, q. 2,814, q. 8,710.

Most contemporaries agreed that differences in the availability of employ-ment for the aged were a major reason for differences in pauperism rates across unions. Booth maintained that old workers were better able to find full- or part-time employment in agriculture than in urban areas, based on the responses he received to a questionnaire on the condition of the local aged population sent to clergy throughout England and Wales.[45] Many of the responses for urban districts noted the absence of work for the aged. In Sheffield there was practically no employment for old men, although "a few act as night watch-men, gather coal on the roads, sweep crossings." In Dewsbury, "men after 60 find work very scarce; mills do not employ them unless skilled," while in Birmingham "the chances of the aged getting casual labour are restricted by the competition of those between 45 and 60."[46]

The responses from rural unions were more mixed, but many reported that work for healthy old people was plentiful. Several unions reported that "field work is available for men as long as they are able to do it." In many agricul-tural districts jobs existed for the old because of the out-migration of younger workers. Booth concluded that in rural districts "old men keep their vigour longer, and even when feeble or ailing can still obtain and do some agricultural work." By contrast, in towns old men "break down at an earlier age," and are the victims of "increased competition for such work as . . . [they] are able to perform." The "effective working life is ten years longer in the country than in the town, or, speaking generally, is as seventy to sixty."[47]

Historians disagree as to the relative availability of jobs in rural and urban districts. Thane contends that "old men could work longest in agriculture," and Macnicol concludes that agricultural districts provided older workers with "a myriad of casual or light employment opportunities." Conversely, Hunt main-tains that "there were more opportunities for old men and women to earn at least part of their own maintenance" in towns than in rural districts. Johnson argues that the occupational data reported in the censuses of 1881 to 1911 do not support the notion "that it was becoming increasingly difficult for [urban] workers to obtain a position after the age of 50," although he found evidence that many urban workers in old age switched from jobs in high-paying sectors to jobs in low-paying sectors.[48]

45. It appears that Booth sent the questionnaire to clergy in all 648 English and Welsh Poor Law unions. He received responses from 360 unions (1894a: 106–7).

46. Similar responses were obtained from Leicester, Darlington, South Shields, Gateshead, Hartlepool, Walsall, Stoke-on-Trent, and Liverpool. Booth (1894a: 108–41, 186–217). Several large cities did not respond to the questionnaire, and for reasons not completely clear, Booth did not report any responses from London unions.

47. Booth (1894a: 150–77, 262–309, 321–22). Spender (1892: 23–46) found that for many urban trades workers' wages declined sharply after age 55, and even earlier for dock workers and other low-skilled workers employed in heavy labor.

48. Thane (2000: 275); Macnicol (1998: 49–50); Hunt (1989: 418); Johnson (1994: 114, 120).

Contemporaries offered additional reasons why old age pauperism rates were lower in rural than in urban unions. Many agricultural laborers had small allotments of land or gardens on which to grow food and perhaps keep a pig. Booth argued that the elderly's housing costs were lower in rural unions, and that neighbors were more likely to offer "friendly assistance in case of need" in rural areas than in towns. Rural neighborliness was countered to some degree by urban charity, but charitable assistance was "more spasmodic" and demoralizing in towns.[49]

Booth also stressed the regional nature of pauperism. He grouped Poor Law unions into six industrial categories, and calculated pauperism rates for persons 65 and older in 1891–92 for a sample of unions in each category.[50] For England and Wales as a whole, old age pauperism was lowest in residential unions, highest in seaports, and similar across manufacturing, mining, and agricultural unions. For each industrial category, pauperism rates were lower in the North than in the Midlands, East, or South. The North-South differential was especially large in purely agricultural districts, where the old age pauperism rate in the North (15.5%) was less than half that in the East (34%) or South (32.5%). The regional differences in pauperism rates *within* industrial categories were larger than the differences across industrial categories.

The differences within industrial categories were caused to some extent by regional wage differentials. Wages in agriculture and the building trades generally are considered to be representative of rural and urban wage rates. Agricultural wages were higher in northern than in southern districts, and, with the exception of high-wage London, wages in the building trades were higher in northern than in southern towns. The higher wage rates in northern districts enabled workers to save more and join friendly societies, and enabled those who continued to work after age 65 to be better able to get by without applying for poor relief. In addition, higher wages enabled children who lived near their aged parents to offer them more financial assistance.[51]

Regional differences in economic circumstances affected pauperism rates in one other way. Children were more likely to assist their aged parents if they lived near them. Other things equal, old people in districts with low out-migration rates would be more likely to have children living nearby, and

49. Parl. Papers, *Royal Commission on the Aged Poor, Minutes of Evidence* (1895, XIV), qq. 5,906–10; Parl. Papers, *Royal Commission on the Aged Poor, Minutes of Evidence* (1895, XV), q. 14,123, q. 15,196, q. 15,246. Booth (1894a: 47–48).

50. Booth (1894a: 16–19). A total of 198 unions were included. The sample omitted unions from London and large cities.

51. Bowley (1900: 59, 63); Hunt (1973: 4–5; 1989: 421). Rural living costs were similar across regions from 1861 to 1911. See Hunt (1973: 80–87). The cost of living was higher in London than in other cities. Real wages for London building trades workers were similar to those of building trades workers in large northern and midlands cities. Great Britain, Board of Trade, *Report of an Enquiry into Working Class Rents, Housing and Retail Prices* (1908), xliv–xlv.

therefore more likely to receive help from their children, than those in districts with high out-migration rates. Out-migration rates were especially high in the low-wage, and rural, South Midlands, East, and South West.[52] As a result, a larger share of old people in the South than in the high-wage North had no children to which they could turn for assistance, and were forced to apply for poor relief when they could no longer support themselves.

Contemporaries noted that pauperism rates were higher in London than in other large cities, and higher than in any other geographical division. These high pauperism rates were not a result of the lax administration of poor relief. London paupers were more than twice as likely to be relieved in workhouses as were paupers in England as a whole. The peculiarities of the metropolis led Booth to conclude that London should be considered "apart from the rest of the country" in analyzing the causes of old age pauperism.[53]

Finally, Booth and other commentators argued that the North's low pauperism rates were to a large extent "due to the character of the people."[54] According to this view, northern workers had bought into the mid-Victorian ethic of respectability and self-help to a much greater extent than had southern workers. Northerners were more likely to have savings accounts and to be members of friendly societies, and therefore less likely to apply for assistance from the Poor Law.

QUANTITATIVE ANALYSIS OF DIFFERENCES IN PAUPERISM ACROSS POOR LAW UNIONS

The cross-sectional dataset includes, for each English Poor Law union in 1891–92, data on the share of aged persons receiving poor relief, population, density, industrial character (manufacturing, mining, shipping, agricultural, residential), the share of the population living in crowded conditions (defined as two or more persons per room), the share of old persons in the population, and the value of rateable property per capita (a measure of unions' overall wealth).[55] The data are used to estimate regression equations to explain variations across English unions in the extent of pauperism among persons aged 65 and older.

52. On migration, see Cairncross (1949), Baines (1985), and Boyer and Hatton (1997). Most migrants were young adults. Regional differences in the share of the population 65 and older largely were driven by differences in migration rates. See Booth (1894a: 11–13). In 1891, the share of the population 65 and older ranged from 5.6% to 7.1% in the four southern registration divisions and from 3.4% to 4.1% in the three northern divisions.

53. Booth (1894a: 14–15, 23–24).

54. Booth (1894a: 15–19, 24).

55. This section draws heavily on Boyer and Schmidle (2009).

There are limitations to the quantitative analysis. Private charity was an alternative to poor relief, and some measure of its availability should be included as an independent variable in the regressions. Unfortunately, data on the availability of charity at the union level do not exist.[56] Nor do data exist on the employment opportunities of aged males or females within a union, other than Booth's categorization of the union's industrial structure. Despite these data limitations, the regression analysis nonetheless yields useful insights into the determinants of variations across unions in old age pauperism.

Table 5.11 presents mean values for several variables for five categories of unions, grouped by population size. It shows the extent to which London unions were different from unions in the rest of England. Outside of the metropolis, the mean share of the aged receiving poor relief was similar across rural and urban unions. Urban unions relieved a larger share of paupers in workhouses than did rural unions, although even here provincial urban unions behaved more like rural unions than London unions. Old people formed a much larger percentage of the population in rural than in urban unions, mainly because of the large amounts of rural-urban migration of young persons.

Regressions to explain the variations in old age pauperism rates across English Poor Law unions are presented in Table 5.12. The dependent variable is defined as the percentage of persons 65 and older who received poor relief other than short-term medical assistance during the 12-month period ending in March 1892.[57] The independent variables include the percentage of paupers relieved in workhouses, population density, the percentage of the population living in crowded conditions, the union's rateable value per capita (the size of the tax base), the number of persons 65 and older per 10,000 population, a series of dummy variables for the industrial character of

56. The literature on privately funded almshouses, a substitute for poor relief, suggests that they provided for only "a small proportion of the elderly," that they "tended to cater for the 're-spectable poor' . . . rather than the indigent or disreputable poor," and that they were more prevalent in southern than northern England. While almshouses were important in some localities, they played a relatively small role in relieving the aged—Goose (2014: 48) estimated that in 1870 the maximum number of residents in English almshouses was 13,360, less than 1% of persons 60 and older, the typical age at which one became eligible to enter an almshouse. The existence of one or more almshouses in a union probably led to a reduction in the number of aged persons on poor relief, but their small size (the typical almshouse held no more than 10 persons) suggests that they had only a minor effect on the pauperism rate. Nor is there reason to expect that the existence of an almshouse affected a union's use of the workhouse test. On the role played by almshouses, see Goose and Basten (2009), Leivers (2009), and Goose (2014).

57. In 1891–92, 2% of paupers 65 and over received only short-term medical assistance outside of the workhouse. For a discussion of the importance of medical assistance provided by the Poor Law, see Digby (1994: 244–53; 2000).

TABLE 5.11. Descriptive Statistics by Size of Poor Law Union

	Population <20,000 (Mean)	Population >20,000 but <50,000 (Mean)	Population >50,000 but <100,000 (Mean)	Population >100,000 (Mean)	London Unions (Mean)
% of population 65 and older receiving poor relief	29.2	27.8	25.8	27.2	42.0
% receiving poor relief other than medical assistance	27.6	26.3	24.7	25.2	38.3
% of paupers relieved in workhouses	31.9	33.1	36.5	46.4	82.3
% of population living in crowded conditions	11.4	10.8	14.5	19.8	34.0
Number 65 and older per 10,000 population	754.2	617.2	454.3	354.3	400.2
Number of Poor Law unions	245	180	75	56	29

Source: Calculated from data reported in Booth (1894a).

the union, and a series of regional dummies; for a subset of rural unions, the weekly wage paid to agricultural laborers also is included.[58] The dependent variable and all independent variables, except the dummies, are measured in logarithms.

Table 5.12 reports the estimated coefficients for the independent variables from three regressions—one including all 585 unions, one excluding the 29 London unions, and one for a subset of rural and semirural unions.[59] The workhouse test had a strong deterrent effect in each regression—a 10% increase in the share of paupers relieved in workhouses led to a 3.5–3.6% decline in the old age pauperism rate. Population density and the share of the population living in crowded conditions had small positive effects on pauperism. Neither the size of a union's tax base nor the size of its aged population had a significant effect

58. Booth grouped unions into seven industrial types—manufacturing, manufacturing and trade, mining, agriculture, agriculture and town, shipping, and residential. The regions in the regressions are defined by Booth and are slightly different from the registration divisions from the census.

59. The complete set of regression results can be found in Boyer and Schmidle (2009).

TABLE 5.12. Regressions to Explain Old Age Pauperism, 1891–92

	All Unions	No London	All Rural
Constant	4.488	4.659	7.112
	(0.485)	(0.482)	(0.789)
% relieved in workhouses	−0.364	−0.360	−0.350
	(0.035)	(0.034)	(0.034)
Rateable value per capita	0.036	−0.011	−0.107
	(0.050)	(0.055)	(0.066)
Density (persons per acre)	0.063	0.059	0.006
	(0.017)	(0.017)	(0.025)
% of population crowded	0.068	0.055	0.051
	(0.026)	(0.026)	(0.027)
No. 65+ per 10,000 population	-0.081	−0.090	−0.210
	(0.076)	(0.075)	(0.123)
Agricultural wage	—	—	−0.516
			(0.127)
London	0.657	—	—
	(0.088)		
North	0.055	0.056	0.034
	(0.053)	(0.052)	(0.059)
Midlands	0.279	0.274	0.190
	(0.048)	(0.047)	(0.055)
East	0.520	0.505	0.329
	(0.057)	(0.056)	(0.070)
South	0.571	0.544	0.391
	(0.051)	(0.050)	(0.060)
South West	0.470	0.457	0.317
	(0.056)	(0.055)	(0.064)
R^2	0.440	0.426	0.444
N	585	556	458

Note: Dependent variable is the share of persons aged 65 and older in receipt of poor relief. The dependent variable and all independent variables, except the dummies, are measured in logarithms. Standard errors are in parentheses.

on the pauperism rate. The coefficients on the dummy variables for industrial character were small and are not reported in the table. Following Booth, the unions were divided geographically into seven regions. The industrial North is the excluded region. The North-South differences in pauperism stressed by contemporaries and shown in Tables 5.4 and 5.6 are clearly revealed in the regressions. Other things equal, pauperism rates in the East, South, and South West were significantly higher than those in the North or industrial North; pauperism rates in the Midlands were above those in northern regions but below those in the South.

Column 3 gives regression results for a subset of rural unions for which agricultural laborers' wage data are available.[60] The agricultural wage had a strong effect on pauperism—a 10% increase in wages led to a 5.2% decline in the old age pauperism rate. The higher workers' incomes were, the better able they were to provide for their old age. Including farm wages reduces the magnitude of the coefficients on the regional dummies somewhat, but they remain significantly different from zero. In other words, the North-South differentials in old age pauperism rates remain even when relief administration, wage rates, and the industrial nature of unions are taken into account.[61] The regional dummies might be serving as proxies for differences in the availability of work outside of agriculture not picked up by the "industrial character" dummies. Job opportunities *within* agriculture also differed across regions—winter employment for the aged must have been especially scarce in the grain-producing South and East.[62] By contrast, the dummy variables might be picking up noneconomic differences across regions.

REGIONAL WELFARE CULTURES?

North-South differentials in pauperism existed long before 1861. The first national count of relief recipients, for April 1802–April 1803, revealed an overall pauperism rate of 14.7% for the four southern registration divisions and 8.3% for the three northern divisions.[63] These regional differentials persisted throughout the nineteenth century. Booth concluded that the North's low pauperism rates were "undoubtedly due to the character of the people," and other commentators agreed. Northerners were deemed to be more likely to have savings accounts and be members of friendly societies than southerners, and to attach a greater stigma to applying for poor relief. The quintessential northern industrial worker was "Rochdale man," described as a "respectable self-helping, self-educating working man with his cooperative society, savings bank and chapel." More recently, King has argued that there were "very substantial . . . differences

---

60. The wage data are from Appendix II of Board of Trade, *Report on the Wages and Earnings of Agricultural Labourers in the United Kingdom* (1900). While I would have preferred to use wage data from an earlier year, the relative level of wage rates across Poor Law Unions probably changed very little over the 10–15 years leading up to 1894. Agricultural wage rates are a good proxy for rural workers' living standards. Hunt (1973: 4); Bowley (1914: 617). The regression analysis uses nominal wages. Hunt (1973: 80–87) concluded that rural living costs "did not vary significantly in different parts of the country."

61. The North-South differentials were not caused by regional differences in the use of private almshouses since almshouses were more prevalent in southern than northern England.

62. Goose (2005: 363–67, 371–76).

63. Parl. Papers, *Abstract of Returns Relative to the Expense and Maintenance of the Poor Law* (1803–4, XIII), pp. 714–15. On regional differentials in pauperism during the eighteenth century, see King (2000).

in entitlement, relief generosity, and relief sentiment" between northern and southern England. In much of the South and East, "custom and a consensual decision-making process created a raft of 'welfare junkies' whose first response when faced with life-cycle stress was to turn to the poor law." By contrast, in the North and West there was "a culture of self-reliance and making do." Southerners were more likely than northerners to apply for poor relief, and local relief administrators were more willing to offer them assistance.[64]

What caused these regional differences in welfare culture, and when did they begin? King maintains that the differences date back to the early eighteenth century if not before—the stingy North and West had "a complex religious history and arguably the most distinctive and potentially puritanical cultures," and also had more developed systems of private charity. Billinge suggests that distinct regional cultures began to develop in the second half of the eighteenth century, as a result of the uneven geographic nature of the industrial revolution.[65]

Distinct regional attitudes toward welfare might have emerged during the heyday of the Old Poor Law from 1795 to 1834. Regional differences in the role of poor relief grew in the late eighteenth century, when the deteriorating economic environment for southern farmworkers led to a sharp increase in demand for public assistance in the grain-producing South and East. The relief of able-bodied laborers and their families was so widespread during the first third of the nineteenth century that the stigma associated with receiving poor relief must have declined. Southerners became accustomed to being on relief, and many came to believe that they had a right to public assistance during hard times.[66] The reforms of 1834 and the Crusade Against Outrelief increased the stigma against accepting relief throughout England, but regional differentials remained.

The aged in Victorian England had grown up under the Old Poor Law— many of those raised in the South and East had lived in families that received child allowances from the parish.[67] The customs established before 1834 might

64. Rose (1977: 185); King (2000: 267–69).

65. King (2000: 268); Billinge (2004).

66. Boyer (1990: 31–43). Contemporaries claimed that the widespread granting of outdoor relief reduced the stigma that the poor attached to applying for assistance. According to the report of the Royal Poor Law Commission, there was among the poor in southern England a "constantly diminishing reluctance to claim an apparent benefit, the receipt of which imposes no sacrifice, except a sensation of shame quickly obliterated by habit, even if not prevented by example." Parl. Papers, *Report on the Administration and Practical Operation of the Poor Laws* (1834, XXVII), p. 25.

67. More than three-quarters of the rural parishes in the South and South East that responded to the Royal Poor Law Commission's Rural Queries granted child allowances to poor workers in 1832. Only 20% of responding northern parishes granted child allowances. Boyer (1990: 153, 169).

have continued to influence the behavior of the aged poor into the 1890s—the shadow cast by Speenhamland was quite long. However, regional differences in attitudes toward welfare should have declined in the last decade of the nineteenth century, as the number of individuals who remembered the period before 1834 fell. This would help to explain the convergence in old age pauperism rates after 1891.

V. The Road to 1908

The 1895 Report of the Royal Commission on the Aged Poor was optimistic about the future trend in old age pauperism. It concluded that "the number of aged poor who seek public relief, while still very large, has much lessened in proportion in the last 30 years. . . . We are encouraged in our hopes for the future by the remarkable growth of thrift, as shown by the savings banks and insurance in friendly societies, which are largely increasing in popularity and importance. The self-reliance and strength of character of the working classes, thus evinced, will greatly aid in the solution of the problems of old age poverty." The report concluded that "no fundamental alterations are needed in the existing system of poor law relief as it affects the aged," although it added that "where outdoor relief is given the amount should be adequate to meet fully the extent of the destitution."[68]

Booth did not share the optimism of the commission's report. He and four other commissioners did not sign the 1895 report, and instead offered a brief report of their own. They argued that the decline in aged pauperism in previous decades had been less impressive than the majority of commissioners supposed, and added that it was "deplorable" that in 1891–92 roughly "three in ten" persons 65 and older were "compelled to apply for parish relief." Moreover, there were large numbers of aged persons "who endure great privations in order to keep off the rates." Such declines in pauperism as had occurred they attributed to the "stricter administration" of the Poor Law and "the increased prosperity of the working classes." However, the administration of relief could not be made any stricter "without fear of a reaction," and the rate of economic growth appeared to be slowing down. Booth and his colleagues recommended that the government create a new commission to examine the costs and benefits of a system of old age pensions outside of the Poor Law and to construct, if possible, a "practicable scheme . . . for the assistance of the aged and respectable poor."[69]

68. The report examined various schemes for government-financed or -assisted pension programs to provide for the aged poor outside of the Poor Law, but rejected each for "financial and economic" reasons. Parl. Papers, *Report of the Royal Commission on the Aged Poor* (1895, XIV), pp. lxxxiii–lxxxvii.

69. Parl. Papers, *Report of the Royal Commission on the Aged Poor* (1895, XIV), pp. xciii–xcvi.

Data on old age pauperism rates after 1892 support Booth's contention that the Royal Commission was overly optimistic about the future. A comparison of Tables 5.2b and 5.3 shows that from January 1, 1892, to March 31, 1906, old age pauperism rates declined in only four southern divisions. In the Midlands, the North, and London, pauperism rates remained constant or increased slightly. For England and Wales as a whole, the old age pauperism rate was nearly identical on the two dates.

Why didn't old age pauperism continue to decline after 1892? From 1891 to 1908 the share of aged paupers relieved in workhouses increased in nine of ten registration divisions. However, the increased use of the workhouse does not necessarily imply that relief administration was becoming stricter. The years 1896–1904 witnessed a sharp increase in capital expenditure on workhouse construction, and much of the increased spending went to upgrading workhouse medical facilities. The improvements in hospital care, particularly in urban unions, made the aged poor more willing to enter workhouses. The stigma effect of workhouse relief, at least as it applied to sick old persons, was declining at the turn of the century.[70]

The "prosperity of the working classes" increased at a much slower rate after 1891 than it had in the previous two decades. From 1891–92 to 1906–7, real full-time wages of manual workers increased by 14.1%, after increasing by 37.9% from 1871–72 to 1891–92. The increase in purchasing power was even smaller in key sectors—real wages in the building trades increased by 8.1% from 1891–92 to 1906–7, and real wages in agriculture increased by 7.8%.[71] Moreover, there was an upward trend in unemployment after 1892. The pressure on living standards was most severe among low-skilled workers, whose employment opportunities deteriorated both absolutely and relative to those of skilled workers.[72] Those who were most likely to turn to the Poor Law for assistance in old age suffered at best a stagnation of income in the decades leading up to the adoption of the Old Age Pension Act.

The Royal Commission on the Aged Poor had called for an increase in the generosity of outdoor relief to make benefits adequate to relieve destitution. However, evidence presented to the Royal Commission on the Poor Laws and Relief of Distress (1905–9) indicated that the called-for increase in benefits did

---

70. Williams (1981: 219); MacKinnon (1986: 326–27). This does not mean that the deterrent effect of the workhouse test no longer existed. In MacKinnon's (1986: 327) words, "the restriction of outrelief was much less likely to force people into the workhouse than were increases in inrelief liable to make the very poor (and the relatives they were dependent on) accept the offer of inrelief."

71. Feinstein (1995: 260–61, 264–65). From 1871–72 to 1891–92, real wages in the building trades increased by 38.7% and real wages in agriculture increased by 32.0%.

72. See Chapter 4.

not occur.[73] Writing in 1909, the Webbs concluded that "the provision for the aged and infirm actually made by the great mass of Boards of Guardians . . . is wholly unsatisfactory." In many unions, outdoor relief benefits were "insufficient to provide even the barest food, clothing and shelter."[74]

The continued high levels of old age pauperism put mounting pressure on the government to adopt a national pension scheme distinct from the Poor Law, and in 1908 Parliament passed the Old Age Pension Act, which provided weekly pensions to poor persons aged 70 and older. The Old Age Pension Act is discussed in Chapter 6.

VI. Conclusion

The estimates of old age pauperism rates for 1861 to 1908 presented here show that large-scale government support for the aged existed long before the welfare state. During the 1860s more than 35% of English persons 65 and older were in receipt of poor relief. The number of aged paupers declined thereafter as a result of the Crusade Against Outrelief and improvements in living standards. Still, in 1908 one-quarter of the population, and more than one-third of working-class persons, 65 and older received poor relief sometime during the year. The share who received relief *at some point* after they turned 65 was even higher. The results support Thomson's conclusion that "a marked willingness to redistribute resources to the aged through communal rather than familial institutions has been evident in Britain for a long time."[75]

The data presented here give some idea of the extent of economic insecurity faced by low-skilled workers in Victorian England. Despite long-run improvements in manual workers' earnings, recourse to the Poor Law remained "the normal method of supplementing income in old age."[76] The rising tide of Victorian economic growth did not raise old boats. It is necessary to realize the extent of working-class insecurity in order to understand Parliament's adoption of the Old Age Pension Act and other social welfare policies in the decade before the First World War.

73. See, for example, the testimony of Baldwyn Fleming, a general inspector of the Local Government Board. Parl. Papers, *Royal Commission on the Poor Laws and Relief of Distress, Appendix Volume I, Minutes of Evidence* (1909, XXXIX), q. 9138.

74. Webb and Webb (1909a: 321–24).

75. Thomson (1986: 367).

76. MacKinnon (1984: 348).

PART II

Constructing the Welfare State

6

Living Standards in Edwardian England and the Liberal Welfare Reforms

The decade and a half from the turn of the twentieth century to the First World War saw an outpouring of work on poverty, economic insecurity, and living standards of the poor. The studies were written by government-appointed commissions, civil servants, academics, and private individuals—they were "local and national, statistical and impressionistic, official and unofficial."[1] With few exceptions, they all reached similar conclusions. Despite growth in the average earnings of manual workers since 1850, economic insecurity and poverty remained widespread at the beginning of the new century. Many within the working class apparently had benefitted little from the rising tide of late Victorian economic growth.

The Liberal government that came to power in 1906 responded to these revelations by adopting several pieces of social welfare legislation that collectively are known as the Liberal Welfare Reforms. The legislation aimed at improving the health of working-class children, reducing poverty among the aged, establishing minimum wages for workers in "sweated industries," and reducing the income insecurity resulting from loss of work due to sickness or unemployment. The Liberal Welfare Reforms represented a sharp about-face in British social policy after seven decades of increasing stinginess toward the poor. The timing of their adoption largely can be explained by the

1. Read (1972: 151).

increased middle-class knowledge of workers' economic insecurity, along with the greater willingness of Parliament to intervene as a result of the growing political voice of the working class.

This chapter examines living standards in Edwardian England, the debate that took place in and out of government over how to deal with poverty and economic insecurity, and the adoption of the Liberal Welfare Reforms. The chapter is divided into four sections. Section I examines working-class living standards in Edwardian Britain. Studies published between 1901 and 1914 indicate that about one in seven working-class households were living in poverty in the decade before the First World War. An additional large number of households lived in constant danger of falling into poverty if the head lost an extended amount of work time due to an accident, sickness, or unemployment.

Section II examines the debate over policy responses, focusing on the Royal Commission on the Aged Poor (1893–95) and the Royal Commission on the Poor Laws and Relief of Distress (1905–9). Section III summarizes the social welfare policies adopted between 1906 and 1911. The safety net these policies created provided a minimum level of assistance outside of the Poor Law to the sick, the unemployed, and the aged, and in doing so reduced the economic insecurity associated with industrial capitalism. However, the new policies left many persons unprotected, and the benefits they provided were far from generous—they were only a tentative step toward the post-1945 welfare state.

Section IV considers the political economy of the Liberal Welfare Reforms, and argues that the social policies adopted were, in part, an unsuccessful attempt by the Liberal government to woo recently enfranchised working-class voters and slow the growing momentum of the Labour Party. Section IV also examines Edwardian Britain in a European mirror, comparing British workers' living standards and social welfare policies with living standards and social policies elsewhere in Europe. Britain's welfare reforms did not take place in isolation—several Western European countries adopted social welfare policies in the decades leading up to 1914.

I. Living Standards in Britain, 1899–1914

A wealth of information exists concerning working-class living standards in the decades leading up to the First World War. The major sources of data include the Board of Trade's wage census of 1906, poverty surveys undertaken by Rowntree in 1899 and Bowley and Burnett-Hurst in 1912–14, and the information collected by the Royal Commission on the Poor Laws and Relief of Distress.[2] This outpouring of information was a result of increased

---

2. Boyer (2004b) provides a detailed discussion of working-class living standards in the decades leading up to the First World War.

middle-class interest in the poor, which can be traced back to the late 1880s and the publication of Booth's initial estimates of poverty in London. Booth found that 30.7% of London's population and 37.4% of the working class were living in poverty, a conclusion that stunned much of middle-class Britain.[3] He followed this work with his study of poverty among the aged discussed in Chapter 5, which, along with the 1895 Report of the Royal Commission on the Aged Poor, revealed both the extent of poverty among the elderly and their need for public assistance.

Booth's pioneering work was followed by Rowntree's 1901 survey of working-class York, *Poverty: A Study of Town Life*. While Booth had defined as poor any household with an average weekly income of 18–21s. or less, Rowntree determined the "poverty line" for families of various sizes by calculating the income required "to provide the minimum of food, clothing, and shelter needful for the maintenance of merely physical health." Families whose income was below the minimum level were described as living in "primary poverty." He defined a second category, "secondary poverty," as consisting of families whose income would have been above the minimum necessary to maintain physical efficiency "were it not that some portion of it is absorbed by other expenditure, either useful or wasteful." Rowntree found that 9.9% of the population of York, and 15.5% of the working class, lived in primary poverty in 1899. Another 17.9% of the population, and 27.9% of the working class, lived in secondary poverty.[4]

The other major study of urban poverty undertaken before the war was Bowley and Burnett-Hurst's 1912–14 investigations of Reading, Northampton, Warrington, Stanley, and Bolton, published in 1915 as *Livelihood and Poverty*.[5] Bowley and Burnett-Hurst's definition of poverty was equivalent to Rowntree's primary poverty—a family was in poverty if its total income was "insufficient for the maintenance of physical health."[6] The top panel of Table 6.1 presents estimates of poverty rates for the five towns surveyed by Bowley and Burnett-Hurst and for York. The share of working-class households living in poverty varied greatly across towns, ranging from 23.2% in Reading to 5.4% in Stanley, a small north-eastern mining town. For each town, the share of working-class *individuals* in poverty was slightly higher than the share of households in

---

3. Booth (1888) contains his initial findings for East London and Hackney. The poverty rates for London as a whole are from Booth (1892b: 2:21).

4. Rowntree (1901: 110–18).

5. Bowley's study of poverty in Reading had been published previously in the *Journal of the Royal Statistical Society*. See Bowley (1913). The analysis of Bolton was published as a supplementary chapter to *Livelihood and Poverty* in 1920.

6. Bowley and Burnett-Hurst (1915: 36–37).

TABLE 6.1. Poverty Rates and Causes of Poverty in York and Bowley's Five Towns

	York 1899	Reading 1912	Northampton 1913	Warrington 1913	Stanley 1913	Bolton 1914
Population	75,812	87,693	90,064	72,100	23,294	180,851
(a) Percentage in Poverty (%)						
Working-class households						
Primary poverty	12.7	23.2	8.2	12.8	5.4	7.8
Working-class population						
Primary poverty	15.5	29.0	9.3	14.7	6.1	8.0
Town population						
Primary poverty	9.9	17.5	7.2	12.2	4.8	
(b) Causes of Poverty (%)						
Chief wage earner:						
Dead or absent	27.5	14.0	25.0	6.0		35.0
Ill or old	10.0	11.0	14.0	1.0		17.0
Out of work	2.6	2.0	3.5	3.0		3.0
Irregularly employed	3.5	4.0	9.0	3.0		6.0
In full work but:						
Low wages	43.7					
Second adult dependent			3.5			
Wage insufficient for 3 children:						
3 children or less		33.0	16.0	22.0		20.0
4 children or more		16.0	7.0	38.0		9.0
Wage sufficient for 3 children but more than 3 children	12.8	20.0	22.0	27.0		10.0

Sources: York: Rowntree (1901: 26, 111–12, 117–20); other towns: Bowley and Burnett-Hurst (1915: 38–44), Bowley and Burnett-Hurst (1920: 237, 240), Bowley and Hogg (1925: 18, 78, 104, 128, 158).

TABLE 6.2. Economic Insecurity in Bowley's Five Towns

Working-Class Households	Reading 1912	Northampton 1913	Warrington 1913	Stanley 1913	Bolton 1914
% of households below poverty line	23.2	8.2	12.8	5.4	7.8
% above, but within 6s. of poverty line	28.8	4.0	17.5	5.0	10.9
% above, but within 6–8s. of poverty line	8.4	3.3	6.1	3.0	4.1
% in poverty or within 6s. of poverty line	51.9	12.3	30.3	10.4	18.7
% in poverty or within 8s. of poverty line	60.3	15.5	36.4	13.4	22.8

Sources: Bowley and Burnett-Hurst (1915: 88, 134, 157, 172), Bowley and Burnett-Hurst (1920: 238).
Note: These estimates understate slightly the true share of households within 6s. or 8s. of the poverty line because I assume that none of the few households with incomes above the poverty line by an unknown amount had incomes within 8s. of the poverty line.

poverty. The share of the total population living in poverty varied from 17.5% in Reading to 4.8% in Stanley.[7]

The reported poverty rates understate by a large amount the extent of economic insecurity among the working class. Table 6.2 presents the share of families with incomes above but close to the poverty line for each of the towns surveyed by Bowley and Burnett-Hurst.[8] A majority of working-class households in Reading had earnings below or within 6s. of the poverty line, as did 30.3% of households in Warrington and 18.7% in Bolton. The share with incomes within 8s. of the poverty line varied from 60.3% in Reading to 13.4% in Stanley. Any event that reduced weekly income or increased expenses by a few shillings would have pushed these families into poverty, at least in the short run.

In 1904 the Board of Trade conducted a survey of nearly 2,000 urban working-class households. Gazeley and Newell, using Bowley's new standard poverty line, found that 12.1–12.3% of the households with complete data had incomes below the poverty line. Fully 40% of households headed by unskilled

7. Mann (1904) and Davies (1909) used similar methods to estimate poverty rates in the rural villages of Ridgmount, Bedfordshire, and Corsley, Wiltshire. Their results suggest that rural poverty rates, at least in southern England, were as high as or higher than urban poverty rates. See Mann (1904: 177, 185), Davies (1909: 105–7, 142–43, 147), and Freeman (2000).

8. Bowley and Burnett-Hurst stressed that their minimum standards of expenditure probably were set too low since few families spent their income solely for the purpose of maintaining physical health. See Bowley and Burnett-Hurst (1915: 36–37).

workers were living in poverty. In addition, a large number of households had incomes slightly above the poverty level, so that "a fairly minor increase in the generosity of the poverty definition would result in a large increase in the poverty rate."[9]

A comparison of the estimated poverty rates with numbers receiving poor relief reveals the extent to which Poor Law data understate the extent of poverty. From 1899 to 1913, the share of the population of England and Wales receiving poor relief at some point over a 12-month period ranged from 4.4% to 5.9%, substantially below the poverty rate in every town except Stanley. In York, 3,451 persons, 4.5% of the population, received poor relief in 1900 (not counting lunatics in asylums), fewer than half of the 7,230 persons living in primary poverty.[10] Large numbers of poor people either did not apply for public assistance or had their applications rejected by local relief officials.

The estimates reported above are snapshots of a community at a point in time. Rowntree was quick to point out that working-class households moved in and out of poverty over time, but that he observed only those in poverty when the survey was undertaken. He maintained that the life of a low-skilled worker was "marked by five alternating periods of want and comparative plenty." The laborer typically lived in poverty for part of his childhood, again during the period from when his second or third child was born until the oldest child reached 14 and began to work, and finally in old age. Rowntree concluded that "the proportion of the community who at one period or other of their lives suffer from poverty to the point of physical privation is therefore much greater, and the injurious effects of such a condition are much more widespread than would appear from a consideration of the number who can be shown to be below the poverty line at any given moment."[11]

The lower panel of Table 6.1 gives the causes of poverty, as estimated by Rowntree and Bowley and Burnett-Hurst, for five towns. The numbers reported are the percentages of households living in poverty due to each cause.[12] In all five towns the principal cause of poverty was deemed to be low wages, or low wages combined with large families. In York, 43.7% of households in poverty were poor because the household's earnings were not large enough to support a moderately sized family of four or fewer children. In nearly three-quarters of these households, the head was a general laborer. Similarly, in 60%

9. Gazeley and Newell (2011: 63–65). Using Rowntree's York standard poverty line, the share of working-class households living in poverty increases to 16.1%. The share of individuals living in poverty was 15.5% using Bowley's poverty line and 17.0% using Rowntree's poverty line.

10. Rowntree (1901: 365–67).

11. Rowntree (1901: 136–38).

12. The estimates for Reading, Northampton, Warrington, and Bolton are from a later study by Bowley and Hogg (1925) and are slightly different from those reported by Bowley and Burnett-Hurst.

TABLE 6.3. Poverty-Line Budgets for a Family of Five

	Rowntree "York" Standard 1899 (s. per week)	Bowley New Standard 1912 (s. per week)	Rowntree Human Needs Standard 1914 (s. per week)
Food	12.75	14.92	15.08
Rent	4.0	5.0[a]	6.0
Clothing	2.25	3.08[b]	5.0
Fuel	1.83	1.58	2.5
Sundries (total)	0.83		6.67
Household			1.67
Personal			5.0[c]
Total	21.67	24.58	35.25
COL index (1906 = 100)	95.4	108.5	112.0
Min. standard 1906 prices	22.71	22.65	31.47
Min. standard 1912 prices	24.65	24.58	34.15

Sources: Minimum budget data from Rowntree (1901: 110); Bowley and Burnett-Hurst (1915: 82); Rowntree (1918: 128–29).

Notes: COL = cost of living. The budgets are for a family consisting of a husband, wife, and three children aged 5–14. In the bottom two rows the three standards have been revalued to take account of price changes over time, using aggregate COL data from Feinstein (1991: 171).

[a]Bowley and Burnett-Hurst excluded rent in their estimate of a minimum standard. Their housing data suggest that the typical family of five paid rent of 5s. per week.

[b]Bowley and Burnett-Hurst's estimate for clothing includes sundries.

[c]Includes "such personal expenses as insurance and sick clubs, recreation, traveling, and numbers of other claims."

of poor households in Warrington and 49% of poor households in Reading, the chief wage earner, although regularly employed, did not earn enough to support a family of three children. The other major causes of poverty were large families and the death or illness of the chief wage earner. Each of the town surveys was undertaken at a time of low unemployment; as a result, unemployment or irregularity of work was the major cause of poverty in only 6.0–12.5% of poor households.[13]

The finding that low wage rates was a major cause of poverty was surprising to many contemporaries, and is worth examining more closely. In order to determine the purchasing power of workers' wages, it is necessary to examine the poverty-line estimates constructed by Rowntree and Bowley. Table 6.3 presents three estimates of the poverty line for a family of five. Rowntree calculated that the weekly expenditures necessary for "merely physical health" for a family consisting of a husband, wife, and three children in York in 1899 was 21.67s. He stressed that the diet allowed was quite meager,

13. In contrast, Booth (1892b: 1:146–49) found that the majority of Londoners in poverty were poor because of the casual or irregular nature of their employment.

and that the budget was "based on the assumption that *every penny earned by every member of the family* went into the family purse, and was judiciously expended upon necessities." Bowley and Burnett-Hurst's "new standard" poverty line, like Rowntree's, estimated the "minimum expenditure needed to maintain physical health."[14] While the two estimates are calculated somewhat differently, when adjusted to take account of differences in prices across years they yield virtually identical necessary minimum weekly expenditures for 1906 and 1912.

The third poverty line, Rowntree's "human needs standard," was meant to "provide for the reasonable human needs of men and women living in a civilized community." It is substantially more generous than either of the previous estimates, mainly in the amount allowed for clothing and personal sundries, including spending on trade union dues, sick clubs, "tram fares to and from work," newspapers, incidental traveling, recreation, beer, and tobacco.[15] At 1906 prices, the human needs standard for a family of five cost nearly 9s. per week more than Bowley's "new standard."

What share of adult males had earnings below that needed to support a family of five? Table 6.4 shows the distribution of weekly earnings for adult working-class males in five towns surveyed by Rowntree and Bowley and Burnett-Hurst. About one-quarter of York workers in 1899 had earnings below 21.67s., the minimum necessary to support a family of five according to Rowntree's original standard. Wage rates varied sharply across the towns studied by Bowley and Burnett-Hurst. The share of adult males with full-time earnings below 24s. was 50.5% in Reading, 27% in Northampton, 32% in Warrington, and 7% in Stanley (the poverty line for a family of five was 24.58s. in 1912). For the five towns combined, somewhere between a quarter and a third of adult males did not earn enough to support a wife and three schoolchildren. The numbers are far more pessimistic if Rowntree's human needs standard is used as the poverty line. Fewer than 15% of adult males in Reading and fewer than one-third in Northampton and Warrington earned enough to support a family of five under the human needs standard.

The data in Table 6.4 are for adult male earnings. When calculating poverty rates, it is necessary to compare *household earnings* (including earnings of wives and children living at home) with the relevant poverty line. Bowley and Burnett-Hurst found that wives or children were employed in 41% of working-class households in Reading, 45% in Warrington, 51% in Northampton, and 31% in Stanley. Combining the households of the four towns, they estimated that "per 100 households" the earning power of all those working was

14. Rowntree (1901: 111, emphasis original); Bowley and Burnett-Hurst (1915: 36–37).
15. Rowntree (1918: 9, 103–5, 128–29).

TABLE 6.4. Distribution of Weekly Wages of Adult Males—Five Towns, 1899–1913

	APPROXIMATE PERCENTAGE OF ADULT MALES IN EACH CATEGORY				
Weekly Wage	York 1899	Reading 1912	Northampton 1913	Warrington 1913	Stanley 1913
Under 20s.	10.0	15.0	13.0	3.5	4.0
20–22s.	16.0	25.0	7.0	15.0	2.0
22–24s.	10.0	10.5	7.0	13.5	3.0
24–26s.	13.0	17.0	9.0	17.0	2.0
26–28s.	6.0	5.0	7.0	6.0	7.0
28–30s.	5.0	2.5	8.0	7.0	7.0
30–31s.	25.0	11.0	22.0	7.5	7.0
31–35s.	6.0	4.0	9.0	7.0	21.0
35–40s.	4.0	6.0	8.0	12.5	19.0
40s. and over	5.0	4.0	10.0	11.0	28.0
Under 24s.	36.0	50.5	27.0	32.0	9.0
24–30s.	24.0	24.5	24.0	30.0	16.0
30s. and over	40.0	25.0	49.0	38.0	75.0

Source: Bowley and Burnett-Hurst (1915: 33).

equivalent to 142 adult males. In the absence of wives and children working, their estimated poverty rates would have been substantially higher.[16]

In sum, on the eve of the First World War 12–15% of urban working-class households had incomes below the poverty line, and an additional 15–20% of households had incomes above but close to the poverty line. The main cause of poverty in these households was the low wage rates paid to male household heads. Rowntree concluded that the going wage for unskilled labor was "insufficient to . . . maintain a family of moderate size in a state of bare physical efficiency," and Bowley and Burnett-Hurst added that a "great part" of poverty was "not accidental or due to exceptional misfortune, but a regular feature of the industries of the towns concerned. . . . To raise the wages of the worst-paid workers is the most pressing social task with which the country is confronted today."[17]

THE HEALTH CONSEQUENCES OF LIVING IN POVERTY

The serious health consequences for both children and adults associated with living in poverty had been known since the pioneering work of Chadwick

16. Bowley and Burnett-Hurst (1915: 28–31). Virtually all children working were aged 14 or older.

17. Rowntree (1901: 133); Bowley and Burnett-Hurst (1915: 41–42).

and others in the 1830s and 1840s.[18] Rowntree documented the relationship between poverty and health by selecting three sections of working-class York—representing the poorest workers, a middle group, and the best paid workers—and comparing infant and child mortality, height, weight, and general physical condition of children across the sections. For each measure, he found a strong negative correlation between health and poverty. Pember Reeves also found that poverty led to a low standard of health from her study of poor families in Lambeth. To her, "the outstanding fact about the children was ... their puny size and damaged health. ... Whatever the exact causes are which produce in each case the sickly children so common in these households, the all-embracing one is poverty."[19]

Poor health for children often translated into poor health for adults. The British public became keenly aware of the adverse health consequences of low living standards during the Boer War of 1899–1902, when approximately 30% of recruits were rejected by medical officers because they did not meet "the army's already shockingly low physical standards." Rejection rates were especially high in large cities—for the two years 1901–2, 35% of London recruits were rejected, as were 37% from Liverpool and 49% from Manchester.[20] Rejection rates were even higher in the mid-1890s—in 1893–96, 40.6% of the 236,000 recruits were rejected due to physical ailments or want of physical development. These numbers understate the share who were deemed physically unfit, because they do not include those rejected by the recruiting officers as unfit for service and therefore not medically inspected. By far the most important cause of rejection was "under chest measurement," followed by defective vision, "under weight," and "under height."[21]

The alarming number of rejections led to the creation in 1903 of the Interdepartmental Committee on Physical Deterioration, whose report of the following year provided additional evidence of "a mass of poverty, sickness, and squalor" in British cities. Sir William Taylor, Director General of the Army Medical Service, concluded in a memorandum to the committee that "the bulk of our soldiers are drawn from the unskilled labour class, and consequently

18. Chadwick ([1842] 1965); Flinn (1965: 3–37); Mokyr (2009: 295–96, 466, 479–81).

19. Rowntree (1901: 198–216); Pember Reeves (1913: 193–94).

20. Searle (2004: 305). The London data are for St. George's Barracks. Data on rejection rates by city are from Parl. Papers, *Report of the Interdepartmental Committee on Physical Deterioration*, vol. 3, App. 6 (1904, XXXII), pp. 2–3.

21. Data on rejection rates for 1893–1902 and causes of rejection are from Parl. Papers, *Report of the Interdepartmental Committee on Physical Deterioration*, vol. 1, App. 1 (1904: XXXII), pp. 96–97. Rowntree (1901: 217–19) maintained that the decline in rejection rates from 1896 to 1900 largely was a result of a lowering of standards and instructions to officers in charge of recruiting "not to send a recruit up for medical examination unless there is a reasonable probability of his passing."

from the stratum of the population living in actual poverty or close to the poverty line." He attributed "the impairment of vigour and physique among the urban poor" to "food insufficient in quantity and probably poor in quality, . . . defective housing, overcrowding and insanitary surroundings." The root cause of all of these factors was low wages. Henry Wilson, Inspector of Factories and Workshops in Newcastle upon Tyne, concluded simply that "it is the wage of the parents which determines the physique of the offspring."[22]

In its 1904 Report the Interdepartmental Committee made a series of recommendations regarding medical inspection of factory employees, reduction in overcrowding and smoke pollution, "systematic instruction" for girls "in the processes of infant feeding and management," policies to ensure the purity of the supply of milk, the systematized medical inspection of schoolchildren, the feeding of needy elementary schoolchildren by local authorities, and increased physical exercise for children in school and in "obligatory evening continuation classes." None of its recommendations dealt with the relationship between low household income and health. The committee concluded that while some might argue they offered "no immediate remedy" to the problems raised in the report, they "are confident that if their recommendations are adopted a considerable distance will have been traversed towards an amendment of the conditions they have described."[23]

Rowntree was far less optimistic about the future. He argued that, so long as "nearly 30 per cent of the population are living in poverty and are ill-housed, ill-clothed, and under-fed . . . a low average standard of physical efficiency among the wage-earning classes is inevitable." In the conclusion to Poverty, he wrote that the existence of so much poverty in "this land of abounding wealth, during a time of perhaps unexampled prosperity . . . is a fact which may well cause great searchings of heart. . . . No civilisation can be sound or stable which has at its base this mass of stunted human life."[24]

SOCIAL COMMENTARY ON THE CONDITION OF ENGLAND

The publication of Rowntree's Poverty was one of the opening salvos in what became an Edwardian debate on the "condition of England" question, perhaps not as famous as the debate of the hungry 1840s but one with as many contributors. Within the following decade many other commentators

---

22. Searle (2004: 375). Taylor's memorandum is in Appendix 1 of Parl. Papers, *Report of the Interdepartmental Committee on Physical Deterioration*, vol. 1 (1904: XXXII), pp. 96–97. Wilson's quote is from his testimony to the committee: vol. 2, q. 1,916, p. 80.

23. Parl. Papers, *Report of the Interdepartmental Committee on Physical Deterioration*, vol. 1 (1904: XXXII), pp. 84–93.

24. Rowntree (1901: 216, 304, emphasis original).

addressed issues of poverty, and the majority reached conclusions similar to Rowntree's. Two who did not were Helen Bosanquet and C. S. Loch, leaders of the Charity Organisation Society. Both responded quickly and negatively to Rowntree's book. They criticized both his (and Booth's) methodology and the very notion of the poverty line. Bosanquet rejected the "crude belief that the Poverty Line is a question of money," and described Rowntree's poverty estimates as "no statistical evidence at all but . . . merely a summary of impressions." She maintained that the economic position of individuals is "dependent upon qualities which are not primarily or obviously economic. . . . All economic problems are ultimately ethical." Loch, Secretary of the COS from 1875 to 1913, referred to Rowntree's estimated poverty rates as "generalizations cloaked in numerical phraseology." In his view, Rowntree's method was "extremely speculative" and "the information on which it is based is far from sufficient." In his 1910 book *Charity and Social Life*, Loch criticized both Booth and Rowntree for forgetting that "poverty is so entirely relative to use and habit and potential ability of all kinds, that it can never serve as a satisfactory basis of social investigation." He concluded, "If we subtract all those whose trouble is due to economic causes wholly or chiefly, we have a large preponderant mass . . . in which the difficulty is not economic but, in the larger sense of the word, moral."[25]

Aside from the criticisms by COS leaders, the response to Rowntree's book was quite positive. Journalist and future Liberal MP Charles Masterman wrote in the *Contemporary Review* that Rowntree's work was "one of the most important pieces of detailed social investigation ever undertaken in England . . . a revelation, in details never before attempted, of the nature of the Abyss in a prosperous provincial city." He added that Rowntree's findings were "apt to soften exultation in modern progress into a certain minor key, and to cause the atmosphere suddenly to grow bleak and chill."[26]

Winston Churchill, still a member of the Conservative Party, read *Poverty* soon after it was published and was "greatly moved by it." In an address to a group of Conservatives in Blackpool, he stated that the book "has fairly made my hair stand on end," and that Rowntree's findings were "terrible and shocking." He wrote an apparently unpublished review of *Poverty* in which he asked readers to "consider the peculiar case of these poor, and the consequences. Although the British Empire is so large, they cannot find room to

25. See Bosanquet (1902: 108–9), Bosanquet (1905: 233), Loch (1902: 8), Loch (1910: 386, 474), and Appendix III (by Loch) to Parl. Papers, *Report of the Interdepartmental Committee on Physical Deterioration*, vol. 1 (1904, XXXII), pp. 109–11. Bowpitt (2000) discusses Rowntree's "early critics."

26. Masterman (1902: 24, 26, 31). Seven years later Masterman (1909) published his own masterpiece, a critique of Edwardian society titled *The Condition of England*.

live in it; although it is so magnificent, they would have had a better chance of happiness, if they had been born cannibal islanders of the Southern seas." Biographer Martin Gilbert stressed the impact that Rowntree's book had on Churchill, stating that "the moment he read it, Churchill's sense of mission was heightened and enhanced." Shortly after finishing *Poverty*, he wrote recommending it to a Conservative friend, and adding: "for my own part, I see little glory in an Empire which can rule the waves and is unable to flush its sewers." Two years later, in May 1904, Churchill left the Conservatives for the Liberal Party, where, as will be discussed later in the chapter, he played an important role in the adoption of the Liberal Welfare Reforms.[27]

Two other important studies of urban working-class communities were published before the First World War: Lady Bell's 1907 book *At the Works*, a study of the north-eastern iron-making town of Middlesbrough; and Pember Reeves's 1913 study of Lambeth, *Round about a Pound a Week*. These works, while influenced by Rowntree's book, were more qualitative in nature, although both examined the weekly expenditures of working-class households. Lady Bell and a small team of visitors investigated 900 ironworkers' households, examining their wages and expenditures, the roles of wives and daughters, and the problems of sickness, accidents, old age, drink and gambling. She found that 125 of the households investigated were "absolutely poor," meaning that they did not have "money enough to buy what are called the necessities of life." Another 175 "were so near the poverty-line that they are constantly passing over it." Adding these two groups together, she concluded that the life of one-third of the households studied was "an unending struggle from day to day to keep abreast of the most ordinary, the simplest, the essential needs."[28]

Bell stressed the income insecurity faced by working-class households, especially those with young children entirely dependent on the income of one breadwinner, where "any illness or accident affecting him at once plunges them into difficulties." When the breadwinner was unable to work, families often were forced to pawn items; homes were "gradually stripped, as, with each fresh need for ready-money, one thing after another is taken to the pawnshop."[29] Old age was another source of insecurity. Bell maintained that one-half or more of ironworkers "are spent by the time they are fifty." Most of the workers investigated dealt with insecurity by joining friendly societies or trade unions

27. See Churchill (1967: 29–31) and Gilbert (1991: 146). Churchill's unpublished review of *Poverty* is included in Churchill (1969: 105–11).

28. Bell (1907: 50–51). It is not clear precisely how Bell and her team determined the number of households living below or near the poverty line. The text does not report the poverty line used or household income for the families investigated.

29. Bell (1907: 49–50, 83–84).

providing sickness benefits. While these helped to smooth income, sickness benefits replaced less than half of lost wage income. Bell concluded that Middlesbrough workers had little "margin in which to remedy mistake and misfortune." If an ironworker "should stumble, either actually or metaphorically . . . he has but a small margin in which to recover himself."[30]

In *Round about a Pound a Week*, Pember Reeves addressed the question: "How does a working man's wife bring up a family on 20s. a week?" To answer it, a committee of the Fabian Women's Group investigated 42 families in Lambeth, south London, where the husband was in regular work and received a regular income of between 18s. and 30s. per week. The men were mainly unskilled laborers. Pember Reeves stressed that these were not the poorest households in the district, and that they included no families where the head was in casual employment.[31]

The investigators found that, at least in Lambeth, it was not possible to adequately bring up a family on a weekly budget of £1. The families lived in houses that were old or badly built, overcrowded, poorly ventilated, and often damp and verminous.[32] Pember Reeves concluded that "the great bulk" of persons living on incomes of less than 30s. per week were "under-fed, under-housed, and insufficiently clothed." The children suffered the most—their diet "is insufficient . . . and utterly unsatisfactory," and as a result "their growth is stunted, their mental powers are cramped, their health is undermined." While many within the middle class labeled poverty as "the result of drink, extravagance, or laziness," Pember Reeves argued that it simply was not possible to "maintain a working man in physical efficiency and rear healthy children" on a weekly income of 20–24s. She concluded that, while it was in the nation's collective interest for its children to be decently fed, clothed, and housed, large numbers of families headed by low-skilled workers were unable to do so at current wage rates.[33]

Taken together, the town surveys revealed that in Edwardian England between one-quarter and one-third of working-class households had weekly incomes that either were below or close to the poverty line at any point in time. The fact that individuals moved in and out of poverty over their life course meant that far more than one-third of working-class individuals were

---

30. Bell (1907: 86, 108, 118–19, 122, 271).

31. Pember Reeves (1913: 8–21); Pember Reeves (1912: 2–3).

32. Pember Reeves (1913: 21–42). Despite its poor quality, housing was expensive. Many families paid 8s. per week in rent, rates, and taxes, which often was one-third or more of their income. The high cost of housing, when necessary heating, lighting, and clothing costs were taken into account, often left only 10s. or less for food.

33. Pember Reeves (1913: 75–80, 145, 213–14, 226–31). In the book's concluding chapter she called for the government to adopt a legal minimum wage or, if that was politically unfeasible, to act as guardian and guarantee "the necessities of life to every child."

in poverty at some point during their lives. The results obtained from the town surveys and the *Report of the Interdepartmental Committee on Physical Deterioration* showed the need for actions to be taken to improve living standards for the lower stratum of manual workers and their families. In the words of Rowntree, "Even if we set aside considerations of physical and mental suffering, and regard the question only in its strictly economic and national aspect, there can be no doubt that the facts set forth . . . indicate a condition of things the serious import of which can hardly be overstated."[34]

II. The Debate over Policy Responses and the Royal Commission on the Poor Laws

The Liberal Welfare Reforms were not adopted out of thin air. Booth's work on *The Aged Poor* and various government reports, discussed in Chapter 5, revealed the extent of poverty and pauperism among working people aged 65 and older, and the Edwardian studies examined above made it clear that income insecurity remained a major problem for working-class households of all ages at the beginning of the twentieth century. These studies led to debates over the state's role in reducing poverty and insecurity, culminating in the adoption of the Liberal welfare policies. This section summarizes the debates over old age pensions, unemployment relief, and the Poor Law.

OLD AGE PENSIONS

The debate over state-provided pensions began in the early 1890s when the Local Government Board first published data on the extent of pauperism among the aged and Chamberlain and Booth put forward proposals for a national system of old age pensions. In March 1891, after the release of information on the number of aged persons receiving poor relief, Chamberlain stated in a speech that it was "deplorable . . . that so large a proportion of the aged people in our land should find themselves at the close of life forced to accept assistance which carries with it the idea of personal degradation." He argued that these "veterans of industry" should be "provided for as respected pensioners," and proposed that Parliament adopt what amounted to a voluntary state-run old age insurance system.[35]

Shortly thereafter Chamberlain set up and chaired a parliamentary committee to consider schemes for old age pensions. He presented a modified version of the committee's proposals in his testimony before the Royal Commission on the Aged Poor in 1893. His proposal involved various schemes,

34. Rowntree (1901: 221).
35. Chamberlain's speech is summarized in the *Times*, March 18, 1891, p. 10.

each of which was voluntary and involved worker contributions as well as a state subvention. A worker seeking old age insurance just for himself would be required to deposit £2.5 in the Post Office Savings Bank at or before turning 25, and make an annual payment of 10s.; the state would add a credit of £10 to the worker's account. Upon reaching 65, the worker would be eligible for a pension of 5s. per week; no benefits were paid to his family if he did not live to 65. A worker who wanted to provide for his wife and dependents could deposit £5 by age 25, and make a £1 annual contribution. In this case the state added £15 to his account. He still received a weekly pension of 5s. upon reaching age 65; however, if he died before 65, a provision would be made for his widow and children (up to age 12). Chamberlain maintained that state contributions would encourage thrift among the working class, and that workers who received pensions would not suffer the humiliation and "loss of self-respect" associated with poor relief.[36]

Booth also offered his first pension proposal in 1891. Unlike Chamberlain, he called for a universal noncontributory pension of 5s. per week for everyone aged 65 or older. He argued that 5s. represented "the minimum cost of life," and that a small pension would not reduce the work effort of the aged, nor would it discourage thrift among those younger than 65. Indeed, a pension, by ensuring that an aged individual could avoid the workhouse, might "make thrift more attractive" to the working class. Booth estimated that his proposal would cost about £17 million and, even assuming a £3 million decline in poor relief spending, he admitted that it would still create "great (perhaps insuperable) financial difficulties."[37]

In 1893 Gladstone appointed the Royal Commission on the Aged Poor, chaired by Lord Aberdare. The membership of the commission included, among others, both Chamberlain and Booth, Loch, the Secretary of the COS, and Charles Ritchie, former President of the Local Government Board. Those who testified before the commission included Booth, Chamberlain, the economist Alfred Marshall, Octavia Hill, and Thomas Mackay of the COS, as well as officials of the Local Government Board and the Board of Trade, Poor Law guardians, officers of friendly societies, and a few members of the working class. The commission's 1895 report examined various schemes for government-financed or -assisted pension/insurance programs to provide for the elderly poor outside of the Poor Law, including those put forward by Booth and Chamberlain, but decided not "to recommend the adoption of any of the schemes . . . in view of the financial and economic difficulties involved." The report further concluded that "no fundamental alterations are needed in

36. Parl. Papers, *Minutes of Evidence Taken before the Royal Commission on the Aged Poor*, vol. 3 (1895, XV), qq. 12,199–12,353.

37. Booth (1891: 634–40).

the existing system of poor law relief as it affects the aged."[38] Neither Booth nor Chamberlain signed the report. They, along with three other members of the commission, wrote a brief Minority Report stressing the stigma attached by the poor to the existing system of poor relief (and their "absolute loathing" of the workhouse) and recommending that the government create a new commission to construct, if possible, a "practicable scheme . . . for the assistance of the aged and respectable poor."[39]

Booth offered a revised plan for universal pensions in 1899, proposing that pensions begin at age 70, and be equal to 7s. per week for men, 5s. for women, and 12s. for married couples. He argued against means testing on the grounds that universality was necessary "to protect the dignity of the pensions" and eliminate any "possible taint of pauperism," although he speculated that a substantial share of the well-to-do would not claim their pensions. He estimated that the total cost of the proposal would be about £16 million.[40]

Chamberlain responded that Booth's new proposal was "absolutely impracticable," and that any system of universal noncontributory pensions was a "gigantic scheme of outdoor relief for everybody—good and bad, thrifty and unthrifty—the waster, drunkard, and idler as well as the industrious."[41] On the other hand, labor organizations in general praised the notion of noncontributory pensions. The National Committee of Organized Labour for the Promotion of Old Age Pensions, founded in 1899, proposed an amended version of Booth's plan (essentially his original proposal), calling for pensions of 5s. a week for men and women beginning at age 65. Pensions were to be funded by general taxation and completely separate from the Poor Law.[42]

The introduction of several pension bills into Parliament in 1899 led Chamberlain, then Colonial Secretary, to appoint the Select Committee on the Aged Deserving Poor, with a charge to determine whether any of the bills submitted could "with advantage be adopted either with or without amendment." The committee recommended adopting means-tested noncontributory pensions of 5–7s. per week for persons 65 and older. To be eligible for a pension, a person must have a weekly income of 10s. or less and must not have received poor relief other than medical relief in the previous 20 years.[43] A departmental committee appointed to examine the "financial aspects" of the Select Committee's

38. Parl. Papers, *Report of the Royal Commission on the Aged Poor* (1895, XIV), pp. lxxxiii–lxxxvii.

39. Parl. Papers, *Report of the Royal Commission on the Aged Poor* (1895, XIV), pp. xciii–xcvi.

40. Booth (1899a: 45–56).

41. Chamberlain's comments regarding universal pensions are reported in the *Times*, May 25, 1899, p. 12.

42. Stead (1909: 59–66).

43. Parl. Papers, *Report from the Select Committee on the Aged Deserving Poor* (1899, VIII), pp. viii–xii.

proposal estimated that in 1901 only 655,000 of the two million persons 65 and older would in fact be eligible for pensions, and that the total cost of the scheme would be about £10.3 million. Parliament did not take action, however, as the Boer War pushed the discussion of pensions onto the back burner, and after the war ended the Treasury opposed the increases in government spending required by the proposal.[44]

THE ROYAL COMMISSION ON THE POOR LAWS
AND THE DEBATE OVER UNEMPLOYMENT RELIEF

The downturn of 1904–5 led Balfour's Conservative government to address the problem of unemployment and examine the state of social welfare policy. In August 1905 Parliament adopted the Unemployed Workmen Act, and four months later, just before leaving office, the Balfour government appointed the Royal Commission on the Poor Laws and Relief of Distress. The commission was charged with inquiring into the workings of the Poor Law and also "into the various means which have been adopted outside of the Poor Laws for meeting distress arising from want of employment, particularly during periods of severe industrial depression; and to consider and report whether any . . . modification of the Poor Laws or changes in their administration or fresh legislation for dealing with distress are advisable."[45]

The commission was chaired by Lord George Hamilton, and its membership included, among others, C. S. Loch, Helen Bosanquet, and Octavia Hill from the COS, the Fabian socialist Beatrice Webb, five Guardians of the Poor, including the socialist George Lansbury, the permanent heads of the Local Government Boards of England, Scotland, and Ireland, three representatives of the Church of England and one of the Roman Catholic Church, two political economists, and Charles Booth, who resigned in 1908 due to ill health. Webb wrote that "the Commission was, in fact, predominantly a body of experts, either in poor law administration or social investigation."[46] Its inquiries lasted for three years, and resulted in two large reports published in February 1909: a Majority Report signed by the chairman and 14 others, and a Minority Report—written by the Webbs—signed by Beatrice Webb and three others.

44. Parl. Papers, *Report of the Departmental Committee on the Aged Deserving Poor* (1900, X), pp. xxiv–xxviii. On the debate concerning pensions from 1891 to 1906, see Hennock (1987: 117–25), Thane (1978), Thane (2000: 198–212), and Macnicol (1998: 65–84, 145–53).

45. Parl. Papers, *Report of the Royal Commission on the Poor Laws and Relief of Distress* (1909, XXXVII), p. 1.

46. Webb (1948: 316–21). Detailed discussions of the Royal Commission can be found in Harris (1972: 245–64), Woodroofe (1977), and McBriar (1987). Webb (1948: chap. 7) offers a behind-the-scenes discussion of the workings of the commission.

As per its charge, the commission examined not only the Poor Law but also other methods of dealing with distress, and in particular policies devoted to relieving the unemployed. Several prominent individuals testified before the commission on the topic of unemployment, including Sidney Webb, William Beveridge, at the time a member of London's Central Unemployed Body, Wilson Fox of the Board of Trade, and professors Bowley and Chapman. Their testimony and the background material they supplied to the commission contain a wealth of information on nineteenth-century unemployment relief, and demonstrate clearly the extent to which the proposals put forward in the Majority and Minority Reports grew out of lessons learned from the successes and failures of previous policies to relieve the unemployed.

Those who testified before the Royal Commission almost universally condemned the use of relief works for assisting the temporarily unemployed, as did Jackson and Pringle, authors of a report for the commission about the effects of unemployment relief since 1886. In a passage quoted approvingly by both the Majority and Minority Reports, Jackson and Pringle concluded that "the Municipal Relief Works, encouraged by Mr. Chamberlain's circular in 1886, have been in operation for twenty years, and must, we think, be pronounced a complete failure—a failure accentuated by the attempt to organise them by the Unemployed Workmen's Act of 1905."[47] The major problem with relief works was that they attracted chronically underemployed workers rather than the temporarily unemployed for whom they were intended. Sidney Webb testified that any attempt to assist skilled workers with work relief was "doomed to failure," because "the practically inexhaustible flood of casual labourers flows in and swamps the register, swamps the relief works, and swamps everything else that a despairing Distress Committee attempts."[48]

Webb, Beveridge, Chapman, Bowley, and Wilson Fox all argued that the recent experiences of the distress committees proved that chronic underemployment was a serious problem, and that no method of unemployment relief could be successful unless the number of surplus laborers in the casual trades was reduced. This could be accomplished through "the organisation of the labour market" by the establishment of a national system of labor exchanges. Labor exchanges would promote the "decasualisation" of trades such as riverside labor by allocating available work so as to give more or less continuous employment to the "better" workmen, and also would reduce unemployment in more skilled occupations by bringing into contact employers

47. Parl. Papers, *Report . . . on the Effects of Employment or Assistance* (1909, XLIV), p. 148. The Chamberlain Circular and the Unemployed Workmen Act are discussed in Chapter 4.

48. Parl. Papers, *Minutes of Evidence . . . of Witnesses Further Relating to the Subject of Unemployment* (1910, XLIX), p. 186.

looking for workers and unemployed workers looking for jobs—that is, by disseminating information.[49]

Several witnesses maintained that public authorities should attempt to "regularise" the national demand for labor by undertaking necessary development projects when the private sector's demand for labor was slack. Bowley put forward the most detailed proposal, recommending that the state set aside funds "in prosperous years, ear-marked for works of construction which need not be done at a particular time, e.g., dock schemes, great building works, school buildings, public parks, improvement of the national roads." He argued that his scheme was much different from the work relief programs of the previous 25 years. Jobs would be "contracted out on the ordinary commercial basis," and there would be no attempt to hire unemployed workers. The scheme would not create an "artificial demand" for labor, "only an adjustment in time of the ordinary demand." Similar, albeit less detailed, proposals were made by Beveridge and Chapman, who stressed that government employment projects must be "rigidly distinguished from the provision of distress works."[50]

Everyone who testified before the commission was impressed with existing trade union unemployment benefits. Unemployment insurance generally was regarded as an efficient method of reducing the distress resulting from cyclical unemployment. Beveridge estimated that in 1905–6 the cost per man-week of relieving unemployed workers was twice as high on work relief projects administered by London's Central Unemployed Body as it was for unemployment insurance administered by London trade unions.[51] Witnesses also agreed that unemployment insurance should be extended to more workers, although there was less agreement on how to achieve this. Webb and Jackson argued that a system of compulsory insurance administered by the government was neither practical nor desirable. They supported instead an extension of the system of voluntary union-provided insurance in which the government paid part of the costs, to encourage unions of low-skilled workers to provide unemployment insurance. Such a subsidy would enable every worker above the grade of casual laborer "to provide against the contingency of unemployment in the method most congenial to himself."[52]

49. See, for example, the statement given by Beveridge to the Royal Commission: Parl. Papers, *Minutes of Evidence . . . of Witnesses Relating Chiefly to the Subject of Unemployment* (1910, XLVIII), pp. 15–16. Beveridge and others stated that casual laborers thrown out of work as a result of "de-casualisation" should be aided by the labor exchanges to find employment in other occupations.

50. The proposals of Bowley, Beveridge, and Chapman are in Parl. Papers, *Minutes of Evidence . . . of Witnesses Relating Chiefly to the Subject of Unemployment* (1910, XLVIII), pp. 467–69, 18, 332.

51. Parl. Papers, *Minutes of Evidence . . . of Witnesses Relating Chiefly to the Subject of Unemployment* (1910, XLVIII), p. 17.

52. Webb suggested the government pay "one half what the trade union paid." Parl. Papers, *Minutes of Evidence . . . of Witnesses Further Relating to the Subject of Unemployment* (1910, XLIX),

Beveridge agreed that trade unions possessed "certain natural advantages" in the provision of unemployment insurance, but argued that insurance also could be administered efficiently by labor exchanges. He disagreed with the Webbs' assertion that many trade unions could not afford to provide unemployment benefits without government assistance. The cost of insurance was relatively small, and "there is no reason why the trade unions themselves should not extend the system of unemployed benefits." Wilson Fox and Llewellyn Smith supported a compulsory state-run system administered by labor exchanges, but with a state subvention in addition to contributions from workers and employers.[53]

The Majority and Minority Reports both proposed adopting a national system of labor exchanges in order to bring the demand and supply of labor "generally and locally in touch with each other." The Majority Report recommended that use of the exchanges be voluntary, although the Board of Trade should "popularise them in every way." The Minority Report recommended that resort to exchanges be "optional for employers filling situations of at least a month's duration," but compulsory for employers in trades where "excessive Discontinuity of Employment prevails."[54]

Both reports supported extending unemployment insurance to a larger share of the workforce. Although the Majority Report did not recommend a specific plan, it noted with approval the system operating in Ghent, Belgium, where the municipality subsidized the provision of unemployment insurance by trade unions. The report concluded that "the establishment and promotion of Unemployment Insurance, especially amongst unskilled and unorganised labour . . . is of such national importance as to justify, under specified conditions, contributions from public funds towards its furtherance." It recommended that a state subsidy be offered not only to trade unions but also to friendly societies providing unemployment benefits to their members. If large numbers of workers remained uninsured, the government could set up a supplementary insurance scheme, administered by the labor exchanges.[55]

The Minority Report rejected the establishment of a state-run compulsory insurance plan, arguing that it would be "financially impracticable" and would have an adverse effect on union membership and organization. It maintained that trade unions possessed certain advantages for dealing with

---

pp. 188–89, 194. Jackson (1910: 34–39) wrote that "a State subsidy . . . is very necessary for the less well-paid trades which have not at present been able to secure sufficient contributions to enable them to pay unemployed benefit to their members."

53. Beveridge (1909: 227–30); Parl. Papers, *Minutes of Evidence . . . of Witnesses Relating Chiefly to the Subject of Unemployment* (1910, XLVIII), pp. 17, 450–53; Smith (1910: 527–28).

54. Parl. Papers, *Report of the Royal Commission on the Poor Laws and Relief of Distress* (1909, XXXVII), pp. 404–5, 630–31; Webb and Webb (1909b: 248–64, 341).

55. Parl. Papers, *Report of the Royal Commission on the Poor Laws* (1909, XXXVII), pp. 415–21.

unemployment, but that, contrary to Beveridge's claim, the high cost of insurance put it beyond the means of all but a small share of better paid artisans. The report proposed that the state adopt a version of the Ghent system, providing unions with "a subvention from public funds, in order to assist them to extend their own insurance against Unemployment."[56]

The Minority Report also called for the government to reduce cyclical unemployment by undertaking ordinary municipal projects "of a capital nature . . . to a greater extent in the years of slackness than in the years of good trade." These projects would be the "opposite of Relief Works," undertaken by "the departments or contractors ordinarily concerned, and by the best of the available workmen and labourers usually engaged in just those kinds of work." Their function was not to relieve distress, but "to prevent, long before they fall into distress, the two or three hundred thousand good and efficient workmen from becoming Unemployed." The Majority Report was more cautious; it supported increasing capital expenditure on public projects during "severe and prolonged" downturns, but warned that proposals for "the regularisation of work . . . must be scrutinised with some care."[57]

In the end, as will be discussed in the following section, the policies adopted by the government to deal with unemployment bore only a faint resemblance to the proposals of either the Majority Report or the Minority Report.

THE DEBATE OVER THE POOR LAW

The Royal Commission was charged with examining the Poor Law and recommending whether any modifications of it were "advisable." Both the Majority and Minority Reports were critical of how poor relief was administered. Their proposed policy responses were similar in some regards and quite different in others. The Majority Report proposed major changes to the Poor Law, while the Minority Report proposed that it be abolished and its functions transferred to specialist (local and national) governmental agencies.

The Majority Report maintained that Poor Law unions were too small to adequately administer relief, that there was a lack of uniformity in relief administration across (and even within) unions, that there was not "proper investigation and discrimination in dealing with applicants" for relief, that the general workhouse was not a suitable "test or deterrent" for able-bodied applicants, and that there was little cooperation between local Poor Law authorities and charitable organizations. It proposed several changes to remedy these defects. Because the poor associated the name Poor Law with "harshness"

56. Webb and Webb (1909b: 288–93, 343).

57. Webb and Webb (1909b: 283–84); Parl. Papers, *Report of the Royal Commission on the Poor Laws* (1909, XXXVII), pp. 411, 633.

and "hopelessness," it should be replaced by the title Public Assistance. The basic unit of relief administration should become the county and the county borough, the Boards of Guardians replaced by a county-wide Public Assistance Authority, and the local poor rate replaced by a county or county borough rate. The day-to-day administration of relief would be done by local committees.[58]

The report recommended that each county and county borough establish a Voluntary Aid Council, which would form a Voluntary Aid Committee to work in cooperation with the Public Assistance Authority in the administration of relief. The main functions of the Voluntary Aid Committees were to assist "(1) persons in distress whose cases do not appear to be suitable for treatment by the Public Assistance Committee, and (2) applicants for Public Assistance whose cases have been referred to the Committee by the Public Assistance Committee." The committees should make "a careful inquiry into the case of every applicant for relief," and the assistance given "should be governed by consistent principles."[59]

As for the methods used to assist the poor, the Majority Report recommended that the general workhouse be abolished and replaced by separate institutions for children, the aged and infirm, the sick, the able-bodied, vagrants, and the mentally ill. Institutions for the aged and the able-bodied should adopt classification systems based on an inmate's conduct "before and after admission," and whenever possible treatment should be "curative and restorative." Outdoor relief, or Home Assistance as the report called it, "should be given only after thorough inquiry, except in cases of sudden and urgent necessity." Those who received assistance in their homes should be subject to supervision by members of the voluntary agencies on a case basis. The supervision "should include in its purview the conditions, moral and sanitary, under which the recipient is living" and the Public Assistance Authority be given "the power to refuse relief . . . where the conditions of living are bad." In general, "every effort should be made to foster the instincts of independence and self-maintenance amongst those assisted."[60]

The Majority Report's stressing of the need for "curative and restorative" forms of assistance followed from its assessment of pauperism's causes. While admitting that some pauperism was a result of economic factors, such as casual employment and low wages, the report stated that issues of character were often at the root of what appeared to be economic causes of pauperism. Government policy by itself could not successfully combat pauperism; it was the

58. Parl. Papers, *Report of the Royal Commission on the Poor Laws* (1909, XXXVII), pp. 596–601.

59. Parl. Papers, *Report of the Royal Commission on the Poor Laws* (1909, XXXVII), pp. 655, 664–65.

60. Parl. Papers, *Report of the Royal Commission on the Poor Laws* (1909, XXXVII), pp. 617–19, 654–55.

duty of all sections of society "by united and untiring effort to convert useless and costly inefficients into self-sustaining and respectable members of the community."[61]

The Minority Report also was highly critical of the local administration of relief, and it too criticized the general mixed workhouse and the lack of uniformity in administration across Poor Law unions. Its main criticism of the existing system, however, was its one-size-fits-all method of assisting the poor. Each relieving officer had to provide for infants, schoolchildren, able-bodied adults, invalids, the sick, the mentally defective, widows, and the aged.[62] In the seven decades since the passage of the Poor Law Amendment Act, several new specialist governmental agencies had been created, dealing with local health, local education, pensions, unemployment, and the mentally defective. Their functions overlapped with those of the Poor Law. Alongside these rival governmental agencies was a "growing stream of private charity and voluntary agencies" uncoordinated with public activity. As a result, the nation was confronted with "an ever-growing expenditure from public and private funds, which results, on the one hand, in a minimum of prevention and cure, and on the other in far-reaching demoralisation of character and the continuance of no small amount of unrelieved destitution."[63]

The Minority Report agreed with the Majority that the Poor Law union was too small to be an efficient unit of relief administration; it did not, however, support replacing local Boards of Guardians by a county-wide Public Assistance Authority.[64] Instead, it called for the Poor Law to be broken up and its functions transferred to existing specialist agencies, administered at the local level by committees of County and County Borough Councils under the supervision of central government agencies.[65]

---

61. According to the report, drink was "the most potent and universal" cause of pauperism. Old age was "hardly in itself a 'cause' of pauperism," although it was a major factor when combined with "low earning power, drink, or thriftlessness." Parl. Papers, *Report of the Royal Commission on the Poor Laws* (1909, XXXVII), pp. 219–27, 643–44.

62. Relieving officers inevitably concentrated their attention "not on the different methods of curative or reformatory treatment that [the applicants] severally require, but on their one common attribute of destitution, and the one common remedy of 'relief,' indiscriminate and unconditional." Webb and Webb (1909a: 574–79).

63. Webb and Webb (1909a: 499–501).

64. Indeed, it accused the Majority Report of proposing to establish "what is practically the same system of Poor Relief, with new members and under another name!" Webb and Webb (1909a: xv–xvi).

65. For example, the care of school-age pauper children would be undertaken by Local Education Authorities, supervised by the Board of Education, and the treatment of the sick undertaken by Local Health Authorities supervised by the Department of Public Health. Webb and Webb (1909a: 516–29).

According to the Minority Report, the scheme proposed by the Majority, like the Poor Law, set as its goal the *relief* of destitution, while their goal was the *prevention* of destitution. The new specialist agencies would assist the poor "*according to the cause or character of their distress.*" The Minority Report asserted that "the mere keeping of people from starving—which is essentially what the Poor Law sets out to do—... cannot, in the twentieth century, be regarded as any adequate fulfilment of social duty." It was cruel to those deserving relief and at the same time "demoralisingly attractive" to the undeserving. By using separate agencies to provide specialized treatment for the poor, it was possible to influence their lives "in such a way as to stimulate personal effort, to strengthen character and capacity to ward off dangers." As these quotes indicate, the authors of the Minority Report, like those of the Majority, believed that the granting of assistance to the poor should build character and promote responsibility.[66]

Shortly after the Majority and Minority Reports were published, a propaganda war began between the two camps. In May 1909, the Webbs set up the National Committee for the Break-Up of the Poor Law and began a publicity campaign in support of the proposals set forth in the Minority Report. This in turn led to the formation of the National Poor Law Reform Association with Lord Hamilton, who had been chairman of the Royal Commission, as President. The association believed that the Poor Law was in "urgent need" of reform, but disagreed with the notion that it should be broken up and replaced by specialist agencies because "a single administration for public assistance is on all grounds better than a divided responsibility by departments." A third group also entered the fray—the local boards of guardians and officials of the Local Government Board's Poor Law Division came out against both the Majority and the Minority Reports and in favor of the status quo. Beatrice Webb, at the end of 1909, put her faith in the results of the upcoming general election; she wrote in her diary, "if the Liberals come in, they must take up a modified version of the Minority Report."[67] She was in for a surprise.

III. The Adoption of the Liberal Welfare Reforms

The Liberal government that came to power in the landslide election of 1906 did not wait for the Royal Commission to report before turning to social policy. The commission had been appointed by the outgoing government, and the new administration felt under no obligation to adhere to its proposals. The Liberal Welfare Reforms, with the exception of labor exchanges, were barely if at all influenced by the Royal Commission. The policies regarding the health

66. Webb and Webb (1909a: 499–500, 518, 590, emphasis original).
67. Webb (1948: 422–41); Woodroofe (1977: 161–63); Hamilton, *Spectator*, May 28, 1910, p. 17.

of schoolchildren and old age pensions were adopted while the commission was still conducting its inquiries, and the government chose to reduce the distress caused by unemployment and sickness by adopting a system of compulsory national insurance, a method of relief on which "the Majority Report was equivocal and the Minority Report positively hostile." The government decided neither to abolish nor to reform the Poor Law; the boards of guardians remained intact until 1929. In the words of Derek Fraser, "never can so important a Royal Commission have produced so little in the way of immediate action."[68] This section summarizes the social welfare policies adopted between 1906 and 1911.

CHILDREN'S HEALTH AND OLD AGE PENSIONS

The first welfare reforms concerned the health of children and were in response to the poor physical state of army recruits during the Boer War and the subsequent recommendations of the *Report of the Interdepartmental Committee on Physical Deterioration*. The 1906 Education (Provision of Meals) Act allowed local authorities to use tax revenue to provide free school meals for needy children. It established the "revolutionary principle" that children had a right to adequate nourishment, and that if their parents "were unable to feed them properly the state should see that they were fed." This was followed a year later by the Education (Administrative Provisions) Act, which implemented school medical inspections and established a medical department in the Board of Education; government grants for the medical treatment of poor children were introduced in 1912. Finally, the Children's Act of 1908 made it a legal offense for a parent to neglect a child's health.[69]

The push for state-provided old age pensions, which had been sidetracked by the Boer War and Treasury opposition, was revived shortly after the Liberals came into power. Prime Minister Asquith and Chancellor of the Exchequer Lloyd George put forward a pension scheme that was noncontributory and means-tested, similar to that proposed by the Select Committee on the Aged Deserving Poor in 1899. After some modifications by Parliament, the Old Age Pension Act was adopted in August 1908 and went into operation in January 1909. It provided a weekly pension of 5s. to individuals aged 70 and older (10s. to couples) with incomes below £21 per annum (about 8s. per week). A sliding scale was introduced that reduced benefits for persons with incomes greater than 8s. per week—pensions were paid to those with incomes as high as £31 10s. (about 12s. per week). Individuals who had received poor relief after

68. Fraser (2003: 176).

69. For a detailed discussion of social welfare legislation for children, see Gilbert (1966a: chap. 3) and Fraser (2003: 161–64). The quote is from Pipkin (1931: 73).

January 1, 1908, initially were not eligible for a pension, although this clause was abolished in 1911.[70]

The number of pension recipients was substantially greater than the government had anticipated. On the last Friday in March 1909, 393,700 persons in England and Wales (38% of the population 70 and older) received a pension from the government (see Table 6.5). This was 164,000 more than the number of persons 70 and older in receipt of poor relief on March 31, 1906. Nearly 90% of pensioners received the maximum benefit of 5s. per week. An additional 175,000–200,000 persons 70 and older received poor relief in March 1909 and were ineligible for a pension. Thus, a majority of persons 70 and older in 1909 received government assistance in the form of either poor relief or a pension.[71] The number of pensioners increased sharply after the Poor Law disqualification was abolished. In March 1911, 57.3% of persons 70 and older received a pension, nearly two-and-a-half times the percentage of persons of the same age who were poor relief recipients five years earlier. A larger percentage of aged women than aged men received a pension, just as a larger percentage of women had received poor relief. Government expenditures on pensions totaled nearly £5.2 million in 1909–10 and over £7.9 million in 1911–12, 26% more than the entire cost of poor relief in 1906–7.[72]

The authors of the 1908 act went to some length to ensure that old age pensions were not associated with the Poor Law—pensions were collected from the local Post Office rather than Poor Law authorities. There was no stigma attached to receiving a pension. Indeed, they were "immensely popular"—old people spending their pension allowance at a shop in Salford "would bless the name of Lloyd George as if he were a saint from heaven." Flora Thompson wrote that the pensions transformed the lives of many aged cottagers in her Oxfordshire village, and recalled that when old people first went to the Post Office to draw their pensions, "tears of gratitude would run down the cheeks of some."[73]

Why was the number of old age pensioners so large? Some of those who received pensions had previously relied on friends, relatives, or private charity, rather than the Poor Law, to supplement their meager incomes. Moreover, the eligibility standards for pensions and poor relief were different—some (immeasurable) share of individuals who were eligible for pensions would not have been deemed destitute enough to grant poor relief. Still, the data suggest that the Poor

70. On the adoption of the Old Age Pension Act, see Macnicol (1998: 155–63), Thane (2000: 217–28), and Gilbert (1966a: chap. 4).

71. On January 1, 1910, there were 195,924 paupers aged 70 and older in England and Wales. Parl. Papers, *Old Age Pensioners and Aged Pauperism* (1913, LV), p. 3.

72. Data on the cost of pensions from Board of Trade, *Seventeenth Abstract of Labour Statistics* (1915: 185). Poor Law expenditures for 1906–7 from Williams (1981: 171).

73. Roberts (1990: 84); Thompson ([1945] 2011: 86).

TABLE 6.5. Number of Old Age Pensioners in England and Wales, 1909–13

	PAUPERS AGED 70+			OLD-AGE PENSIONERS			
	1906	1909	1910	1911	1912	1913	
Total	229,474	393,700	441,489	613,873	642,524	668,646	
Males	88,098			218,158	232,966	245,418	
Females	141,376			395,715	409,558	423,228	
% getting 5s.		87.4	89.5	92.7	93.9	94.2	
	% OF PERSONS AGED 70+ RECEIVING POOR RELIEF (1906) OR PENSIONS						
Total	23.4	38.0	41.9	57.3	60.0		
Male	21.4			49.2			
Female	24.9			63.0			

Sources: Data on paupers aged 70 and older in March 1906 from Parl. Papers, *Royal Commission on the Poor Laws and Relief of Distress, Appendix Vol. XXV, Statistical Memoranda* (1910, LIII), pp. 176–93. Data on number of old-age pensioners from Board of Trade, *Seventeenth Abstract of Labour Statistics* (1915: 184).

Note: For both paupers and pensioners, data are for one day in late March of the year.

Law statistics understate, perhaps by a substantial amount, the extent of poverty among the aged. In the first decade of the twentieth century, a large number of old people lived on quite low incomes without applying for poor relief. The fact that they did so is evidence that the working class attached a stigma to the receipt of poor relief, especially in a workhouse. Commenting on the unexpectedly large number of pensioners, Lloyd George stated in 1909, "What strikes you is their horror of the Poor Law . . . this pension act has disclosed the presence amongst us of over 600,000 people, the vast majority of whom were living in circumstances of great poverty, yet disclaimed the charity of the public."[74]

TRADE BOARDS

Appeals for minimum wage legislation began before Rowntree's survey of York and the Board of Trade's 1906 wage census revealed that large numbers of low-skilled adult males were paid wages that were not sufficient to maintain a family of five. In their 1897 book, *Industrial Democracy*, the Webbs called for the adoption of legal minimum wages for both men and women, "determined by practical inquiry as to the cost of the food, clothing, and shelter physiologically necessary, according to national habit and custom, to prevent bodily deterioration." The minimum wage would be different for men and women, and perhaps also for urban and rural districts. It would not correspond to and would be lower than a "living wage," but it would be a boon to unskilled men and women in unregulated, parasitic trades.[75]

While support for a national minimum wage was never strong, the 1890s witnessed increasing pressure for legislation regulating wages in so-called sweated industries dominated by women workers. At the instigation of the Women's Trade Union League, in 1906 the *Daily News* sponsored a Sweated Industries Exhibition in London, at which visitors could learn about working conditions in 45 sweated trades. The exhibition led to the formation of the National Anti-Sweating League. This pressured the Liberal government to create the Select Committee on Homework, whose 1908 report proposed the establishment of wage boards in certain trades "to fix minimum time and piece rates of payment for Home Workers in those trades."[76]

In March 1909, Winston Churchill, President of the Board of Trade, introduced a Trade Boards Bill into the House of Commons. It passed with little

74. Thane (2000: 227–28). Budd and Guinnane (1991) found that some Irish pensioners misrepresented their age in order to collect a pension before reaching 70. Some English pensioners also might have exaggerated their age.

75. Webb and Webb (1897: 774–78).

76. Schmiechen (1984: 162–70); Morris (1986: 195–207); Parl. Papers, *Report from the Select Committee on Home Work* (1908, VIII), p. xviii.

opposition in July. The Trade Boards Act established boards to set minimum hourly wages in four trades—ready-made and wholesale bespoke tailoring, paper box making, chain making, and machine lace finishing. Each trade board was to be made up of equal numbers of employer and employee representatives plus several independent members nominated by the Board of Trade and was to set general minimum hourly wages and minimum piece rates that would enable an average worker to earn the minimum time rate. Once approved by the Board of Trade, minimum wages were to be enforced by the levy of fines for noncompliance.

Some 250,000 workers were employed in these trades, including approximately 175,000 women. The Trade Boards Act gave the Board of Trade authority to create additional boards in trades where wages were "exceptionally low as compared with other employments," and in 1913 boards were established in sugar confectionery and food preserving, shirt making, hollow ware making, tin box making, and linen and cotton embroidery. In determining which trades to include, the Board of Trade was guided largely by information on women's wages contained in the 1906 wage census; it chose the "lowest paid trades" where the workforce was dominated by women. The number of women employed in trades covered by trade boards in 1914 was about 325,000, nearly 10% of females employed outside of domestic service or agriculture.[77]

For each of the industries covered by the act, the initial rates for women set by the trade boards exceeded the average weekly wage of female workers in 1906. The gap between the previous average wage and the board-determined minimum varied substantially across trades, and was particularly large in lace making, hollow ware, and tin box making. It is not possible to determine how many women experienced wage increases as a result of the act or the magnitude of the average increase in their weekly income, but some idea of the Trade Boards Act's effects on wages can be obtained from data for the tailoring and box-making trades reported by Tawney and Bulkley. Tawney, using wage data for 11,372 women employed in ready-made tailoring from the 1906 wage census, estimated that at least 38% of women engaged in tailoring should have received a wage increase as a result of the establishment of minimum rates. Roughly a third of those who received increases had their weekly wages raised by up to 1s. 6d. per week, another third received an additional 1s. 6d.–2s. 6d. per week, and the final third received an additional 2s. 6d.–4s. per week. Bulkley estimated that 52% of the 2,934 women employed in box making in the wage census should have had their wages raised. Because the majority of women in tailoring and box making worked on piece rates, the new minimum

---

77. For more on the Trade Boards Act, see Bean and Boyer (2009), Sells (1923), Blackburn (2007), and Hatton (1997).

rates also caused some of those with weekly earnings above the minimum set by the board to receive wage increases.[78]

The 1909 act applied to a relatively small number of poor women workers, and largely ignored the pressing issue of the low wage rates of adult male unskilled laborers. For this reason, it was criticized by some contemporaries for being too cautious a measure, and historians have echoed these criticisms. For example, Blackburn referred to the act as a "modest reform" and contended that "what was required was a much more radical measure . . . a national minimum wage based on an agreed living income." Even if one focuses only on female low-wage workers, the Trade Boards Act was a modest reform. Labor leader Joseph Hallsworth concluded after the act's extension in 1913 that "a very large amount of sweating . . . still continued in trades not covered by the Boards, and particularly among women and girls."[79]

However, the adoption of a more radical policy, such as a national minimum wage, was not politically feasible in 1909. The evils of the sweating system had been known since the late 1880s, and yet despite the lobbying efforts of various groups, it took two decades for Parliament to adopt legislation addressing the issue. Tawney wrote that "the weight of ignorance and prejudice, as well as reasoned opposition, to be overcome" in adopting the Trade Boards Act "was enormous." The opposition to a national minimum wage for adult males would have been far stronger, since many reformers who supported regulating women's employment contracts were opposed to regulating those of men. Churchill, when introducing the bill to Parliament, felt it necessary to emphasize that "these methods of regulating wages by law are only defensible as exceptional measures to deal with diseased and parasitic trades."[80]

LABOR EXCHANGES AND NATIONAL INSURANCE

Both the Majority and Minority Reports of the Royal Commission supported the adoption of a national system of labor exchanges for bringing together employers looking for workers and unemployed workers looking for jobs. The major proponent for labor exchanges before 1909 was William Beveridge. In 1906, as a member of the Central (Unemployed) Body for London, Beveridge proposed the establishment of a metropolitan network of labor exchanges. A year later, he testified before the Royal Commission

---

78. Sells (1923: 80); Tawney (1915: 77–78); Bulkley (1915: 32–33).

79. Blackburn (1999: 111, 107); Hallsworth (1925: 9). See also Blackburn (1991; 2007).

80. Tawney (1927: 19); Churchill (1969: 879). Checkland (1983: 216) wrote, regarding the adoption of a national minimum wage before the First World War, that "for any government to contemplate so far-reaching an interference in the labour market and in income distribution was as yet unthinkable."

that the most important cause of unemployment was "the normal overstocking of each occupation with labour as the direct result of want of organisation in the demand for labour and want of fluidity in the supply," and concluded that "the first step in the solution of the unemployment problem must be the organisation of the labour market" by a national system of labor exchanges. Shortly after Churchill became President of the Board of Trade in 1908, he offered Beveridge a position as a civil servant. Beveridge largely was responsible for the Labour Exchanges Bill that Churchill introduced in Parliament in the spring of 1909. The bill was adopted with little opposition.[81]

The Labour Exchanges Act authorized the Board of Trade to establish and maintain labor exchanges "in such places as they see fit." Their use was to be voluntary for both employers and workers—workpeople seeking employment registered at the local exchange and employers notified the exchange of vacancies. The role of the exchange was to fill each vacancy with the best qualified workman in the area; if no suitable workmen were available locally, the exchange passed the job information on to other exchanges. By December 1910, 147 exchanges had been established, and by 1912 there were 414 exchanges covering the entire country. The number of workers registered increased from about 1.4 million in 1910 to nearly 3 million in 1913, while the number of vacancies filled rose from 374,00 in 1910 to 922,000 in 1913. The share of adult male registrants for whom work was found ranged from 27.5% in 1911 to 32.8% in 1912. Placement rates were slightly higher for adult women and substantially higher for boys and girls under age 17, over 40% of whom were found jobs each year.[82]

At the same time that Beveridge was working on labor exchanges, Llewellyn Smith, Permanent Secretary of the Board of Trade, was drafting a system of national unemployment insurance. In his May 1909 speech to the House of Commons announcing that he was about to introduce a labor exchanges bill, Churchill stated that in the near future the government would propose a system of national unemployment insurance. He argued that labor exchanges and unemployment insurance were "complementary . . . they mutually support and sustain each other." Labor exchanges provided the "apparatus for finding work and testing willingness to work" without which no unemployment insurance scheme can work. Churchill reminded the House that both the Majority and Minority Reports of the Royal Commission to Investigate the Poor Laws called for the adoption of labor exchanges. He did not add that neither report supported a compulsory system of unemployment insurance.[83]

81. Harris (1997: 153–73); Parl. Papers, *Minutes of Evidence . . . of Witnesses Relating Chiefly to the Subject of Unemployment* (1910, XLVIII), pp. 6–7, 15–17.

82. Beveridge (1930: 295–306). Data on number of registrants and placement rates are from Board of Trade, *Seventeenth Abstract of Labour Statistics* (1915: 13).

83. Churchill (1909: 253–65).

The battle over Lloyd George's 1909 Finance Bill, which resulted in two general elections in the following year, delayed government action on unemployment until May 1911. During this time Churchill, Llewellyn Smith, and Beveridge continued to iron out the details of their unemployment insurance policy. There were several issues to be settled. Churchill quickly determined that the system would be mandatory, although, at least initially, only a limited number of industries would be included. He rejected a voluntary state-aided system on the grounds that it would attract mainly those "bad risks" who were "most liable to be unemployed," which would be fatal to the system's financial stability. He insisted that employers contribute to the scheme, along with workers and the state; in doing so he rejected the adoption of a Ghent-style system, in which unemployment insurance was run by trade unions with a subvention from the state. A scheme that included only trade unionists would assist those who were "most able to aid themselves" without helping workers who "under existing conditions, have not been able to make any effective provision." Churchill insisted that receipt of unemployment benefits not be conditional on the behavior of the unemployed person. In a memo to Llewellyn Smith titled "Notes on Malingering," he wrote that a worker who had paid his contributions into the scheme and lost his job as a result of drunkenness should still receive unemployment benefits. In his words, "I do not like mixing up moralities and mathematics. . . . Our concern is with . . . the fact of unemployment, not with the character of the unemployed."[84]

The finalized unemployment insurance scheme was introduced to Parliament on May 4, 1911, as Part II of the National Insurance Bill. It established compulsory unemployment insurance (UI) in a limited number of industries—building, construction of works, shipbuilding, mechanical engineering, iron founding, construction of vehicles, and sawmilling—chosen because unemployment in them was "not only high and chronic, but marked by seasonal and cyclical fluctuations." Some 2.25 million workers were covered—about 20% of employed adult males, and roughly one-third of those "engaged in purely industrial work." Workers and their employers each contributed 2.5d. per week to the UI fund, and the state contributed 1.67d. An unemployed worker received a weekly benefit of 7s. for a maximum of 15 weeks in any 12-month period, subject to the provision that he had paid five weekly contributions for every week of benefit.[85]

The scheme was administered through local labor exchanges—a workman claimed and received his benefit at the exchange, and "proved his unemployment and capacity to work by signing an unemployed register there in working hours daily." The system was meant to be self-supporting. Contributions were

84. Churchill (1909: 265–67); Harris (1972: 302–9); Gilbert (1966b: 855–56).
85. Fraser (2003: 188); Churchill (1909: 267–68).

paid into and benefits paid out of an unemployment fund. If an extended period of high unemployment exhausted the fund, it could borrow from the Treasury, which under certain circumstances could adjust the contribution or benefit levels to restore solvency. As an olive branch to organized labor, unionized workers in insured trades could draw benefits from their trade union rather than a labor exchange, and the state agreed to repay unions, in both insured and uninsured trades, "one-sixth of any unemployed benefit paid by them to their members from their own resources."[86]

At the same time the Board of Trade was working on an unemployment insurance scheme, officials in the Treasury, under the leadership of Chancellor Lloyd George, were developing a scheme of health insurance. Lloyd George's interest in health insurance dated from his 1908 trip to Germany to examine their system of national insurance. While his purpose was to learn about pensions, he returned impressed by the fact that German national insurance affected "the great mass of German people in well-nigh every walk of life." In a speech at Swansea in October, he stated that the Old Age Pension Act was just the beginning of needed social reforms: "We are still confronted with the more gigantic task of dealing with the rest—the sick, the infirm, the unemployed, the widows, and the orphans."[87]

Lloyd George realized from the beginning that, unlike pensions, health benefits were too costly to be financed by taxation alone. He therefore called for a system of insurance, in which workers and employers, along with the state, contributed to the cost of health benefits. Like Churchill, he believed that the payment of contributions earned workers a right to benefits, and he insisted that benefits be provided even to those who became sick due to their own negligence. The Webbs, among others, strongly objected to both the contributory nature of health insurance and to the idea that workers had a right to benefits regardless of their conduct. Beatrice Webb described the scheme as "rotten" in her diary, and criticized the "naïve delight" among those in the governing class at making workmen pay part of the costs. She also wrote that the "unconditionality" of benefits "constitutes a grave defect. The state gets nothing for its money in the way of conduct, it may even encourage malingering."[88]

The bill proposed by Lloyd George provided benefits only to those who contributed to the system; aside from maternity benefits, dependents of the

86. Beveridge (1930: 266–69); Harris (1972: 332–34).

87. Hennock (1987: 149–50); Gilbert (1966a: 231–32, 294).

88. Webb (1948: 430, 475–77). William Braithwaite, a civil servant who worked with Lloyd George in writing the health insurance bill, described a "Homeric" breakfast meeting between the Chancellor and the Webbs. Before Lloyd George could speak, "Mr. and Mrs. Webb, singly and in pairs, leap down his throat.... The Chancellor was unable to get a word in, and was evidently partly amused and partly annoyed." Braithwaite (1957: 115–16).

insured were not covered. It provided a weekly benefit to ease the effects of the interruption of earnings caused by illness, and medical treatment to reduce time away from work. A 1910 report by government actuaries argued that "it is the husband's and not the wife's health which it is important to insure. So long as the husband is in good health and able to work adequate provision will be made for the needs of the family, . . . whereas when the husband's health fails there is no one to earn wages." The policy was meant to reduce workers' economic insecurity, and not to improve the health of the working class. The Webbs were especially critical of this aspect of the scheme, arguing that the government's role should be to prevent or cure sickness, not simply to reduce the income loss caused by sickness.[89]

It turned out to be more difficult to get health insurance through Parliament than unemployment insurance. Lloyd George had to deal with three powerful interest groups, all of whom feared the effects of national health insurance— friendly societies, industrial assurance companies, and the British medical profession. As a result, the act adopted in 1911 was substantially different from that proposed in 1908. For example, Lloyd George's original proposal included widow's and orphan's pensions, but these were dropped in response to the strenuous objections of the friendly societies, who viewed them as a form of funeral benefit. Lloyd George responded to friendly societies' more general objections to national insurance in his April 1909 budget speech, arguing that there were several million people in Britain "who either cannot be persuaded or perhaps cannot afford to bear the expense of the systematic contributions" required to become members of friendly societies, and that nothing "short of an universal compulsory system can ever hope to succeed adequately in coping with the problem."[90]

The government's health insurance scheme was introduced in May 1911 as Part I of the National Insurance Bill. There followed several months of negotiations both within Parliament and between the government and interest groups, in particular the British Medical Association and the industrial insurance industry. Indeed, the passage of the bill provided "an almost classic history of lobby activity." Lloyd George compromised on some points, while at the same time appealing to the public to support his health insurance scheme. In a speech at Birmingham on June 12, he famously stated,

> This year, this Session, I have joined the Red Cross. I am in the ambulance corps. I am engaged to drive a wagon through the twistings and turnings and ruts of the Parliamentary road. . . . Now there are some who say I am in a great hurry. I am rather in a hurry, for I can hear the moanings of the wounded,

89. Gilbert (1966a: 315); Webb (1948: 478–79).
90. Gilbert (1966a: 294–300).

and I want to carry relief to them in the alleys, the homes where they lie stricken, and I ask you, and through you, I ask the millions of good-hearted men and women who constitute the majority of the people of this land—I ask you to help me to set aside hindrances, to overcome obstacles, to avoid the pitfalls that beset my difficult path.[91]

The act that was adopted in December 1911 established a system of compulsory health insurance covering all workers aged 16 and over earning less than £160 per year. The system was contributory—workers paid 4d. per week, their employers 3d., and the state 2d. In return, an insured man received 10s. per week when sick (an insured woman 7.5s.), payable from the fourth day of illness, for up to 13 weeks. Thereafter, weekly benefits for both men and women were 5s. for an additional 13 weeks. The scheme was administered by approved societies, who set up local branches or committees to deal with the insured. Insured workers received free medical treatment from a doctor whom they could select from a list of those employed by an approved society, and were eligible to obtain treatment in a tuberculosis sanatorium. Dependents of insured workers did not receive medical treatment, except for a 30s. maternity benefit payable to an insured worker's wife at childbirth.

The Liberal Welfare Reforms, considered together, represent a major shift in British social welfare policy. They provided a minimum level of assistance outside of the Poor Law to the sick, the unemployed, and the aged, and in doing so reduced the economic insecurity associated with industrial capitalism. They also led to a sharp increase in social welfare spending—government spending on old age pensions alone in England and Wales in 1913 was 29% greater than total spending on indoor and outdoor poor relief in 1908.

However, the new policies left many working-class individuals unprotected, and the benefits they provided were far from generous—the safety net created by the Liberal Welfare Reforms was full of holes. The Old Age Pension Act did not cover workers aged 65–70, national unemployment insurance covered only one in five adult males, and those for a maximum of 15 weeks, medical benefits were not provided to the dependents of insured workers, and the Trade Boards Act, even after the creation of additional Boards in 1913, covered only one in ten women employed outside of agriculture or domestic service. The reforms did not address the fact that wage rates for many unskilled workers were "insufficient to . . . maintain a family of moderate size in a state of bare physical efficiency."[92] Some of the policies, in particular the

91. Gilbert (1966a: 356–57); Fraser (2003: 180–83); Braithwaite (1957: 176–77).

92. See Rowntree (1901: 133) and Bowley and Burnett-Hurst (1915: 41–42). There also were odd inconsistencies across programs. A worker covered by unemployment insurance who lost his job received 7s. per week; the same worker received 10s. per week if he was unable to work due to sickness.

Trade Boards Act and national unemployment insurance, must be viewed as experiments, and indeed their coverage was extended after the First World War. The Liberal Welfare Reforms were a step, but a tentative one, toward the post-1945 welfare state.

IV. The Political Economy of the Liberal Welfare Reforms

What led Parliament in 1906–11 to seemingly turn its back on the ideology of self-help and adopt a series of social welfare policies, after decades of stinginess toward the poor? The reforms were not a foregone conclusion given the Liberal Party's victory in the 1906 election, as the Liberals had not campaigned for the adoption of social welfare policies. There were, as has been discussed, economic and humanitarian reasons to adopt such programs. The studies by Booth and Rowntree revealed large numbers of working-class households living near or below the poverty line, with little or no savings, whose heads were not members of friendly societies or trade unions, and who did not apply for poor relief either out of shame or fear of the workhouse. However, the public's increasing awareness of the large gaps in the public-private safety net did not, at least before 1906, lead to a strong call for state intervention. Masterman, writing in 1901, lamented the decline in public interest in "the problems of poverty and the possibilities of social reform" since the 1880s. The dawn of the twentieth century had brought with it a wave of imperialism, and the problems of the poor had ceased "to trouble the public mind."[93]

To explain the timing of the Liberal reforms, it is necessary to add a political economy dimension to the story. This section examines the role played by the increase in the franchise and the rise of the Labour Party in leading the Liberals to turn to social reform, and also compares the timing of welfare legislation in Britain with that of its continental neighbors and economic competitors.

THE ROLE OF POLITICAL VOICE

Lindert has argued convincingly that the fall and rise of social welfare spending in Victorian and Edwardian Britain cannot be understood without including political voice. The Great Reform Act of 1832 gave the vote to the middle class, and increased the size of the parliamentary electorate by nearly 65%. The newly enfranchised, many of whom were petty capitalists and shopkeepers, largely were opposed to generous poor relief spending.[94] The Reform Act of 1867—Disraeli's "leap in the dark"—granted the vote to all household heads

---

93. Masterman (1901: 1–4).
94. See Lindert (2004: 71–73, 80–83) and Acemoglu and Robinson (2006: 3).

living in boroughs (including a substantial share of urban working-class males) and increased the electorate by 85%.[95]

In 1884 the Third Reform Act extended the franchise to household heads living in the counties, increasing the electorate by a further 88%. The act gave most agricultural laborers and coal miners the vote. In 1885, the parliamentary electorate totaled 5.7 million, or 63% of the adult male population. The Redistribution of Seats Act of 1885 increased the representation of northern cities and created single-member constituencies in both boroughs and counties. Liverpool gained six seats in Parliament, Birmingham gained four, and Manchester and Sheffield each gained three. The working-class districts of Tower Hamlets and Hackney in East London each gained five seats. Some of the new urban constituencies were "overwhelmingly middle-class or working-class," which encouraged "the development of a class-based electoral system." The acts of 1884 and 1885 thus produced "a 'mass' electorate . . . in which the traditional parties who ignored the wishes of manual workers would do so at their peril."[96]

The Liberal Party seemed to most contemporaries to be the logical home for the newly enfranchised, but the party did not go out of its way to appeal to working-class voters, and it paid a heavy price at the polls. The general elections of 1886, 1895, and 1900 were "resounding Liberal defeats."[97] Working-class dissatisfaction with the two major parties led in 1893 to the founding of the Independent Labour Party (ILP), which in 1900 merged with other Socialist groups to form the Labour Party.

The 1906 election was a landslide victory for the Liberals, who gained a 243-seat majority over the Conservatives. The election also saw a fivefold increase in the number of votes cast for Labour, and an increase in the number of Labour MPs from 2 to 29. The Labour Party *had* campaigned for the adoption of social welfare policies—its election manifesto stated that underfed schoolchildren, the aged poor, and the unemployed had been neglected by Parliament, and ended with an appeal to workers: "You have it in your power to see that Parliament carries out your wishes."[98]

Some Liberals recognized the threat posed by Labour even before 1906. Lloyd George, for one, understood that the Liberal Party needed to provide workers with an attractive alternative to socialism. In a 1904 speech he warned

---

95. The number of voters in English and Welsh boroughs increased by 138% as a result of the act. In 1871, 44.7% of adult males were on the electoral registers in boroughs, as compared to 19.7% in 1861 (Hoppen 1998: 253). Lindert (2004: 72) estimates that the share of UK adult men who had the right to vote increased from 18.0% in 1866 to 31.4% in 1868.

96. Searle (1992: 49–50); Youngs (1979; 1991).

97. Searle (1992: 51).

98. Craig (1989: 18); Dale (2000: 10–11).

his fellow Liberals that "unless we can prove . . . that there is no necessity for a separate party to press forward the legitimate claims of Labour, you will find that . . . the Liberal Party will be practically wiped out and that, in its place, you will get a more extreme and revolutionary party." A year later Lord Crewe wrote the Liberal leader, Campbell-Bannerman, that the party was on "trial as an engine for securing social reforms. . . . It has to resist the ILP claim to be the only friend of the workers."[99]

Once in power, Lloyd George and others began to call for social welfare legislation. In October 1906, Lloyd George, then President of the Board of Trade, stated in a speech at Cardiff that if the Liberal Parliament would do something "to remove the national degradation of slums and widespread poverty and destitution" and provide "an honourable sustenance for deserving old age, . . . then the Independent Labour party will call in vain upon the working men of Britain to desert Liberalism that is so gallantly fighting to rid the land of the wrongs that have oppressed those who labour in it." Churchill, at the time Under-Secretary of State for the Colonies, also recognized the political benefits to be reaped from the adoption of social welfare legislation. In 1907 he wrote to the editor of the *Westminster Review* that the working classes "will not continue to bear, they cannot, the awful uncertainties of their lives. Minimum standards of wages and comfort, insurance in some effective form or other against sickness, unemployment, old age—these are the questions and the only questions by which parties are going to live in the future."[100]

The Liberal government's achievements on the reform front were modest in its first two years in power, consisting mostly of free school lunches and medical inspections for poor children. The "tempo of reform dramatically quickened" when, in 1908, with the Liberals' popularity declining as a result of rising unemployment, and after losing five by-elections, the gravely ill Campbell-Bannerman resigned as Prime Minister and was replaced by Asquith. The resulting Cabinet reshuffling increased the power of the "social Liberals," and in particular Lloyd George and Churchill, "the heavenly twins of social reform"—Lloyd George became Chancellor of the Exchequer and Churchill replaced him as President of the Board of Trade.[101]

The "social Liberals" strongly supported social welfare programs on political as well as national efficiency and humanitarian grounds. They believed that the adoption of old age pensions and national sickness and unemployment insurance would be popular enough among working-class voters to slow the growth of the Labour Party. In a 1908 letter to his brother, Lloyd George wrote that the Old Age Pension Act before Parliament would appeal "straight to the

99. Grigg (1978: 77); Searle (2004: 361).
100. Lloyd George (1910: 36); Hay (1978: 72).
101. Searle (2004: 362–66); Churchill (1967: 238).

people" and thus "help to stop the electoral rot." He lashed out at Labour in a speech at Swansea in October 1908, stating that while the Liberal government "was extending the mercy of a small pension to the aged who have won it by a life of toil, . . . incredible as it may seem, it was attacked with spiteful savagery by socialists on the flank." Churchill also stressed how the Liberal government's social policies were superior to the socialism advocated by Labour. In a speech at Dundee in the fall of 1908, he stated, "Socialism wants to pull down wealth, Liberalism seeks to raise up poverty. . . . Socialism assails the maximum pre-eminence of the individual—Liberalism seeks to build up the minimum standard of the masses."[102]

As predicted by Lloyd George, the Old Age Pension act was "immensely popular" with the working class. He and Churchill believed that health and unemployment insurance also would be popular. Churchill wrote the Prime Minister in December 1908 that the government should put forward a program of national sickness and unemployment insurance, and predicted that it "would not only benefit the state but fortify the party." At the time of its passage, many members of the opposition also believed that national insurance would yield political benefits to the Liberals. Austen Chamberlain, a leading Conservative, commented in 1911, "Confound Ll. George. He has strengthened the Government again. His sickness scheme *is* a good one and he is on the right lines this time."[103]

In the event, national insurance turned out to be less popular with the working class than old age pensions, due in large part to differences in how the programs were funded. Pensions were noncontributory, while national insurance required weekly deductions from workers' wages. Workers liked the extension of the safety net and reduction in economic insecurity provided by health and unemployment insurance, but did not like the decline in their disposable income. The more militant among the working class argued that what was needed was not compulsory state-based insurance, but steady work and higher wages. Once these were secured, workers would be able to protect themselves.[104]

The Liberal Welfare Reforms did not yield the positive political bump that Lloyd George and Churchill had hoped to achieve—they did not "stop the electoral rot" in the long run. Working-class voters came to believe that their interests would be better served by a working-class party than by a middle-class party catering to the working class. There was "a growing feeling in the country that the Liberal Party was no longer the party of the working classes, but that in some perceived if indefinable way the Labour Party was."[105]

102. Searle (2004: 366); George (1958: 220); Lloyd George (1910: 58); Churchill (1967: 255).

103. Churchill (1969: 862–64).

104. Thane (1984); Searle (1992: 111–13).

105. McKibbin (1974: 70–71); Searle (1992: 68–76, 112–20).

EDWARDIAN BRITAIN IN A EUROPEAN MIRROR

How did British workers' living standards and social welfare policies at the turn of the century compare with living standards and social policies in other European countries? Table 6.6 presents data for seven measures of the standard of living for nine European countries circa 1900–1910: GDP per capita, real wages for manual laborers, life expectancy at birth, heights of adult males, literacy, school enrollment, and annual discretionary hours. GDP per capita is measured in 1990 international dollars. The real wage series is an index, with British wages in 1904–8 equal to 100. The school enrollment rate is defined as the number of primary and secondary school students per 1,000 children aged 5–14. Annual discretionary (leisure) time is defined as 4,160 hours minus the average annual number of hours worked.[106]

Many economists believe that income, measured by either GDP per capita or real wages, is the best measure of living standards. Higher incomes enable workers to purchase more of what they value most, be it more nutritious food, better housing, better health care, education for their children, or more beer. Richer countries will have healthier and better educated workers. Others view income as a measure of command over resources, an input to well-being rather than an indicator of well-being, which is better measured by life expectancy, health, education, and voluntary leisure time. Height by age is a function of net nutrition in childhood and adolescence, and therefore a proxy for health. Workers gain satisfaction from leisure as well as income. The decline in annual hours of work that occurred in virtually all industrialized nations after 1870 "did not come about as an accident," and resulted in a significant increase in workers' well-being.[107]

Britain's ranking in the league table depends on which measure of the standard of living is being considered. In 1900 Britain was the richest nation in Europe, with a per capita GDP 19% greater than Belgium and one-third greater than Germany. British workers' material living standards, as measured by real wages, were higher than those of other European workers. They also enjoyed more leisure time than workers on the continent, to go with their higher income.

When well-being is compared using biological or schooling measures, however, the rankings of European nations change. Life expectancy at birth was

106. I chose 4,160 hours as the maximum length of the work year. It is equal to 52 times 80 hours per week. This assumes that the remaining 88 hours in the week are necessary for sleep, meals, chores, and commuting to and from work. Fogel (2000: 184) estimates that sleep, meals, chores, and commuting took 13 hours per day.

107. See Sen (1987), Steckel and Flood (1997), Fogel (2000: 184–86), Kuznets (1952: 63–69), Nordhaus and Tobin (1973), and Williamson (1984).

TABLE 6.6. Measures of Living Standards, Europe 1900–1910

	GDP per Capita 1900	Real Wages 1904–8	Life Expectancy 1910	Adult Male Heights 1900	Literacy Rate 1910	School Enrollment 1900	Annual Discretionary Hours 1900
United Kingdom	4,714.0	100.0	53.4	169.3	92.5	728	1,504
Belgium	3,975.0	86.2	49.6	165.8	86.6	374	1,096
Denmark	3,592.7	93.7	57.7	168.8	97.0	731	1,418
France	3,097.7	76.1	50.4	166.6	88.1	636	1,045
Germany	3,526.0	87.4	49.0	169.0	97.0	772	1,104
Italy	2,359.3	45.6	47.2	163.8	60.7	371	1,146
Netherlands	3,704.0	78.5	56.1	170.0	92.5	465	1,123
Norway	2,049.3	89.5	57.2	170.4	97.0	718	1,416
Sweden	2,930.3	91.5	57.0	172.5	98.5	705	1,415

Sources: GDP per capita: Maddison (2003). Real wages: Williamson (1995). Revised series for Belgium, Netherlands, Norway, and the United Kingdom constructed by O'Rourke and Williamson (1997) obtained from the authors. Life expectancy: Crafts (1997). Adult male heights: Data for France, Germany, Netherlands, Sweden, and United Kingdom from Steckel and Floud (1997); data for Belgium, Denmark, Italy, and Norway from Floud (1994). Literacy: Flora (1973). School enrollment: Lindert (2004: vol. 2), and revised numbers from his UC Davis website. Discretionary time: Calculated by author using data on annual hours worked from Huberman (2012: 149); Norway calculated as average of Denmark and Sweden.

Note: See text for definition of variables.

three to four years lower in Britain than in Scandinavia or the Netherlands, although British workers lived longer, on average, than those in Germany, France, and Belgium. The data for adult male heights tell a similar story—on average, men were taller in Sweden, Norway, and the Netherlands than in Britain, and German men were nearly as tall as their British rivals. Nor was Britain a leader in education. Literacy was highest in Scandinavia and Germany, and the share of children attending school was highest in Germany.

Why weren't high-wage British workers healthier and better educated than their European counterparts? In part the answer has to do with differences in social policies across countries. Urban death rates declined relatively slowly in Victorian Britain, largely because cities were slow to construct sewers and water systems. The reason for this tardiness in public health investment is similar to the reason for Britain's increasingly stingy welfare policy after 1834. The urban middle class—shopkeepers, landlords, and other small tradesmen—who had been given the franchise in 1832, voted in municipal elections to keep their regressive property taxes as low as possible. This meant blocking expensive investments in public health infrastructure. Britain's slow growth in educational attainment up to 1891 also was due in part to its "elite democracy"; the major acts of Parliament (1870, 1891) that led to mass primary education were not adopted until after the reform acts of 1867 and 1884 extended the franchise to the working class.[108]

Table 6.6 raises another perplexing issue—how can the fact that British wages were higher than wages on the continent be reconciled with the poverty estimates of Rowntree and Bowley? Perhaps urban poverty rates were even higher in Europe than in Britain. Unfortunately, there are no comparable poverty surveys of German or French towns with which to test this hypothesis. Moreover, there was no "condition of Germany" debate comparable to the "condition of England" debate discussed in Section I. A recent comparative study of British and German workers' living standards suggests an answer. Broadberry and Burhop compared British and German real wages in 12 occupations in 1905 and found that while skilled workers' wages were 10–30% lower in Germany, wages for unskilled engineering laborers were the same in the two countries. In other words, the skill premium was higher in Britain than in Germany. They conclude that the relatively low wages of unskilled British workers makes it "easier to understand the persistence of large pockets of poverty in Europe's highest wage economy."[109]

---

108. On public health investments, see Hennock (1973), Williamson (1990: chap. 10), Szreter (1988; 1997), and Sandberg and Steckel (1997, 143–45). On Britain's lag in educational attainment, see Lindert (2004: chap. 5).

109. Broadberry and Burhop (2010: 419–23). Their conclusion fits well with the findings of Rowntree and Bowley that the major cause of poverty in Edwardian cities was the low wages

TABLE 6.7. Social Welfare Legislation and Spending, Europe Pre-1914

(A) ADOPTION DATE FOR SOCIAL WELFARE LEGISLATION

	Accident Insurance	Old Age Pensions	Sickness Insurance	Unemployment Insurance
United Kingdom	1897	1908	1911	1911
Belgium	1903	1900(V)	1894	1907(V)
Denmark	1898	1891	1892(V)	1907(V)
France	1898	1900(V)	1898(V)	1905(V)
Germany	1884	1889	1883	—
Italy	1898	1898(V)	1886(V)	—
Netherlands	1901	1913	1913	—
Norway	1894	—	1909	1906(V)
Sweden	1901	1913	1891(V)	—

(B) SOCIAL TRANSFERS AS A PERCENTAGE OF GROSS DOMESTIC PRODUCT

	1880	1890	1900	1910
United Kingdom	0.86	0.83	1.00	1.38
Belgium	0.17	0.22	0.26	0.43
Denmark	0.96	1.11	1.41	1.75
France	0.46	0.54	0.57	0.81
Germany	0.50	0.53	0.59	NA
Italy	0.00	0.00	0.00	0.00
Netherlands	0.29	0.30	0.39	0.39
Norway	1.07	0.95	1.24	1.18
Sweden	0.72	0.85	0.85	1.03

Sources: Adoption dates for social legislation from Huberman and Lewchuk (2003: 11). Data on social transfers from Lindert (2004: 12–13).
Note: V indicates a voluntary program.

The decades leading up to the First World War witnessed the adoption of social welfare legislation throughout Northwestern Europe; the Liberal Welfare Reforms did not take place in isolation. The spread of legislation and the increase in spending on social welfare programs have been documented by Flora and Alber, Lindert, and Huberman.[110] Table 6.7 shows the adoption dates of old age pensions and accident, sickness, and unemployment insurance

---

paid to unskilled laborers. Broadberry and Burhop's finding that wages for unskilled laborers in the engineering trades were equal in Britain and Germany appears not to jive with Williamson's (1995) estimate that laborers' wages were 13% lower in Germany than in Britain (see Table 6.6). Williamson's wage data are for laborers in the building trades, and his estimate is similar to Broadberry and Burhop's finding that wages for building trades laborers were 14% lower in Germany than in Britain.

110. See Flora and Alber (1981), Lindert (1994; 2004), Huberman and Lewchuk (2003), and Huberman (2012).

policies for nine Northwestern European nations and gives decadal levels of social spending as a share of national product from 1880 to 1910 for the same nations.

The data reported in panel (a) show that Britain was a laggard in the adoption of sickness insurance and old age pensions. Six of the nine countries adopted some form of sickness insurance before 1900, although in four cases the policies were subsidized voluntary schemes. The share of workers covered by sickness plans varied widely across nations. According to Flora and Alber, in 1910, the year before the adoption of the National Insurance Act, 55% of the economically active population in Denmark was eligible for sickness benefits, as compared to 51% in Germany, 27% in Sweden, 17% in France, 12% in Belgium, and 6% in Italy.[111] Five countries adopted old age pension plans before Britain, although the Belgian, French, and Italian plans were voluntary. The leader, in terms of number of economically active workers covered, was Germany. On the other hand, Britain was the first country to adopt a compulsory unemployment insurance scheme, albeit one that covered only one in five adult male workers. The voluntary unemployment benefit schemes adopted in Europe in the first decade of the twentieth century covered few workers—about 9% of Danish and 4% of Belgian workers were eligible for unemployment benefits in 1910.[112]

Flora and Alber constructed an index of social insurance coverage consisting of a "weighted average of the percent of the labor force covered" by old age pensions and sickness, unemployment, and accident insurance. This indicates, not surprisingly, that in the first decade of the century coverage was highest in Germany, followed by Denmark. With the adoption of the Old Age Pension Act in 1908, Britain overtook Denmark, and after the passage of the National Insurance Act coverage rates were higher in Britain than in any other European country. Britain's lead was short-lived, however, as it was overtaken by Sweden in 1913. On the eve of the First World War, Britain was one of three leading European "welfare" states, along with Sweden and Germany, in terms of worker coverage.[113]

While the number of workers covered by social insurance increased rapidly in the decades leading up to the First World War, government spending on social welfare programs remained tiny in all European countries, as can be seen

111. Flora and Alber (1981: 75). Hennock (2007: 180) estimates that in 1911 German membership in sickness funds of all kinds equaled about 14.25 million, which was 36.1% of the population aged 15–64. This percentage, while far below that reported by Flora and Alber, still leaves German coverage second in rank, behind only Denmark.

112. Flora and Alber (1981: 76–77).

113. Flora and Alber (1981: 54–57). Hennock (2007: 172–81) estimates that in 1913–14 the share of the working-age population eligible for sickness benefits was 48.5% in England and Wales and 46.7% in Germany.

in panel (b) of Table 6.7. In 1910 only the three Scandinavian countries and Britain spent more than 1% of gross domestic product on social transfers. By contrast, in 1995 the ratio of social transfer spending to GDP exceeded 20% in all nine countries, and exceeded 30% in Denmark and Sweden. A comparison of panels (a) and (b) shows that there is not a one-to-one correspondence between social insurance coverage and social spending. The reason for this is that in some countries government-mandated social insurance programs were not paid for by taxpayer contributions. Germany is a prime example. The entire cost of German sickness insurance up to 1914 was borne by workers, who paid two-thirds of the costs, and their employers, who paid the remaining one-third. The state provided a small subsidy to the old age and invalidity insurance fund, but in 1908 this equaled only 0.12% of German national product. In the words of Lindert, "the famous Bismarckian social insurance involved almost no redistribution through government budgets."[114]

To what extent were the Liberal Welfare Reforms modeled on European, and in particular German, precedents? Daniel Rodgers maintained that Churchill, Lloyd George, and the Liberals were "eager policy borrowers, scavengers across the boundaries of national political cultures." Beveridge (1907) and Lloyd George (1908) visited Germany to study its social welfare policies, and both came back impressed with the German system of social insurance. Journalist Harold Spender, who accompanied Lloyd George on his visit, wrote, "The German example has taught us this great lesson—that the principle of insurance, which is used so freely in our own country to protect the prosperous, . . . may be even more successfully extended to protect the unprosperous. . . . Within a few years, practically the whole of the working classes of Germany will be made immune from the quadruple risks of old age, accident, invalidity and sickness, while the State that has brought that about will be contributing little more than the cost of administration." Churchill compared British private voluntary insurance with German compulsory insurance in a January 1908 letter to Wilson Fox and concluded that the "enormous advantage" of the German system was that "it catches everybody," whereas the British system offered no provision for "the residue" who "have neither the character nor the resources" to provide for themselves. Eleven months later, after becoming President of the Board of Trade, he wrote the Prime Minister recommending that the government "thrust a big slice of Bismarckianism over the whole underside of our industrial system, and await the consequences."[115]

The fact that the Liberals were influenced by German policies does not mean, however, that the British social welfare reforms were simply adaptations

114. Lindert (2004: 12–13); Lindert (1994: 9–14).
115. Rodgers (1998: 229–32); Hennock (1987: 133–38, 149–51); Spender (1909: 27); Churchill (1969: 759, 862–64).

of German prototypes. Consider the three main social welfare policies: old age pensions, sickness insurance, and unemployment insurance. German old age and invalidity insurance was funded mainly by contributions from workers and their employers. In contrast, the British system of old age pensions was financed completely out of general tax revenue; it was noncontributory and means-tested. Because British pensions were paid to "persons rather than to wage earners . . . from the first they reached at least three times as many persons." The British system was modeled on the noncontributory pension schemes adopted in Denmark in 1891 and New Zealand in 1898, not the German program.[116]

The German sickness insurance program was funded completely by contributions from workers and employers, with workers paying two-thirds of the cost. The British system was similar in the sense that workers and employers contributed to the fund—in both the German and British plans, employers paid one-third of the weekly contributions (3d. per worker per week in Britain). However, the British government contributed 2d. per worker per week out of tax revenue, so that workers paid only 44% of the cost (4d. per week). In the words of Lloyd George, workers received 9d. for a contribution of 4d.

Great Britain was the first country to adopt a compulsory system of unemployment insurance. Ten years earlier the city of Ghent, Belgium, had adopted a voluntary unemployment insurance scheme in which the municipality subsidized the provision of the insurance by trade unions. Ghent-type systems quickly spread to cities throughout Western Europe, and by 1908 national schemes for subsidizing voluntary (mainly trade union) unemployment insurance funds were adopted by France, Denmark, and Norway. It was hoped that government subsidies would lead additional unions—including unions of low-skilled workers—to offer unemployment benefits to their members, although in this regard the plans were not especially successful. The Minority Report of the Poor Law Commission proposed that Britain adopt a version of the Ghent system, and the Majority Report also noted the Ghent system with approval. In the end, however, Churchill rejected a Ghent-type system and insisted that employers, as well as workers and the state, contribute to the scheme. The resulting British system therefore differed from all previous unemployment insurance plans.

In sum, while Britain was a bit of a latecomer in the adoption of state-supported social welfare programs, it caught up in 1908–11. On the eve of the First World War, it was a leader in social welfare protection, measured either by the share of persons covered or by expenditures as a share of national income.

---

116. Rodgers (1998: 230); Abbott (1918: 9–10).

Britain expanded its social safety net in the 1920s, as we will see in Chapter 7, and remained a leader in social welfare throughout the interwar period.

V. Conclusion

The decade that began with the death of Queen Victoria in 1901 and ended with the passage of the National Insurance Act marked a watershed in British social welfare policy. The Liberal Welfare Reforms provided assistance to the working class, which was outside of the Poor Law and therefore did not involve "the stigma of pauperism." Parliament did not, however, break up the Poor Law as the Webbs had called for, and it continued to play an important role during the interwar years, assisting those who fell through the cracks in the safety net.

Late Victorian and Edwardian Britain witnessed an explosion of information on working-class living standards, which revealed that poverty and insecurity remained serious problems despite decades of economic growth—trickle down clearly was not sufficient to eliminate economic distress among the lower stratum of the working class. The findings disturbed middle-class Britain on both humanitarian and national efficiency grounds and helped turn the tide of public opinion in favor of government-supported social safety nets. The drive for welfare reform was further encouraged by the granting of political voice to a large share of the working class and the Liberal government's attempt to slow the growth of the Labour Party.

In terms of the funding of social policy, the Liberal Welfare Reforms marked a sharp break from the past. The Poor Law and municipal relief works were financed out of local taxation. In contrast, old age pensions were funded entirely by the central government, and national insurance was financed by contributions from employers, workers, and the state. By increasing the central government's role in the funding of social welfare policies, the Liberal Welfare Reforms helped pave the way for the rise of the welfare state in the 1940s.

7

Social Welfare Policy and Living Standards between the Wars

The British economy slid into recession in 1921 and remained depressed up to the beginning of the Second World War. The social welfare system adopted in 1906–11 and extended during the 1920s was put to a serious test by the prolonged slump, and has been criticized by historians, and some contemporaries, for not being up to the task. There is no doubt that the safety net had many holes in it, and that the protection it offered to working-class households was inferior to that provided by the welfare state adopted after the Second World War. Still, it is important to keep in mind that the interwar economy was hit by economic shocks that were unprecedented in nature. No one in 1911, or 1920, anticipated the extent of these shocks or the pressure that would be put on the social welfare system as a result of them.

This chapter shows what happened to workers' living standards between the wars and examines the extent to which social welfare policies were successful in alleviating poverty and maintaining the well-being of working-class households in an era of unprecedentedly high unemployment. Section I describes the structural/regional nature of interwar unemployment. Section II examines the interwar changes in the social insurance system, focusing on the government's continuing balancing act of providing for the unemployed, the sick, and the old while at the same time attempting to minimize expenditures. Section III reveals the important role played by the Poor Law, which served as a residual safety net, assisting those who fell through the cracks of the social insurance programs. While the Liberal Welfare Reforms were expected to greatly reduce the Poor Law's role, numbers receiving poor relief increased sharply in the 1920s. Many of those relieved were unemployed able-bodied males and their families, who had been virtually eliminated from the relief roles by 1900.

Section IV examines trends in working-class living standards, broadly defined. Despite the high interwar unemployment rates, both material and biological measures of living standards improved from 1920 to 1938. The health of working-class children improved even in the distressed areas, which can be interpreted as evidence of the beneficial effects of government social policies. Section V summarizes the findings of the several town-level social surveys undertaken between the wars and uses information from the surveys to examine the role of social welfare policies in alleviating distress.

I. Interwar Unemployment

Any examination of workers' living standards and welfare policy in interwar Britain must first and foremost confront the issues created by the depressed state of the economy, and in particular by the exceedingly high unemployment rates. From 1921 to 1938, the unemployment rate among insured workers averaged 14.2%; among all workers it averaged 10.9% (see Table 7.1). The economic distress was not simply cyclical in nature—the annual unemployment rate among insured workers did not fall below 9.7% throughout the period. These consistently high unemployment rates created major problems for the financing of the unemployment insurance system, as will be discussed below.

The average unemployment rate between the wars was substantially higher than in 1870–1913 or 1947–73. There is not space here to explain the reasons for this high unemployment; it must suffice to state that it had several causes, including, but not limited to, the global economic disruption caused by the First World War, major shocks to the economy, the decline in exports, the increase in structural turbulence, and, to some extent, poor economic policy choices.[1] The government officials who constructed the unemployment insurance system did not anticipate the high unemployment rates, and the methods used to finance the system had to be altered in the face of the enormous costs of unemployment relief. The relief of the unemployed became "the major social problem of the time."[2]

The interwar economy suffered from severe structural problems. Unemployment was especially high in coal mining, iron and steel, shipbuilding, and cotton textiles. These were "old" industries that had been key growth sectors

---

1. For a detailed analysis of interwar unemployment, see Thomas (1988), Hatton (1986; 2004), Crafts (1987), Eichengreen (1987), Benjamin and Kochin (1979), and Garside (1990). Hatton and Boyer (2005) offer a comparison of unemployment rates across eras.

2. Burns (1941: 35).

TABLE 7.1. Unemployment Rates, 1921–38

	Insured Unemployed/ Insured Employees	Total Unemployed/ Total Employees
1921	17.0	12.2
1922	14.3	10.8
1923	11.7	8.9
1924	10.3	7.9
1925	11.3	8.6
1926	12.5	9.6
1927	9.7	7.4
1928	10.8	8.2
1929	10.4	8.0
1930	16.1	12.3
1931	21.3	16.4
1932	22.1	17.0
1933	19.9	15.4
1934	16.7	12.9
1935	15.5	12.0
1936	13.1	10.2
1937	10.8	8.5
1938	12.9	10.1
Average 1921–38	14.2	10.9

Source: Feinstein (1972: T128, Table 58).

in the Victorian economy, and they were heavily dependent on exports. On the other hand, unemployment was relatively low in gas, water and electricity, electrical engineering, chemicals, automobiles and aircraft, railway service, and the distributive trades. Some of these—electricity and electrical engineering, motor vehicles, and chemicals—were "new" industries that specialized in producing consumer durables for the domestic market. The average unemployment rate for 1923–38 exceeded 20% in each of the four old "staple" industries; it was below 10% in gas, water and electricity, electrical engineering, railways, and the distributive trades.[3]

The high-unemployment industries had something else in common; they were concentrated in northern England, southern Wales, and Scotland. In contrast, the "new" industries tended to locate in the South Midlands and the South East, near London, the largest consumer market in the country. As a result of the regional concentration of old and new industries, the extent of unemployment differed greatly across regions. From 1925 to 1938,

3. Unemployment rates by industry from Department of Employment and Productivity, *British Labour Statistics: Historical Abstract 1886–1968* (1971: 314–15, Table 164).

unemployment rates were substantially higher in the North, Wales, Scotland, and Northern Ireland than in London, the South East, or South West. The average unemployment rate for 1923–38 was over 20% in Wales and Northern Ireland and nearly 18% in the North and Scotland, but only 12% in the Midlands and 8–8.5% in the South East and London. At the peak of the depression, in 1932, the unemployment rate was 36.5% in Wales and exceeded 25% in the North, Scotland, and Northern Ireland, but was below 15% in London and the South East.[4]

Differences in unemployment rates across cities were quite large for the same reasons. Table 7.2 shows unemployment rates for adult males in London and 15 provincial cities in three years, 1927, 1932, and 1936. In 1927, a relatively prosperous interwar year, the unemployment rate was below 7% in London and Leicester. It was 15% or higher in seven cities, all in the North of England, Wales, or Scotland, and exceeded 30% in Sunderland, located in the coal-producing North East. In 1932, unemployment was roughly 15% in London and below 22% in five provincial cities, but exceeded 35% in Glasgow, Sheffield, Swansea, and Sunderland. Finally, in 1936, when adult male unemployment was below 11% in London and Birmingham, it exceeded 30% in Liverpool, Swansea, and Sunderland. The distress faced by workers and their families was not evenly distributed across Britain. In the words of contemporary economist Henry Clay, the situation was one "in which a limited number of districts are faced with an entirely unprecedented volume of unemployment."[5] The consequences of this concentration of distress are discussed in Sections II and III.

Another aspect of interwar unemployment needs to be mentioned. The average duration of a spell of unemployment was relatively long throughout the period, and it increased over time. The "average interrupted spell" of unemployment increased from 22.3 weeks in September 1929 (the first date it can be measured) to 31.6 weeks in June 1932 and 42.9 weeks in June 1935. The share of the unemployed out of work for 12 months or longer increased from 10.7% in September 1929 to 21.0% in December 1932 and remained above 20% through the fall of 1938. Both the average duration of an unemployment spell and the share out of work for a year or more were substantially higher during the interwar years than in late Victorian and Edwardian Britain.[6]

4. Regional unemployment rates from Garside (1990: 10) and monthly issues of the *Ministry of Labour Gazette*.

5. Clay (1930: 54).

6. Data on average duration of unemployment spells and the share of applicants unemployed for 12 months or longer from Crafts (1987: 419–22). The "average interrupted spell length" measures "how long on average the unemployed had been out of work at the moment of observation." Thomas (1988: 98–115) provides a detailed discussion of unemployment duration in interwar Britain and alternative ways to calculate average duration of unemployment. Thomas

TABLE 7.2. Unemployment Rates of Adult Males by City, 1927–36

	1927	1932	1936
London	6.4	14.8	10.1
Bristol	12.5	24.2	14.7
Southampton	9.9	24.7	13.5
Birmingham	8.0	20.6	7.4
Nottingham	8.3	21.1	17.7
Leicester	5.2	16.2	11.1
Manchester	8.2	20.2	14.7
Liverpool	17.1	34.1	31.7
Leeds	11.2	26.5	17.1
Sheffield	16.3	39.8	20.0
Newcastle	18.7	31.6	23.5
Sunderland	30.4	52.1	39.6
Edinburgh	10.4	20.7	20.2
Glasgow	15.4	38.0	28.2
Cardiff	15.0	33.2	27.9
Swansea	19.8	41.3	34.0

Source: Monthly *Local Unemployment Index* published by the Ministry of Labour.
Note: For 1927, each city's unemployment rate was calculated as the average of the March and July unemployment rates. For 1932 and 1936, it was calculated as the average of the January and July unemployment rates.

Beveridge maintained that "from the point of view of effect on the unemployed person, differences in the duration of unemployment . . . are of first importance." Any given unemployment rate can reflect high turnover and short duration or low turnover and long duration. A labor market in which many workers were unemployed for short periods of time functioned much differently, and had different implications for the welfare costs on the unemployed, than one in which a smaller number of workers were unemployed for long periods. Contemporaries agreed that the welfare costs of long-term unemployment were especially high in interwar Britain. E. W. Bakke found that long periods of unemployment led to the "slow death" of ambition and industriousness among workers. Similarly, the Pilgrim Trust concluded in its report *Men without Work* that long-term unemployment made many men diffident; they "find it more and more difficult to face repeated failures and . . . finally give up looking for work," even though they "have not in any way become used to unemployment."[7]

(1990: 36–43) presents estimates of average duration of unemployment spells in Victorian and Edwardian England.

7. Beveridge (1944: 65); Bakke (1933: 70–72); Pilgrim Trust (1938: 172–73).

II. The Interwar Social Security System

The social welfare system established in 1906–11 and extended in the 1920s consisted of several independently administered programs—unemployment insurance, sickness and disability insurance, old age pensions, widows' and orphans' insurance, and the Poor Law. The Poor Law was viewed as a program of last resort, to be used by those who either did not qualify for national insurance or pensions or had reached the maximum duration of insurance benefits. It is important to begin by reviewing the changing rules regarding generosity and eligibility for unemployment and sickness insurance, and old age pensions.

CHANGES IN THE UNEMPLOYMENT INSURANCE SYSTEM

The unemployment insurance (UI) system initiated by the 1911 National Insurance Act covered only one in five adult males. It was far from generous—an unemployed worker was eligible to receive a weekly benefit of 7s. for a maximum of 15 weeks within an "insurance year." The supposed problem of "malingering" was guarded against by requiring five weekly contributions to the UI fund for each week of benefits received. That is, an insured worker who made 50 weekly contributions would be eligible for no more than ten weeks of benefit.

In 1920 Parliament extended unemployment insurance to all manual workers other than those engaged in agriculture or domestic service, and to all nonmanual workers with annual incomes below £250. The Unemployment Insurance Act set weekly benefits at 15s. for men and 12s. for women (Table 7.3). The maximum duration of benefits remained at 15 weeks per year; the number of weekly contributions required to receive a week of benefits was increased from five to six. A worker had to make at least 12 contributions to the fund to be eligible for benefits.[8]

The government anticipated that the average unemployment rate among covered workers in the 1920s would be lower than that anticipated in 1911. Alfred Watson, the government actuary, estimated that for the workers included in the UI scheme as of 1920, the average annual unemployment rate measured "over a series of years, *i.e.*, a trade cycle" was 5.3%. He arrived at this number using estimates of unemployment by industry supplied by the Ministry of Labour. The projected unemployment rate for industries covered by the 1911 act—building, construction of works, shipbuilding, mechanical engineering, iron founding, construction of vehicles, and sawmilling—was

---

8. To pay for the higher benefits, employers' and workers' weekly contributions to the UI fund each were raised from 2.5d. to 4d. per week, while the state's contribution increased from 1.67d. to 2d. On the Unemployment Insurance Act of 1920, see Gilbert (1970: 63–74), Royal Commission on Unemployment Insurance, *Final Report* (1932: 15–21), and Beveridge (1930: 274–75).

6.5%. The projected rate was 3.0% for cotton and woolen textiles, 1.5% for mining, and 1.0% for railways.[9]

Within months of the act's adoption it became apparent that Watson's estimates were far too optimistic. The unemployment rate among insured workers, which was under 4% when the act was adopted, increased to 8.2% in January 1921, 17.8% in June (during a coal strike), and 16.1% in December, and did not fall below 12% in 1922.[10] Parliament responded to the higher unemployment rates with a series of acts. The Unemployment Insurance Act of March 1921 enabled unemployed workers who did not meet the contributory requirements to draw emergency or "uncovenanted" benefits (essentially benefits paid in advance of a worker's contributions) for an additional time, provided they met certain conditions. The ability to claim emergency benefits was meant to be temporary, but it was continued in some form for a decade. The March 1921 act also increased weekly benefits to 20s. for men and 16s. for women. The increase in benefits was short-lived; on June 30 they returned to the levels set in 1920.[11]

Table 7.3 shows the changes in weekly UI benefits in the interwar period. Benefits were not related to family size in either 1911 or 1920—single men and married men with families received identical payments. By 1921, however, it had become clear that benefits were inadequate to maintain an unemployed married worker with dependent children. The Unemployed Workers' Dependents (Temporary Provisions) Act of November 1921 introduced dependents' benefits. An unemployed married man received an additional 5s. per week to support his wife (or housekeeper), and 1s. for each dependent child.[12] The dependents' allowance initially was meant to last only for six months, but was made permanent in 1922. Its introduction raised the weekly benefits of unemployed workers with families substantially—a married man with two dependent children received 22s. per week from 1922 to 1924. Benefits were raised an additional six times, and cut once, between 1924 and 1938. The cost of living declined almost continually from 1920 to 1934, so that real benefits increased over time.

9. Watson (1920: 75–76, 80).

10. Hilton (1923: 191).

11. The increase in benefits was paid for, in part, by an increase in contributions by employers, workers, and the state. The March 1921 act increased total weekly contributions per worker from 10d. to 13.75d.; however, before the new rates took effect they were raised again by the July 1921 Unemployment Insurance (No. 2) Act to 18.75d. per week (of which 8d. was paid by the employer, 7d. by the worker, and the remainder by the state). On the Unemployment Insurance Acts of 1921, see Deacon (1976: 16–18, 21), Burns (1941: 35–48), Gilbert (1970: 76–80), Beveridge (1930: 274–77), and Royal Commission on Unemployment Insurance, *Final Report* (1932: 18–21).

12. To help defray the cost of these benefits, total weekly contributions were raised to 25.75d. (10d. paid by the employer, 9d. by the worker, and 6.75d. by the state).

TABLE 7.3. Unemployment Benefits, 1913–39

	WEEKLY UNEMPLOYMENT INSURANCE BENEFITS (S.)							REAL BENEFITS
	Single Man	Single Woman	Adult Dependent	Dependent Child	2 Adults and 2 Children	2 Adults and 3 Children	COL Index	2 Adults and 2 Children
1913	7	7	0	0	7	7	100.0	100.0
1920	15	12	0	0	15	15	244.9	87.5
1921								
January 1–March 2	15	12	0	0	15	15	221.8	96.6
March 3–June 29	20	16	0	0	20	20	221.8	128.8
June 30–November 9	15	12	0	0	15	15	221.8	96.6
November 10–December 31	15	12	5	1	22	23	221.8	141.7
1922	15	12	5	1	22	23	180.2	174.4
1923	15	12	5	1	22	23	172.5	182.2
1924								
January 1–August 13	15	12	5	1	22	23	172.5	182.2
August 14–December 31	18	15	5	2	27	29	172.5	223.6
1925	18	15	5	2	27	29	172.5	223.6
1926	18	15	5	2	27	29	169.5	227.6
1927	18	15	5	2	27	29	164.8	234.0
1928								
January 1–April 18	18	15	5	2	27	29	163.3	236.2
April 19–December 31	17	15	7	2	28	30	163.3	244.9

1929	17	15	7	2	28	30	161.8	247.2

1929	17	15	7	2	28	30	161.8	247.2
1930								
January 1–March 12	17	15	7	2	28	30	155.6	257.1
March 13–December 31	17	15	9	2	30	32	155.6	275.4
1931								
January 1–October 7	17	15	9	2	30	32	144.8	296.0
October 8–December 31	15.25	13.5	8	2	27.25	29.25	144.8	268.8
1932	15.25	13.5	8	2	27.25	29.25	141.7	274.7
1933	15.25	13.5	8	2	27.25	29.25	138.6	280.9
1934								
January 1–June 30	15.25	13.5	8	2	27.25	29.25	138.6	280.9
July 1–December 31	17	15	9	2	30	32	138.6	309.2
1935								
January 1–October 30	17	15	9	2	30	32	141.7	302.4
October 31–December 31	17	15	9	3	32	35	141.7	322.6
1936	17	15	9	3	32	35	144.8	315.7
1937	17	15	9	3	32	35	152.5	299.8
1938								
January 1–March 30	17	15	9	3	32	35	154.1	296.7
March 31–December 31	17	15	10	3	33	36	154.1	305.9
1939	17	15	10	3	33	36	158.7	297.1

Sources: Benefit data from Royal Commission on Unemployment Insurance, *Final Report* (1932: 20) and Burns (1941: 368). Cost of living (COL) data from Feinstein (1995: 265).

As a result of increases in spending brought about by the high number of applicants and the increased benefit rates, the UI fund, which had been in surplus when the 1920 act was adopted, "sank steadily deeper into debt" during the 1920s. In an attempt to contain costs, Parliament adopted two "tests" meant to disqualify "malingerers" and those with household incomes above a certain level.[13] The "genuinely seeking work" test was introduced in Clause 3(b) of the Unemployment Insurance Act of March 1921. Those receiving uncovenanted benefits had to prove, by convincing a Local Employment Committee, that they were "genuinely seeking whole-time employment but unable to obtain such employment." A "means test" was introduced in February 1922, stipulating that married persons whose partners were employed and single persons living with their parents or other relatives should be denied uncovenanted benefits unless they could convince the Local Employment Committee that refusal of benefits would "cause serious hardship." The rules regarding both the genuinely seeking work test and the means test were altered several times during the interwar period to tighten up the administration of the UI system by denying benefits to the "undeserving." The enforcement of the tests led to the disqualification of large numbers of applicants for UI benefits.[14]

OTHER CHANGES IN THE SOCIAL SECURITY SYSTEM

The changes in the unemployment insurance system were mirrored by changes in other social welfare programs established before the war. The National Health Insurance Act of 1920 extended compulsory health insurance to cover all persons aged 16–70 engaged in manual labor and other employed persons earning less than £250 per year. In response to wartime inflation, the weekly sickness benefit was increased from 10s. to 15s. for insured men and from 7.5s. to 12s. for insured women, and disability benefits for both men and women were raised from 5s. in 1911 to 7.5s. in 1920. The maximum duration of sickness benefits was extended to 26 weeks, after which those still unable to work could collect the smaller disability benefits. To pay for the higher benefits, employers' weekly contributions were raised by 2d. and workers' contributions by 1d.

---

13. According to Deacon (1976: 17–18), "If it was politically necessary to provide benefits in advance of contributions, it was economically vital to restrict that provision to a minimum. . . . The more lax the contributory conditions for benefit, the more urgent the need to devise alternative ways of protecting the fund."

14. From the introduction of the genuinely seeking work test in March 1921 to April 1928 the share of claims that were disallowed varied from a high of 17.0% in 1927 to a low of 6.1% in March–October 1921. Deacon (1976: Appendix II). See also Burns (1941).

In 1921, Parliament adopted the National Health Insurance (Prolongation of Insurance) Act, enabling individuals to retain their eligibility for sickness and disability benefits despite prolonged spells of unemployment. The act was meant to be temporary, but was continued each year until a permanent scheme of extended benefits was adopted in 1928.[15]

Unlike unemployment benefits, which were raised several times after 1920, weekly sickness benefits remained at 15s. throughout the interwar years, and did not include dependents' benefits. In 1920, UI benefits and sickness benefits were equal for adult males, at 15s. per week, with no dependents' allowance, but the gap between the two benefits increased over time—from 1924 through 1928, a married man with two children received 27s. per week in unemployment benefits; if unable to work due to sickness, he received only 15s.

Parliament increased the level of noncontributory old age pensions in 1919 to 10s. per week for persons aged 70 and older with annual incomes below £26.42 (about 10s. per week); those with incomes above £26.42 but below £47.88 received a smaller pension. The high unemployment rates of the 1920s led to calls for lowering the pensionable age to 65. In 1925 Parliament adopted the Widows', Orphans', and Old Age Contributory Pensions Act, under which all wage earners who contributed to the National Health Insurance plan became entitled to a 10s. a week pension between the ages of 65 and 70 (£1 for married couples). Widows' pensions of 10s. per week were payable to women under 70 upon the death of their husband, with additional benefits for dependent children—5s. per week for the first child under 14 (16 if still in school) and 3s. for any other children. A person in receipt of a pension under the scheme would, upon reaching age 70, automatically receive a pension under the previous Old Age Pensions Act without having to satisfy the means test. Like sickness benefits, old age pensions remained at 10s. per week (£1 for a couple) throughout the interwar period. Whether these pensions were sufficient for an individual or couple to live on largely depended on how much rent they paid.[16]

---

15. Hohman (1933: 130–37); Harris (1920); Cohen (1932: 5–6). The 1920 act also increased the maternity benefit from 30s. to 40s.; if both husband and wife were insured, the benefit was 80s. Employers' contributions were higher, and workers' contributions lower, for workers earning less than 4s. per day.

16. Children who lost both parents received an orphan's pension of 7.5s. per week up to age 14, or 16 if still in school. The new benefits were funded by increased contributions to national health insurance. For men, the employer and the worker each paid 9d. per week; for women, the employer paid 7d. per week and the worker 6d. The state contributed £4 million a year for ten years, and thereafter an amount determined by Parliament. Parl. Papers, *Seventh Annual Report of the Ministry of Health, 1925–1926* (1926, XI), pp. 123–25; Hohman (1933: 38–47); Cohen (1932: 52–53, 60–61, 98–100); Bowley and Hogg (1925: 15).

THE GENEROSITY OF SOCIAL SECURITY BENEFITS

As Table 7.3 shows, unemployment insurance benefits were raised at various points after 1924. Wage rates remained roughly constant from 1924 to 1930 and then declined—the average benefit/wage ratio therefore increased over time. Contemporary economist Edwin Cannan and more recently Daniel Benjamin and Levis Kochin have argued that the high interwar unemployment rates were caused in part by the generous level of UI benefits, and the resulting high benefit/wage ratios. According to Benjamin and Kochin, the existence of generous UI benefits led firms and workers to adopt implicit labor contracts involving "more temporary layoffs and less wage variation" during downturns. Generous UI benefits also increased the duration of the average spell of unemployment because they lowered the cost of job search and of leisure.[17] Subsequent research by Ormerod and Worswick, Eichengreen, Hatton and Bailey, and others pointed out numerous problems with Benjamin and Kochin's work. The most recent study, Hatton and Bailey's analysis of unemployment incidence in London in 1929–31 using individual level data, found that when an individual's skill level and industry are taken into account, the benefit/wage ratio did not have a significant effect on unemployment incidence.[18]

While economists in recent decades have focused on the effect of UI benefits on the level of unemployment, many contemporaries were more concerned with whether benefits provided adequate support for the unemployed and their families. One way to measure the adequacy of benefits is to compare them with estimates of the poverty line. Bowley and Hogg, in their reanalysis of poverty in the five towns originally studied in 1912–14, estimated that in 1924 the poverty line for a family consisting of a husband, wife, and two children was 25.25s. per week, excluding rent. If average weekly rent was equal to 7–8s., then minimum weekly expenditure for a family of four was 32.25–33.25s. An unemployed worker with a dependent wife and two children received weekly UI benefits of 22s. up to August 1924, and 27s. thereafter. Even after the substantial increase in benefits in 1924, a family of four receiving UI benefits required an additional 5.25s. per week just to reach a poverty line income. The gap between UI benefits and the poverty line increased with family size. The minimum necessary weekly expenditure for a child aged 5–14 was 5s., while the increase in UI benefits for each additional child was 2s. An unemployed worker with a wife and three children (two aged

---

17. See Cannan (1927: 398; 1930) and Benjamin and Kochin (1979).

18. Hatton and Bailey (2002). See also Ormerod and Worswick (1982), Collins (1982), Eichengreen (1987), and Crafts (1987).

5–14 and one under 5) would receive UI benefits of 29s., but have minimum weekly expenditures of at least 37.25s.[19]

Despite increases in 1928 and 1930, UI benefits remained below minimum necessary expenditures in the early 1930s. Bowley and Caradog Jones constructed poverty lines for London in 1929 and Merseyside in 1929–30, respectively. For a family consisting of a husband, wife, and two children aged 10 and 4, minimum necessary expenditure, including rent, was 36.67s. in London and 32.58s. in Merseyside.[20] Benefit levels for a family of four were equal to 28–30s. in 1929–30, which was 2.6–4.6s. below the poverty line in Liverpool, and even further below the poverty line in high-cost London. As before, the gap between UI benefits and the poverty line was greater for those with more children because the expenses of an additional child were larger than the additional UI benefits. The inadequacy of UI benefits in the 1920s was recognized by many contemporaries. Both the Association of Poor Law Unions and the Trades Union Congress submitted documents to the Blanesburgh Committee in 1926 proposing that UI benefits be raised by enough to make supplemental poor relief unnecessary.[21]

The situation changed by the mid-1930s, as a result of both increasing UI benefits and declining living costs. In 1935 the weekly benefit for a dependent child (under 14) increased from 2s. to 3s., raising the benefit for a family of four to 32s. per week. George estimated that in 1936 the poverty line for a family of four, excluding rent, was 22.25s. for the five towns surveyed by Bowley in 1924, 22.17s. for London, and 20.92s. for Merseyside. According to Rowntree, average weekly working-class rent in 1936 was 9.5s. (10s. in London). Thus, UI benefits for a family of four were about equal to the poverty line in London and Bowley's five towns, and slightly above the poverty line in Merseyside.[22] Even the larger dependents' allowance, however, was below the minimum cost of supporting an additional child, and the weekly benefits paid to families with three or more children remained below the poverty line.

The extent of economic hardship created by the relatively low level of UI benefits depended on the earnings of other members of the claimant's family and the amount of household savings. Households where the wife or one or more children living at home were working did not require full maintenance, and often had incomes well above the poverty line even if the household head

---

19. Bowley and Hogg (1925: 6–7, 37, 69, 90, 118, 144, 175). The median weekly rent for working-class houses in 1924 was 7.17s. in Warrington, 7.58s. in Bolton, 8.58s. in Northampton, and 9s. in Reading and Stanley.

20. Bowley (1932: 74); Caradog Jones (1931: 225). The poverty line estimate for London reported in the text excludes two items included by Bowley: 1.33s. per week for insurance and 1s. for traveling.

21. Deacon (1976: 43–44).

22. George (1937: 90–91); Rowntree (1937: 86–93).

was unemployed. On the other hand, in families where the household head was the sole source of income, unemployment often led to hardship. The probability of suffering hardship increased with the duration of unemployment. The Pilgrim Trust's 1936 survey of the long-term unemployed found that 30% of those out of work for more than 12 months had incomes below the poverty line and that some 41% of those wholly dependent on unemployment benefits were in poverty. Moreover, the probability of living in poverty increased with "the number of children under working age" in the family.[23]

The benefits paid to those unable to work due to sickness or disability were substantially smaller than unemployment benefits, and far below the poverty line for all households with children. The inadequacy of sickness benefits was made clear by the 1926 Report of the Royal Commission on National Health Insurance. The report admitted that the existing disability benefit of 7.5s. per week "is obviously not sufficient for the maintenance even of a single man. . . . The sickness benefit of 15s. is very near the margin for the single man and insufficient for the man with dependents." It went on to question why sickness benefits were smaller than unemployment benefits, arguing that both benefits "are designed to alleviate the distress arising from the cessation of income due to causes beyond the worker's control, and the question whether these causes are to be sought in ill-health or in the failure of employment has no bearing on the needs of dependents."[24]

Despite evidence that sickness and disability benefits were not sufficient for individuals with dependents, there was strong opposition from friendly societies to increasing benefits. Both the Manchester Unity Oddfellows and the Independent Order of Rechabites submitted statements to the Royal Commission objecting to any increase in standard benefits. They maintained that "Voluntary Societies make ample provision for any person who requires a larger amount of benefit than is provided under National Health Insurance."[25]

The Majority Report of the Royal Commission concluded that the low level of sickness benefits was "difficult to defend," and also that there was "no logical reason" why the rate of benefit should be cut in half after 26 weeks of illness. Still, the report rejected, on financial grounds, proposals to increase standard benefits to match the level of unemployment benefits and to raise disability benefits. It stated, possibly in response to pressure from the friendly societies, that individuals were free to obtain additional benefits through voluntary insurance and added that "there are advantages, moral and otherwise, in such a

23. Pilgrim Trust (1938: 105, 109–13, 424).

24. Parl. Papers, *Report of the Royal Commission on National Health Insurance* (1926, XIV), pp. 25–26.

25. Royal Commission on National Health Insurance (1925), *Appendix to Minutes of Evidence*, pt. II, Appendices VII, VIII, pp. 209–11.

mixed system." The report supported the adoption of dependents' allowances of 2s. per week for a wife and each child under age 14 in the case of sickness, and 1s. per week in the case of disability. However, not even this relatively low-cost proposal was adopted by Parliament, and sickness and disability benefits remained at the rates set in 1920.[26]

The 10s. per week old age pension benefit was less than either the unemployment or sickness benefit for a single adult. A couple who each were over 70 received 20s. per week, although a couple in which only one member was 70 received only 10s. in benefits. Bowley and Hogg estimated that in 1924 the minimum weekly expenditure for a person over 70 was 5.83s. for food, clothing, and lighting. An aged individual living alone and with no other source of income would be in poverty if his or her expenditures on rent and fuel exceeded 4.17s. per week. Similarly, an elderly couple would be able to stay out of poverty so long as they spent less than 8.33s. per week on rent and fuel. Individuals and couples who lived with other family members and paid little or no rent were seldom in poverty. In 1929 London, the minimum weekly expenditure for an "inactive" person over 65 was 7.5s., excluding rent; for a couple, it was 12.83s. Llewellyn Smith concluded that a Londoner over 70 "living alone with no resources except pension would in the year 1929 be commonly below the poverty line, while old couples living together and both drawing pensions would be usually above the line." He added that elderly persons living with relatives were seldom in poverty. Parliament realized the potential inadequacy of public old age pensions, and included a provision in the 1919 Old Age Pensions Act permitting persons in receipt of pensions to apply for supplementary assistance from the Poor Law.[27]

In sum, there were many cracks in the interwar social security system, due to the fact that eligibility for benefits was not universal and due to the inadequacy, and in some cases limited duration, of benefits paid to those in need. Persons who did not qualify for benefits, as well as many in receipt of inadequate unemployment, sickness, or disability benefits or widows' or old age pensions, were forced to turn to the Poor Law for assistance.

III. The Role of the Poor Law in the Interwar Social Security System

Social insurance and pensions were meant to replace the Poor Law, but the shocks to the interwar economy instead created a new role for poor relief as a supplement to social insurance. Table 7.4 presents data on the number of poor

26. Parl. Papers, *Report of the Royal Commission on National Health Insurance* (1926, XIV), pp. 137–43, 281, 318–20; Hohman (1933: 178–80).

27. Bowley and Hogg (1925: 15, 81–82); Bowley (1932: 76–77); Smith (1932: 193–94).

TABLE 7.4. Number of Poor Relief Recipients: England and Wales, 1910–39

	NUMBER RELIEVED (DAY COUNT)			% OF POPULATION RELIEVED (OFFICIAL)	NUMBER RELIEVED (YEAR COUNT) Total (1,000s)	% OF POPULATION RELIEVED (REVISED)	% RELIEVED INDOORS
	Indoor (1,000s)	Outdoor (1,000s)	Total (1,000s)				
1910	275	540	815	2.3	1,752	4.9	33.7
1911	275	508	783	2.2	1,683	4.7	35.1
1912	267	408	676	1.9	1,453	4.0	39.6
1913	265	412	677	1.9	1,456	4.0	39.1
1919	184	285	469	1.3	1,008	2.7	39.2
1920	181	298	479	1.3	1,030	2.7	37.8
1921	193	347	540	1.4	1,161	3.1	35.7
1922	209	1,147	1,356	3.6	2,915	7.7	15.4
1923	214	1,398	1,612	4.2	3,466	9.1	13.3
1924	215	1,062	1,277	3.3	2,746	7.2	16.8
1925	213	915	1,128	2.9	2,425	6.3	18.9
1926	217	1,011	1,227	3.2	2,638	6.8	17.7
1927	221	1,735	1,956	5.0	4,205	10.8	11.3
1928	221	997	1,218	3.1	2,619	6.7	18.1
1929	221	891	1,113	2.8	2,393	6.1	19.9
1930	217	850	1,067	2.7	2,294	5.8	20.3
1931	209	762	971	2.4	2,088	5.2	21.5
1932	196	859	1,055	2.6	2,268	5.7	18.6
1933	191	1,087	1,278	3.2	2,748	6.8	14.9
1934	184	1,154	1,338	3.3	2,877	7.1	13.8
1935	178	1,223	1,401	3.5	3,012	7.5	12.7
1936	170	1,170	1,340	3.3	2,881	7.1	12.7
1937	161	1,105	1,266	3.1	2,722	6.7	12.7
1938	153	912	1,065	2.6	2,290	5.6	14.4
1939	149	928	1,077	2.6	2,316	5.7	13.8

Source: Data on the number relieved (day count) and the official percentage of the population receiving relief from Williams (1981: 161–62).
Note: The estimated numbers relieved in column 5 were calculated by assuming that the ratio of number relieved in 12 months to number relieved on one day was equal to 2.15, the ratio of the year count to the day count from the pauper census of 1906–7.

relief recipients for England and Wales from 1910 to 1939. After declining from 815,000 in 1910 to under 500,000 in 1919 and 1920, the official (day) count of relief recipients increased to 1,356,000 in 1922, and remained above one million for all but one year from 1922 to 1939. The official day count substantially understates the number who received relief over a 12-month period. Column 5 presents estimates of the number relieved at some point in the calendar year, assuming that the ratio of the year count to the day count was 2.15, its level in 1906–7. This indicates that over two million persons received poor relief every year from 1922 to 1939; the share of the population relieved varied from 5.2% in 1931 to 10.8% in 1927. The way in which poor relief was administered also changed. After increasing from the 1870s to 1913, the share of Poor Law recipients relieved in workhouses dropped dramatically in the 1920s, returning to its level before the Crusade Against Outrelief (column 7).[28]

Both the increase in numbers receiving relief and the decline in the share relieved in workhouses were the result of a shift in policy regarding granting outdoor relief to able-bodied adults. In Edwardian England virtually no able-bodied adult males were assisted by the Poor Law. In the 1920s, large numbers of able-bodied males and their families were granted outdoor relief. Throughout the decade, a third or more of relief recipients were unemployed workers and their dependents. The unemployed accounted for a larger share of relief recipients in London and urban Poor Law unions than in other, more rural, unions.

There were substantial year-to-year fluctuations in numbers receiving poor relief due to unemployment, caused largely by changes in the level of UI benefits and the administration of unemployment insurance. Table 7.5 shows the number of unemployed persons receiving poor relief in June and December of each year from 1922 to 1938. The share of the unemployed in receipt of poor relief exceeded 20% in the summers of 1922 and 1926 (the year of the General Strike) and was above 10% as late as December 1934, but was below 3% in 1930–31 and 1937–38. Many of the unemployed assisted by the Poor Law in 1922–23 were receiving supplemental benefits, made necessary by the fact that their UI benefits were not adequate to support their families. After an increase in benefit rates in August 1924, the number of the unemployed receiving poor relief fell by 28,000 from June to December, despite the fact that the number of unemployed persons increased by 163,000. The removal of the maximum duration of insurance benefits in 1928 followed by the abolition of the genuinely seeking work clause in March 1930 caused a sharp drop in the

---

28. The number of relief recipients given in columns 1–3 does not include casuals or the insane. The ratio of the year count to the day count is from the pauper census of 1906–7. Parl. Papers, *Royal Commission on the Poor Laws and Relief of Distress, Appendix Vol. XXV, Statistical Memoranda* (1910, LIII), p. 562.

TABLE 7.5. Numbers Receiving Poor Relief Due to Unemployment: Great Britain, 1922–38

| | Total Number Unemployed (1,000s) | NUMBER OF UNEMPLOYED RECEIVING POOR RELIEF | | Percentage of Unemployed Receiving Poor Relief |
		Excluding Dependents (1,000s)	Including Dependents (1,000s)	
1922 June	1,504	356	1,244	23.7
1922 December	1,409	239	833	17.0
1923 June	1,256	205	710	16.3
1923 December	1,188	174	607	14.6
1924 June	1,099	141	491	12.8
1924 December	1,262	113	396	9.0
1925 June	1,388	117	407	8.4
1925 December	1,217	162	566	13.3
1926 June	1,743	452	1,573	25.9
1926 December	1,432	264	906	18.4
1927 June	1,091	157	514	14.4
1927 December	1,201	154	517	12.8
1928 June	1,285	120	415	9.3
1928 December	1,355	112	386	8.3
1929 June	1,193	95	326	8.0
1929 December	1,377	94	320	6.8
1930 June	1,913	43	150	2.2
1930 December	2,493	59	199	2.4
1931 June	2,720	66	216	2.4
1931 December	2,708	101	326	3.7
1932 June	2,882	130	407	4.5
1932 December	2,830	168	518	5.9
1933 June	2,545	165	491	6.5
1933 December	2,313	192	573	8.3
1934 June	2,179	203	615	9.3
1934 December	2,172	222	662	10.2
1935 June	2,089	175	479	8.4
1935 December	1,947	173	467	8.9
1936 June	1,778	150	397	8.4
1936 December	1,697	144	381	8.5
1937 June	1,423	31	73	2.2
1937 December	1,733	30	72	1.7
1938 June	1,880	27	66	1.4
1938 December	1,908	28	67	1.5

Source: Burns (1941: 53, 343, 360).

share of the unemployed receiving poor relief, from 12.8% in December 1927 to 2.2% in June 1930.

Major changes to the unemployment insurance system in the fall of 1931, including the reinstatement of a household means test and a reduction in benefit levels, led to another increase in the number of unemployed persons receiving poor relief. The share of the unemployed on relief roles increased from 2.4% in June 1931 to 10.2% in December 1934, despite a sharp fall in the total number unemployed. The increased reliance on the Poor Law was reversed by the implementation of the Unemployment Act of 1934, which created the Unemployment Assistance Board to assist able-bodied unemployed workers who were not eligible for insurance. The act was implemented in two stages, the first in January 1935 and the second, after various delays, in April 1937. The implementation of the second stage virtually eliminated the Poor Law's role in assisting the unemployed. From December 1936 to June 1937, the number of unemployed receiving poor relief fell from 144,000 to 31,000, representing 2.2% of those without work.[29] In sum, the Poor Law served as a safety net for those who fell through the cracks in the UI system. Whenever the administration of unemployment insurance was "tightened up," the cracks became larger and the number of individuals forced to turn to the Poor Law for assistance increased.

It is not possible to determine how many of those who were disqualified for unemployment insurance applied for poor relief. However, in the spring of 1931 the Royal Commission on Unemployment Insurance enlisted independent investigators to undertake local investigations regarding "the extent to which disallowed claimants apply for outdoor relief from the Poor Law Authority, and if they do not so apply, how they find means of support." Investigations were undertaken in eight major urban areas: London, Liverpool, Manchester, Sheffield, Hull, Tyneside, Southampton, and Glasgow.[30] Data were reported on 2,354 men, women, and juveniles who were disallowed benefits between February and March 1931. Each individual in the sample was visited by an investigator, who sought to determine how many of those denied benefits found

---

29. On the role of the Unemployment Assistance Board and the reasons for the implementation delay, see Burns (1941: 149–56) and Garside (1990: 72–83). The Poor Law's role in assisting the unemployed was further reduced by the adoption of the Unemployment Insurance (Agriculture) Act in 1936, establishing a separate unemployment insurance scheme for agricultural workers.

30. Royal Commission on Unemployment Insurance, *Appendices to the Minutes of Evidence*, pt. III (1931: 105). The commission took advantage of ongoing social surveys in three of the urban areas—Caradog Jones's investigation of Merseyside, Ford's investigation of Southampton, and Owen's investigation of Sheffield.

other employment, how many "possessed or had access to private resources which enabled them to live," and how many applied for poor relief.[31]

Table 7.6 shows that one-third of those denied benefits were able to find employment for part or all of their spell of disallowance, although most of the work was low-skilled, and the duration of some jobs was brief. The ability to find employment varied substantially across demographic groups and across cities. In general, single women and juveniles found it easier to find work than married men; the group least likely to find employment was married women. Those living in urban areas with high unemployment rates found it especially difficult to obtain jobs; in Liverpool and Glasgow, only one in five married men who were denied benefits were able to find work, as compared to one-half of married men in Southampton. To make matters worse, the jobs obtained by adult men typically were of short duration.

Only 17% of those denied benefits were in receipt of poor relief. This number, however, is deceiving. Very few women or juveniles, and only 13% of single men, received poor relief, and the sample was "overweighted with females and single men." Some 52.2% of married (and widowed) men were in receipt of public assistance; in Liverpool and Hull, more than two-thirds of married men denied benefits turned to the Poor Law for help, while Southampton relieved only 7.1% of married men denied benefits. The report summarizing these findings found that the large differences across cities in the share of married men receiving poor relief were not due to differences in "the state of local sentiment towards the poor law," but rather to "the varying intensity of poverty in each locality," and concluded that a "very lively dread of falling on the rates . . . still prevails in most areas . . . even though, in the light of modern conditions, it is unfounded."[32]

Not all persons denied UI benefits either found work or applied for poor relief. The vast majority of juveniles, and most single men and women under age 25, lived at home and were maintained by their parents. Over 80% of married women denied benefits had husbands who were either employed or receiving benefits. The situation was different for married men who were denied assistance—over 80% of them either found work or were in receipt of poor relief. Only 5.1% of married men denied benefits had a wife in work or receiving benefits, and 21.6% obtained assistance from relatives, typically employed sons

31. The date of visitation "varied between one and thirteen or more weeks after disallowance;" in nearly 80% of cases it occurred at least six weeks after disallowance. Royal Commission on Unemployment Insurance, *Appendices*, pt. III (1931: 107–9, 113, 119). Of the 2,354 persons sampled, 1,120 were adult men, 1,072 were adult women, and 162 juveniles. In his general report, R. C. Davison admitted that both women and juveniles were oversampled relative to adult males.

32. Royal Commission on Unemployment Insurance, *Appendices*, pt. III (1931: 111–12).

TABLE 7.6. Means of Support for Persons Disqualified for Unemployment Insurance

PERCENTAGE WITH VARIOUS MEANS OF SUPPORT

Means of Support	London	Liverpool	Hull	Manchester	Sheffield	Southampton	Tyneside	Glasgow	Total
Employment									
Single men	37.4	15.4	38.2	36.6	23.9	29.3	34.9	34.5	33.1
Married men	38.8	20.0	28.9	31.7	28.9	50.0	32.6	20.2	30.3
Total men	38.0	18.7	33.6	34.1	26.7	34.5	33.9	25.8	31.8
Single women	49.5	32.0	37.1	63.3	42.0	47.2	33.0	37.4	43.9
Married women	24.6	11.1	40.0	22.9	7.1	25.0	15.6	15.1	18.7
Total women	35.7	23.3	37.9	39.5	26.9	41.7	35.6	24.9	32.1
Juveniles	41.2	0.0	47.6	0.0	57.1	58.6	27.8	44.0	47.5
Total	37.2	20.9	36.2	37.3	29.5	42.4	34.2	26.4	33.0
Poor relief									
Single men	3.5	38.5	28.9	7.3	22.5	7.3	10.5	14.6	13.1
Married men	36.4	68.6	68.4	51.2	58.9	7.1	51.1	51.7	52.2
Total men	17.9	60.4	48.7	29.3	42.9	7.3	22.4	33.1	31.9
Single women	3.6	0.0	3.2	6.1	3.6	0.0	1.2	6.5	3.5
Married women	3.8	5.6	12.0	5.7	5.9	0.0	3.1	2.4	4.4
Total women	3.7	2.3	5.7	5.9	4.6	0.0	1.7	4.1	3.9
Juveniles	0.0	0.0	0.0	0.0	0.0	0.0	5.6	8.0	1.9
Total	10.2	33.0	30.4	15.4	19.8	3.0	17.1	16.7	17.0
Male unemployment rate	16.3	29.5	21.7	13.4	21.1	7.4	31.1	24.7	21.6

Source: Royal Commission on Unemployment Insurance, *Appendices to the Minutes of Evidence*, pt. III (1931: 112, 119).

or daughters living at home. Slightly more than one in five married men either received a pension or had private or "other" means.[33]

The report summarizing the investigation noted that "relations and friends were a stand-by for all classes." It added, however, that there was "a darker side to this picture of mutual help rendered by members of a family group to one another. . . . The burden of maintaining the disallowed persons was, in greater or less degree, usually a cause of hardship to others." In such cases "the burden was not removed; it was only spread." The report concluded that "the picture is not, in the main, a cheerful one." There was "ample evidence of suffering," although "the only class on which the full brunt of poverty falls as a direct result of disallowance of benefit, is that of the married men who have families to maintain."[34] In sum, despite the expansion of the unemployment insurance system after 1920, at any point in time substantial numbers of the unemployed either did not receive UI benefits, because they had exceeded the maximum duration or did not meet the contributory requirements, or received benefits that were not adequate to meet their household's needs. Many of these turned to the Poor Law for assistance.

A substantial and increasing number of recipients of sickness and disability benefits and old age pensions also found it necessary to supplement their benefits with poor relief. On January 1, 1922, 145,846 adults were in receipt of outdoor relief on account of their own sickness, accident, or bodily infirmity, nearly two-thirds of whom were women. The number receiving relief, and the share who were men, increased throughout the interwar period—on January 1, 1929, there were 259,000 recipients of poor relief on account of sickness or infirmity, 46% of whom were men, while on January 1, 1936, there were over 408,000 recipients, 54% of whom were men. From 1922 to 1936, the number of adult men relieved on account of their own sickness or infirmity increased by more than a factor of four.[35] A majority of those receiving poor relief were not covered by the national health insurance system. Some, however, used poor relief to supplement inadequate sickness or disability benefits.

The Royal Commission on National Health Insurance found evidence of widespread use of the Poor Law to supplement sickness benefits. The Vice-President of the Association of Poor Law Unions of England and Wales testified before the commission that individuals with dependents who were in receipt

33. Royal Commission on Unemployment Insurance, *Appendices*, pt. III (1931: 112–13). These shares sum to more than 100%, since may of those denied benefits relied on more than one form of assistance.

34. Royal Commission on Unemployment Insurance, *Appendices*, pt. III (1931: 113).

35. Great Britain, Ministry of Health, annual reports on *Persons in Receipt of Poor-Law Relief* for 1922–30, and *Persons in Receipt of Poor Relief* for 1931–38. The number of adult men receiving relief on account of sickness, etc. increased from 51,554 in 1922 to 220,142 in 1936.

of sickness benefits "are bound to come for Poor Law assistance, unless they have some other resources." Evidence for the cities of Birmingham, Liverpool, Reading, and Halifax indicated that up to 10% of those in receipt of sickness benefits found it necessary to turn "to the Guardians for further aid." Looked at another way, in Liverpool one-quarter of those in receipt of poor relief due to sickness or infirmity also were receiving health insurance benefits; in Birmingham over 60% of those receiving poor relief due to sickness also were in receipt of insurance benefits.[36]

As noted above, the 1919 Pensions Act permitted persons in receipt of old age pensions to receive supplemental assistance from the Poor Law. The number of elderly persons receiving both old age pensions and outdoor relief increased steadily, from slightly more than 19,000 in 1922 to over 88,000 in 1929, 162,000 in 1934, and nearly 227,000 in 1938.[37] The New Survey of London Life and Labour found that in 1929–30 about one in six persons in receipt of old age pensions also received outdoor relief. The share receiving outdoor relief varied greatly by living situation: "Nearly half of those living alone were found to be receiving domiciliary poor relief in addition to their pensions, while only one in five of those living in couples and only one in nine of those living with relatives were in receipt of such relief." The share of old age pensioners receiving poor relief was higher in London than elsewhere—Hohman estimated that for England and Wales as a whole 9% of those in receipt of pensions were also receiving poor relief.[38]

As a result of the cracks in the social security safety net, some of the costs of relieving the unemployed, the sick and disabled, and the aged fell back onto the traditional source of assistance, the local Poor Law union. The total number of households who fell through the cracks was relatively small, and someone looking solely at the aggregate data might argue that the financial burden resulting from the increased demand for relief could easily be met by local Poor Law authorities. If the households needing assistance had been distributed roughly equally across Poor Law unions, the increased burden on individual unions would have been manageable. Unfortunately, interwar unemployment was concentrated in a few regions, and as a result the demand for poor relief fell heavily on a small number of unions. In 1929 more than four out of five able-bodied recipients of poor relief lived in just 50 of the 631 Poor Law unions in England and Wales, containing about 35% of the

36. Royal Commission on National Health Insurance (1925), *Minutes of Evidence*, vol. 4, q. 21,673; Parl. Papers, *Report of the Royal Commission on National Health Insurance* (1926, XIV), p. 138; Hohman (1933: 174–76); Witmer (1932: 104–5).

37. Great Britain, Ministry of Health, annual reports on *Persons in Receipt of Poor-Law Relief* for 1922–30, and *Persons in Receipt of Poor Relief* for 1931–38.

38. Smith (1932: 194–95); Hohman (1933: 49).

population, while some 400 unions "have not been touched by the problem of able-bodied pauperism."[39]

Throughout the 1920s the entire cost of poor relief fell on local Poor Law unions. The high concentration of relief recipients in South Wales, northern England, and parts of Scotland led to sharp increases in the poor rate levied on local property owners. The economic downturn not only caused an increased demand for relief but also caused the rateable value of industrial property to decline. As had occurred during the hungry 1840s and the Lancashire cotton famine, local authorities in the high-unemployment areas responded to the sharp increase in rates by demanding help from the central government, arguing that it was unjust for localities to be held responsible for assisting the unemployed—"unemployment was due to national causes" and therefore unemployment assistance should be a national charge.[40]

Unions that were unable to raise a sufficient amount from the rates to meet their "abnormal expenditures" were permitted to borrow, subject to approval by the Ministry of Health. However, this proved to be a costly short-run solution to a long-term problem, because "the necessity of making interest and capital payments on these loans was, in view of the continuance of unemployment into the 1930's, yet one more burden adding to the hopeless financial position of authorities in the distressed areas in later years."[41]

The burden on local taxpayers in the distressed areas was relieved somewhat in 1929 by Parliament's adoption of the Local Government Act, which abolished Poor Law unions and transferred the administration of poor relief to the counties and county boroughs. The act cut the number of Poor Law authorities from 631 to 145, and thereby greatly enlarged the size of local tax bases. The widening of the basis of taxation reduced poor rates in the distressed areas, but did not eliminate the variations in Poor Law expenditures across locations. The total cost of outdoor relief for the year ending March 1931, expressed as a rate per pound of rateable value, was 6.60s. in the Welsh borough of Merthyr Tydfil, 4.81s. in Glamorgan, and 4.06s. in county Durham, but less than 1s. in Bristol, Birmingham, and London. The per capita cost of outdoor relief was 21.92s. in Merthyr Tydfil and exceeded 10s. in 15 English and Welsh counties and county boroughs, but was less than 3s. in 45 counties and county boroughs.[42] The high unemployment rates of 1933–34 caused the already high

---

39. Clay (1930: 52).

40. Clay (1930: 52–53); Burns (1941: 56–57); Robson (1934: 124).

41. Burns (1941: 30, 58). Poor Law unions obtained the power to borrow by the Local Authorities (Financial Provisions) Act of 1921.

42. Royal Commission on Unemployment Insurance, *Appendices to the Minutes of Evidence,* pt. VII (1931: 461–65). The costs reported understate the actual poor rate in each location, as they do not include the cost of indoor relief or other costs related to the Poor Law.

poor rates in the distressed areas to increase, to 15.60s. per pound of rateable value in Merthyr Tydfil, 8.52s. in County Durham, and 8.42s. in Glamorgan.[43] The heavy financial burden on Poor Law authorities in the distressed areas of southern Wales and northern England was not eliminated until the spring of 1937, when the Unemployment Assistance Board assumed responsibility for those unemployed workers unable to satisfy "the modest contributory conditions of the transitional payments scheme" and also for recipients of UI benefits who required supplementary allowances.[44] The transfer of the cost of assisting those unemployed workers who fell through the cracks of the UI system from local authorities to the central government greatly reduced tax burdens in the distressed areas.

IV. Living Standards in Interwar Britain

How successful was the interwar safety net in reducing economic distress among the working class? To answer this question, it is necessary to examine poverty rates and trends in living standards in interwar Britain.

Perhaps surprisingly, given the high level of unemployment throughout the period, both real wages and biological indicators of working-class living standards (life expectancy, infant mortality, and height by age) showed improvement during the interwar years. Real wages on average increased by 15% from 1913 to 1924, and then increased by 18% from 1924 to 1938. The annual rate of growth of real wages for 1913–38, 1.21%, was about the same as in 1856–1913 (1.24%), and was much more rapid than that for 1899–1913.[45] Moreover, unlike the trend in late Victorian and Edwardian England, wage rates increased more rapidly for unskilled than for skilled workers. From 1906 to 1924, the average annual earnings for unskilled workers increased by 123%, from £60 to £134, while earnings for skilled manual workers increased by 88%, from £97 to £182. In real terms, unskilled wages increased by 18.4% and skilled wages remained constant—the ratio of unskilled to skilled wages increased from 62% in 1906 to 74% in 1924. This "major compression of the skill differential" occurred in several industries. From 1913–14 to 1923–24, the ratio of unskilled to skilled wages increased from 67% to 75% in the building trades, from 55% to 74% in shipbuilding, from 59% to 72% in engineering, and from 53% to 68% in railways. The relative gains of the unskilled were maintained in most sectors throughout the remainder of the interwar period. In 1937–38, the ratio of

43. Ministry of Labour, *Reports of Investigations into the Industrial Conditions in Certain Depressed Areas* (1934: 89–90, 167–68).

44. Burns (1941: 153–57).

45. Wage data from Feinstein (1995: 263–65). The annual rate of growth in real wages for 1899–1913 was 0.29%. Estimates of annual growth rates in wages from Boyer (2004b: 284).

unskilled to skilled wages was 75% in the building trades and engineering and 72% in shipbuilding. In railways the ratio declined slightly over time, although in 1937–38 it remained above the prewar level.[46]

Several reasons have been given for the decline in the skill differential during and after the war. Knowles and Robertson contended that the decline largely was caused by "the practice of granting flat-rate [wage] increases" to both skilled and unskilled workers in response to wartime inflation, and in general "to the effect of institutional factors connected with the character of collective bargaining." Bowley maintained that unemployment insurance enabled unskilled workers, more than skilled, "to exert pressure (without an actual trade dispute) against reduction in wages." He added that the increase in unskilled wages at the end of the war was supported by the British public, who believed that living standards "should be at a level worthy of the heroes of the war," and that during the deflation of the early 1920s public opinion opposed any reductions in unskilled workers' wages "more than commensurate with the fall in prices."[47]

The relatively large increase in unskilled workers' wages was caused in part by the spread of Trade Boards to more industries as a result of the 1918 Trades Boards Act, which empowered the Minister of Labour to establish boards in trades where "no adequate machinery exists for the effective regulation of wages." The act changed the criteria for the establishment of Trade Boards from the prevention of sweating to the setting up of wage standards in poorly organized trades. Sells maintained that the act had two additional objectives: "to prevent a sudden fall in wages immediately after the War . . . [and] to adjust wages upon a fair basis in the future." Eleven boards were established in 1919 and 22 in 1920; by the end of 1921 44 Trade Boards were in place in Great Britain. Few additional boards were established thereafter; in 1937 there were 47 boards in operation, covering 1.14 million workers, 73% of whom were women.[48]

A comparison of average weekly wage rates with Trade Board rates "for the lowest grades of experienced adult workers, male and female" suggests that the existence of Trade Boards cushioned the fall in nominal wages for low-skilled workers during the deflation of 1920–22. From 1920 to 1923, average nominal wages declined by 25%, while Trade Board rates fell by 16% for men and 19% for women. After 1923, Trade Board rates moved virtually in lockstep with

---

46. Aggregate estimates of skilled and unskilled wages from Routh (1965: 88, 97–98). Data for individual occupations from Knowles and Robertson (1951: 111). The quote is from Broadberry and Burhop (2010: 421).

47. Knowles and Robertson (1951: 121–22); Bowley (1930: 153–55).

48. Sells (1923: 3–6, 84, 269–70); Sells (1939: 366); Hatton (1997). An additional 15 boards were established in Ireland in 1919–20.

average wage rates.[49] Sells concluded that the boards placed "a floor in the entire wage structure" and supplied "a yardstick for determination of agreed wage rates in organized industries." Moreover, by limiting the decline in nominal wages in the early 1920s, "the wage boards are to be credited further with the steady upward trend of real wages and therefore of potential purchasing power which all workers have enjoyed since 1916."[50]

The social surveys undertaken before the First World War found low wages to be a major cause of poverty. Bowley, in his prewar study of poverty in five towns, had declared the raising of unskilled workers' wages to be "the most pressing social task with which the country is confronted to-day." Writing a decade later, in 1925, he added, "It has needed a war to do it, but that task has been accomplished. . . . There is no doubt that the weekly wages of unskilled men have approximately doubled in ten years, while the cost of the minimum standard has risen by the summer of 1924 by about 70 per cent."[51] The effect of increasing wages on poverty rates will be examined in more detail in the next section.

The interwar years witnessed a substantial improvement in several biological measures of living standards. Life expectancy at birth for males in England and Wales increased from 51.5 in 1910–12 to 55.6 in 1920–22 and 58.7 in 1930–32, while that for females increased from 55.4 in 1910–12 to 59.6 in 1920–22 and 62.9 in 1930–32. Much of the increase was a result of the sharp decline in infant mortality rates. However, from 1910–12 to 1930–32 life expectancy at age 15 increased by 2.6 years for males and 2.9 years for females. Longevity also improved for middle-aged adults—life expectancy at age 45 increased by 1.6 years for men and 2 years for women.[52]

Panel (a) of Table 7.7 shows infant mortality rates for England and Wales and for various divisions. Infant mortality fell throughout the interwar period, from 90.9 per thousand live births in 1916–20 to 55.6 per thousand births in 1936–40. The decline occurred in each division in each five-year period. From 1916–20 to 1931–35, the rate of decline was most rapid in London and small urban areas, where infant mortality fell by 33%, but it also declined by 24% in Wales, which was plagued by high unemployment throughout the interwar years. Panel (b) gives infant mortality rates by region and type of registration

49. Data on Trade Board rates from Sells (1939: 376–77). Data on average wage rates from Chapman (1953: 27). The average Trade Board minimum rates were close to, and in a few cases above, the rates paid to laborers in noncovered trades. In 1935, the average Trade Board rate "exceeded the average wage of coal miners and was only marginally lower than that earned by building labourers and by adult males in the textile trades." Hatton (1997: 25).

50. Sells (1939: 278).

51. Bowley and Hogg (1925: 20–21).

52. Life expectancy estimates for England and Wales from Great Britain, Office of Population Censuses and Surveys (1985: 25).

TABLE 7.7. Infant Mortality Rates in Interwar England and Wales

(A) INFANT MORTALITY RATES, 1911–40

	1911–15	1916–20	1921–25	1926–30	1931–35	1936–40
England/Wales	108.7	90.9	74.9	67.9	62.2	55.6
England/Wales	119.6	100	82.4	74.7	68.4	61.2
London	120.0	100	78.6	71.1	67.2	
County boroughs	122.2	100	85.6	76.5	69.7	
Other urban districts	125.0	100	85.4	74.8	67.2	
Rural districts	117.5	100	84.7	77.4	71.6	
North	118.7	100	86.4	76.4	69.5	
Wales	127.3	100	88.6	80.8	75.9	

(B) INFANT MORTALITY RATES BY ADMINISTRATIVE AREAS (PER 1,000 LIVE BIRTHS), 1930

	North	Midlands	South	Wales	England/Wales
London			59		59
County boroughs	75	61	54	69	68
Other urban districts	65	52	45	66	56
Rural districts	63	50	44	65	53
All areas	70	54	52	67	60

(C) PERCENTAGE DECLINE IN INFANT MORTALITY FROM 1911–15 TO 1930

	North	Midlands	South	Wales	England/Wales
London			46		46
County boroughs	43	50	43	43	45
Other urban districts	47	47	46	46	48
Rural districts	43	40	40	36	41
All areas	44	47	45	42	45

Sources: Data for panel (a) from Registrar General, *Statistical Review of England and Wales for the Year 1935* (1938: 14–18), and Mitchell (1988: 59). Data for panels (b) and (c) from Registrar General, *Statistical Review of England and Wales for the Year 1930* (1932: 9–10).

district in 1930. Not surprisingly, infant mortality was highest in county boroughs in the North and Wales and lowest in rural districts and small urban districts in the South. However, the high infant mortality rates in the northern and Welsh industrial districts predated the interwar economic distress, and panel (c) shows that from 1911–15 to 1930 infant mortality in these districts declined at a rate similar to that for England and Wales as a whole.

Height by age is perhaps a better measure of health than mortality rates. Eveleth and Tanner contend that "the average values of children's heights and weights reflect accurately the state of a nation's public health and the average

TABLE 7.8. Heights of Adult Men and Schoolchildren

(A) MEAN HEIGHTS OF ADULT MEN BY BIRTH COHORTS (CENTIMETERS)

	1901–5	1906–10	1911–15	1916–20	1921–25	1926–30	1931–35	1936–40
Great Britain	171.29	171.53	171.60	171.90	172.82	173.60	173.86	173.87

(B) HEIGHTS OF SCHOOLCHILDREN IN BRITISH TOWNS BY DATE OF OBSERVATION (CENTIMETERS)

	1908–11	1912–15	1916–19	1920–23	1924–27	1928–31	1932–35	1936–39
Age 5								
Boys	101.4	101.9	102.2	103.1	104.0	104.1	104.8	105.7
Girls	101.0	101.8	102.2	102.5	103.4	104.2	104.7	105.5
Age 8								
Boys	117.4	118.3	119.2	119.7	121.0	121.8	123.1	123.7
Girls	114.9	117.2	117.3	118.8	119.6	120.5	121.3	122.4
Age 12								
Boys	135.0	134.9	135.6	135.3	136.4	137.9	139.0	139.6
Girls	135.2	135.5	135.4	135.9	137.3	138.6	139.8	141.1

Sources: Data in panel (a) from Hatton and Bray (2010: 411). Data in panel (b) from Hatton and Martin (2010b: 507).

nutritional status of its citizens."[53] Table 7.8 presents estimates of movements in the average heights of adult males and schoolchildren. Panel (a) shows that adult males born in 1930–35 were on average 2.26 cm taller than those born 20 years earlier, in 1911–15. During the entire transwar period, from 1911–15 to 1951–55, adult male heights increased by 0.99 cm per decade, slower than the rate of increase from 1871–75 to 1911–15, but nearly double the growth per decade from 1951–55 to 1976–80.[54] Panel (b) gives the heights of school-children aged 5, 8, and 12 in British towns, by date of observation. The interwar improvement in heights for each age group is striking. From 1912–15 to 1936–39, 5-year-old boys and girls grew on average by 3.8 and 3.7 cm, 8-year-old boys and girls grew by 5.4 and 5.2 cm, and 12-year-olds grew by 4.7 and 5.6 cm. The height data indicate that, on average, the health of children improved substantially in interwar Britain.

What caused this surprising increase in heights? Broadly speaking, in-creases in height are caused by increases in nutrition (food intake) and improvements in the disease environment. Nutrition is determined largely by per capita food consumption within households, which in turn is a func-tion of family income and family size. Boyd Orr concluded from his mid-1930s study of the relationship between income, diet, and health that "the

53. Eveleth and Tanner (1976: 1); Oddy (1982: 121–25); Hatton (2014: 349–50).
54. Hatton (2014: 351–52).

diet of nearly one-half of the population, though sufficient to satisfy hunger, is deficient for health." The negative effects of a poor diet were "accentuated in children," who require a diet rich in protein, minerals, and vitamins. He found that boys from families with low per capita incomes were shorter than those from more well-to-do households, and that poorer children were more prone to "deficiency diseases" such as rickets and anemia. Despite these findings, he concluded that the picture was "much brighter than any picture of pre-war days." Annual per capita consumption of fruit, fresh vegetables, butter, eggs, and cheese increased substantially from 1909–13 to 1934, and the improvement in diet was accompanied by an "improvement in national health"—children were taller and healthier than they had been before the war, and the sharp decline in infant mortality had led to an increase in life expectancy of about seven years.[55]

As noted above, real wages increased during the interwar period at a rate about equal to that for 1856–1913. This rate of increase was not large enough on its own to cause the sharp increase in heights. Hatton and Martin contend that the growth in per capita food consumption in interwar Britain was driven less by rising wages than by declining fertility rates, which reduced the number of children per family. From 1906 to 1938 the average number of children in working-class families declined from 3.6 to 2.0; the 55% increase in average per capita real weekly income (from 11.7s. to 17.4s. in 1938 shillings) largely was a result of falling family size. Hatton and Martin estimate that the decline in number of children accounts for about a quarter of the increase in children's heights in interwar Britain.[56]

The disease environment also improved. The late nineteenth and early twentieth centuries witnessed a rapid increase in urban public health expenditures on sanitation and clean water, which led to a reduction in death rates due to cholera, typhus, typhoid, and infant diarrhea.[57] Children's health also improved as a result of a decline in overcrowding, defined as more than two persons per room. The Registrar General's *Statistical Review* for 1932 showed that the death rate for children under age 5 was positively related to overcrowding—the effect of overcrowding on mortality risk from bronchitis, pneumonia, measles, and whooping cough was especially pronounced. From 1921 to 1931, the share of the population of England and Wales living in overcrowded conditions declined from 9.6% to 6.9%, in part because of an increase in home building aided by subsidies for the construction of low-cost housing, and partly as a consequence of the decline in family size. Whatever the cause, the decline

---

55. Boyd Orr (1937: 8–9, 23–28, 39–49).

56. Hatton and Martin (2010b: 515–17). Average per capita food expenditure increased from 6.7s. to 8.7s. per week from 1906 to 1938. See also Hatton and Martin (2010a: 174–79).

57. Szreter (1997); Bell and Millward (1998: 242–45).

in infectious diseases resulting from the decline in overcrowding led to an improvement in children's health, and an increase in heights.[58]

The increase in heights, along with the decline in mortality rates and the increase in wage rates, suggests that working-class material and biological living standards improved during the interwar years. Not all contemporaries or historians agree with this conclusion. Hutt's 1933 book, *The Condition of the Working Class in Britain*, was a severe indictment of interwar living standards. Patterned after Engels's similarly titled 1845 work, the book offered detailed pictures of working-class life in the distressed areas of South Wales, Lancashire, and Clydeside. Hutt showed that in working-class wards in Liverpool, Manchester, Glasgow, and other cities, infant mortality rates in 1931 exceeded 100 per thousand live births, and that in many urban districts infant mortality increased sharply from 1930 to 1931. He concluded that these data demonstrated "the grave effects of prolonged trade depression on the health of the working class." Pollitt, in his introduction to Hutt's book, concluded that "the stark reality is that in 1933, for the mass of the population, Britain is a hungry Britain, badly fed, clothed and housed."[59]

Historian Charles Webster also was critical of conclusions reached using national data. While admitting that national averages "seem to offer unquestionable evidence supporting an optimistic interpretation of trends in health during the interwar period," he added that "closer attention to the data relating to infant mortality, however, suggests a more diverse and less flattering picture." For urban districts throughout northern England, Scotland, South Wales, and Northern Ireland, "the improvement in mortality rates during the interwar period was real but small in extent," and in many areas large differences in mortality between middle- and working-class districts did not decline over time. Webster questioned the accuracy of much of the information regarding working-class health contained in governmental reports, and criticized the effectiveness of government social welfare policies. He concluded that mortality and morbidity data raised "the question of the degree of benefit derived by the lower social classes from the expansion of social welfare services during the interwar period."[60]

Hutt and Webster maintained that the most distressed regions did not share in whatever improvements in health occurred in interwar Britain, and therefore that the picture presented by national data was misleading. However, more recent research suggests that health improved even in the distressed areas

58. Office of Population Censuses and Surveys, *Registrar General's Statistical Review of England and Wales for the Year 1932* (1935: 32–36); Carr-Saunders and Jones (1937: 16); Burnett (1986: 226–49); Hatton and Martin (2010b: 513–17).

59. Hutt (1933: 41–42, 83–86, 117–18); Pollitt (1933: xii).

60. Webster (1982: 111–15, 123–25).

during the interwar years. Winter examined movements in infant mortality rates in all metropolitan and county boroughs in England and Wales and found that the statistical variance across locations was "astonishingly uniform" over time; "whatever their experience of unemployment, virtually all urban areas went through the process of infant mortality decline together." He concluded that "unemployment was not the decisive cause of fluctuations in infant mortality rates during this period."[61] Winter's findings are supported by the data in panel (c) of Table 7.7, which show that from 1911–15 to 1930 infant mortality rates declined by 43% in county boroughs in the distressed North and Wales, compared to a decline of 45% for England and Wales as a whole.

Bernard Harris examined the relationship between unemployment and children's heights in interwar Britain for eleven towns, including three south-eastern towns with relatively low unemployment rates (Cambridge, Croydon, and Reading) and four located in depressed areas with high unemployment rates (Glasgow, Rhonda, Leeds, and Wakefield). The average heights of 5-year-old boys increased in each of the towns. The extent of the increase varied across towns, but only by a relatively small amount. Harris's statistical analysis indicated that changes in unemployment had a significant effect on changes in height in only about half of the towns he examined, and that the magnitude of the effect was small.[62]

How should one interpret the relatively weak relationship between unemployment rates and changes in heights? Harris maintained that his results were "not altogether surprising" since variations in unemployment would not have a large effect "on the *average* standard of children's health unless they led to a big enough reduction in the incomes of enough people to have an effect on the community as a whole." He did not view the weak relationship as evidence of the positive effects of government social policies in maintaining children's health. The "main reason" why high unemployment had little effect on children's health "in the most depressed areas was not the generosity of the benefit system, but the appallingly low standard of health experienced by the children of those in work."[63]

In my opinion, the data support a different interpretation of interwar social policy. Historians who argue that social policy was ineffective because health improved faster in the South of England than in the depressed areas are approaching the issue from the wrong direction. The fact that health did not decline, and even improved somewhat, in the depressed areas should be interpreted as evidence of the beneficial effects of government social policies. The

61. Winter (1983: 233, 247–48).

62. Harris (1988: 173–77); Harris (1994: 32–38); Harris (1995: 136–42); Floud and Harris (1997: 106–10).

63. Harris (1994: 38); Harris (1988: 176–77).

question that should be asked is this: what would have happened to children's health in the 1920s and 1930s in the absence of unemployment benefits and other social policies? Most of the unemployed received weekly UI benefits that were substantially less than their previous earnings, so that a family in which the male breadwinner was unemployed experienced a decline in household income. However, the combination of unemployment benefits, income earned by other household members, and poor relief enabled many, although certainly not all, families to avoid serious economic distress even when the household head fell out of work. Children living in families where the head was unemployed experienced a decline in nutrition, but its magnitude in most cases was small.

Consider what the condition of households where the head was out of work would have been if unemployment insurance did not exist. The absence of UI benefits would have compelled virtually all unemployed workers to turn to the Poor Law for assistance. The resulting increase in demand for relief would have created an enormous financial burden for Poor Law unions in the distressed areas. The transference of the administration of poor relief to counties and county boroughs in 1929 would have relieved the pressure on local taxpayers somewhat, but several counties and county boroughs still would have found it very difficult to assist all of the unemployed. Many unions/counties/county boroughs would have been forced to reduce benefits to quite low levels. Even if Parliament had responded to the crisis by providing grants or loans to distressed areas, the reduction in income and children's nutrition for the families of the unemployed would have been much greater than what actually occurred under national unemployment insurance. Under these circumstances, the distressed areas almost certainly would have experienced increases in infant mortality rates and a reduction in the heights of schoolchildren.

The data on wage rates, infant mortality, and heights suggest that both earnings and health improved, albeit slowly, during the interwar years. To determine the effects of the economic downturn and government social policies on poverty rates, it is necessary to turn to the interwar social surveys.

V. Interwar Poverty Surveys

Several surveys similar to the prewar surveys by Rowntree and Bowley were undertaken during the interwar period. These included Bowley and Hogg's reinvestigation of Reading, Northampton, Warrington, Stanley, and Bolton in 1923–24, Bowley and Llewellyn Smith's survey of London in 1929–30, Caradog Jones's survey of Merseyside in 1929–30, Ford's 1931 survey of Southampton, Owen's 1931 survey of Sheffield, Rowntree's 1936 reinvestigation of York, and Tout's 1937 survey of Bristol. All of the studies except those by Rowntree and Tout calculated poverty rates using the methodology developed by Bowley for

TABLE 7.9. Poverty Rates and Causes of Poverty, 1923–24

	Northampton	Warrington	Reading	Stanley	Bolton
(A) PERCENTAGE IN POVERTY (%)					
Working-class households	4.0	7.9	11.3	7.5	4.9
Working-class population	4.2	7.9	11.9	7.2	4.3
All households[a]	2.8	6.6	7.9	7.0	3.7
Working-class households (Rowntree's "human needs" line)[b]	8.6	17.2	24.2	16.1	10.7
(B) CAUSES OF POVERTY (%)					
Chief wage earner:					
Dead or absent	21.9	11.8	27.2	38.3	13.6
Ill or old	21.9	9.2	16.3	14.9	34.1
On strike	3.1	7.9	3.3		
Out of work	18.8	30.3	19.6	14.9	38.6
Irregularly employed	25.0	10.5	5.4		4.5
In full work but:					
Low wages					
Second adult dependent		3.9	2.2		
Wage insufficient for 3 children:					
3 children or less		3.9	7.6	2.1	4.5
4 children or more	3.1	6.6	2.2		
Wage sufficient for 3 children but more than 3 children	6.3	14.5	12.0	29.8	4.5
Other members unemployed		1.3	4.3		

Source: Bowley and Hogg (1925: 17–18, 78, 104, 128, 158, 197).
[a]The estimates for the percentage of all households in poverty are from Hatton and Bailey (1998: 576).
[b]The estimated poverty rates obtained using Rowntree's "human needs" standard are from Linsley and Linsley (1993: 103).

his prewar town surveys, which in turn largely was based on that developed by Rowntree for his original 1899 survey of York. While each survey made minor adjustments to Bowley's assumptions, the poverty lines for the cities are reasonably comparable.[64]

Table 7.9 presents estimates of poverty rates for the towns surveyed by Bowley and Hogg in 1923–24, and Table 7.10 shows estimated poverty rates for the six cities surveyed between 1929 and 1937. For each town, poverty rates for the working-class population and working-class households, as reported in the surveys, are presented in panel (a). The third row gives estimates of the share of all households living in poverty, as calculated by Hatton and Bailey,

64. On the calculation of poverty lines for each of the town surveys, see Gazeley (2003: 77–90), George (1937), and Linsley and Linsley (1993).

while the fourth row gives estimated poverty rates using Rowntree's more generous "human needs" standard, discussed below. Panel (b) gives the causes of poverty in each town.

The share of working-class households living in poverty in the towns surveyed in 1923–24 varied from 4.0% in Northampton to 11.3% in Reading. For four of the towns, the share of households in poverty was much lower in the 1920s than it had been before the war. Bowley and Hogg described the improvement as "very striking." Moreover, the principal causes of poverty in 1923–24 were different than those found in 1912–14. Before the war, the major causes of poverty were low wages, large families, and the death or illness of the chief wage earner. The increase in wages and decline in family size during and after the war greatly reduced the importance of these factors as causes of poverty. Bowley and Hogg concluded that "the proportion of families, in which a man is normally earning, found to be in poverty was in 1924 only one-fifth of the proportion in 1913, if full employment is assumed." However, the economic disruption of the interwar period meant that full employment could not be assumed, and unemployment was a much more important cause of poverty in 1924 than in 1912–14. In Northampton, Warrington, and Bolton, unemployment or underemployment was the principal cause of poverty in more than 40% of poor working-class households. The other major causes of poverty were the death or illness of the chief wage earner, old age, and, in Stanley, large families. Even with the increase in unemployment, however, "the proportion in poverty in 1924 was little more than half that in 1913."[65]

Table 7.10 shows that for the cities surveyed between 1929 and 1937 the share of working-class households in poverty ranged from 6.5% in York in 1936 to 21.3% in Southampton in 1931. Merseyside, Southampton, and Sheffield were surveyed during a time of high unemployment—in each of these locations, and in York, a majority of the households in poverty were poor because the chief wage earner was unemployed or underemployed.[66] The other major causes of poverty were the death or illness of the chief wage earner and old age—these factors accounted for about one-third of the households in poverty in London, York, and Bristol.

The authors of the surveys stressed that the poverty line represented, in the words of Rowntree, "the minimum sum on which physical efficiency could be maintained." Bowley referred to the poverty line as "a standard below which a

---

65. Bowley and Hogg (1925: 16–21, 25). The adult male unemployment rate when the surveys were undertaken was about 7% in Reading, 8% in Northampton, 10% in Bolton, and 13% in Warrington.

66. The author of the Southampton study estimated that if the survey had been done in 1928 or 1929, the poverty rate would have been 13–15%, about two-thirds its 1931 level. Ford (1934: 118).

TABLE 7.10. Poverty Rates and Causes of Poverty, 1929–37

	London 1929–30	Merseyside 1929–30	Southampton 1931	Sheffield 1931–32	York 1936	Bristol 1937
(A) PERCENTAGE IN POVERTY (%)						
Working-class households	9.8	16.1	21.3	15.4	6.5	10.7
Working-class population	9.1	16.0	21.5	17.1	6.8	11.8
All households[a]	7.1	10.9	15.0	12.6	4.0	7.8
Working-class households (Rowntree's "human needs" line)[b]	22.2	37.1	42.9		31.1	10.7
(B) CAUSES OF POVERTY (%)						
Chief wage earner:						
Dead or absent	24.5	13.6[c]	2.8	10.0	9.0	13.3
Ill or old	8.5		14.6	18.2	23.5	24.2
Out of work	48.0	39.9	63.8	66.6	44.5	32.0
Irregularly employed			2.3		5.9	
Self-employment or hawking		23.3				6.5
In full work but:						
Low wages				5.2	9.2	
Second adult dependent			4.7			0.2
Wage insufficient for 3 children:						
3 children or less	5.25		4.7			8.1
4 children or more	2.25		4.7			9.0
Wage sufficient for 3 children but more than 3 children	11.5				8.0	4.0
Other			2.3			2.7

Sources: London: Bowley (1934: 87–88, 108); Merseyside: Jones (1934: 164, 166, 174); Southampton: Ford (1934: 119, 129); Sheffield: Owen (1933: 24, 28); York: Rowntree (1941: 108, 110); Bristol: Tout (1938: 25, 37, 44, 46).

[a] The estimates for the percentage of all households in poverty are from Hatton and Bailey (1998: 576).

[b] The sources for the poverty rates obtained using Rowntree's human needs standard are as follows: York: Rowntree (1941: 11, 34–36); London: Hatton and Bailey (1998: 584–85); Merseyside, Southampton: Linsley and Linsley (1993: 103). Tout's (1938: 25) estimate for Bristol is based on a poverty line similar to that constructed by Rowntree.

[c] The data on causes of poverty in Merseyside do not sum to 100%.

family is *prima facie* in want."[67] For his 1936 reinvestigation of poverty in York, Rowntree calculated two distinct poverty lines. One represented "a standard of bare subsistence," comparable to his 1899 poverty line. This yielded the "primary" poverty rate of 6.5%. The second and more generous poverty line, which he referred to as a "human needs standard," represented the amount of income necessary to secure "a healthy life." While food consumption for a family consisting of a husband, wife, and three children was similar under the two standards, the human needs standard allowed a few more shillings per week for clothing and household sundries than the primary poverty standard, and allowed 9s. per week for personal sundries.[68] Using the "human needs" poverty line, Rowntree found that 31.1% of working-class families in York were living in poverty in 1936. His estimate, along with estimates of the share of working-class families with incomes below the "human needs" standard for other cities calculated by Linsley and Linsley and by Hatton and Bailey, are given in row 4 of Tables 7.9 and 7.10.[69] Under the more generous standard, the poverty rate in 1923–24 ranged from 8.6% in Northampton to 24.2% in Reading. The share of households with incomes below the human needs standard increased sharply after 1928; it was 37.1% in Merseyside in 1929–30 and 42.9% in Southampton in 1931.

Not surprisingly, the causes of poverty differ depending on which poverty standard is adopted. Rowntree calculated the principal causes of poverty in York in 1936 under both standards. As shown in Table 7.10, the main causes of primary poverty were unemployment (44.5%) and the illness or old age of the chief wage earner (23.5%). Using the human needs standard, the principal causes of poverty were "inadequate wages of workers in regular employment" (32.8%), unemployment (28.6%), and old age (14.7%).[70]

How high would interwar poverty rates have been in the absence of existing social welfare policies? The data necessary to answer this question do not exist,

67. Rowntree (1941: 102); Bowley and Hogg (1925: 14). George (1937: 74) described the poverty line as "a standard of living so low, that while persons below it are living in extreme poverty, those just above it would commonly be regarded as very poor."

68. The poverty line for a family of five under the first standard was 30s. 7d. per week in 1936; under the second standard it was 43s. 6d. Both estimates are net of rent. Under personal sundries Rowntree included payments for unemployment and health insurance, contributions to sick and burial clubs, money for traveling to and from work, money for a daily newspaper, a wireless, stamps, and writing paper, and 3s. 4d. for "beer, tobacco, presents, holidays, books, travelling, etc." See Rowntree (1941: 27–31) and Linsley and Linsley (1993: 93–96).

69. Rowntree (1937); Rowntree (1941: 28–32, 101–2, 108); Linsley and Linsley (1993: 102–3); Hatton and Bailey (1998: 584).

70. An additional 9.5% of persons were in poverty as a result of "inadequate earnings of other persons." This included laborers in casual occupations, small shopkeepers, and persons "engaged in selling goods from door to door." The causes of poverty are discussed in detail in Rowntree (1941: 38–100).

but it is possible to use information from the social surveys to get an idea of the share of poor persons who received social welfare benefits of one form or another. Several of the surveys undertaken in the 1930s discuss the important role played by social services in the lives of the poor. Caradog Jones found that 36% of the families included in the Merseyside survey were "in receipt of some form of social income." The chief sources of social benefits for poor families were public assistance (poor relief) and unemployment benefits; the recipients of public assistance were "the most [economically] depressed of all families." For families above the poverty line, the chief sources of social income were old age pensions and unemployment benefits. In constructing estimates of the number of families living in poverty, Jones included social income, other than public assistance, as a part of family income. He made no attempt to calculate what the share of working-class families living in poverty would have been in the absence of social income, other than to conclude that "if we regard a family as being in poverty if they fail to reach the minimum standard without outside assistance, then it is clear that 16 per cent. is not the full measure of poverty in our sample."[71]

The role of social benefits in assisting the poor was as large or larger in Southampton, where 81% of families below the poverty line and 47% of all families surveyed were in receipt of income from one or more social services. Three-quarters of families below the poverty line received more than half of their income from social services, and about one-half of families in poverty received *all* of their income from social services. Column 1 of Table 7.11 shows that the two main sources of social income were unemployment benefits and old age pensions.[72]

In Sheffield, 56% of the working-class families surveyed in 1931–32, and 90% of families below the poverty line, were in receipt of some form of social income. Unemployment benefits were the main source of social income in Sheffield, as in Merseyside and Southampton (Table 7.11, columns 2–4). One-half of the families in poverty received unemployment benefits, 41% received public assistance (poor relief), and one quarter received old age pensions, widow and orphan pensions, or disability benefits. Owen, the author of the Sheffield report, concluded that "the part played by social income in maintaining the standard of living is, of course, very important. . . . Had it not been for the receipt of social income (leaving public assistance relief out of account) rather more than sixty per cent of the families would have been below the poverty line at the time when the investigation was made."[73]

71. Jones (1931: 235–43). See also Jones (1934).

72. Ford (1934: 119, 131–43).

73. In other words, the receipt of social income reduced the working-class poverty rate in 1931–32 by more than two-thirds. Owen (1933: 41–43).

TABLE 7.11. Types of Social Income Received: Southampton and Sheffield

| | PERCENTAGE OF FAMILIES IN RECEIPT OF SOCIAL INCOME | | | |
| | Southampton | Sheffield | | |
Type of Social Income	All Families	All Families	Below Poverty Line	Above Poverty Line
Unemployment benefit	26.5	34.3	50.2	29.5
Health insurance	4.3	1.1	4.2	1.2
Old age pension	13.6	11.0	10.1	11.1
Widow's pension	5.4	8.9	8.8	9.2
Disability pension	NA	1.8	7.4	0.8
War pension	1.6	3.0	1.9	3.2
Public assistance	2.1	8.6	41.1	2.2
Miscellaneous	0.5	0.4	0.0	0.5
All Sources	47.0	56.2	90.2	48.5

Sources: Data for Southampton from Ford (1934: 133–35). Data for Sheffield from Owen (1933: 42).

The survey of Bristol, conducted in the summer of 1937, coincided with a business cycle peak, so it is not surprising that the share of working-class families in receipt of social service income was lower than in Sheffield or Southampton. Still, 32% of the families surveyed, and 71% of families below the poverty line, received social income from one or more sources. Unlike previous town surveys, the Bristol survey included public assistance as part of family income. If public assistance is omitted from income, the share of working-class families below the poverty line increases from 10.7% to 12.1%.[74]

Rowntree did not report the share of York's working-class families in receipt of social income in 1936. He did, however, estimate that slightly more than two-thirds of the income of families in primary poverty, and 38% of the income of families below the "human needs standard," came from social benefits. For both definitions of poverty, the largest source of social income was unemployment benefits, followed by state (old age and widows) pensions and public assistance.[75] At the turn of the century the only source of social income was the Poor Law; York's expenditure on poor relief in 1901 was £5,950. In 1936 "the total sum distributed in York from public funds for the benefit of

74. Social income was not reserved for the poor—slightly more than one-quarter of working-class families with incomes 200% or more above the poverty line "rely on the social services for some of their income." Tout (1938: 29, 47–48).

75. In those families below the human needs standard in which the head was unemployed, social benefits accounted for 80% of total income; in families where the head was too old to work, social benefits accounted for two-thirds of income. Rowntree (1941: 42–43, 117–19).

the sick, the unemployed, the aged, widows and orphans, and those who from any cause were destitute, was . . . over eighteen times as much as in 1901, after allowing for the difference in the value of money." Rowntree stressed that this "remarkable growth of social services" was an important cause of the decline from 1899 to 1936 in the share of families living in primary poverty. He also noted that the "the average per capita deficiency" of income for those below the primary poverty line declined substantially from 1899 to 1936. This also was due in large part to the increase in social spending.[76]

Contemporaries did not agree on how to interpret the information on social income contained in the interwar surveys. The fact that so many re-cipients of social income were found to be still living in poverty led some to focus on the inadequacy of benefits. Gertrude Williams, while admitting that poverty rates would have been substantially higher in the absence of unemployment insurance benefits, concluded that the fact "that the number in poverty varies still so greatly in accordance with the extent and duration of unemployment points to the limitations of the system." Llewellyn Smith, on the other hand, stressed the beneficial effects of social income, writing that "some of the concomitants of poverty which in the past caused the greatest anxiety and distress, e.g. actual destitution and physical want, or the fear of it, have been removed or very largely reduced by the operation of the Social Services." He added, "The outstanding fact is that in the years through which we have been passing National Insurance and Pensions have stood between the people and a state of distress and suffering which it would be terrible to contemplate."[77]

With the exception of Owen's estimate noted above, none of the authors of the interwar surveys, or other contemporaries, attempted to determine what the share of families living in poverty would have been in the absence of social income. Nor did they attempt to measure the effect of social income on the average poor family's income deficit, the so-called intensity of poverty. This last point is especially important. Amartya Sen contends that the "head-count measure" of poverty is inadequate because it "pays no attention whatever to the extent of income shortfall of those who lie below the poverty line: it matters not at all whether someone is just below the line, or very far from it in acute misery and hunger." To determine the effects of social welfare policies on the poor, it is necessary to calculate not only how many families were raised out of poverty by the receipt of social income, but also the extent to which social income reduced the average income deficit for those remaining in poverty. Social welfare benefits might have ameliorated the poverty problem without

---

76. Rowntree (1941: 117–20, 214, 454–55).
77. Williams (1936: 314–15); Smith (1932: 10, 27).

TABLE 7.12. Percentage in Poverty in London: With and Without Social Income

Percentage in Poverty	INCLUDES SOCIAL INCOME		NO SOCIAL INCOME	
	NSLLL	Rowntree/ Linsley	NSLLL	Rowntree/ Linsley
Households	8.2	19.2	15.1	23.3
Individuals	9.9	21.0	14.3	23.7
Males 14–64	6.4	14.6	9.2	16.4
Females 14–64	7.1	16.1	10.9	18.9
Children <14	17.4	32.4	19.7	33.0
Elderly 65+	10.0	35.5	43.7	55.8
Average income deficit (% of minimum needs)	21.4	24.1	60.2	49.2
Intensity index	1.7	4.6	9.1	11.5

Source: Hatton and Bailey (1998: 584, 587).

raising any families above the poverty line, by reducing the size of the average poor family's poverty deficit.[78]

Tim Hatton and Roy Bailey, using the surviving records from the New Survey of London Life and Labour (NSLLL), estimated the impact of social income on both the poverty rate and the intensity of poverty for London in 1929–31. The results of their calculations are reported in Table 7.12. The first two columns report estimated poverty rates using the NSLLL poverty line and the Rowntree/Linsley human needs scale. The estimated poverty rates were calculated using gross income, and therefore differ slightly from those reported in Table 7.10, which were calculated using income and needs net of rent.[79] In order to determine the impact of social income on the rate of poverty, Hatton and Bailey deduct all state benefits, including public assistance, from household income and recalculate the number living in poverty. Columns 3 and 4 report the share of households and individuals below the NSLLL and Rowntree poverty lines "when all state benefits are excluded from income." For the NSLLL scale, the share of households below the poverty line increases from 8.2% to 15.1% in the absence of social income; for the Rowntree/Linsley human needs scale, the share in poverty increases from 19.2% to 23.3%. The demographic group most affected by the loss of social income is the

78. Sen (1979: 295). In like manner, Watts (1968: 325) argued that "poverty is not really a discrete condition. One does not immediately acquire or shed the afflictions we associate with the notion of poverty by crossing any particular income line. The constriction of choice becomes progressively more damaging in a continuous manner." See also Atkinson (1987) and Sen (1997).

79. Hatton and Bailey (1998: 584–86) found that the poverty rate was two to three percentage points lower when calculated "on a gross basis than when calculated net of rent."

elderly—for the NSLLL scale, the share of persons 65 and older below the poverty line increases from 10% to 43.7% when social income is deducted. For each demographic group, the increase in poverty resulting from deducting social income is smaller for the Rowntree/Linsley scale than for the NSLLL scale; "social security benefits were not typically high enough to carry many households up to and beyond" the more generous Rowntree scale.[80]

Hatton and Bailey determined the effect of social income on the intensity of poverty by calculating the "average income deficit for households in poverty as a percentage of the minimum needs" both including and excluding social income. The next to last row in Table 7.12 shows that, in the absence of social benefits, the average income deficit for those below the poverty line increases from 21.4% to 60.2% of minimum needs for the NSLLL scale, and from 24.1% to 49.2% under the Rowntree/Linsley scale. The receipt of social benefits substantially raised the living standards of families who remained below the poverty line, making them "less poor." They measure the overall effect of social security policies by multiplying the average income deficit for those in poverty and the share of households below the poverty line—the resulting measure of "the intensity of poverty" is reported in the table's bottom row. The deduction of social income causes the intensity of poverty to increase sharply for both scales.[81]

In sum, the social surveys undertaken between 1929 and 1937 show that large numbers of working-class families, both above and below the poverty line, were in receipt of one or more forms of social income. While Hatton and Bailey's estimates indicate that the social security system reduced the share of working-class families in poverty by a relatively modest amount, they also show that social income "effectively filled much of the poverty gap" that existed in the 1930s. The condition of the working class would have been substantially worse in the absence of the government safety nets.[82]

VI. Conclusion

The interwar British economy was subjected to severe economic shocks and unprecedentedly high unemployment rates. The social welfare system that dealt with the resulting economic distress was a hodgepodge, with separate programs providing unemployment benefits, sickness and disability benefits, old age pensions, and widows' and orphans' pensions. The Poor Law served as a residual safety net, assisting those who fell through the cracks of the government social programs.

80. Hatton and Bailey (1998: 586–88).
81. Hatton and Bailey (1998: 586–88).
82. Hatton and Bailey (1998: 595).

This chapter has revealed both the positive and negative aspects of the interwar social welfare system. The existence of unemployment and sickness benefits enabled many, though not all, families to avoid serious economic distress even when the household head was out of work. Old age pensions kept large numbers of persons 65 and older from falling into poverty. The social surveys clearly show the important role played by social welfare policies— between a third and a half of all working-class families in the surveys undertaken in the 1930s received social income of some form. In the absence of social benefits, both the share of families below the poverty line and the average income deficit for those in poverty would have been substantially larger.

However, there were many cracks in the interwar social welfare system, due in part to the fact that eligibility for benefits was not universal, and in part to the inadequacy, and sometimes limited duration, of benefits paid to those in need. Many of those who did not qualify for benefits, as well as many in receipt of inadequate benefits, turned to the Poor Law for supplementary assistance. Throughout the 1920s the cost of poor relief continued to fall on local Poor Law unions, which at times put the unions in which relief recipients were concentrated under severe financial pressure. The 1929 Local Government Act widened the tax base and reduced poor rates in the distressed areas, but substantial differences across locations remained.

The problems associated with the interwar social security system were well known at the time. An influential 1937 *Report on the British Social Services* by the independent Political and Economic Planning group criticized the "haphazard" nature of and "large range of gaps" in public social policies, and called for the appointment of a Permanent Statutory Committee to review the existing social services and recommend "necessary changes in their structure or their method of operation." Four years later, in the midst of the Second World War, the Minister without Portfolio set up the Inter-departmental Committee on Social Insurance and Allied Services with William Beveridge as its chair, and directed it "to inquire into the wide range of anomalies that had arisen as a result of the haphazard and piecemeal growth of the social security system over the previous fifty years."[83] As will be seen in Chapter 8, the government got far more than it bargained for.

---

83. Political and Economic Planning (1937: 9–10, 167–70, 178–80); Harris (1997: 365).

8

The Beveridge Report and the Implementation of the Welfare State

> The plan for a universal coverage by a basic insurance marks the highest point which England has reached on her road to social security. . . . The people of England in their long pilgrimage have come at last "to the top of the hill called Clear," whence they can see opening before them the way to freedom with security.
>
> —DE SCHWEINITZ, *ENGLAND'S ROAD TO SOCIAL SECURITY*

The Beveridge Committee issued its report, *Social Insurance and Allied Services*, in December 1942 under the name of the chairman alone. The other committee members, all drawn from the civil service, were instructed by their superiors not to sign the report, and Arthur Greenwood, the Minister without Portfolio, had notified Beveridge in January that the report "will be your own report . . . the departmental representatives will not be associated in any way with the views and recommendations on questions of policy which it contains." There were several reasons for Greenwood's decision—from the start Beveridge had "dominated and even monopolized" the committee's proceedings, his interpretation of the committee's charge and his policy proposals went far beyond what the government had intended, and ministers did not want to commit the government to a proposal for postwar reconstruction that, in the words of the Chancellor of the Exchequer, "involves an impracticable financial commitment."[1]

1. Beveridge (1942: 19); Harris (1997: 373–76); Barnett (1986: 27–28).

As early as July 1941, after only one meeting of the committee, Beveridge made it clear that he planned to do far more than inquire into the anomalies resulting from the piecemeal growth in social policy and make recommendations for tidying it up. In a short memo titled "Social Insurance—General Considerations," he wrote, "The time has now come to consider social insurance as a whole; as a contribution to a better new world after the war. How would one plan social insurance now if one had a clear field, that is to say if one could plan an ideal scheme, using all the experience gained in the past, but without being hampered by regard for vested interests of any kind?"[2]

Social Insurance and Allied Services, hereafter referred to as the Beveridge Report, proposed a rationalization and extension of contributory social insurance to provide subsistence benefits covering all "principal causes of interruption or loss of earnings," a system of children's allowances, and the "establishment of comprehensive health and rehabilitation services." The report was greeted with great enthusiasm by the working classes, if not by the government, and sold over 600,000 copies within a year of issue. The *Times* stated, on the day after the report was issued, "Beveridge and his colleagues have put the nation deeply in their debt, not merely for a confident assurance that the poor need not always be with us, but for a masterly exposition of the ways and means whereby the fact and the fear of involuntary poverty can be speedily abolished altogether." It added that the report's central proposals "must surely be accepted as the basis of government action."[3]

The Beveridge Report has been viewed as both an end and a beginning. Many see the report as marking the beginning of a new and more inclusive and generous phase of government social policy, the blueprint for the British welfare state. Others contend that many of Beveridge's assumptions were backward-looking, and that his proposals largely were the culmination of the social policies of the previous four decades.[4] Karl de Schweinitz, in the epigraph to this chapter, describes the report in Bunyanesque language, with the British people after a long pilgrimage being led by the shepherd Beveridge to the top of Mount Clear, from which they could see the Celestial City of social security.

2. This short document contains the germ of many of the ideas that appear in the 1942 report and has been called "the first draft of the Beveridge Report." It can be found in the Beveridge Papers, LSE Archives (BEVERIDGE/9A/41/1).

3. *Times*, "Freedom from Want," December 2, 1942: 5. The *Financial Times* was less enthusiastic. In an editorial titled "From Cradle to Grave," it noted that the report represented the view of only one person, stressed the plan's high cost, and concluded that any move to put it into practice in the near future "would be inopportune, to say the least." *Financial Times*, "From Cradle to Grave," December 2, 1942: 2.

4. On Beveridge's backward-looking assumptions, see Glennerster and Evans (1994) and Veit-Wilson (1992).

This chapter examines the Beveridge Report and the beginnings of the postwar welfare state. Section I provides a detailed look at the report's main proposals, and discusses how, in Beveridge's view, these proposals would eliminate the "giant evil" of want. Section II examines the debate over the Beveridge Report within the government, the adjustments made to his proposals, and the implementation of social welfare legislation after the war, concluding with a discussion of the extent to which the adoption of the welfare state eliminated poverty in the 1950s.

I. The Beveridge Report

The call for a comprehensive overhaul and extension of British social policies did not begin with the Beveridge Report. A wave of "New Jerusalemism" hit Britain in the summer of 1940, and lasted throughout the war. Those calling for a postwar New Jerusalem or New Britain included Bishop (later Archbishop of Canterbury) William Temple, H. G. Wells, historians Arnold Toynbee and E. H. Carr, Harold Laski, J. B. Priestley, and many others.[5] Carr, for example, in a leader in the *Times* on July 1, 1940, titled "The New Europe," wrote that it was a good time to reflect on the values "for which we fight." "If we speak of democracy, we do not mean a democracy which maintains the right to vote but forgets the right to work and the right to live. . . . If we speak of equality we do not mean a political equality nullified by social and economic privilege. If we speak of economic reconstruction, we think less of maximum production (though this too will be required) than of equitable distribution."[6] The January 4, 1941, special issue of the magazine *Picture Post* put forward "A Plan for Britain," which called for "a job for every able-bodied man" and "a National Minimum—a standard below which no one should be allowed to fall, in employment or out, in sickness or in health, during widowhood or in old age." To achieve the national minimum, the report called for the adoption of a national minimum wage, a system of child allowances, "an all-in contributory scheme of social insurance," the abolition of means tests, and the establishment of a new Ministry of Social Welfare. It also proposed "a state medical service . . . and a complete overhaul of education."[7] The following month, the General Council of the Trades Union Congress proposed major revisions to the system of national health insurance and criticized the confusing nature of the existing social insurance programs, which they described as "a whole lot of schemes

---

5. Barnett (1986: 11–24).

6. *Times*, "The New Europe," July 1, 1940: 5. For another example, see Priestly (1967: 51–58).

7. Excerpts from "A Plan for Britain" and introductory comments from the editor of *Picture Post* can be found in Hopkinson (1970: 15, 90–99). I thank Amanda Goodall for bringing the report to my attention.

purporting to deal with the same problem, but each providing a different kind of remedy."[8] Finally, the policy think tank Political and Economic Planning, in a July 1942 paper on "Planning for Social Security," proposed the adoption of "a national Plimsoll Line of goods and services for all classes, based on a 'decent' Human Needs Standard," a national health service, and the merger of all existing income-maintenance programs into a Ministry of Social Security.[9]

The extent to which public support for reforming the social welfare system was a result of the war has been debated by historians. Some contend that the experience of war created social solidarity, which increased public support for an extension of the social safety net. According to Richard Titmuss, the evacuation from Dunkirk, the Blitz, and the threat of invasion caused a major shift in British public opinion toward collectivism. In his words, Dunkirk "summoned forth a note of self-criticism, of national introspection, and it set in motion ideas and talk of principles and plans." The "dangerous period" from June 1940 to May 1941 "was most fruitful for social policy and action." Historian Paul Addison added that "the demand for social reform at home sprang up suddenly [in the summer of 1940] as a gust of wind on a still day, and continued to blow with increasing force."[10]

Other historians, including Beveridge's biographer José Harris, maintain that the effect of the war on social policy has been overstated. They stress that "the breach with the past was less abrupt . . . [and] the aura of consensus was weaker" than Titmuss and others contend.[11] Many of those who called for social reform during the war had supported such reform before 1939. When Tawney asserted in his pamphlet *Why Britain Fights* that one of Britain's postwar goals must be to create "opportunities by which all can participate, according to their powers, in the treasures of civilization," he was reiterating what he had been writing for two decades.[12] Beveridge, in the concluding paragraphs of his report, echoed Tawney, the *Picture Post*, and others when he stated that "the purpose of victory is to live . . . [in] a better world than the old one," and that his proposals were a sign to the British people and the world that "the object of government in peace and war is not the glory of rulers or of races, but the happiness of the common man."[13] There seems little doubt, however,

8. Beveridge (1953: 296–97). The Trades Union Congress's statement is in Parl. Papers, *Social Insurance and Allied Services, Appendix G: Memoranda from Organisations*, Paper 3 (1942–43, VI), pp. 13–17.

9. A condensed version of the Political and Economic Planning report is contained in its memorandum to the Beveridge Committee. Parl. Papers, *Social Insurance and Allied Services, Appendix G*, Paper 7 (1942–43, VI), pp. 34–37.

10. Titmuss (1950: 508–9); Addison (1975: 104).

11. Harris (1992); Harris (1997: 367–69); Leaper (1992: 20–23); Lowe (1990).

12. Tawney (1941: 46). The quote is similar to statements in Tawney (1920) and (1931).

13. Beveridge (1942: 171).

that even if many of the persons advocating social reform after May 1940 had called for similar policies in the 1930s, their statements were now being heard by more receptive ears, not only from the political left but also from the growing "progressive Centre."[14]

THE BEVERIDGE REPORT'S PROPOSALS

The main planks of Beveridge's plan are well known, but bear repeating. The report began by stating that Britain's existing social insurance policies, while "hardly rivalled" by any other industrial nation, were complex and inefficient as a result of their piecemeal growth. Not all persons or risks were covered by the existing schemes, and benefit rates in some schemes were too low. The problems with the existing programs were made clear by an examination of the interwar social surveys. Beveridge concluded that the chief cause of poverty for between three-quarters and five-sixths of the families below the poverty line in the cities surveyed was the "interruption or loss of earning power." They had somehow fallen through the cracks in the safety net. For most of the remaining households in poverty, the cause was the large size of their families.[15]

Rather than patch the existing schemes, Beveridge recommended the creation of a new comprehensive and coordinated system of social insurance, together with a program of children's allowances. In an address given at Oxford five days after the release of the report, he stated that his program was meant to provide "a national minimum of income," to ensure that "everyone at all times, in virtue of contributions made by him, and as of right without any means tests, has the minimum income necessary to meet his responsibilities." By providing income security for the British people, his plan would abolish want, one of the "five giant evils" on the road to reconstruction. Additional government policies would be necessary to provide freedom from the other giant evils: disease, ignorance, squalor, and idleness.[16]

The plan covered all British citizens, not just the working class. To be eligible for benefits, an individual made compulsory weekly contributions to the insurance fund, or had contributions made on his or her behalf. The contribution was set at a flat rate—all insured persons made the same weekly payment to the social insurance fund. In return for their contributions, individuals received benefits when their earnings were interrupted due to unemployment, sickness, accident, disability, or retirement, or by the death of the breadwinner, and also received maternity and funeral benefits. These benefits also were provided at a flat rate, "irrespective of the amount of the earnings which have been interrupted

14. Addison (1975: 17–18).
15. Beveridge (1942: 5–7).
16. Beveridge (1943: 92); Beveridge (1942: 6).

by unemployment or disability or ended by retirement." The weekly benefit was the same for each principal cause of interrupted earnings—unemployment, sickness, disability, and retirement. It would be generous enough to "provide by itself the income necessary for subsistence in all normal cases," and would "continue so long as the need lasts, without means test."[17]

Despite the extension of social insurance to cover virtually all needs, there still would be some people who were not eligible for benefits, either because they did not meet the contributory conditions or the conditions for benefit, or were "in need through causes not suitable for insurance," such as deserted wives. All persons not covered by insurance would be covered by National Assistance. The level of assistance should be enough to meet individuals' "needs adequately up to subsistence level, but it must be felt to be something less desirable than insurance benefit; otherwise the insured persons get nothing for their contributions." Unlike insurance benefits, assistance would be subject to a means test. It would be funded completely by the national exchequer. The adoption of national assistance would effectively mark the end of the Poor Law.[18]

Beveridge admitted that freedom from want could not be achieved simply by his plan for social insurance and national assistance. It required, in addition to insurance, the adoption of children's allowances, a comprehensive system of health and rehabilitation services, and policies to maintain employment and prevent mass unemployment. The interwar social surveys found that between one-sixth and one-quarter of poor families were in poverty due to their large number of children. A flat rate insurance benefit could not be set high enough to provide families of every size with a subsistence income, so some system of child allowances was necessary. However, the payment of child allowances only to families in receipt of social insurance benefits would create serious disincentive effects, since persons with large numbers of children might receive as much or more in benefits when unemployed or sick than they earned in wages when working. Beveridge therefore proposed the adoption of a universal system of children's allowances payable to all families regardless of income, "subject to the omission of the first child when the parent is earning." Allowances should continue up to age 16 for children "in approved full time education." Universal children's allowances would serve an additional purpose—they would help to reverse the decline in the birth rate. The allowances would be paid for out of general taxation.[19]

17. Beveridge (1942: 121–22, 10–11).

18. Beveridge (1942: 141–42).

19. Beveridge (1942: 154–58). In his words, "with its present rate of reproduction, the British race cannot continue; means of reversing the recent [downward] course of the birth rate must be found."

The abolition of want also required the adoption of a comprehensive national health service. In his December 6 Oxford address, Beveridge argued that equal access to health care must be regarded as part of the national minimum. The national health service would ensure that all citizens had access to whatever medical treatments they required, including home and hospital care, access to specialists, nursing and midwifery, dental care, and postcare rehabilitation, "without remuneration limit and without an economic barrier at any point to delay recourse to it." Medical services would be provided to every citizen "without a treatment charge." The goal was for every citizen to be "as well as science applied to the prevention and cure of Disease can make him." The report raised many issues regarding the organization and financing of health care that it did not address in any detail, and called for a further enquiry into the topic.[20]

Finally, the success of social insurance in abolishing want hinged on the maintenance of employment, by which Beveridge meant the abolition of mass unemployment and of long-term ("year after year") unemployment for individual workers. Mass unemployment would create severe financial pressure on the social insurance fund, while the idleness associated with long-term unemployment demoralized individuals. The report did not propose how to maintain employment at a high level, other than to call for the state to use its powers "to whatever extent may prove necessary to ensure for all, not indeed absolute continuity of work, but a reasonable chance of productive employment." However, in addresses given around the time of the report's publication, Beveridge discussed his views regarding employment policy in more detail. He argued that the destruction of idleness, the "fifth giant," was the most important postwar aim. Unless idleness was destroyed, "the other aims of reconstruction . . . are out of reach in any serious sense and their formal achievement is futile." The reduction of unemployment required a fluid labor market and national planning to relate the nation's needs and resources to each other, which in turn required some encroachment by the state into the field of private enterprise in certain sectors of the economy. Beveridge admitted that private enterprise is "a ship that has brought us far on the journey to higher standards of living and of leisure," but added that the interwar period has shown that it is "a ship for fair weather and open seas." The abolition of mass unemployment required that the state play a larger role in postwar economic affairs.[21]

Part of the cost of social security was to be paid for by weekly contributions from workers. In addition, employers would make a weekly contribution on behalf of each employee, which they should view as "a proper part of the cost of production" because social security would create a healthier and more efficient

20. Beveridge (1942: 158–63); Beveridge (1943: 94).
21. Beveridge (1942: 163–65); Beveridge (1943: 50–60).

workforce. The state also would contribute to the cost of social security out of general taxation. Thus, the Beveridge Plan continued the "tripartite scheme of contributions" begun with the 1911 National Insurance Act. The division of costs among the three groups varied across programs. Beveridge envisioned that workers' and employers' joint contributions would cover two-thirds of the cost of unemployment benefits, five-sixths of the costs of retirement pensions, disability benefits, and widow's benefits, and some undesignated share of the cost of health care. The state would provide one-third of the cost of unemployment benefits, one-sixth of the cost of pensions and disability benefits, and the entire cost of children's allowances and national assistance. It also would pay for the National Health Service, with some assistance from local governments through local rates and from the social insurance fund.[22]

While some reformers argued that the cost of social security should be borne entirely out of general taxation, Beveridge defended the use of workers' contributions on two grounds. First, he claimed that the British people preferred contributing to the insurance fund rather than receiving benefits as a free allowance from the state—"there is a psychological desire to get something for which you have paid." Nor did they want contributions to vary according to income. They wanted, to use a later phrase, "something for something" rather than "something for nothing." Second, Beveridge believed that a contributory system helped "to keep the Social Insurance Fund self-contained." The existence of a self-contained fund would make clear to the public that benefits could be increased only if their contributions also increased, and would help to ensure that the British people did not come to view the state as "the dispenser of gifts."[23]

The weekly benefit paid to those experiencing an interruption of earnings would be adequate both "in amount and in time." Beveridge stressed that the proposed rate of benefit "is intended in itself to be sufficient without further resources to provide the minimum income needed for subsistence in all normal cases." Moreover, benefits "will continue indefinitely without means test, so long as the need continues." In the concluding section, he reiterated that a rate of benefits "materially below" that proposed in the report could not "be justified on scientific grounds as adequate for human existence." Lower benefits or pensions would mean "that the cost of unemployment or sickness or childhood is borne . . . indirectly in privation and lowered human efficiency."[24]

The report concluded by addressing a question: is the abolition of want "a practicable post-war aim"? In his answer, Beveridge turned first to the information contained in the interwar social surveys. Despite the fact that a substantial

22. Beveridge (1942: 107–16).
23. Beveridge (1942: 11–12); Harris (1997: 409). Beveridge referred to social security benefits funded entirely from taxation as the "Santa Claus state."
24. Beveridge (1942: 122, 170).

share of families were found to be in poverty in each of the cities surveyed, the "great bulk" of working-class families had incomes that were far above the "minimum for subsistence." Beveridge calculated that in East London in 1929 the aggregate surplus income of working-class families above the (primary) poverty line exceeded the aggregate deficit of those below by a factor of 30. For York in 1936, using the more generous human needs standard, the surplus of those above the standard exceeded the deficit of those below by more than a factor of eight. He concluded that the abolition of want in interwar Britain "was easily within the economic resources of the community"; its existence was "a needless scandal due to not taking the trouble to prevent it."[25]

The social surveys, along with other economic and biological evidence, showed that living standards had increased substantially in the previous three or four decades. However, this increasing prosperity did not eliminate poverty. The moral, according to Beveridge, was that "new measures to spread prosperity are needed. . . . Abolition of want cannot be brought about merely by increasing production, without seeing to correct distribution of the product." In more recent terminology, trickle down by itself had proved insufficient to cure poverty. But there was a second, more encouraging, moral as well. The growth in living standards since 1900 had occurred despite the waste of four years of war and the disruption of the international economy following the war. The moral was that there was no reason to believe that the current war would bring an end to economic progress, making the plan for social security an unaffordable luxury. In sum, when the war ends the "abolition of want by re-distribution of income" will be within the means of the British people, and the new distribution, if properly designed and financed, need have no disincentive effects and "can increase wealth, by maintaining physical vigour."[26]

THE GENEROSITY OF BENEFITS

Historians have debated what precisely Beveridge meant by his proposal that the level of benefits should be "sufficient without further resources" and "adequate for human existence." Were his proposed benefits based on Rowntree's primary poverty (physical efficiency) standard, on his human needs standard, or somewhere in between these two? Beveridge admitted in Part I of the report that it was not easy to define a subsistence income: "Determination of what is required for reasonable human subsistence is to some extent a matter of judgment; estimates on this point change with time, and generally, in a progressive community, change upwards." Harris maintains that Beveridge "concluded that insurance benefits must be related to the wider concept of

25. Beveridge (1942: 165–66).
26. Beveridge (1942: 165–67).

'human needs'" and that he envisioned Rowntree's human needs standard "as the basis upon which all state cash benefits should be calculated in the social security arrangements of the future." On the other hand, Veit-Wilson contends that Beveridge used the term "subsistence" to refer to the primary poverty standard, and that the benefit rates contained in his report "represented not a *living* income but a state contribution towards one which recipients would have had to supplement in other ways if they wished to live social lives." He goes on to argue that by adopting a physical efficiency standard but implying that benefit levels were "adequate" and "sufficient for all normal needs," Beveridge was being "consciously ambiguous" or "perhaps even mendacious."[27]

Glennerster and Evans are only slightly less critical. They point out that Beveridge's insistence on flat-rate insurance contributions (and therefore rejection of progressive funding) "made irreconcilable his objectives of subsistence adequacy and universal coverage." The maximum rate of individuals' contributions was constrained by the ability of the low-skilled to pay. This in turn meant that benefits could be set above a minimum level only if the state agreed to contribute a substantial subsidy to the social insurance fund, which was not politically or financially feasible. Faced with this dilemma, Beveridge chose to "sacrifice the principle of subsistence to the requirements of his other principles."[28]

How do Beveridge's benefit rates compare to Rowntree's human needs and physical efficiency standards? Veit-Wilson points out that Beveridge's benefit level for a single man or woman was "two-thirds or less" of Rowntree's human needs scale, although he admits that the allowances for children set by Beveridge were more generous than those set by Rowntree.[29] Gazeley found that the relationship between Beveridge's recommended benefits and Rowntree's human needs scale differed substantially across family types. For a couple with no children or one child, Beveridge's rate was 75–78% of Rowntree's human needs scale, for a couple with three children the scales were the same, and for a couple with four children Beveridge's rate was slightly above Rowntree's scale. Gazeley calculated that Beveridge's recommended benefits for families with one to four children were 31–35% above Rowntree's primary poverty scale, which would seem to go against Veit-Wilson's conclusion that

27. Beveridge (1942: 14); Harris (1997: 382); Veit-Wilson (1992: 282–84, 296–97). Timmins (1995: 52) disagrees with the charge that Beveridge was "consciously ambiguous." He concludes that Beveridge made "no real attempt to hide the essential arbitrariness" of his method for arriving at benefit rates.

28. Glennerster and Evans (1994: 57, 61–62); Timmins (1995: 59).

29. Veit-Wilson (1992: 284, 294); Veit-Wilson (1994: 103–5). The main reason for the large discrepancy between the two scales is that Beveridge included little for personal sundries, such as beer, tobacco, a wireless, or a daily newspaper, expenses that Rowntree included in his human needs scale. Rowntree (1937: 98–101).

the approach used by the Beveridge Committee in setting benefit scales "was indistinguishable in principle and . . . in composition from the primary poverty measures described by Rowntree in 1899."[30]

Why didn't Beveridge set benefits at a higher level? Despite his 1941 statement that the committee should devise an "ideal scheme" of social security, Beveridge, in writing the report, faced two constraints, one perhaps self-imposed, the other real. The first constraint revolved around an issue that by 1942 already had been debated for over a century—the effect of public assistance on work incentives. At the beginning of the report, Beveridge wrote that one of the "guiding principles" he adhered to in making recommendations was that "the State in organising security should not stifle incentives, opportunity, responsibility; in establishing a national minimum, it should leave room and encouragement for voluntary action by each individual to provide more than that minimum for himself and his family." The role of social insurance was to guarantee "the minimum income needed for subsistence"; setting benefits much above subsistence would create work disincentives and would be "an unnecessary interference with individual responsibilities."[31] Veit-Wilson, Glennerster and Evans, and others, perhaps rightly, have criticized Beveridge for accepting the Victorian concept of "less eligibility." Still, the concern of many economists, government officials, and politicians over the possible disincentive effects of state benefits put Beveridge under some constraint in setting benefit levels.

Even if Beveridge had not been bothered by questions of less eligibility, he could not have avoided the issue of cost. Concern among government officials regarding the possible cost of his scheme began months before the report was released. One of those concerned about affordability was Keynes, who was very enthusiastic about the general scheme. A major reason for this concern was the fact that no one knew what British national income would be when the war ended—forecasts varied from £6.5 billion or less to £7 billion. In a note to Sir Richard Hopkins at Treasury in June 1942, Keynes wrote that "to commit

30. Gazeley (2003: 153–56). Hatton and Bailey (1998: 580–83) compared the Rowntree/Linsley human needs scale with the Beveridge scale for London in 1930 prices, and obtained results similar to those found by Gazeley. Excluding rent, the Beveridge poverty line for a single adult male was 60.9% of the Rowntree line. However, for a couple the Beveridge line was 4.7% above the Rowntree line, and for a couple with three children it was 10.2% above the Rowntree line.

31. Beveridge (1942: 6–7, 14, 76, 118–22, 143, 154, 170, 293). Compare Beveridge with Wells's ([1905] 1967: 155) comments on incentives in *A Modern Utopia*: "The modern Utopia will give a universal security . . . but it will offer some acutely desirable prizes. The aim of all these devices, the minimum wage, the standard of life, provision for all the feeble and unemployed and so forth, is not to rob life of incentives but to change their nature, to make life not less energetic, but less panic-stricken and violent and base." At a memorial service held for Wells shortly after his death, Beveridge read from *A Modern Utopia*, calling it "the book which had influenced him most" (Smith 1986: 484). Beveridge's 1948 book *Voluntary Action* stressed the important role of voluntary organizations in postwar Britain.

ourselves here and now or in the near future to what we could only afford on the assumption of a national income comfortably in excess of £m6,500 would be very imprudent." Keynes opposed Beveridge's plan for fixed weekly contributions on theoretical grounds, as they were in effect a poll tax on workers and an employment tax on firms. However, he argued that such contributions should be retained "in order that the additional charges on the Budget may not look altogether too formidable."[32]

Beveridge met with Keynes several times during the spring and summer of 1942 to iron out the plan's finances. Keynes suggested ways to reduce costs by about £100 million, some of which Beveridge accepted. In the end, Keynes concluded that "Beveridge has made a manful effort to meet the financial criticisms which have been made," that he made "very large concessions from the first version of the scheme," and that his revised proposals were not "open to serious criticism on purely financial grounds." On the last point he was overly optimistic. The Chancellor of the Exchequer, Kingsley Wood, believed that even the revised proposal was financially impractical and premature. He wrote Churchill in November complaining that Beveridge and others were assuming that the war's end would usher in a Golden Age of prosperity, and added "the time for declaring a dividend on the profits of the Golden Age is the time when those profits have been realized in fact, not merely in the imagination."[33]

In sum, as Veit-Wilson admits, there were political reasons for many of the ambiguities in the Beveridge Report. Those regarding costs and the level of benefits were to a large degree conscious, as Beveridge was trying to construct a document acceptable both to those demanding a New Britain and to the Treasury. However, not all the blame for the ambiguities should be assigned to Beveridge. In an October memo, Keynes wrote Hopkins that he had asked Beveridge to "speak less precisely" about the level at which postwar benefits and contributions would be set. Keynes believed that the report was a "grand document," and he wanted to maximize the probability of getting a version of it adopted by Parliament. The best way to do that was to keep some of the financial details a bit vague.[34]

II. Debate over and Implementation of the Welfare State

On December 2, 1942, the day after his report was issued as a Command Paper, Beveridge discussed his "Plan for Social Security" in a radio address. He concluded the address with an appeal to the Prime Minister. The plan, he said, "is a completion of what was begun a little more than thirty years ago when

32. Keynes (1971: 204, 206, 216, 223–24). In another note to Hopkins, Keynes referred to "the 'fiction' of a contributory system," and then offered several reasons for retaining it.
33. Keynes (1971: 220–55); Timmins (1995: 45).
34. Keynes (1971: 246–47, 255).

Mr. Lloyd George introduced National Health Insurance, and Mr. Winston Churchill, then President of the Board of Trade, introduced Unemployment Insurance. . . . The Minister who thirty years ago had the courage and imagination to father the scheme of Unemployment Insurance, a thing then unknown outside Britain, is the man who is leading us to victory in this war; I'd like to see him complete as well the work that he began in social insurance then."[35] The reaction of Churchill and the Cabinet to the report was far less positive than Beveridge had hoped. The Cabinet was divided, with reactions ranging from positive to lukewarm to damning. This is not surprising given the coalition government, but there was division not only across parties but also within both the Conservative and Labour parties. On January 12, 1943, Churchill circulated a note to the Cabinet stating that a "dangerous optimism" regarding the possibilities for postwar Britain was growing among the public. The government needed to be cautious because the state of the postwar economy was uncertain, and the Beveridge proposals might prove to be unaffordable. He therefore asked Cabinet ministers to refrain from making promises about the future, "because I do not wish to deceive the people by false hopes and airy visions of Utopia and El Dorado."[36]

Parliament debated the Beveridge Report on February 16–18, 1943. Churchill had recently returned from Casablanca and was ill with pneumonia, but sent another note to the Cabinet on February 14 regarding how to handle the debate. The note's tenor was different from that of the previous month. He wrote that Beveridge's "approach to social security, bringing the magic of averages nearer to the rescue of the millions, constitutes an essential part of any post-war scheme of national betterment." A government body should be set up to examine the feasibility of the particular proposals, and to reshape them in preparation for legislation. He added, however, that the government could not at this point make any commitments regarding postwar policy. This would be a task for the Parliament elected after the war, which could mold social legislation to existing economic conditions.[37]

The debate did not go well for the government. Its three main speakers— Sir John Anderson on the 16th, Sir Kingsley Wood on the 17th, and Herbert Morrison on the 18th—gave somewhat conflicting views on the Beveridge Report. Anderson unenthusiastically stated that the government approved the scheme in principle but would make no "binding commitment." Wood emphasized the need for a cautious approach and stated that the government's duty was to "weigh all the financial implications of the Beveridge plan so that hopes incapable of fulfilment should not be held out." Morrison, in the most

---

35. Beveridge (1943: 86).
36. Churchill (1950: 861); Timmins (1995: 44–46); Addison (1975: 220–21).
37. Churchill (1950: 862).

positive speech, reiterated that the government needed to "watch finance," but stressed that it accepted most of Beveridge's "fundamental principles." The division at the end of the debate produced 121 votes against the government, including 97 from Labour. This represented an "unprecedented rebellion," the most votes against the government up to this point in the war.[38]

The *Economist*'s leader of February 20 criticized Anderson and Wood for the lack of vision, courage, and "practical idealism" in their speeches, which "outraged Parliament and a large part of the public." It added, "The Government must say Yes or No. They cannot sit on the fence. . . . Is the prevention of want to be a first charge in any event?" The political fallout from the government's position quickly became apparent. There were six by-elections in February, a "general election in miniature," and the Beveridge Report figured prominently in each of them. In five of the elections, all Conservative-held seats, the government candidate won by a very small majority against an Independent candidate, and in four contests the Conservative vote declined by an average of eight percentage points. A Home Intelligence department's survey in late February found that a "disappointed majority" thought the government was "trying to kill or shelve the Report," which "augurs ill for the future of social security."[39]

The outcome of the parliamentary debate, the results of the by-elections, and the Home Intelligence reports regarding public opinion caused Churchill to modify his position on social security. He still doubted whether the Beveridge Plan was affordable, and he wanted to focus on winning the war before worrying about the peace, but the strength of public and parliamentary support for the Beveridge Plan forced his hand. According to Addison, "reconstruction . . . flowed around and past [Churchill], like a tide cutting off an island from the shore."[40]

On March 21, 1943, the Prime Minister made a radio address to the nation titled "After the War," which focused on postwar reconstruction. Throughout much of the address Churchill sounded once more like the "young

38. Addison (1975: 223–25); Timmins (1995: 46–48); Barnett (1986: 30); *Times*, "Financing the Beveridge Proposals," February 18, 1943: 4; *Times*, "Beveridge Plan Division," February 20, 1943: 2; *Financial Times*, "Premier May Seek a Confidence Vote," February 19, 1943: 1. One of the votes against the government was cast by Lloyd George, his last vote in the House of Commons. In his autobiography, Beveridge (1953: 323–25, 331–33) wrote that after his report was published members of the government ignored him, and that "the Government boycott of me became formal and explicit" after the parliamentary debate. He added: "no member of the Government of any party, other than the Minister of Information, spoke to me about my Report after it had been made, or discussed any of its proposals with me."

39. *Economist*, "The Parting of the Ways," February 20, 1943: 225–26; *Economist*, "By-Elections," March 6, 1943: 293; Addison (1975: 225–27); Timmins (1995: 48).

40. Addison (1975: 126); Lowe (1990: 158); Timmins (1995: 48–49).

redistributor" of the decade before the First World War. After stating that he refused to tell "fairy tales" to the British people or to make premature pledges "to impose great new expenditure on the State," he proceeded to "peer through the mists of the future to the end of the war." He advocated the government adopt a four-year plan covering "five or six large measures" concerning social policy. Without mentioning the Beveridge Report (although he once referred to "my friend Sir William Beveridge"), Churchill said the time was ripe for "another great advance" in social security, and he and his colleagues in the government were "strong partisans of national compulsory insurance for all classes for all purposes from the cradle to the grave." He also called for government employment policies, education reform, child allowances, and a national health service, stating that "there is no finer investment for any community than putting milk into babies. Healthy citizens are the greatest asset any country can have." No promises could be made during the war, but the government will undertake "every preparation, including, if necessary, preliminary legislative preparation . . . so that when the moment comes everything will be ready."[41]

The government began preparing for postwar social policy shortly thereafter. A White Paper on *A National Health Service* was issued in February 1944 by the Ministry of Health, followed by White Papers on *Employment Policy* in May and *Social Insurance* in September, both issued by the Ministry of Reconstruction. The proposals laid out in these papers were similar to those made by Beveridge. *A National Health Service* stated that the government planned to provide every man, woman, and child with "a comprehensive service covering every branch of medical and allied activity, from the care of minor ailments to major medicine and surgery" free of charge. Funding of the health service mainly would come from national and local taxation, although part would come from contributions "under whatever social insurance scheme is in operation."[42]

The White Paper on *Social Insurance* was in some ways remarkably similar to the Beveridge Report. It began by stating it was the government's duty "to plan for the prevention of individual poverty resulting from those hazards of personal fortune over which individuals have little or no control." Like the Beveridge Plan, the White Paper proposed to cover the entire population, to increase the level of unemployment and sickness benefits and retirement pensions, to create a system of family allowances, and to include a system of National Assistance for those who fell through the safety net. Insurance benefits would be funded by a "tripartite scheme of contribution," with a combination

---

41. Churchill's speech is in James (1974: 6755–65). The description of the pre-1914 Churchill as "the young redistributor" is from Lindert (2003: 316).

42. Parl. Papers, Ministry of Health, *A National Health Service* (1943–44, VIII), pp. 5, 46–47.

of employee and employer contributions paying for five-sixths of most insurance benefits (except unemployment) and the state contributing the remaining one-sixth; the contribution for unemployment benefits would be shared equally between employees, employers, and the state. Family allowances and national assistance would be funded entirely by the Exchequer.[43]

The White Paper accepted Beveridge's notion of a flat rate of contributions and flat rate of benefits. However, the benefits were in some cases less generous than those envisioned by Beveridge. The White Paper stated it was "not practicable" to adopt "a subsistence basis for benefits" for two main reasons. First, the insurance scheme, which "must necessarily deal in averages of need and requirement," could not be adapted to the nearly "infinite variety of individual conditions." Second, the scheme's contributory nature meant that any increase in benefits required an increase in employee contributions. The benefit level should be set to provide "a reasonable insurance against want" while taking into account the "maximum contribution which the great body of contributors can properly be asked to bear." The White Paper also set the weekly cash allowance for each child at a level below that set by Beveridge. Finally, while Beveridge proposed that unemployment and sickness benefits be continued as long as needed, the White Paper set limits on both, calling sickness benefits of unlimited duration "psychologically unwise" and unemployment benefits subject to abuse. It concluded by thanking Beveridge for his "comprehensive and imaginative Report" and noting that much of his plan was embodied "in the proposals set out in this White Paper." It then ended with a flourish, stating that the proposed plan provides "against every one of the main attacks which economic ill-fortune can launch against individual well-being and peace of mind," and calling social insurance "a necessary means . . . to achieving positive effort and abundant living."[44]

The Ministry of Reconstruction produced its White Paper on *Social Insurance* without input from Beveridge, who wrote that by March 1943 "it became clear to me that the Beveridge Report was no longer my concern." The following month he began an investigation of policies to maintain full employment, which led to his book *Full Employment in a Free Society*, published in November 1944, six months after the publication of the White Paper on *Employment Policy*, which had been produced quickly to ensure it would appear before Beveridge's book. Beveridge responded by adding a postscript to *Full*

---

43. Parl. Papers, Ministry of Reconstruction, *Social Insurance*, pt. I (1943–44, VIII), pp. 5–7.

44. Parl. Papers, Ministry of Reconstruction, *Social Insurance*, pt. I (1943–44, VIII), pp. 7–9, 17, 40. The White Paper set unemployment and sickness benefits at the nominal level suggested by Beveridge, but the increase in prices by 1944 was higher than he had predicted, so that in real terms benefit levels were lower. According to Abel-Smith (1992: 14), few members of Parliament, aside from the recently elected Beveridge, criticized the decision to set benefits below the subsistence level.

Employment criticizing the White Paper for underestimating "the seriousness of the disease" of unemployment and for its inadequate practical proposals.[45]

The White Paper began by stating that after the war "the maintenance of a high and stable level of employment" would be *one* of the government's "primary aims and responsibilities." It added, however, that government policy by itself could not guarantee a high level of employment, which required in addition expanding export markets, reasonably stable wages and prices, and "sufficient mobility of workers between occupations and localities." The White Paper proposed two main policies to maintain a high level of employment. The first involved the use of countercyclical public investment. Local authorities should annually submit to the appropriate departments five-year programs of capital expenditure. The government would consolidate these proposals, and adjust public spending upward or downward as needed to maintain employment at a high level. During periods of declining private investment, it would, "by granting loan sanctions or otherwise facilitating finance, bring forward projects which otherwise might have had to wait for a later opportunity." The other policy involved varying weekly social insurance contributions of workers and employers according to the state of the economy, to maintain a high level of private consumption. Contribution rates would be lowered when unemployment was above the "estimated average level" and raised when unemployment was below average. The decline in payroll deductions during downturns would increase workers' disposable income and thus "help to maintain demand for consumers' goods." The idea of varying contribution rates according to the state of the economy was originally suggested by economist James Meade in the spring of 1942, and was discussed briefly in the Beveridge Report.[46]

The White Paper's discussion of the budgetary effects of its policy recommendations was confusing and ambiguous due to its attempt to be acceptable to both Keynesian and orthodox economists within the government. It stated that none of its major proposals "involves deliberate planning for a deficit in the National Budget in years of sub-normal trade activity," but added that this "does not mean a rigid policy of balancing the Budget each year regardless of the state of trade." In other words, the budget need not be balanced "in a particular year" but it "must be balanced over a longer period." This period could not be too long, since any "undue growth of national indebtedness" would reduce public confidence in the economy.[47]

45. Beveridge (1953: 328–31); Beveridge (1944: 259–74).

46. Parl. Papers, Ministry of Reconstruction, *Employment Policy* (1943–44, VIII), pp. 3–6, 15–24; Keynes (1971: 208–9); Beveridge (1942: 164–65).

47. Parl. Papers, Ministry of Reconstruction, *Employment Policy* (1943–44, VIII), pp. 24–26. On the debate among government economists regarding policies in the White Paper, see Peden (1983; 1988), Tomlinson (1987), and Booth (1987).

The White Paper was "epoch-marking," but according to Beveridge it did not go far enough, being "an anti-cycle policy" when what was needed was a program that "takes as its aim freedom from idleness and sets out a Policy of Full Employment to achieve that aim." *Full Employment in a Free Society* provided just such a policy. Beveridge asserted that the government should use its "responsibilities and powers" to maintain full employment, which he defined as "having always more vacant jobs than unemployed men . . . [jobs] at fair wages, of such a kind, and so located that the unemployed men can reasonably be expected to take them." To accomplish this task, the state would have to substantially increase its role in the economy. First, and most important, it needed to ensure that national income was large enough to provide jobs for all those who were available to work—in Beveridge's term, it needed to maintain "at all times adequate total outlay." But large regional differences in unemployment between the wars demonstrated that adequate outlay was not enough; jobs and workers needed to be brought together. To do this, the government should create a National Investment Board that would, among other things, control the location of industry. It would be empowered to prohibit firms from locating in areas where employment already was plentiful and to encourage them to locate in areas where jobs were needed most. Finally, full employment requires a flexible labor supply, which should be promoted by policies to secure the "organized mobility of labour." Because "changes in the demand for labour are inseparable from progress . . . if and when change is necessary, men and women shall be willing to change their occupations and their places of work, rather than cling to idleness."[48]

Whereas the White Paper was ambiguous in not defining what it meant by a "high" level of employment, Beveridge argued that the government should strive for an unemployment rate of no more than 3%. The few without work would be seasonally or frictionally unemployed; Beveridge described them as "the irreducible margin of labour required to be standing by at every moment to make change possible . . . a shifting body of short-term unemployed who could be maintained without hardship by unemployment insurance." He admitted that his estimate of full employment was far more optimistic than other estimates, or his own earlier estimates for that matter—in his 1942 report he had assumed that after the war the average unemployment rate would be about 8.5%, although he hoped it would be possible to reduce it below that number. Most if not all economists in the government thought his estimate wildly optimistic. Even Keynes, in a note to Beveridge shortly after *Full Employment* was published, wrote, "No harm in aiming at 3 per cent unemployment, but I shall be surprised if we succeed."[49]

48. Beveridge (1944: 17–19, 29, 32, 36, 131–35, 166–75, 272).
49. Beveridge (1944: 126–28); Beveridge (1942: 164); Keynes (1971: 381).

Only one plank of the welfare state was put into place by the Coalition government. In June 1945, a month after VE Day and a few weeks before the general election, Parliament adopted the Family Allowances Act, authorizing the payment to all families of 5s. per week for each child after the first, up to school-leaving age. The benefit rate was that suggested by the White Paper on *Social Insurance*, and below that supported by Beveridge. Benefits were paid for out of general taxation, and were not means tested.[50]

In late May, shortly after the breakup of the coalition government, Churchill called for a general election to be held on July 5. While the election manifestoes of the Conservative and Labour parties differed on many major issues, both called for the adoption of compulsory national insurance, a national health service, and policies to maintain employment at a high level. The Conservative Manifesto proposed to adopt the policies recommended by the White Papers on *Social Insurance, A National Health Service*, and *Employment Policy*, and stressed the important role that private enterprise must play in promoting the economic growth necessary for the adoption of social security. The Labour Manifesto asserted that while all parties claimed to support social legislation, Labour had "led the fight" for social security while the Conservatives were in power, and only "the Labour Party is prepared to achieve it." The manifesto argued that the Conservatives support full employment if it can be obtained "without interfering too much with private industry," while Labour was willing "to keep a firm public hand on industry in order to get jobs for all." Labour supported "planned investment in essential industries" and control over the location of new factories to ensure that there would be "no depressed areas in the New Britain."[51]

Many explanations have been offered for Labour's landslide victory in the 1945 general election. The issues considered most important by the British people in the run-up to the election, as revealed by polling, were housing, full employment, and social security. In the words of Peter Hennessy, these issues "were Beveridge's 'Giants on the Road to Recovery' translated into voters' preoccupations and, given Labour's greater emphasis upon them and the Conservatives' lack of credibility as giant-killers, translated into voting intentions as well." The electorate, "with memories of the 1930s still fresh" in their minds, did not "trust the Tories with the reconstruction of Britain." Viewed this way, Labour's victory was a victory for the Beveridge Plan. Ironically, Beveridge, who had won a 1944 by-election as a Liberal, lost his seat to a Conservative, one of the few Conservative gains in the election.[52]

---

50. On the reasons why allowances were set at 5s. per week rather than Beveridge's suggested 8s., see Macnicol (1980: 192–94). The first family allowances were not paid until August 1946.

51. The Election Manifestos are in Craig (1970: 87–105).

52. Hennessy (1992: 85); Timmins (1995: 62); Beveridge (1953: 347–49); Morgan (1984: 36–44).

The Labour government quickly went to work implementing the welfare state. The National Health Service Act was adopted in 1946, although the British Medical Association engaged in a running battle with Aneurin Bevan, the Minister of Health, almost up to the day the law went into effect, July 5, 1948. The year 1946 also saw the adoption of the National Insurance Act, which represented "the core of the Beveridge Report." It provided flat-rate sickness and unemployment benefits, retirement pensions, widows' benefits, maternity and funeral grants, and guardians' allowances, paid for by flat-rate contributions by employees and employers, and by general taxation. The weekly benefit rate for unemployment, sickness, and retirement was 26s. for a single individual and 42s. for a married couple. These nominal benefits were slightly greater than the provisional level of postwar benefits (24s. and 40s.) included in the Beveridge Report. Beveridge obtained his benefit rate by taking the benefits he had calculated for 1938 and increasing them by 25% to account for wartime inflation. The Minister for National Insurance, James Griffiths, wrote that he increased benefits by 2s. "to maintain the Beveridge level," meaning that wartime inflation had been somewhat greater than Beveridge had assumed. Griffiths informed the House of Commons that "we have in this way endeavoured to give a broad subsistence basis to the leading rates." However, Abel-Smith contends that both the Coalition and Labour governments had "fiddled" with the cost of living index, so that it understated the actual increase in prices for poorer working-class families. As a result, Griffith's benefits were below those set by Beveridge in real terms. To make matters worse, the act did not index benefit levels to take account of annual changes in the cost of living—benefits were to be reviewed every five years, and adjusted then if necessary. When the insurance scheme came into operation on July 5, 1948, prices were 72% greater than in 1938 while benefits were only 31% greater than those originally set by Beveridge; in real terms "benefit rates were nearly a third below what Beveridge had recommended as necessary for subsistence." Thus, from the beginning benefits failed to meet one of the key criteria envisioned by Beveridge and the government. For reasons that are not clear, this erosion of the purchasing power of social insurance benefits did not receive much attention in the late 1940s.[53]

The National Assistance Act, adopted in May 1948, was the final plank in Labour's welfare state. The act abolished the Poor Law, in the 350th anniversary year of its enactment, and replaced it with the National Assistance Board to act as a residual relief agency. In doing so it shifted the responsibility and cost of assisting those who fell through the cracks of the social insurance system from local and county authorities to the central government. The act provided means-tested cash allowances to persons either who were not eligible

53. Timmins (1995: 112–38); Morgan (1984: 151–63, 170–73); Beveridge (1942: 89–90, 150); Abel-Smith (1992: 14–15); Peden (1985: 153–54).

for national insurance or whose insurance benefits needed to be supplemented. Beveridge had argued that the level of national assistance should be "less desirable" than insurance benefits. In practice, this often turned out not to be the case. Assistance benefits were set slightly below insurance benefits, but those receiving assistance typically had their "full actual rent" paid in addition, so that some recipients received more than they would have if they had been eligible for insurance benefits.[54]

Labour's election manifesto also had pledged a policy of "jobs for all" and elimination of the depressed areas. The fulfillment of this pledge turned out to be easier than expected. Although the unemployment rate reached 12% during the "Great Freeze" in February 1947, it was down to 2.9% two months later, and remained at that level or below until reaching 3.0% in January 1959. From June 1948 through December 1951 the peak U.K. unemployment rate was a mere 2.0%, in January 1949. The only region that could be classified as depressed between 1949 and 1955 was Northern Ireland, where the average unemployment rate was 7.2%. The North of England, Scotland, and Wales, each of which had severe unemployment problems between the wars, had unemployment rates averaging less than 3.0% from 1949 to 1955. Unemployment rates in the South of England during this period averaged less than 1.5%, and in the Midlands less than 1.0%.[55]

What role did the Labour government play in maintaining full employment? It helped to reduce unemployment in the depressed areas by influencing the geographic distribution of new jobs, using financial inducements and coercion to get firms to locate new plants in the North, Scotland, or Wales rather than in the South or South Midlands, where employment was plentiful. Some historians also contend that the government helped to keep the aggregate unemployment rate low through the use of Keynesian demand-management policies, and most working-class voters at the time viewed Labour as "the party of full employment, the party which had exorcized for ever the ghosts of Jarrow, Wigan, and Merthyr Tydfil." The notion that government policy played an important role in maintaining full employment has been disputed by economists. Matthews, in a seminal 1968 paper, raised "serious objections" to the view that full employment was a result of "the Keynesian revolution." He argued that the postwar decline in demand deficiency was not a result of expansionary fiscal policy because the government "persistently had a large current account surplus." Rather, postwar Britain experienced "a gigantic cyclical boom," driven by a high and sustained level of private investment. Tax incentives helped prolong the boom, but it largely was a historical accident, a

---

54. Abel-Smith (1992: 14–16); Chambers (1949: 70–71).

55. Great Britain, Department of Employment and Productivity, *British Labour Statistics: Historical Abstract 1886–1968* (1971: 306, 316, 328).

result of pent-up investment opportunities that had been stifled by two world wars and the interwar slump. This does not mean, of course, that government full employment policy failed, but rather that, in the words of Cairncross, it was "rarely put to the test in the 1950s and 1960s. . . . The government never had to handle a situation in which full employment was really in jeopardy."[56]

National Insurance and the National Health Service were brought into operation on July 5, 1948, the third anniversary of Labour's election victory. Two days earlier an article in the *Daily Mail* summed up the public's anticipation: "On Monday morning you will wake up in a new Britain." Griffiths, who as Minister of National Insurance had done much to bring the day about, wrote in his memoirs, "Beveridge called for a crusade to slay the five giant evils which afflicted our society—poverty, ignorance, disease, squalor, and idleness. Within three years of our electoral victory, the Labour Government had provided the legislative framework and created the organization designed to rid our country of all five."[57]

To what extent did the new policies reduce the poverty rate? In 1951 Rowntree provided an estimate of the effects of the new social policies in his third survey of York, *Poverty and the Welfare State*, coauthored with G. R. Lavers. The book's purpose was to examine "how far the various welfare measures which have come into force since 1936 have succeeded in reducing poverty." Rowntree and Lavers estimated the percentage of working-class persons and households living in poverty in 1950 (using a poverty standard comparable to that of 1936) and compared it to the percentage found by Rowntree to be living in poverty in his 1936 survey. They found that York experienced a "remarkable decrease in poverty" between the two surveys. In 1936, 31.1% of the working-class population was living in poverty; in 1950, only 2.8% of working-class individuals and 4.6% of working-class households were in poverty. The causes of poverty also changed over time. In 1936 the major causes had been unemployment and inadequate wages of persons in regular employment, whereas in 1950 no families were in poverty because of the unemployment of the chief wage earner, and only 1% of the poor were in poverty because of low wages. The main causes of poverty were old age (68.1% of poor families) and sickness (21.3%). The government announced an increase in retirement pensions shortly after the survey was undertaken, and Rowntree and Lavers estimated that if the more generous pensions had been in force when the survey was done the share of working-class households in poverty would have been 1.95% rather than 4.64%.[58]

56. Morgan (1984: 180–84); Timmins (1995: 133); Matthews (1968); Cairncross (1981: 374).
57. Timmins (1995: 127); Griffiths (1969: 88).
58. Rowntree and Lavers (1951: 1, 26–36). Rowntree was 80 years old when the survey was undertaken. Hatton and Bailey (2000: 522–26, 537–41) discuss the extent to which the 1950 poverty scale was indeed comparable to Rowntree's 1936 human needs scale.

To determine the extent to which the "remarkable" reduction in poverty was due to the adoption of welfare legislation, Rowntree and Lavers adjusted social insurance benefits and contributions to 1936 levels, and deducted from household income "the value of food subsidies, family allowances, school milk, cheap milk for infants, and free school meals where granted." These calculations revealed that in the absence of post-1936 welfare programs some 22.2% of working-class individuals and 24.7% of families would have been living in poverty. Without the welfare state, the share of persons or families in poverty in 1950 would have been lower than in 1936, but still would have been quite high. Finally, Rowntree and Lavers calculated what the share in poverty would have been in 1950 if the welfare state was in place but the unemployment rate in York was 8.8%, its level in 1936. In this scenario, 9.1% of working-class families and 7.9% of individuals would have been in poverty. The recent welfare legislation "substantially reduced the amount and the severity of poverty" that resulted from unemployment. In sum, if the welfare state had not rid the country of poverty, it had reduced poverty rates to very low levels.[59]

The book was published less than two weeks before the 1951 election and, as might be expected, it made quite a splash. Its findings were "eagerly seized on by the Labour Party as impartial and irrefutable evidence of . . . the benefits of their rule." The *Manchester Guardian* hailed "the ending of poverty," and Lavers himself claimed that "to a great extent poverty has been overcome by the Welfare State."[60]

No other town-level surveys similar to that of Rowntree and Lavers were undertaken during the 1950s. Perhaps as a result, most Britons at the time assumed that the social welfare policies adopted in 1945–48 had virtually eliminated poverty. This was unfortunate, because in recent decades Atkinson et al. and Hatton and Bailey have shown that there were problems with Rowntree and Lavers's analysis and that their results were seriously misleading. Hatton and Bailey reanalyzed the surviving data from the 1950 survey and found that 8.9–11.8% of working-class households and 5.7–8.6% of individuals were in poverty. That is, the actual poverty rate in York was roughly twice that reported by Rowntree and Lavers. Hatton and Bailey also recalculated what the poverty rate in 1950 would have been in the absence of post-1936 welfare programs and found that the welfare reforms caused the share of working-class households in poverty to decline by 9.8 percentage points, about "half that suggested by Rowntree and Lavers." What caused Rowntree and Lavers to underestimate the poverty rate and overestimate the effects of the welfare state? It appears that "a number of different biases crept in during the process of measurement."

---

59. Rowntree and Lavers (1951: 36–40, 46–49).

60. Kynaston (2009: 28); Hatton and Bailey (2000: 517). Rowntree, like Beveridge, was a supporter of the Liberal Party, and one wonders how he felt about Labour politicians' use of his conclusions.

These biases mostly went in the same direction, and in combination produced overly optimistic results.[61]

Hatton and Bailey's findings support the notion that the welfare reforms of 1945–48 should be viewed "as a set of incremental changes to social security, rather than as the birth of an entirely new system." They also support the views of academics who had questioned Rowntree and Lavers's results from the beginning. As early as 1952, Peter Townsend argued that there was "reason to doubt" both the findings of the third survey of York and the role played by the welfare state in reducing poverty. He maintained that since the war prices were increasing faster than insurance benefits and that as a result "the benefits conferred under the National Insurance scheme have been increasingly inadequate in recent years in providing for the necessities of subsistence, even in the stringent Beveridge sense of 'subsistence.'" To the extent that the rate of poverty had declined since the war, it was due more to full employment and rising wages than to the welfare state.[62]

The optimism of the 1950s was dealt a blow in 1965, when Townsend and coauthor Brian Abel-Smith, in *The Poor and the Poorest*, presented new information that led to what has been called "the rediscovery of poverty." Abel-Smith and Townsend examined the extent of poverty in 1953–54 using household-level expenditure data collected by the Ministry of Labour and the Rowntree-Lavers poverty standard adjusted to take price changes from 1950 to 1953–54 into account. They found that 4.1% of persons in their national sample (and 5.4% of households) were in poverty in 1953–54, as compared to Rowntree and Lavers's estimated 1.7% of the population of York in 1950. Another 4.0% of persons lived in households with expenditures less than 20% above the poverty line, and 6.6% were in households with expenditures between 20% and 40% above the poverty line. Some 14.7% of the persons in their sample, "representing about 7½ millions in the population," were living either in poverty or at the margins of poverty.[63]

Abel-Smith and Townsend's analysis of poverty in 1953–54 together with Hatton and Bailey's reanalysis of poverty in York in 1950 present a different and less optimistic picture than that contained in Rowntree and Lavers's book. The extent of poverty had indeed declined since the 1930s, but the combination of economic growth, full employment, and the adoption of the postwar social security system had failed to eliminate poverty.

61. Atkinson et al. (1981); Hatton and Bailey (2000: 526–36).

62. Hatton and Bailey (2000: 536). Townsend's 1952 essay is included in Townsend (2010: 136–47).

63. Abel-Smith and Townsend also examined poverty in 1953–54 and 1960 using a "national assistance standard," and estimated that the percentage of persons living in households with expenditure/income less than 140% of the government's national assistance scale increased from 7.8% in 1953–54 to 14.2% in 1960. Abel-Smith and Townsend (1965: 16–17, 35–36, 57–58).

III. Conclusion

The information presented in this chapter shows that the set of policies proposed in the Beveridge Report and the resulting welfare legislation of 1945–48 were to a large extent the logical extension of—in Beveridge's words "a completion of"—the expansion of the role of government in social welfare policy that began with the Liberal Welfare Reforms of 1906–11. This does not mean, however, that Beveridge should be described as backward-looking, or that the importance of the postwar legislation should be downplayed. Beveridge's proposals were different from the Edwardian or interwar social welfare policies in at least three important respects. First, while the earlier legislation covered only the working class, and in some cases only the poor, the Beveridge Plan was universal, covering the entire British population. Second, the National Health Service, as proposed by Beveridge and adopted by the Labour government in 1948, went far beyond the health benefits provided before the war. One of the most, if not *the* most, important aspects of the National Health Service was its notion of equal treatment—all citizens were to have equal access "to whatever medical treatments they required." Third, the Beveridge proposals shifted much of the cost of social security to the central government, and thus to general taxation. Family allowances were completely paid for by general taxation, and most of the costs of the National Health Service also were funded by the Exchequer. The adoption of National Assistance and the abolition of the Poor Law shifted the entire cost of residual relief from the localities and the counties to the national government.

In sum, while the Beveridge Plan should not be considered as revolutionary, it was far more than a simple extension of the Liberal Welfare Reforms. Because of the adoption of the National Health Service, universal coverage, and equality of treatment, Britain after 1948 deserves to be referred to as a welfare state, while Edwardian Britain and interwar Britain do not. Unfortunately, despite the enthusiasm with which the welfare state was greeted by the British public, the policies adopted in 1945–48 did not reduce poverty and insecurity to negligible levels. Those historians such as de Schweinitz, quoted at the beginning of this chapter, who maintained that the Beveridge Plan marked the culmination of Britain's quest to eliminate economic insecurity, were mistaken. Beveridge may have enabled the British people to glimpse the Celestial City of social security, but neither he nor the postwar Labour government were able to lead them to the gates. The social welfare legislation of the 1940s did not represent "the end of the road of social reform."[64]

64. On the definition of a welfare state, see Briggs (1961). Titmuss (1956: 6).

The rediscovery of poverty in the 1960s led to a sharp increase in the attention given by academics to the effects of social welfare legislation, and the amount written on post-1950 British social policy is immense. I have little to add to this literature, and so this book ends where many histories of the welfare state begin, with the adoption of the postwar Labour reforms. The next and concluding chapter summarizes the major issues raised in the book and the changing nature of British social policy from the 1830s to 1950.

9

What Was Gained

What have we learned from this examination of economic insecurity and social welfare policy from the 1830s to the adoption of the postwar welfare reforms? First, the road to the welfare state of the 1940s was not a wide and straight thoroughfare through Victorian and Edwardian Britain. Rather, the road was narrow and winding, with an occasional rut and several sharp turns, so that Victorian travelers had little idea where it was leading. It began to straighten out only in the brief Edwardian era. As the previous chapters have made clear, the story of British social policy from 1830 to 1950 is really two separate stories joined together in the years immediately before the Great War. The first is a tale of increasing stinginess toward the poor by the central and local governments, while the second is the story of the construction of a national (and universal) safety net, culminating in the Beveridge Report and Labour's social policies of 1946–48. The prototype for the welfare reforms of the twentieth century cannot be found in the Victorian Poor Law.

The path of British social spending up to the adoption of the Liberal Welfare Reforms is summarized in Figures 9.1 and 9.2, which show the trends in real per capita spending on poor relief from 1831 to 1871 and the pauperism rate (year count) from 1859 to 1908.[1] Government social spending fell sharply after the adoption of the 1834 Poor Law Amendment Act. From 1831–34 to 1837–40, real per capita relief spending fell by 45%, from slightly more than

---

1. Figure 9.2 reports the share of the population receiving poor relief beginning in 1859, because a consistent and comparable series of the number of relief recipients exists from that year onward. More speculative estimates of the share receiving poor relief from 1829 to 1858 are presented in Figure 1.3. The trend in the share receiving relief for 1829–58 is similar to the trend in real per capita relief spending.

9s. to 5s. per person (in 1834 currency). It then fluctuated between 4.7s. and 6.5s. per person from 1841 through 1871, with peaks occurring in 1842–43 and 1847–48, the worst years of the hungry 1840s, and during the crisis of the late 1860s. Figure 9.2 extends the story to 1908, using data on the percentage of the population in receipt of poor relief at some point during the year.[2] The pauperism rate was 9% or above throughout the period 1859–72, peaking at 10.9% during the Lancashire cotton famine and again at 9.8% in 1869–71. It dropped sharply during the 1870s, falling to 6.5% in 1876 and 5.8% in 1884, after which it remained below 6% up to the First World War. Estimates of poor relief spending as a percentage of GDP for England and Wales, reported in Figure 1.4, tell a similar story. Relief spending declined from 2.0% of GDP in 1816–33 to 1.1% in 1835–50 and 0.8% from 1871 to 1908.[3]

Some of the decline in social spending was a result of increases in manual workers' real wages and in working-class self-help. Indeed, COS officials and other contemporary observers, as well as some historians, have stressed that economic growth led to a decline in the need for welfare spending. I do not dispute that, on average, workers' living standards improved over the second half of the nineteenth century, and that as a result the need for skilled workers to turn to the Poor Law during unemployment or old age declined, and in some cases disappeared. Working-class savings and membership in mutual insurance societies greatly increased in late Victorian Britain. However, the data presented in Chapter 3 show that at the time of Queen Victoria's death in 1901 self-help was outside the sphere of the bottom third of the income distribution. Low-skilled workers' households remained economically insecure despite late nineteenth-century economic growth.

If the long-term fall in social spending was driven by demand, it should have declined gradually from the 1830s up to the turn of the century as living standards improved. Figures 9.1 and 9.2 show that this is not what happened. Most of the decline occurred in two short bursts in the 1830s and 1870s. The steep decline in social spending in the second half of the 1830s was followed by three decades of fluctuations around a flat trend, and the sharp fall in the pauperism rate in the 1870s was followed by a very gradual decline in the 1880s and then little if any change from 1891 to 1908. The two sharp declines were the

---

2. The pauperism rate (year count) is constructed by multiplying the official "day count" of paupers in England and Wales by 2.24 for the years 1859–1900 and by 2.15 for 1901–8, and dividing the total by the population. See the notes and sources in Appendix 1.2. As discussed in Chapter 1 and elsewhere, I consider the estimated year count to be a better measure of the number of poor relief recipients than the official day count. See MacKinnon (1988) and Lees (1998: 180–82).

3. My estimates of poor relief spending as a share of GDP are slightly different than those reported by Lindert (1998: 114; 1994: 11), although the trends are similar. The differences in our estimates are due mainly to my using more recent estimates of GDP.

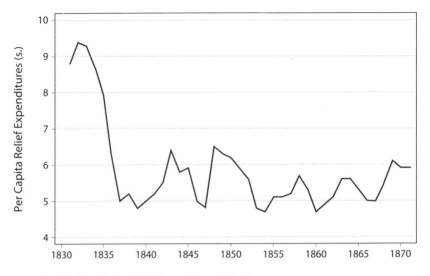

FIGURE 9.1. Real Per Capita Relief Expenditures, 1831–71

FIGURE 9.2. Share of Population Receiving Poor Relief, 1859–1908

result of changes in government policy—the implementation of the Poor Law Amendment Act after 1834 and the Crusade Against Outrelief in the 1870s.

The Crusade Against Outrelief should be viewed as a second attempt by middle-class reformers to implement the "ideal" system of poor relief advocated by the Report of the Royal Commission to Investigate the Poor Laws. The Poor Law Commission established by the 1834 Poor Law Amendment Act succeeded in driving down relief spending, but, as shown in Chapter 2, it failed to abolish the payment of outdoor relief to the able-bodied. It became clear to reformers during the crisis of the 1860s that the "principles of 1834" were not being enforced in northern industrial cities or working-class districts of London. Many placed the blame for the crisis on the failure of the poor to protect themselves against income insecurity through self-help. In turn, they blamed the behavior of the poor largely on the easy availability of generous outdoor relief and unregulated private charity. To these reformers, the solution to the problem seemed obvious—a return to the "principles of 1834." The result was the Crusade Against Outrelief of the 1870s. Poor Law unions throughout England and Wales, but especially in urban districts, adopted some form of the workhouse test and made outdoor relief substantially more difficult to obtain. In the words of Michael Rose, the crisis of the 1860s "provided the opportunity for a radical restructuring of the system. This restructuring was a major step towards achieving the ideals of the 1834 reformers. . . . The New Poor Law was a creation of the 1860s and 1870s rather than of the 1830s."[4]

After seven decades of increasing stinginess toward the poor, British social policy did an abrupt about-face in 1906–11 with the adoption of the Liberal Welfare Reforms. The reforms caused an immediate sharp increase in government social spending—in 1906, spending on indoor and outdoor poor relief for England and Wales totaled £6.35 million; seven years later, in 1913, government spending on poor relief and noncontributory old age pensions was £14.3 million, an increase of 125%.[5] The Old Age Pension Act and the National Insurance Act laid the foundations on which the interwar social welfare policies and the post-1945 welfare state were constructed.

There are no simple explanations for the changes in social welfare policy from the 1830s to the 1940s, and in particular for the Crusade Against Outrelief and the Liberal Welfare Reforms. To explain these major policy shifts, it is necessary to take into account economic issues, such as actual (or anticipated) changes in cost, and therefore in taxes, but also changes in the franchise, and changes in information and public opinion. I consider each of these in turn.

THE ROLE OF THE FRANCHISE

As Lindert has stressed, political voice, at both the national (parliamentary) and local levels, mattered in decisions regarding social spending. The parliamentary franchise was extended to the middle class by the Reform Act of 1832 and later to most urban skilled working-class males in 1867 and to household

4. Rose (1981: 52).
5. Williams (1981: 171); Board of Trade, *Seventeenth Abstract of Labour Statistics* (1915: 185). The figure for 1913 underestimates total social welfare spending because it does not include government contributions to unemployment and sickness benefits.

heads living in the counties, including most agricultural laborers and coal miners, in 1884. Each of the reform acts led to a shift in the political balance of power. Many of the petty capitalists, shopkeepers, and other "self-employed males" who gained the franchise in 1832 were opposed to generous poor relief spending because it increased their taxes, and some also believed that it reduced the productivity and morality of the working class. They were likely supporters of the ideals put forward by the Report of the Royal Poor Law Commission, and their increased political power helps to account for the adoption of the Poor Law Amendment Act and the sharp decline in real per capita relief spending from 1834 to 1840 and its stagnation for several decades thereafter.[6]

The short-run effects of the Second and Third Reform Acts were not as straightforward. The 1867 act increased the parliamentary electorate by 85%, and made skilled working men the majority of the electorate in many urban boroughs, while the Municipal Reform Act of 1869 similarly increased the franchise in local elections. How can this increase in workers' political voice be reconciled with the Crusade Against Outrelief of the 1870s? Why didn't the newly enfranchised workers push for more generous public relief? Despite contemporaries' descriptions of the Second Reform Act as "a great experiment" and "a leap in the dark," the effects of the franchise reforms of 1867 and 1869 "proved less dramatic than they at first appeared." Workers' voice in national politics remained weak even after 1867, since "most of the new voters were corralled within the largest towns."[7] Moreover, the changes in the franchise brought about by the Municipal Reform Act did not extend to elections for Boards of Guardians—even after 1869 urban skilled workmen were excluded from the local administration of the Poor Law, and therefore had no direct impact on the crusade. Even with these caveats, however, the fact that the newly enfranchised workers appear to have done little to resist the adoption of the workhouse test in urban boroughs is, at first glance, surprising.

There was no unified working-class community in Victorian Britain. Within the working class, as within the middle class, there were "infinite gradations" in social scale, status consciousness, and "a jockeying for social superiority." Many within the working class viewed households in receipt of poor relief as being of lower social status. The stigmatization of poor relief recipients was directed more toward the able-bodied than toward the sick or the aged—receipt of poor relief was "more or less disgraceful according as the pauper is presumably more or less able to support himself by labour."[8]

Here it is useful to consider another concept discussed by Lindert, social affinity. Those artisans who felt affinity with their lower-skilled working-class

---

6. Lindert (2004: 71–73, 80–83).
7. Hoppen (1998: 253–59); Acemoglu and Robinson (2006: 3).
8. Bosanquet (1896: 3–4); McKibbin (1990: 11, 37); Cannan (1895: 385–86).

brethren were likely to support generous tax-funded poor relief, while those who felt themselves socially superior to the low-skilled were more likely to support lower taxes and stingier relief. Some historians contend that the so-called labor aristocracy "should be grouped with the middle class, many of whose prejudices about keeping down the rates and maintaining social order they probably shared, and a large gap should be marked between them and the mass" of manual workers.[9] An unmeasurable, but possibly large, share of newly enfranchised skilled urban workers sided with the middle class in favor of tax cuts and in support of the workhouse test.

The Third Reform Act (1884) extended the franchise to include lower-skilled workers, increasing the parliamentary electorate by 88%, and the 1885 Redistribution of Seats Act increased the representation of northern cities in Parliament and created single-member constituencies in both boroughs and counties. Some of the new urban constituencies were "overwhelmingly middle-class or working-class," which encouraged "the development of a class-based electoral system."[10] The extension of the franchise led, in 1893, to the formation of the Independent Labour Party (ILP). The following year Robert Blatchford called on workers to reject the Conservative and Liberal parties and adopt socialism in his influential book, *Merrie England*, writing, "Neither of the Political Parties is of any use to the workers. . . . These Party Politicians do not in the least understand what the rights, the interests, or the desires of the workers are; if they did understand they would oppose them implacably." The working class should "return working men representatives, with definite and imperative instructions, to Parliament and to all other governing bodies."[11]

At the local level, the democratization of the Poor Law occurred in 1893–94. In 1893 the qualification to vote in Board of Guardian elections was reduced to occupying a property with a "rateable value of £5 per annum," which extended the franchise to most working-class householders. The 1894 Local Government Act abolished plural voting and ex-officio members of Boards of Guardians, and reduced the property qualification for serving as a guardian.[12] For the first time,

9. Lindert (2004: 186–88); Clark (1966: 132). Mill ([1848] 1909: 393) wrote in 1848 that "the line of demarcation" between different classes of workers was so complete "as to be almost equivalent to an hereditary distinction of caste." Taylor-Gooby (2013: 34–36, 50–58) presents evidence that in the United Kingdom there still is a stigmatization of poverty among those of working age and that the stigmatization is growing.

10. After 1884 about 60% of adult males had the franchise. Searle (1992: 49–50; 2004: 133).

11. Blatchford (1894: 198–99). At the same time that Blatchford appealed to workers to accept socialism, an old and frustrated Friedrich Engels admitted to a fellow socialist that he was "driven to despair by these English workers . . . with their essentially bourgeois ideas and viewpoints." Marx and Engels (1953: 537).

12. Hurren (2007: 214–41); Keith-Lucas (1952: 40–44); MacKay (1899: 582–84); Webb and Webb (1929: 232–33).

the working class was able to participate in the local administration of the Poor Law. Historians do not agree on the extent to which working-class voters exerted their newly won voice at the local level. Mackay, writing in 1900, admitted that "the civic enthusiasm engendered in the last ten years has increased the number of those who are anxious to take part in local administration," but concluded that "there does not appear to be much difference in the electorates before and after 1894." Similarly, Thane reported that voter turnout in local elections "was usually low even after the local franchise changes in 1894." More recently, however, Hurren argued that the democratization of the Poor Law "sounded the death knell" of the Crusade Against Outrelief. In the "crusading" Brixworth union, the newly enfranchised workers "organised to reclaim lost outdoor relief benefits. Most wanted welfare reform within the poor law because only by taking control . . . could they ensure that their everyday material lives were improved." She concluded that "what mattered to contemporaries . . . is that those in power perceived that there was a pressure from below and that they needed to react accordingly."[13] The effect of the democratization of the Poor Law on the local administration of poor relief needs to be studied in more detail.

An independent working-class political voice grew slowly but steadily after the formation of the ILP. In the 1900 general election the newly formed Labour Party, initially a loose combination of the ILP with other socialist organizations and trade unions, contested 15 seats and won 2. Six years later, Labour contested 50 seats in the 1906 general election and elected 29 MPs. The Labour Party had campaigned for the adoption of social welfare policies, and its relatively strong showing in 1906 was duly noted by Lloyd George, Churchill, and other members of the Liberal government. The welfare reforms of 1906–11 were in part an attempt by the Liberal Party to appeal to working-class voters, as discussed in Chapter 6. The political voice of the working class, and workers' adherence to the Labour Party, grew stronger during the interwar period, aided by the extension of the vote to all adult males over 21 and most women 30 and older in 1918 and to all women 21 and older in 1928. The crucial role of working-class votes in driving social policy became clear in 1945, when Labour's landslide victory in the general election led to the adoption of the social policies that together formed the welfare state.

THE ROLE OF PUBLIC OPINION AND INFORMATION

Another lesson from this book is that public opinion matters for social policy. If the public believes that most poor people are destitute through no fault of their own, they are more willing to support tax-funded generous public

13. See MacKay (1899: 583), Thane (1984: 878), Webb and Webb (1929: 233), Hurren (2007: 241–45), and Keith-Lucas (1952: 43–44).

assistance than if they believe that poverty largely is a result of laziness, lack of thrift, and drunkenness. The views of the middle and upper classes toward the poor, in particular regarding the reasons for their destitution, changed over time. In the years leading up to the Poor Law Amendment Act, when only the top of society could vote, numerous influential observers criticized the behavior of poor relief recipients, and many placed the blame for the apparent deterioration in the poor's character on the administration of the Poor Law. These criticisms were summarized in the Royal Poor Law Commission's 1834 report, which maintained that generous outdoor relief reduced workers' skill, diligence, and honesty, and caused labor productivity to decline. On the other hand, relieving the able-bodied in well-regulated workhouses would restore the industry and "frugal habits" of the poor and improve their "moral and social condition."[14]

The middle-class belief that workers could and should protect themselves against income insecurity grew after 1834—the concept of self-help was "one of the favourite mid-Victorian virtues." The opening line of Smiles's book *Self-Help* is "Heaven helps those who help themselves." He goes on to say, "The spirit of self-help is the root of all genuine growth in the individual. . . . No laws, however stringent, can make the idle industrious, the thriftless provident, or the drunken sober." Smiles was convinced that all manual workers earned enough to provide against income loss. If a worker set aside a few of the pennies he earned, "some weekly into a benefit society or an insurance fund, others into a savings' bank . . . he will soon find that this attention to small matters will abundantly repay him, in increasing means, growing comfort at home, and a mind comparatively free from fears as to the future."[15]

The crisis of the Poor Law in the 1860s prompted a renewed interest in the character of the poor. Why were so many able-bodied persons still applying for relief? Why weren't they protecting themselves against misfortune by saving and joining insurance-providing friendly societies? The answer, according to many, was similar to that given in 1834—the generous nature of poor relief made it unnecessary for workers to practice self-help. This belief that the Poor Law, combined with indiscriminate private charity, was a "mighty engine for evil" that reduced self-reliance among the working class led to the formation of the COS and to the Crusade Against Outrelief. The fact that the number of relief recipients fell by one-third in the 1870s after Poor Law unions restricted the granting of outdoor relief reinforced public opinion that many of those who had received poor relief in the past had been lacking in character and were "undeserving" of assistance. Indeed, the propaganda of the COS was

14. Royal Commission to Investigate the Poor Laws, *Report on the Administration and Practical Operation of the Poor Laws* (1834: 68–71, 261–63). See Boyer (1990: 52–65) and Poynter (1969).
    15. Briggs (1987: 37); Smiles ([1866] 2002: 17, 254).

so strong that working-class attitudes toward the Poor Law also hardened, so that many, though by no means all, of the poor went to great lengths to avoid applying for public relief.

Middle-class attitudes toward the poor began to soften, albeit slowly, in the decades following the Crusade Against Outrelief. The shift in public opinion was part of a growing debate regarding the limits of laissez-faire liberalism. The last third of the nineteenth century witnessed a "rise of collectivism." While market failures had been perceived in the 1830s and 1840s, especially with regard to child labor in factories and public health, after 1865 mounting evidence of the limitations of the free market economy began to shift public opinion toward government intervention. Parliament responded by adopting a series of measures restricting the employment and regulating the hours of children, young persons, and adult women, regulating working conditions and safety in factories and mines, giving legal recognition to trade unions, and enabling local authorities to use tax revenue to construct sanitation systems.[16]

Beatrice Webb attributed the change in middle-class attitudes in the 1880s to a new class-consciousness of sin, "a growing uneasiness, amounting to conviction, that the industrial organisation, which had yielded rent, interest and profits on a stupendous scale, had failed to provide a decent livelihood and tolerable conditions for the majority of inhabitants of Great Britain."[17] This "growing uneasiness" was encouraged by the publication of numerous works regarding poverty in London, the most influential of which were Mearns's *The Bitter Cry of Outcast London* (1883) and Booth's *Life and Labour of the People in London* (1892). Mearns's pamphlet was not the first study to depict the dire state of the London poor, but its impact was "immediate and cataclysmic." Indeed, *The Bitter Cry of Outcast London* has been described as "perhaps the most influential single piece of writing about the poor that England has ever seen."[18]

If Mearns opened the eyes of the middle class, Booth's finding that 30% of London's population was living in poverty stunned them. His results were particularly unsettling to the notion that most of the poor were "undeserving." Booth's analysis of the causes of poverty revealed that a majority of the "very poor" (families with incomes less than 18s. per week) and two-thirds of the "poor" (weekly incomes of 18–21s.) were in poverty due to low pay or lack of

16. Dicey (1905: 64–69, 258–301); Paul (1980: 31–34); Mokyr (2009: 479–85).

17. Webb (1926: 178–83).

18. Wohl (1968: 189); Gilbert (1966a: 28). See also Wohl (1970), Fraser (2003: 144–50), and Himmelfarb (1991: 57–65). Henry Mayhew's letters in the *Morning Chronicle* in 1849–50 also opened the eyes of the middle class to the plight of London's poor, but, in the words of Thompson (1967: 43), their "protective shell of Podsnappery... healed quickly." By the early 1860s Mayhew was viewed as "quaint."

work; fewer than one-in-five were in poverty due to idleness, thriftlessness, or drinking. The deserving poor far outnumbered the undeserving. Moreover, few of these deserving poor applied for or received public assistance. The two poorest districts in East London, St. George in the East and Bethnal Green, had poverty rates of 48.8% and 44.7%; in 1881 these same two districts had pauperism rates of 3.4% and 3.2%.[19]

The rediscovery of poverty in the 1880s led to a softening of middle-class attitudes toward the poor and to governmental inquiries into working-class housing, the aged poor, and distress from want of employment. The change in public opinion can be seen in economist Alfred Marshall's 1893 testimony before one of these inquiring bodies, the Royal Commission on the Aged Poor. Marshall stated, "The problem of 1834 was the problem of pauperism, the problem of 1893 is the problem of poverty. . . . Extreme poverty ought to be regarded, not indeed as a crime, but as a thing so detrimental to the State that it should not be endured." However, public interest in poverty and social policy appeared to diminish in the late 1890s, leading Masterman in 1901 to bemoan "the wide indifference to social reform" expressed by both the middle and working classes.[20]

This indifference changed shortly thereafter. The "terrible and shocking" condition of the poor revealed in Rowntree's *Poverty: A Study of Town Life*, also published in 1901, along with the equally shocking revelation that 30% of Boer War recruits were deemed by medical officers to be physically unfit, revived the public's interest in social policy. Rowntree added a new dimension to the debate, arguing that the issue was not simply the suffering of the poor, but also the problem of national economic efficiency. The economic competition of Germany, Belgium, and the United States made it imperative that Britain raise the mental and physical efficiency of its workforce. Rowntree's book was followed by additional studies of urban working-class communities by Lady Bell, Pember Reeves, and Bowley and Burnett-Hurst, and by the *Report of the Interdepartmental Committee on Physical Deterioration*. These studies reinforced Rowntree's finding by showing the great distress suffered by the lower stratum of manual workers and their families. In combination, they led to a reawakening of the public to the plight of the poor, which helped to bring about the adoption of the Liberal Welfare Reforms.

19. Booth published his initial estimates for East London and Hackney in two articles in the *Journal of the Royal Statistical Society* (1887; 1888). The poverty and pauperism rates for St. George in the East and Bethnal Green are from Booth (1888: 284, 331). His reported "figures of pauperism are the average of the first fifteen weeks in 1888." The first edition of *Life and Labour of the People* was published in 1889.

20. Parl. Papers, *Royal Commission on the Aged Poor, Minutes of Evidence*, vol. 3 (1895, XIV), q. 10,358. See also Marshall's comments in qq. 10,272 and 10,379. Masterman (1901: 4).

Finally, war influenced people's attitudes toward the poor. Within two weeks of the signing of the armistice ending the First World War, Lloyd George vowed to make Britain "a fit country for heroes to live in." The first important step in this process occurred before the war ended—the 1918 Representation of the People Act enfranchised all males aged 21 and older and women aged 30 and older who met a minimum property qualification. In the two immediate postwar years, before the sharp rise in unemployment, Parliament adopted several social policies. The 1918 Trade Boards Act established 33 new trade boards within two years, the 1919 Housing and Town Planning Act provided subsidies to local authorities for the construction of working-class housing, the Unemployment Insurance Act of 1920 extended unemployment insurance to all manual workers other than those engaged in agriculture or domestic service, and the National Health Insurance Act of 1920 extended compulsory health insurance to cover all persons aged 16–70 engaged in manual labor.

The economic shocks of the interwar period slowed the reforming impulse, but it was rekindled by the beginning of the Second World War. As discussed in Chapter 8, the call for a postwar New Jerusalem or New Britain began in the summer of 1940 and continued throughout the war. The common sacrifices being made by Britons both on the battlefield and in the bombed cities led to an increased affinity of the middle for the working class, and many came to believe along with Tawney that one of the goals of the war effort should be that all British citizens be enabled to participate "in the treasures of civilization." The message of the Beveridge Report was sown on well-prepared fields. Labour's landslide victory in the 1945 general election ensured that the call for a New Britain would be translated into the adoption of the welfare state.

THE ROLE OF COSTS

Social welfare policies cannot be had free of charge. The important issue of the cost of social policies, and who will pay for them, is entwined with the issues of political voice and public opinion. No one likes to pay taxes, especially if they think that the benefits are going to another (perhaps undeserving) group. The call for cuts in social spending in the 1830s and 1870s were influenced by the fear of rising taxes as much as by the belief that many of the poor were not deserving of assistance. Numerous critics of the Old Poor Law argued that local poor rates would increase continually if the payment of generous outdoor relief to able-bodied males was not eliminated, and the 1834 Report of the Royal Poor Law Commission predicted that the substitution of workhouses for outdoor relief would lead to a fall in local rates and an increase in land values.[21] Local rates did indeed decline following the

---

21. Boyer (1990: 194–204); Royal Commission to Investigate the Poor Laws, *Report on the Administration and Practical Operation of the Poor Laws* (1834: 63–67).

adoption of the New Poor Law, but the crisis of the 1860s led to a renewed fear of increasing taxes.

The Crusade Against Outrelief largely was driven by a desire to reduce taxes on the part of the middle class. The Union Chargeability Act of 1865, which placed the entire cost of poor relief on the Poor Law union rather than on the parishes and directed that each parish's contribution to the union common fund be based on the value of its taxable property, shifted a large share of the cost of poor relief from working-class to middle-class parishes. The resulting increase in poor rates in wealthier districts sparked a middle-class reconsideration of the proper role of the Poor Law, and they swallowed the rhetoric of the Charity Organisation Society hook, line, and sinker. By restricting outdoor relief and offering the poor assistance in workhouses, middle-class-dominated boards of guardians believed that they would both reduce their taxes and improve the morals of the working class.[22]

The Union Chargeability Act was the first major step in shifting the cost of social welfare policies, and additional shifts continued up through the adoption of the welfare state in the 1940s. The extent of this cost shifting is worth considering. The Poor Law was administered at the local level and funded by a local property tax. The 1834 Poor Law Amendment Act grouped parishes into Poor Law unions, but each parish within a union remained responsible for relieving its own poor. As a result, there were large differences in poor rates across parishes within unions. These differences grew during downturns, when increasing demand for assistance forced many urban working-class parishes to raise their poor rates to high and unsustainable levels. The 1861 Irremovable Poor Act shifted some of the cost of relief from the parish to the union, and this shift was completed four years later by the Union Chargeability Act. Still, relief of the poor remained the responsibility of local authorities, and poor rates varied substantially across Poor Law unions.

The Liberal Welfare Reforms began the process of shifting the cost of social welfare from local taxpayers to the central government, employers, and workers. The 1908 Old Age Pension Act was funded completely out of general taxation, while unemployment and sickness insurance were funded by contributions from workers, employers, and the state. Government pensions led to a sharp drop in the number of aged persons collecting poor relief, and

22. As discussed in Chapter 3, the effect of the Crusade Against Outrelief on local taxes was not as straightforward as its leaders believed. While the increased use of the workhouse test reduced the number of applicants for relief, this did not necessarily translate into a reduction in poor rates because the administrative cost of relieving the poor in workhouses was far greater than the cost of giving them outdoor relief. The declines in Poor Law spending and taxes associated with the crusade were smaller than most reformers claimed they would be, and in some Poor Law unions the crusade might have led to an increase in poor rates. The extent of workhouses' deterrent effects and the high administrative costs of indoor relief are discussed in MacKinnon (1987), Kiniria (2016), and Lindert (2004: 51–55).

TABLE 9.1. Spending on Social Services: Great Britain, 1925 and 1938–39

(A) EXPENDITURES IN 1925 (£ MILLION)

	Expenditures Met by Contributions From:				
	Central Government	Local Authorities	Employers	Workers	Total
Unemployment insurance	13.2		19.2	17.5	49.9
Health insurance	7.0		14.0	13.0	34.0
Widows', orphans' pensions	4.0		11.0	11.0	26.0
Old age pensions	25.8				25.8
Poor law relief	3.5	34.5			38.0
Total social spending	53.5	34.5	44.2	41.5	173.7
% of overall social spending	30.8	19.9	25.4	23.9	100.0
Total spending as % of GDP					4.2

(B) EXPENDITURES IN 1938–39 (£ MILLION)

	Expenditures Met by Contributions From:				
	Central Government	Local Authorities	Employers	Workers	Total
Unemployment insurance	62.2		22.5	22.2	106.9
Health insurance	7.7		14.6	15.3	37.6
Widows', orphans' pensions	17.0		15.9	17.3	50.2
Old age pensions	48.4				48.4
Poor law relief (outdoor)		26.3			26.3
Total social spending	135.3	26.3	53.0	54.8	269.4
% of overall social spending	50.2	9.8	19.7	20.3	100.0
Total spending as % of GDP					5.4

Sources: Data for 1925 from Jones (1927: 709). Data for 1938–39 from Beveridge (1942: 241). GDP data from Feinstein (1972: T13).

a shift in the cost of maintaining the elderly poor from local authorities to the Treasury.[23] Unemployment and sickness benefits also reduced poor relief spending, though by a smaller amount since few adults between the ages of 16 and 60 turned to the Poor Law for assistance. The effect of the new policies on the distribution of social spending can be seen in panel (a) of Table 9.1, which shows that in 1925 local authorities contributed only £34.5 million (20%) out of a total cost of social services of £173.7 million. The central government contributed £53.5 million (31%), mainly for old age pensions, and the joint contribution of employers and workers was £85.7 million (49%).

23. From March 1906 to January 1913, the number of persons 70 and older in receipt of poor relief fell by 75%. Parl. Papers, *Old Age Pensioners and Aged Pauperism* (1913, LV), pp. 8–9.

The 1929 Local Government Act abolished Poor Law unions and trans-ferred administration of poor relief to the counties and county boroughs. This reduced the number of Poor Law authorities in England and Wales from 631 to 145, which greatly enlarged the size of local tax bases and reduced, but did not eliminate, variations in poor rates across locations. The Unemployment Act of 1934 further shifted costs from counties and county boroughs to the central government and virtually eliminated the role of the Poor Law in assisting the unemployed. Panel (b) of Table 9.1 shows how social services were financed in 1938–39. The increased role of the central government stands out—it con-tributed one-half of the total cost of social spending, up from 31% in 1925. The table does not include spending on institutional poor relief and therefore understates expenditures by local authorities. If we assume that total Poor Law spending in 1939 was £40 million, the central government still paid 48% of the total cost of social spending, as compared to 14% paid by local authorities.[24]

Finally, the 1948 National Assistance Act, a part of Labour's welfare state, abolished the Poor Law and replaced it with the National Assistance Board to act as a residual relief agency. The act shifted the responsibility and cost of assisting those who fell through the holes in the social safety net to the central government. In so doing, it completed the process of transferring the costs of social welfare policies from local authorities to the Treasury that had begun 40 years earlier with the Old Age Pension Act. Table 9.2 summarizes the changes over time in how social policies were financed.

The shifting of the costs of social welfare from parishes to unions to counties to the central government was accompanied by changes in the people who paid for the social welfare policies. The nineteenth-century poor rate was a property tax assessed on "land, houses, and buildings of every description" within the par-ish. It largely was paid by employers of labor and the lower middle class (shop-keepers, landlords, tradesmen, etc.), although workers, as occupiers of dwelling houses, paid part of the tax. The actual amount that workers contributed is dif-ficult to measure. Working-class dwellings represented a majority of the total number of assessments in both urban and rural locations, but assessments on workers' dwellings were small (typically less than £8, often less than £4), and occupiers often were excused from paying the poor rate "on account of poverty." Data for 1848/9 suggest that assessments on working-class dwellings represented *at most* 14–28% of the poor rate in Lancashire cities, and no more than 10% of the poor rate in rural Suffolk. If workers were able to shift some of the tax onto their landlords, their actual contributions to the poor rate were even smaller.[25]

---

24. According to the data reported in Mitchell (1988: 418, 424), total spending on poor relief by local authorities was £35.4 million in 1925 and £40.7 million in 1939.

25. These estimates assume that all assessments valued at less than £8 were on working-class dwellings. See Chapter 2, Section II. Data on the distribution of poor rate assessments from Parl.

TABLE 9.2. Sources of Spending on Social Security

	GOVERNMENT		Employers	Workers	Other	Total
	Local	Central				
1830	100.0	0.0	0.0	0.0	0.0	100.0
1880	100.0	0.0	0.0	0.0	0.0	100.0
1911	64.6	35.4	0.0	0.0	0.0	100.0
1925	19.9	30.8	25.4	23.9	0.0	100.0
1938–39	9.8	50.2	19.7	20.3	0.0	100.0
1950						
Social insurance	27.6		30.7	37.4	4.2	100.0
Social security	61.9		15.6	17.8	4.7	100.0
1960						
Social insurance	19.1		39.0	38.8	3.2	100.0
Social security	58.7		17.9	20.0	3.4	100.0

Sources: Expenditure data for 1911 from Williams (1981:171) and *Seventeenth Abstract of Labour Statistics* (1915: 185). Sources for 1925 and 1938–39 are given in Table 9.1. Expenditure data for 1950 and 1960 from Flora et al. (1983: 548).

Note: Some rows do not sum to 100.0 due to rounding. For definitions of social insurance and social security, see text.

The Liberal Welfare Reforms changed the method of funding social spending. The 1911 National Insurance Act was the first to institute a "tripartite scheme of contribution," with workers, employers, and the state all contributing to the cost of unemployment and sickness benefits. Beveridge's social insurance scheme also was funded by a tripartite system of contribution, and the 1946 National Insurance Act was paid for by flat-rate contributions by employees and employers, and by general taxation.

As the social safety net widened and became more generous, workers' contributions to its funding increased. In 1925 and 1939 workers directly paid 20–25% of the cost of social services. The Beveridge Plan and the postwar welfare legislation continued, and extended, the use of workers' contributions for social security. Table 9.2 shows that in 1950 and 1960 workers directly paid more than one-third of the cost of social insurance.[26] When social security is defined more broadly to include public health, national assistance, and family allowances, each of which was financed mainly from tax revenue, workers'

Papers, *Returns Relating to Rating of Tenements in Lancashire, Suffolk, Hampshire, and Gloucestershire* (1849, XLVII), pp. 2–15. Data on the value of rateable property for counties, parishes, and large towns in 1847 from Parl. Papers, *Return of Amount Levied for Poor and County Rates, etc.* (1847–48b, LIII).

26. Social insurance includes unemployment, health, pension, and occupational injury insurance.

direct contributions fall to about 20% of total costs. However, workers' payroll deductions substantially understate their total contribution. Some (perhaps most) of employers' contributions were passed on to workers in the form of lower wages, and the central government's customs and excise taxes fell to some extent on workers. All told, workers in interwar Britain paid more than one-third of the cost of social services, while in the 1950s workers paid one-half or more of the cost of social insurance, and as much as one-third of the cost of social security, broadly defined.[27]

In response to arguments that the cost of social security should be borne entirely out of general taxation, Beveridge claimed that the British people did not want "something for nothing." Workers supported contributing to a tripartite scheme because it enabled them to obtain "security not as a charity but as a right." A system of social services funded entirely by general taxation would have been considered an extravagance by a large share of the British electorate in 1945. Many, including some within the postwar Labour government, would have viewed the necessary increase in government spending as too high a price to pay even for increased income security.

The relatively heavy taxation of labor is a general characteristic of European welfare states, as Lindert and Kato have shown.[28] Workers largely pay for the benefits they receive. This should not be surprising, given that a major plank of Britain's social security program was a compulsory and comprehensive system of social insurance. The welfare state reduces economic insecurity not only by relieving poverty, but also by providing individuals with an insurance mechanism to facilitate consumption smoothing over the life cycle. Falkingham and Hills estimate that in the late 1980s individuals financed, on average, between two-thirds and three-quarters of the lifetime benefits they received "through their *own* lifetime tax payments." The remaining one-quarter to one-third of benefits represented transfers across people, from the "lifetime rich" to the "lifetime poor." The welfare state's consumption-smoothing "piggy bank" function is quantitatively larger than its redistributive "Robin Hood" function.[29]

---

27. Beveridge estimated that in 1945 workers' direct contributions through payroll deductions would equal 28% of the cost of social services, employers' contributions 20%, and general taxation 50%. He calculated that when the costs of institutional medical services and workers' compensation were added to social spending, in 1938–39 workers' direct contributions equaled 16% of the total cost of social services. Finally, he estimated that the share paid by workers would decline gradually over time, from 28% in 1945 to 20% in 1965, as a result of changes in contributions for retirement pensions. Beveridge (1942: 107–19).

28. Lindert (2004: 235–45); Kato (2003).

29. Hills (2004: 195–97); Falkingham and Hills (1995: 137–49); Hills (2017: 47–73); Barr (2001: 1–7).

THE ROLE OF SELF-HELP AND THE
STIGMATIZATION OF THE POOR LAW

The mid-Victorian ethos of respectability and self-help assumed that virtually all working-class households, by practicing "simple industry and thrift," could protect themselves against income loss due to unemployment, sickness, or old age. The aggregate data presented in Chapters 2 and 3 suggested that the Victorian self-help movement was a resounding success in terms of its own objectives—membership in friendly societies and insurance-providing trade unions, and working-class deposits in savings banks, increased greatly in the second half of the nineteenth century. Workers responded to the cutbacks in outdoor relief initiated during the 1870s by protecting themselves against financial insecurity, as Smiles and other Victorian commentators predicted.

However, the chapters also make it clear that the aggregate data tell only a part of the story. Self-help by itself was not enough. While most working-class households had savings accounts in 1901, the average balance in these accounts was only £4–5, the equivalent of 2–4 weeks' pay for manual workers. Nor did friendly societies adequately protect the working class against insecurity. For one thing, low-skilled workers found it difficult to make the weekly contribution of 6d.–1s. required by friendly societies offering sickness and old age benefits. As a result, membership in such societies largely remained outside the sphere of the bottom one-third of the income distribution. It would be incorrect to suggest that no low-skilled workers joined such societies, but in general "friendly society membership was the badge of the skilled worker."[30]

Friendly societies did not cover a major source of financial insecurity— unemployment. The moral hazard issues associated with the provision of unemployment benefits simply were too costly. Trade unions of skilled craft workers were able to monitor their members' eligibility for benefits and search activity at relatively low cost, and most craft unions provided some form of unemployment benefits. However, the irregularity of employment in most low-skilled occupations raised the cost of insurance substantially above what the unskilled could afford to pay, and few unions of low-skilled workers provided benefits. As late as 1908, only 12% of the adult male workforce in England and Wales was eligible for unemployment benefits.

To remain eligible for friendly society benefits, members had to continue paying their dues month in and month out. Those who fell into arrears often were fined and/or disqualified from receiving benefits; if they remained in arrears long enough, they could be suspended from the society. In addition, some (unknown) percentage of workers who joined friendly societies as young

---

30. Johnson (1985: 57–63); Gilbert (1966a: 166–67).

men quit them before reaching an age where sickness rates rose.[31] The share of workers who were protected against income loss due to sickness throughout their adult years thus was smaller than the membership data suggest. In sum, the assumption held by Smiles and other Victorians that almost all manual workers, so long as they were thrifty, could protect themselves against income insecurity, was not correct at any point from 1850 to 1914. In the words of Eric Hopkins, "Although working-class self-help . . . achieved great things by 1914, it had proved inadequate as a means of succor for the working classes as a whole. Put simply, the very poorest did not have the resources to help themselves."[32]

Another option for those suffering financial hardship during "critical life situations" was to turn to relatives and neighbors for help. Data reported in Chapter 5 show that large numbers of aged persons, especially females, received assistance from their children, and many resided with younger relatives, usually, but not always, their children. Married couples often lived near their parents—this was true in mid-nineteenth-century Preston and in Bethnal Green a century later—which enabled children and parents to assist each other as necessary. Unemployed, sick, or widowed individuals also turned to kin for assistance. However, the amount of aid that could be obtained from working-class kinfolk often was small, especially during cyclical downturns when hardship was widespread. Those who assisted kinfolk in need often created hardship for themselves—their relatives' "burden was not removed; it was only spread." In sum, kinship networks played an important but limited role in income smoothing.[33]

After 1870, if not before, the working class attached a stigma to the acceptance of poor relief. The stigmatization of poor relief increased over time, largely due to increased use of the workhouse and COS propaganda. It was strongest for able-bodied adults, but existed even for the elderly. The extent of stigmatization at the beginning of the twentieth century was revealed by Rowntree's poverty estimates and also by the enormous number of applicants for Old Age Pensions. As discussed in Chapter 6, Rowntree found that the number of persons living in primary poverty in York in 1899 was more than double the number of persons receiving poor relief at some point during the year—half of those in poverty were not applying for public assistance. Some of this was due to fear of the workhouse, but much was due to the stigmatization

---

31. Emery and Emery (1999: 50–51, 102–16, 128–32); Emery (2008). Emery and Emery found that 28% of Canadian Odd Fellows were in arrears in 1919 and 58% in 1929. To my knowledge, data on the number of friendly society members in arrears in late Victorian or Edwardian England do not exist.

32. Hopkins (1995: 227).

33. Anderson (1971: 56–67, 136–61); Dupree (1995: 328–45, 350); Young and Willmott (1957); Royal Commission on Unemployment Insurance, *Appendices*, pt. III (1931: 113).

of relief. The impact of the Old Age Pension Act was even more surprising. In March 1912 the number of persons in receipt of a means-tested pension in England and Wales was 642,524, 60% of the population aged 70 and older, and 280% more than the number of relief recipients 70 and older in 1906. Many contemporaries, including Lloyd George, interpreted the large difference between the number of paupers and pensioners as evidence of the extent of the stigma the working class attached to the Poor Law.[34] In combination, the stigmatization of the Poor Law and the inability of self-help to protect the low-skilled meant that around the turn of the twentieth century many within the bottom one-third of working-class households effectively had no safety net against the very distinct possibility of falling into destitution as a result of negative income shocks—they were not members of friendly societies, had little savings, and were unwilling to apply for poor relief.

The substitution of new government social programs for the Poor Law reduced, but did not eliminate, the stigmatization of public assistance—the "non-take-up" of benefits remains an issue in Europe today. In his recent book *Inequality*, Atkinson stresses that "the capacity of a transfer scheme to provide effective income support depends on how that support is viewed by the potential beneficiaries," and adds that the take-up rate is determined in part by how social policies are financed, and by whether they are means-tested or universal. Individuals attach less stigma to benefits that they contributed to directly through payroll deductions than to benefits that they paid for indirectly through income tax; the act of direct contribution gives one a "right" to benefits. They also attach a greater stigma to targeted means-tested benefits than to universal benefits. It appears that Beveridge was correct both in insisting that social security should cover all British citizens and that benefits not be means-tested, and in supporting workers' direct contributions to the social insurance scheme on the grounds that "there is a psychological desire to get something for which you have paid."[35]

Concluding Thoughts on the Poverty Line, Insecurity, and Social Policy

In *David Copperfield*, Dickens had Mr. Micawber explain the difference between happiness and misery as follows: "Annual income twenty pounds, annual expenditure nineteen [pounds] nineteen [shillings] and six [pence], result happiness. Annual income twenty pounds, annual expenditure twenty pounds

34. Rowntree (1901: 365–67); Parl. Papers, *Old Age Pensioners and Aged Pauperism* (1913, LV), pp. 7–8; Thane (2000: 227–28).

35. Atkinson (2015: 210–12, 229–31); Atkinson (2014: 52–55); Beveridge (1942: 11–12). For an earlier call for a universal social security system, see Tawney (1931: 153).

ought and six, result misery."[36] This notion that a small decline in income can create immense hardship is sometimes assumed by those who use the poverty line as a measure of the extent of destitution—simply substitute the word poverty for misery. All households above the poverty line are assumed to have an adequate income, while those below it are assumed to be indigent. But economic hardship does not work that way. The state of privation is a continuum—one can become more or less poor by a small change in income, but one doesn't shift from happiness to misery that easily.

The estimated poverty rates from the various town surveys reported in Chapters 6 and 7 convey useful information, but they are an incomplete measure of the extent of economic insecurity. Head counts of poverty do not reveal how many households have incomes above but close to the poverty line. These households are non-poor by definition, but they are economically insecure—if the main breadwinner was unable to work for several weeks due to sickness or unemployment many such households would be plunged into destitution. Nor do head counts reveal anything about the "intensity of poverty," the magnitude of the average income deficit of the households living in poverty. Surely it matters whether the average poor family's weekly income was two shillings or eight shillings below the poverty line.

The inadequacy of poverty head counts is shown in Table 9.3, which presents data on working-class living standards for the five towns surveyed by Bowley and Burnett-Hurst in 1912–14. The second row gives the share of households with incomes above but within 8s. of the poverty line (the near-poor), and row three gives the results obtained from adding these households to the share with incomes below the poverty line. Some 60% of Reading's working-class households had weekly incomes no more than 8s. above the poverty line, as did 36% of Warrington's and 23% of Bolton's households. Similarly, in 1899 one-third of York's working-class population lived in households with incomes no more than 6s. above the poverty line. All of these households, both the poor and the near-poor, were economically insecure.[37]

Another way to measure the extent of economic hardship is to estimate the share of working-class families living in comparative comfort, with incomes high enough to withstand small negative income shocks without experiencing acute distress. There is no good measure of what constitutes a "comfortable" income; here I pick (arbitrarily) a household income of 40s. (£2) per week, slightly less than 16s. above the poverty line for a family of five in 1912.[38] The

36. Dickens ([1850] 2004: 174).

37. A family of five with an income 8s. above the poverty line in 1912 would be about 33% above the poverty threshold. Rowntree (1901: 142–43) reported only the number of working-class persons living in households with incomes no more than 2s. or 6s. above the poverty line.

38. The poverty line for a family of five in 1912, by Bowley's measure, was 24.6s. See Table 6.3.

TABLE 9.3. Poverty and Economic Insecurity in Bowley's Five Towns

Households	Reading 1912	Warrington 1913	Northampton 1913	Stanley 1913	Bolton 1914
% of households below poverty line	23.2	12.8	8.2	5.4	7.8
% above, but within 8s. of poverty line	37.1	23.6	7.3	7.9	15.0
% in poverty or within 8s. of poverty line	60.3	36.5	15.5	13.4	22.8
% with incomes 16s. or more above the poverty line	15.4	36.1	59.7	65.8	48.4
% of those in poverty 6s. or more below poverty line	36.8	17.1	14.0	45.5	23.1
Estimated average poverty gap (s.)	6.1	3.9	3.5	6.2	4.2

Source: Bowley and Burnett-Hurst (1915: 88, 134, 157, 172; 1920: 238).

fourth row of Table 9.3 shows that households with weekly incomes that were 16s. or more above the poverty line constituted nearly two-thirds of working-class families in Stanley and 60% of families in Northampton, but only 36% of families in Warrington and 15% of families in Reading.

The last two rows present evidence on the intensity of poverty. The share of poor households with weekly incomes more than 6s. *below* the poverty line ranged from 14% in Northampton and 17% in Warrington to 37% in Reading and over 45% in Stanley. The final row reports the estimated average income deficit (poverty gap) for households with incomes below the poverty line. Not only did Reading have a large number of poor or near-poor households, but the average weekly income deficit of its poor households was relatively high, at 6.1s. Only a small share of Stanley's households had incomes below the poverty line, but those that did had an average income deficit of 6.2s. A comparison of Warrington and Bolton shows that, while the poverty rate was five percentage points higher in Warrington, the average income deficit of the poor was larger in Bolton.

The inadequacy of head count measures of poverty becomes especially clear when evaluating the effects of government social policies. Consider the following scenario. Suppose the government instituted a welfare policy that raised no poor households above the poverty line, but reduced the average weekly income deficit for those in poverty from 6s. to 2s. Commentators who focus on poverty head counts would deem the policy to be a failure, despite the fact that it raised the incomes of poor households by an average of 4s. per week. The proper way to evaluate social welfare policies is to determine their effects not just on the poverty head count but also on the intensity of poverty. For example, Hatton and Bailey show that, although the interwar social security system reduced the poverty rate by a relatively small amount, it improved the condition of the poor by eliminating "much of the poverty gap" that existed in the 1930s.[39]

Those who focus on head counts also miss the positive effects that social welfare policies have on persons with incomes above the poverty line. Social policies not only raise the poor out of poverty but also keep the near-poor from falling into poverty when they experience negative income shocks. The interwar town surveys discussed in Chapter 7 found that large numbers of households above the poverty line received social income in one or more forms, most frequently unemployment benefits or old age pensions. The interwar safety net, like most social welfare policies, reduced the economic insecurity faced by the non-poor as well as the poor.

Another issue needing to be confronted is the relationship between social welfare policies and inequality. Marx, Nolan, and Olivera concluded from a survey of recent studies that there exists "a strong empirical relationship" between social spending and inequality. In their words, "no advanced economy achieved a low level of inequality and/or relative income poverty with a low level of social spending. . . . Conversely, countries with relatively high social spending tended to have lower inequality and poverty." Is the sharp rise in income and wealth inequality since 1980 associated with changes in social spending? Atkinson argues that it is. In response to calls for "rolling back the welfare state," Britain and other Western economies reduced social insurance benefits (or did not increase them in line with rising prices) and reduced benefit coverage, especially for the unemployed. Atkinson contends that "a renewal of social insurance, raising the level of benefits and extending their coverage," is necessary to reduce inequality to pre-1980 levels.[40]

All of the industrialized West, and not just Britain, greatly increased the scope of their social welfare policies between the wars and especially after the Second World War. On the eve of the First World War, Britain and the Scandinavian countries were the only European nations that spent more than 1% of their gross domestic product on social transfers.[41] By 1930, social transfer spending exceeded 2% of GDP in seven European nations, including Britain. The immediate postwar period saw the rise of welfare states throughout Western Europe, North America, and the Antipodes. These welfare states took various forms. Esping-Andersen contends that there are three distinct welfare state regimes—the Anglophone liberal/market-based welfare states,

---

39. Hatton and Bailey (1998: 587–88, 595).

40. Marx, Nolan, and Olivera (2015: 2081); Atkinson (2015: 205, 223–31).

41. Denmark, the leader in social spending, devoted 1.75% of its GDP to social transfers. See Table 6.7.

the conservative/corporatist welfare states of continental Europe, and the Nordic social-democratic welfare states. More recently, a fourth regime, the Southern European model, has been identified.[42] The postwar era witnessed a sharp increase in social spending in all welfare state regimes. In 1960 social spending exceeded 10% of GDP in eight of the nine European nations included in Table 6.7. A decade later it exceeded 15% in each of these nations except Britain, where it was 13.2% of GDP. In relative terms, social spending grew slowly in Britain. In 1910 and 1930, Britain was among the leaders in social spending; by 1970 British spending was closer to that of the United States and Canada than to that of its Northern European neighbors.[43] Britain also seems to have changed regimes in terms of Esping-Andersen's typology. Beveridge's 1942 model and Labour's social welfare legislation of 1945–48 were largely social-democratic, but over time the British system has become more liberal and residualist.[44]

What we have learned here provides a useful perspective for examining the current welfare debates. The idea that most poor people are lazy, thriftless, or thoughtless is not new—it has been argued by the "haves" since the eighteenth century, if not earlier. The evidence for Victorian England shows that the assertion is unfair—the advocates of self-help "never took proper account of the precarious economic circumstances of working-class life."[45] The assumption that low-skilled workers, assuming they were thrifty, could protect themselves against income loss due to sickness, unemployment, and old age was incorrect throughout the nineteenth century and remains incorrect today.

The findings presented here show that government crackdowns on welfare, such as occurred in the 1830s and 1870s, were far better at reducing relief roles than at reducing poverty or insecurity. Politicians then, and now, celebrate policy-induced reductions in numbers on welfare, but largely ignore the economic conditions of those pushed off the roles. As Solow observed, they don't ask "what has happened to the former welfare recipients or to the working poor. . . . They may be living with relatives who cannot afford them, or on the street."[46] We await the twenty-first-century incarnations of Booth and Rowntree to reveal how many of those no longer receiving welfare as a result of recent reforms remain in poverty.

42. Lindert (2004: 11–15); Esping-Andersen (1990: 21–32); Garland (2016: 59–80); Ferrera (1996). On the development of the welfare state in various Western European nations, see Baldwin (1990).

43. Lindert (2004: 11–15). In 1970 social spending as a share of GDP ranged from 22.5% in the Netherlands to 10.4% in the United States. Britain remained in last place among the nine countries in terms of social spending as a share of GDP in both 1990 and 2000. See Lindert (2017: 40).

44. Garland (2016: 78–80). On Britain's "rejection of Beveridge," see Lowe (1994).

45. Johnson (1985: 217–18).

46. Solow (1998: 42–43).

Finally, the book has revealed insecurity's amazing persistence. Perhaps the most important lesson to be learned is that economic growth does not necessarily lead to economic security. Insecurity was the scourge of preindustrial agrarian societies. When the vast majority of people lived near the subsistence level, a downward shift in the yield of the grain harvest brought about by bad weather or blight often led to misery and destitution for a large share of the population. As Tawney reminds us, the insecure peasant "curses the weather." The industrial revolution brought immense wealth but also led to a new form of economic insecurity, which switched from an agrarian problem associated with the supply of food to an industrial problem associated with fluctuations in the wage income and employment of household heads. Beveridge, writing in 1942, looked back on four decades of rising living standards and noted that "growing general prosperity . . . diminished want, but did not reduce want to insignificance." He concluded that "new measures to spread prosperity are needed. . . . Abolition of want cannot be brought about merely by increasing production."[47]

The post-1945 boom led to a further decline in economic insecurity, which, largely due to the expansion of social welfare policies, fell to very low levels in the Nordic and Low Countries and France. However, the level of insecurity stabilized in the 1970s, and in Britain, the United States, and some other affluent nations insecurity increased after 1980. Hacker contends that insecurity lives on, and is growing, in twenty-first-century America, as a result of rising income volatility, the rising threat of "catastrophic medical costs," and "the massively increased risk that retirement has come to represent."[48]

The persistence of economic insecurity over time has been overlooked or dismissed by those economists, politicians, and pundits who, like Nobel Prize winner Robert Lucas, stress "the apparently limitless potential of increasing production" for "improving the lives of poor people." The evidence presented here suggests that faith in economic growth and trickle-down as a solution to poverty and insecurity is misplaced. The business cycles and job reallocation associated with economic growth create income volatility for households, and increasing globalization has raised job insecurity in many sectors of the economy. Moreover, recent growth has been accompanied by rising inequality—those at the bottom of the income ladder have benefited the least. The "unequal gains" of post-1970 growth have done little to reduce insecurity among the working poor. In Keynes's words, there is a "tendency for wealth to be distributed where it is not appreciated most."[49] Economic growth may be necessary for reducing insecurity, but it is not sufficient.

47. Beveridge (1942: 166–67).

48. On rising levels of economic insecurity in Britain and the United States since 1980, see Osberg and Sharpe (2002: 305–9; 2005: 317–22; 2014: S57–62, S72) and Hacker (2008: chap. 1).

49. Lucas (2004: 8); Lindert and Williamson (2016: chap. 9); Keynes (1926: sec. III).

Lloyd George, an early leader in the war against poverty and insecurity, concluded his April 1909 speech introducing the People's Budget to Parliament by stating that the money raised by it would be used "to wage implacable warfare against poverty and squalidness," and added, "I cannot help hoping and believing that before this generation has passed away we shall have advanced a great step towards that good time when poverty, and the wretchedness and human degradation which always follow in its camp will be as remote to the people of this country as the wolves which once infested its forests."[50] He lived long enough to see and support the Beveridge Plan, which mapped out "the way to freedom with security," but passed away shortly before Labour's landslide victory in the 1945 general election. The implementation of National Insurance, the National Health Service, and National Assistance in 1948 held out the hope that Lloyd George's vision of "that good time" was about to be fulfilled. Unfortunately, it has become clear in the past half century that the adoption of the welfare state was not the end of the road to economic security. The road continues.

50. Lloyd George (1910: 143).

REFERENCES

Official Publications

Great Britain, Board of Trade (1887). *Statistical Tables and Report on Trade Unions*. London: HMSO.

Great Britain, Board of Trade (1895). *Seventh Annual Report on Trade Unions*. London: HMSO.

Great Britain, Board of Trade (1900). *Report on the Wages and Earnings of Agricultural Labourers in the United Kingdom*. London: HMSO.

Great Britain, Board of Trade (1900). *Sixth Abstract of Labour Statistics of the United Kingdom*. London: HMSO.

Great Britain, Board of Trade (1902). *Eighth Abstract of Labour Statistics of the United Kingdom*. London: HMSO.

Great Britain, Board of Trade (1905–17). *Labour Gazette*. Various issues. London: HMSO.

Great Britain, Board of Trade (1907). *Eleventh Abstract of Labour Statistics of the United Kingdom, 1905–06*. London: HMSO.

Great Britain, Board of Trade (1908). *Rates of Wages and Hours of Labour in Various Industries*. Unpublished.

Great Britain, Board of Trade (1908). *Report of an Enquiry into Working Class Rents, Housing and Retail Prices*. London: HMSO.

Great Britain, Board of Trade (1908). *Twelfth Abstract of Labour Statistics of the United Kingdom*. London: HMSO.

Great Britain, Board of Trade (1910). *Earnings and Hours of Labour of Workpeople of the United Kingdom. III.—Building and Woodworking Trades in 1906*. London: HMSO.

Great Britain, Board of Trade (1912). *Fifteenth Abstract of Labour Statistics of the United Kingdom*. London: HMSO.

Great Britain, Board of Trade (1912). *Report on Trade Unions in 1908–10*. London: HMSO.

Great Britain, Board of Trade (1915). *Seventeenth Abstract of Labour Statistics of the United Kingdom*. London: HMSO.

Great Britain, Board of Trade (1927). *Eighteenth Abstract of Labour Statistics of the United Kingdom*. London: HMSO.

Great Britain, Board of Trade (1937). *Twenty-Second Abstract of Labour Statistics of the United Kingdom*. London: HMSO.

Great Britain, Board of Trade (1940). *Eighty-Third Statistical Abstract for the United Kingdom, for Each of the Fifteen Years 1924 to 1938*. London: HMSO.

Great Britain, Central Statistical Office (1957, 1962). *Annual Abstract of Statistics*. London: HMSO.

Great Britain, Department of Employment and Productivity (1971). *British Labour Statistics: Historical Abstract 1886–1968*. London: HMSO.

Great Britain, Local Government Board (1871–1919). *Annual Reports of the Local Government Board*. London: HMSO.

Great Britain, Ministry of Labour (1917–39). *Ministry of Labour Gazette.* Various issues. London: HMSO.

Great Britain, Ministry of Labour (1927–39). *Local Unemployment Index.* London: HMSO.

Great Britain, Ministry of Labour (1934). *Reports of Investigations into the Industrial Conditions in certain Depressed Areas.* London: HMSO.

Great Britain, Office of Population Censuses and Surveys (1932). *Registrar General's Statistical Review of England and Wales for the Year 1930.* London: HMSO.

Great Britain, Office of Population Censuses and Surveys (1935). *Registrar General's Statistical Review of England and Wales for the Year 1932.* London: HMSO.

Great Britain, Office of Population Censuses and Surveys (1938). *Registrar General's Statistical Review of England and Wales for the Year 1935.* London: HMSO.

Great Britain, Office of Population Censuses and Surveys (1985). *Mortality Statistics, Serial Tables: Review of the Registrar General on Deaths in England and Wales, 1841–1980.* London: HMSO.

Great Britain, Parliamentary Papers (1803–4, XIII). *Abstract of Returns Relative to the Expense and Maintenance of the Poor Law.*

Great Britain, Parliamentary Papers (1834, XXVII). *Report on the Administration and Practical Operation of the Poor Laws.*

Great Britain, Parliamentary Papers (1837–38, XXVIII). *Fourth Annual Report of the Poor Law Commissioners for England and Wales.*

Great Britain, Parliamentary Papers (1842, XXII). *Reports of the Inspectors of Factories for the Half Year Ending the 31st December 1841.*

Great Britain, Parliamentary Papers (1842, XXII). *Reports of the Inspectors of Factories . . . for the Half Year Ending June 30, 1842.*

Great Britain, Parliamentary Papers (1842, XXXV). *Report of the Assistant Poor Law Commissioners . . . on the State of the Population of Stockport.*

Great Britain, Parliamentary Papers (1843, VII). *Report from the Select Committee on Distress (Paisley).*

Great Britain, Parliamentary Papers (1844, XL). *Return of Average Annual Expenditure of Parishes in Each Union in England and Wales.*

Great Britain, Parliamentary Papers (1846, XXXVI). *A Copy of Reports Received by the Poor-Law Commissioners in 1841, on the State of the Macclesfield and Bolton Unions.*

Great Britain, Parliamentary Papers (1847, XI). *Report from the Select Committee on Settlement and Poor Removal.*

Great Britain, Parliamentary Papers (1847–48, LIII). *Return of the Comparative Expenditure for Relief of the Poor . . . in the Six Months Ending Lady-Day in 1846, 1847 and 1848.*

Great Britain, Parliamentary Papers (1847–48, LIII). *Return of Amount Levied for Poor and County Rates, etc.*

Great Britain, Parliamentary Papers (1849, XLVII). *Returns Relating to Rating of Tenements in Lancashire, Suffolk, Hampshire, and Gloucestershire.*

Great Britain, Parliamentary Papers (1854–55, XIII). *Report from the Select Committee on Poor Removal.*

Great Britain, Parliamentary Papers (1861, IX). *First Report from the Select Committee on Poor Relief (England).*

Great Britain, Parliamentary Papers (1862, X). *Third Report from the Select Committee on Poor Relief.*

Great Britain, Parliamentary Papers (1862, XLIX, Pt. 1). *Return of Number of Paupers in Receipt of Relief (in Cotton Manufacturing Districts), 1858, 1861 and 1862.*

Great Britain, Parliamentary Papers (1863, LII). *Return of Number of Paupers in Receipt of Relief, January–August 1858, 1862 and 1863.*

Great Britain, Parliamentary Papers (1864, IX). *Report from the Select Committee on Poor Relief.*

Great Britain, Parliamentary Papers (1864, XXV). *Sixteenth Annual Report of the Poor Law Board, 1863–64.*

Great Britain, Parliamentary Papers (1866, XIII). *First Report from the Select Committee on Metropolitan Local Government.*

Great Britain, Parliamentary Papers (1867, XXXIV). *Nineteenth Annual Report of the Poor Law Board, 1866–67.*

Great Britain, Parliamentary Papers (1867, LX). *Return Relating to Poor Relief, etc. (Metropolis).*

Great Britain, Parliamentary Papers (1868–69, XXXI). *Minority Report of the Royal Commission on Trades Unions.*

Great Britain, Parliamentary Papers (1870, XXXV). *Twenty-Second Annual Report of the Poor Law Board.*

Great Britain, Parliamentary Papers (1870, LVIII). *Returns Relating to Pauperism and Relief, etc. (Metropolis).*

Great Britain, Parliamentary Papers (1872, XXVIII). *First Annual Report of the Local Government Board.*

Great Britain, Parliamentary Papers (1874, XXIII). *Fourth Report of the Commissioners Appointed to Inquire into Friendly and Benefit Building Societies.*

Great Britain, Parliamentary Papers (1887, XXXVI). *Sixteenth Annual Report of the Local Government Board, 1886–87.*

Great Britain, Parliamentary Papers (1890–91, LXVIII). *Return . . . of Paupers over Sixty.*

Great Britain, Parliamentary Papers (1892, XXXVI). *Royal Commission on Labour: Rules of Associations of Employers and of Employed.*

Great Britain, Parliamentary Papers (1892, LXVIII). *Return for Each Union and Parish in England and Wales of Number in Receipt of In-Door and Out-Door Relief, January 1892.*

Great Britain, Parliamentary Papers (1892, LXVIII). *Return . . . of Paupers over Sixty-Five.*

Great Britain, Parliamentary Papers (1893–94, XXXIX, Pt. 1). *Royal Commission on Labour, Fourth Report, Minutes of Evidence.*

Great Britain, Parliamentary Papers (1893–94, LXXXII). *Agencies and Methods for Dealing with the Unemployed.*

Great Britain, Parliamentary Papers (1895, IX). *Third Report from the Select Committee on Distress from Want of Employment.*

Great Britain, Parliamentary Papers (1895, XIV). *Report of the Royal Commission on the Aged Poor.*

Great Britain, Parliamentary Papers (1895, XIV). *Royal Commission on the Aged Poor, Vol. II, Minutes of Evidence.*

Great Britain, Parliamentary Papers (1895, XV). *Royal Commission on the Aged Poor, Vol. III, Minutes of Evidence.*

Great Britain, Parliamentary Papers (1899, VIII). *Report from the Select Committee on the Aged Deserving Poor.*

Great Britain, Parliamentary Papers (1900, X). *Report of the Departmental Committee on the Aged Deserving Poor.*

Great Britain, Parliamentary Papers (1904, XXXII). *Report of the Interdepartmental Committee on Physical Deterioration.*

Great Britain, Parliamentary Papers (1905, LXXXIV). *British and Foreign Trade and Industrial Conditions.*

Great Britain, Parliamentary Papers (1908, VIII). *Report from the Select Committee on Home Work.*

Great Britain, Parliamentary Papers (1909, XXXVII). *Report of the Royal Commission on the Poor Laws and Relief of Distress.*

Great Britain, Parliamentary Papers (1909, XXXIX). *Royal Commission on the Poor Laws and Relief of Distress, Appendix Volume I. Minutes of Evidence.*

Great Britain, Parliamentary Papers (1909, XLI). *Royal Commission on the Poor Laws and Relief of Distress, Appendix Volume IV. Minutes of Evidence.*

Great Britain, Parliamentary Papers (1909, XLIV). *Royal Commission on the Poor Laws and Relief of Distress, Report . . . on the Effects of Employment or Assistance Given to the "Unemployed" since 1886 as a Means of Relieving Distress outside the Poor Law.*

Great Britain, Parliamentary Papers (1910, XLVIII). *Royal Commission on the Poor Laws and Relief of Distress, Minutes of Evidence . . . of Witnesses Relating Chiefly to the Subject of Unemployment, Appendix Volume VIII.*

Great Britain, Parliamentary Papers (1910, XLIX). *Royal Commission on the Poor Laws and Relief of Distress, Minutes of Evidence . . . of Witnesses Further Relating to the Subject of Unemployment, Appendix Volume IX.*

Great Britain, Parliamentary Papers (1910, LIII). *Royal Commission on the Poor Laws and Relief of Distress, Appendix Volume XXV, Statistics Relating to England and Wales.*

Great Britain, Parliamentary Papers (1911, LXXIII). *The Rules and Expenditure of Trade Unions in Respect of Unemployed Benefits.*

Great Britain, Parliamentary Papers (1913, LV). *Old Age Pensioners and Aged Pauperism.*

Great Britain, Parliamentary Papers (1913, LXXVIII). *1911 Census of England and Wales, Vol. X, Occupations and Industries.*

Great Britain, Parliamentary Papers (1922, XVII). Ministry of Health, *Persons in Receipt of Poor-Law Relief (England and Wales), 1922.*

Great Britain, Parliamentary Papers (1926, XI). Ministry of Health, *Seventh Annual Report of the Ministry of Health, 1925–1926.*

Great Britain, Parliamentary Papers (1926, XIV). *Report of the Royal Commission on National Health Insurance.*

Great Britain, Parliamentary Papers (1928–29, XVI). Ministry of Health, *Persons in Receipt of Poor-Law Relief (England and Wales), 1929.*

Great Britain, Parliamentary Papers (1933–34, XXI). Ministry of Health, *Persons in Receipt of Poor Relief (England and Wales), 1934.*

Great Britain, Parliamentary Papers (1934–35, XVII). Ministry of Health, *Persons in Receipt of Poor Relief (England and Wales), 1935.*

Great Britain, Parliamentary Papers (1942–43, VI). *Social Insurance and Allied Services, Appendix G: Memoranda from Organisations.*

Great Britain, Parliamentary Papers (1943–44, VIII). Ministry of Heath, *A National Health Service.*

Great Britain, Parliamentary Papers (1943–44, VIII). Ministry of Reconstruction, *Employment Policy.*

Great Britain, Parliamentary Papers (1943–44, VIII). Ministry of Reconstruction, *Social Insurance, Part I.*

Great Britain, Poor Law Board (1849–70). *Annual Reports of the Poor Law Board.* London: HMSO.

Great Britain, Poor Law Commission (1835–48). *Annual Reports of the Poor Law Commissioners.* London: HMSO.

Great Britain, Royal Commission on National Health Insurance (1925). *Minutes of Evidence Taken before the Royal Commission on National Health Insurance.* 4 vols. London: HMSO.

Great Britain, Royal Commission on Unemployment Insurance (1931). *Appendices to the Minutes of Evidence.* London: HMSO.

Great Britain, Royal Commission on Unemployment Insurance (1932). *Final Report.* London: HMSO.

Great Britain, Royal Commission to Investigate the Poor Laws (1834). *Report on the Administration and Practical Operation of the Poor Laws.* London: B. Fellows.

Newspapers, Magazines, and Archival Material

Bank of England. "A Millennium of Macroeconomic Data." Broadberry et al. estimates of nominal GDP data. www.bankofengland.co.uk/statistics/research-datasets.

Bauer, Lord Peter. House of Lords Debates June 29, 1983. Vol. 443, cc252–359.

Beveridge, William H. "Social Insurance–General Considerations." Beveridge Papers, LSE Archives (BEVERIDGE/9A/41/1)

Economist. "By-Elections." March 6, 1943, p. 293.

Economist. "The Parting of the Ways." February 20, 1943, pp. 225–26.

Economist. Various issues, 1847–48, 1861–62.

Financial Times. "From Cradle to Grave." December 2, 1942, p. 2.

Financial Times. "Premier May Seek a Confidence Vote." February 19, 1943, p. 1.

Goss, Frank. Autobiographical manuscript. Brunel University Research Archive. http://bura .brunel.ac.uk/handle/2438/10909.

Spectator. Comments by Lord Hamilton, May 28, 1910, p. 17.

Thomas, Ryland, and Samuel H. Williamson (2017). "What Was the U.K. GDP Then?" *MeasuringWorth.* www.measuringworth.com/ukgdp/.

Times. "Beveridge Plan Division." February 20, 1943, p. 2.

Times. Chamberlain's comments regarding universal pensions, May 25, 1899, p. 12.

Times. "Financing the Beveridge Proposals." February 18, 1943, p. 4.

Times. "Freedom from Want." December 2, 1942, p. 5.

Times. "The New Europe." July 1, 1940, p. 5.

Times. "Summary of Chamberlain's Speech." March 18, 1891, p. 10.

Webb Local Government Collection in the British Library of Political and Economic Science. Part 2: The Poor Law. Vol. 307.

Secondary Sources

Abbott, Edith (1918). *Democracy and Social Progress in England.* Chicago: University of Chicago Press.

Abel-Smith, Brian (1992). "The Beveridge Report: Its Origins and Outcomes." *International Social Security Review* 45: 5–16.

Abel-Smith, Brian, and Peter Townsend (1965). *The Poor and the Poorest: A New Analysis of the Ministry of Labour's Family Expenditure Surveys of 1953–54 and 1960.* London: Bell.

Acemoglu, Daron, and James A. Robinson (2006). *Economic Origins of Dictatorship and Democracy.* Cambridge: Cambridge University Press.

Addison, Paul (1975). *The Road to 1945: British Politics and the Second World War.* London: Jonathan Cape.

Adshead, Joseph (1842). *Distress in Manchester: Evidence of the State of the Labouring Classes in 1840–42.* London: Henry Hooper.

Anderson, Michael (1971). *Family Structure in Nineteenth Century Lancashire.* Cambridge: Cambridge University Press.

Anderson, Michael (1977). "The Impact on the Family Relationships of the Elderly of Changes since Victorian Times in Governmental Income-Maintenance Provision." In Ethel Shannas and Marvin Sussman, eds., *Family, Bureaucracy, and the Elderly.* Durham, N.C.: Duke University Press. Pp. 36–59.

Arnold, R. Arthur (1865). *The History of the Cotton Famine*. London: Saunders, Otley.

Ashbridge, Pauline (1997). "Paying for the Poor: A Middle Class Metropolitan Movement for Rate Equalisation 1857–1867." *London Journal* 22: 107–22.

Ashforth, David (1985). "Settlement and Removal in Urban Areas: Bradford, 1834–71." In Michael E. Rose, ed., *The Poor and the City: The English Poor Law in Its Urban Context, 1834–1914*. New York: St. Martin's. Pp. 58–91.

Ashworth, Henry (1842). "Statistics of the Present Depression of Trade at Bolton; Showing the Mode in Which It Affects the Different Classes of a Manufacturing Population." *Journal of the Statistical Society of London* 5: 74–81.

Atkinson, A. B. (1987). "On the Measurement of Poverty." *Econometrica* 55: 749–64.

Atkinson, A. B. (1999). *The Economic Consequences of Rolling Back the Welfare State*. Cambridge, Mass.: MIT Press.

Atkinson, A. B. (2014). *Public Economics in an Age of Austerity*. London: Routledge.

Atkinson, A. B. (2015). *Inequality: What Can Be Done?* Cambridge, Mass.: Harvard University Press.

Atkinson, A. B., et al. (1981). "Poverty in York: A Re-analysis of Rowntree's 1950 Survey." *Bulletin of Economic Research* 33: 59–71.

Bain, George S., and Robert Price (1980). *Profiles of Union Growth: A Comparative Statistical Portrait of Eight Countries*. Oxford: Basil Blackwell.

Baines, Dudley E. (1985). *Migration in a Mature Economy*. Cambridge: Cambridge University Press.

Bakke, E. W. (1933). *The Unemployed Man: A Social Study*. London: Nisbet.

Baldwin, Peter (1990). *The Politics of Social Solidarity: Class Bases of the European Welfare State 1875–1975*. Cambridge: Cambridge University Press.

Bane, Mary Jo, and David Ellwood (1986). "Slipping Into and Out of Poverty: The Dynamics of Spells." *Journal of Human Resources* 21: 1–23.

Barnett, Correlli (1986). *The Audit of War: The Illusion and Reality of Britain as a Great Nation*. London: Macmillan.

Barnett, Henrietta (1918). *Canon Barnett: His Life, Work, and Friends*. London: John Murray.

Barnsby, George J. (1971). "The Standard of Living in the Black Country during the Nineteenth Century." *Economic History Review* 24: 220–39.

Barr, Nicholas (2001). *The Welfare State as Piggy Bank: Information, Risk, Uncertainty, and the Role of the State*. Oxford: Oxford University Press.

Baxter, R. Dudley (1868). *National Income. The United Kingdom*. London: Macmillan.

Bean, Jessica S., and George R. Boyer (2009). "The Trade Boards Act of 1909 and the Alleviation of Household Poverty." *British Journal of Industrial Relations* 47: 240–64.

Bell, Frances, and Robert Millward (1998). "Public Health Expenditures and Mortality in England and Wales, 1870–1914." *Continuity and Change* 13: 221–49.

Bell, Lady Florence (1907). *At the Works: A Study of a Manufacturing Town*. London: Edward Arnold.

Benjamin, Daniel, and Levis Kochin (1979). "Searching for an Explanation of Unemployment in Interwar Britain." *Journal of Political Economy* 87: 441–78.

Beveridge, William H. (1909). *Unemployment: A Problem of Industry*. London: Longmans.

Beveridge, William H. (1930). *Unemployment: A Problem of Industry*. 2nd ed. London: Longmans, Green.

Beveridge, William H. (1942). *Social Insurance and Allied Services*. London: HMSO.

Beveridge, William H. (1943). *The Pillars of Security*. New York: Macmillan.

Beveridge, William H. (1944). *Full Employment in a Free Society*. London: G. Allen and Unwin.

Beveridge, William H. (1948). *Voluntary Action: A Report on Methods of Social Advance*. London: Macmillan.

Beveridge, William H. (1953). *Power and Influence*. London: Hodder and Stoughton.

Billinge, Mark (2004). "Divided by a Common Language: North and South, 1750–1830." In Alan R. H. Baker and Mark Billinge, eds., *Geographies of England: The North-South Divide, Imagined and Material*. Cambridge: Cambridge University Press. Pp. 88–111.

Blackburn, Sheila (1991). "Ideology and Social Policy: The Origins of the Trade Boards Act." *Historical Journal* 34: 43–64.

Blackburn, Sheila (1999). "A Very Moderate Socialist Indeed? R. H. Tawney and Minimum Wages." *Twentieth Century British History* 10: 107–36.

Blackburn, Sheila (2007). *A Fair Day's Wage for a Fair Day's Work? Sweated Labour and the Origins of Minimum Wage Legislation in Britain*. Aldershot: Ashgate.

Blatchford, Robert (1894). *Merrie England*. London: Clarion Office.

Blaug, Mark (1963). "The Myth of the Old Poor Law and the Making of the New." *Journal of Economic History* 23: 151–84.

Blaug, Mark (1964). "The Poor Law Report Reexamined." *Journal of Economic History* 24: 229–45.

Blunden, G. H. (1895). *Local Taxation and Finance*. London: Swan Sonnenschein.

Boot, H. M. (1984). *The Commercial Crisis of 1847*. Hull: Hull University Press.

Boot, H. M. (1990). "Unemployment and Poor Law Relief in Manchester, 1845–50." *Social History* 15: 217–28.

Booth, Alan (1987). "The War and the White Paper." In Sean Glynn and Alan Booth, eds., *The Road to Full Employment*. London: Allen & Unwin. Pp. 175–95.

Booth, Charles (1888). "Condition and Occupations of the People of East London and Hackney, 1887." *Journal of the Royal Statistical Society* 51: 276–339.

Booth, Charles (1891). "Enumeration and Classification of Paupers, and State Pensions for the Aged." *Journal of the Royal Statistical Society* 54: 600–643.

Booth, Charles (1892a). "The Inaugural Address of Charles Booth, Esq., President of the Royal Statistical Society. Session 1892–93. Delivered 15th November, 1892." *Journal of the Royal Statistical Society* 55: 521–57.

Booth, Charles (1892b). *Life and Labour of the People in London*. 2 vols. London: Macmillan.

Booth, Charles (1892c). *Pauperism, a Picture and the Endowment of Old Age, an Argument*. London: Macmillan.

Booth, Charles (1894a). *The Aged Poor in England and Wales*. London: Macmillan.

Booth, Charles (1894b). "Statistics of Pauperism in Old Age." *Journal of the Royal Statistical Society* 57: 235–53.

Booth, Charles (1899a). *Old Age Pensions and the Aged Poor*. London: Macmillan.

Booth, Charles (1899b). "Poor Law Statistics as Used in Connection with the Old Age Pension Question." *Economic Journal* 9: 212–23.

Bosanquet, Helen (1896). *Rich and Poor*. London: Macmillan.

Bosanquet, Helen (1902). *The Strength of the People: A Study in Social Economics*. London: Macmillan.

Bosanquet, Helen (1904). "Wages and Housekeeping." In C. S. Loch, ed., *Methods of Social Advance*. London: Macmillan. Pp. 131–46.

Bosanquet, Helen (1905). "The Poverty Line." In *Occasional Papers of the C.O.S.*, 3rd series. London: Charity Organisation Society. Pp. 221–35.

Bowley, A. L. (1900). *Wages in the United Kingdom in the Nineteenth Century*. Cambridge: Cambridge University Press.

Bowley, A. L. (1913). "Working-Class Households in Reading." *Journal of the Royal Statistical Society* 76: 672–701.

Bowley, A. L. (1914). "Rural Population in England and Wales." *Journal of the Royal Statistical Society* 77: 597–652.

Bowley, A. L. (1930). *Some Economic Consequences of the Great War.* London: Thornton Butterworth.

Bowley, A. L. (1932). "The House Sample Analysis." In H. L. Smith, ed., *The New Survey of London Life and Labour. Volume III. Survey of Social Conditions. (1) The Eastern Area.* London: P. S. King. Pp. 29–96.

Bowley, A. L. (1934). "The House Sample Analysis." In H. L. Smith, ed., *The New Survey of London Life and Labour. Volume VI. Survey of Social Conditions. (2) The Western Area.* London: P. S. King. Pp. 29–117.

Bowley, A. L. (1937). *Wages and Income in the United Kingdom since 1860.* Cambridge: Cambridge University Press.

Bowley, A. L., and A. R. Burnett-Hurst (1915). *Livelihood and Poverty: A Study in the Economic Conditions of Working-Class Households in Northampton, Warrington, Stanley and Reading.* London: G. Bell.

Bowley, A. L., and A. R. Burnett-Hurst (1920). *Economic Conditions of Working-Class Households in Bolton, 1914: Supplementary Chapter to "Livelihood and Poverty."* London: G. Bell.

Bowley, A. L., and M. H. Hogg (1925). *Has Poverty Diminished?* London: P. S. King.

Bowpitt, Graham (2000). "Poverty and Its Early Critics: The Search for a Value-Free Definition of the Problem." In Jonathan Bradshaw and Roy Sainsbury, eds., *Getting the Measure of Poverty: The Early Legacy of Seebohm Rowntree.* Aldershot: Ashgate. Pp. 23–38.

Boyd Orr, John (1937). *Food Health and Income: Report on a Survey of Adequacy of Diet in Relation to Income.* 2nd ed. London: Macmillan.

Boyer, George R. (1988). "What Did Unions Do in Nineteenth Century Britain?" *Journal of Economic History* 48: 319–32.

Boyer, George R. (1990). *An Economic History of the English Poor Law, 1750–1850.* Cambridge: Cambridge University Press.

Boyer, George R. (1997). "Poor Relief, Informal Assistance, and Short Time during the Lancashire Cotton Famine." *Explorations in Economic History* 34: 56–76.

Boyer, George R. (2002). "English Poor Laws." In Robert Whaples, ed., *EH.Net Encyclopedia.* http://eh.net/encyclopedia/english-poor-laws.

Boyer, George R. (2004a). "The Evolution of Unemployment Relief in Great Britain." *Journal of Interdisciplinary History* 34: 393–433.

Boyer, George R. (2004b). "Living Standards, 1860–1939." In Roderick Floud and Paul Johnson, eds., *The Cambridge Economic History of Modern Britain*, vol. 2. Cambridge: Cambridge University Press. Pp. 280–313.

Boyer, George R. (2009). "Insecurity, Safety Nets, and Self-Help in Victorian and Edwardian Britain." In David Eltis and Frank Lewis, eds., *Human Capital and Institutions: A Long Run View.* Cambridge: Cambridge University Press. Pp. 46–89.

Boyer, George R. (2016). "'Work for Their Prime, the Workhouse for Their Age': Old Age Pauperism in Victorian England." *Social Science History* 40: 3–32.

Boyer, George R., and Timothy J. Hatton (1997). "Migration and Labour Market Integration in Late Nineteenth-Century England and Wales." *Economic History Review* 50: 697–734.

Boyer, George R., and Timothy J. Hatton (2002). "New Estimates of British Unemployment, 1870–1913." *Journal of Economic History* 62: 643–75.

Boyer, George R., and Timothy Schmidle (2009). "Poverty among the Elderly in Late Victorian England." *Economic History Review* 62: 249–78.

Brabrook, E. W. (1898). *Provident Societies and Industrial Welfare.* London: Blackie and Son.

Braithwaite, William J. (1957). *Lloyd George's Ambulance Wagon*. London: Methuen.

Briggs, Asa (1961). "The Welfare State in Historical Perspective." *European Journal of Sociology* 2: 221–58.

Briggs, Asa (1987). "Samuel Smiles: The Gospel of Self-Help." *History Today* 37(5): 37–43.

Broadberry, Stephen, and Carsten Burhop (2010). "Real Wages and Labor Productivity in Britain and Germany, 1871–1938: A Unified Approach to the International Comparison of Living Standards." *Journal of Economic History* 70: 400–427.

Broadberry, Stephen, et al. (2015). *British Economic Growth, 1270–1870*. Cambridge: Cambridge University Press.

Brown, Kenneth D. (1971). *Labour and Unemployment, 1900–1914*. Newton Abbot: David & Charles.

Bruce, Maurice (1968). *The Coming of the Welfare State*. London: Batsford.

Budd, John W., and Timothy Guinnane (1991). "Intentional Age-Misreporting, Age-Heaping, and the 1908 Old Age Pensions Act in Ireland." *Population Studies* 45: 497–518.

Bulkley, M. E. (1915). *The Establishment of Legal Minimum Rates in the Boxmaking Industry under the Trade Boards Act of 1909*. London: G. Bell.

Burnett, John (1986). *A Social History of Housing 1815–1985*. 2nd ed. London: Methuen.

Burnette, Joyce (2008). *Gender, Work and Wages in Industrial Revolution Britain*. Cambridge: Cambridge University Press.

Burns, Eveline M. (1941). *British Unemployment Programs, 1920–1938*. Washington, D.C.: Social Science Research Council.

Cage, R. A. (1981). *The Scottish Poor Law 1745–1845*. Edinburgh: Scottish Academic Press.

Cage, R. A. (1987). "The Nature and Extent of Poor Relief." In R. A. Cage, ed., *The Working Class in Glasgow, 1750–1914*. London: Croom Helm. Pp. 77–97.

Cairncross, A. K. (1949). "Internal Migration in Victorian England." *Manchester School* 17: 67–87.

Cairncross, A. K. (1981). "The Postwar Years 1945–77." In Roderick Floud and D. N. McCloskey, eds., *The Economic History of Britain since 1700. Vol. 2: 1860 to the 1970s*. Cambridge: Cambridge University Press. Pp. 370–416.

Cannan, Edwin (1895). "The Stigma of Pauperism." *Economic Review* 5: 380–91.

Cannan, Edwin (1927). *An Economist's Protest*. London: P. S. King.

Cannan, Edwin (1930). "The Problem of Unemployment." *Economic Journal* 40: 45–55.

Caplan, Maurice (1978). "The New Poor Law and the Struggle for Union Chargeability." *International Review of Social History* 23: 267–300.

Carr-Saunders, A. M., and D. Caradog Jones (1937). *A Survey of the Social Structure of England and Wales: As Illustrated by Statistics*. 2nd ed. Oxford: Clarendon.

Chadwick, Edwin ([1842] 1965). *Report on the Sanitary Condition of the Labouring Population of Gt. Britain*. Edinburgh: Edinburgh University Press.

Chambers, Rosalind (1949). "The National Assistance Act, 1948." *Modern Law Review* 12: 69–72.

Chapman, Agatha L. (1953). *Wages and Salaries in the United Kingdom 1920–1938*. Cambridge: Cambridge University Press.

Charity Organisation Society (1886). *On The Best Means of Dealing with Exceptional Distress*. London: Cassell.

Charity Organisation Society (1908). *Report of the Special Committee on Unskilled Labour*. London: Charity Organisation Society.

Checkland, S. G. (1983). *British Public Policy, 1776–1939: An Economic, Social, and Political Perspective*. Cambridge: Cambridge University Press.

Churchill, Winston S. (1909). *Liberalism and the Social Problem*. London: Hodder and Stoughton.

Churchill, Winston S. (1950). *The Second World War. Volume IV. The Hinge of Fate*. London: Cassell.

Churchill, Randolph S. (1967). *Winston S. Churchill. Volume II. Young Statesman, 1901–1914*. Boston: Houghton Mifflin.

Churchill, Randolph S. (1969). *Winston S. Churchill. Companion Volume II, Parts 1 and 2.* Boston: Houghton Mifflin.

Clark, G. Kitson (1966). *The Making of Victorian England.* New York: Atheneum.

Clay, Henry (1930). *The Post-war Unemployment Problem.* London: Macmillan.

Clegg, Hugh A., Alan Fox, and A. F. Thompson (1964). *A History of British Trade Unions since 1889. Volume 1: 1889–1910.* Oxford: Oxford University Press.

Cohen, Percy (1932). *The British System of Social Insurance.* New York: Columbia University Press.

Collins, Michael (1982). "Unemployment in Interwar Britain: Still Searching for an Explanation." *Journal of Political Economy* 90: 369–79.

Crafts, N. F. R. (1987). "Long Term Unemployment in Britain in the 1930s." *Economic History Review* 40: 417–31.

Crafts, N. F. R. (1997). "The Human Development Index and Changes in Standards of Living: Some Historical Comparisons." *European Review of Economic History* 1: 299–322.

Craig, F. W. S. (1970). *British General Election Manifestos 1918–1966.* Chichester: Political Reference Publications.

Craig, F. W. S. (1989). *British Electoral Facts 1832–1987.* Aldershot: Parliamentary Research Services.

Crowther, M. A. (1981). *The Workhouse System 1834–1929: The History of an English Social Institution.* London: Batsford.

Dale, Iain (2000). *Labour Party General Election Manifestos, 1900–1997.* London: Routledge.

Davies, M. F. (1909). *Life in an English Village.* London: T. Fisher Unwin.

Deacon, Alan (1976). *In Search of the Scrounger: The Administration of Unemployment Insurance in Britain 1920–1931.* London: G. Bell.

Dearle, Norman B. (1908). *Problems of Unemployment in the London Building Trades.* London: J. M. Dent.

de Schweinitz, Karl (1943). *England's Road to Social Security: From the Statute of Laborers in 1349 to the Beveridge Report of 1942.* Philadelphia: University of Pennsylvania Press.

Dicey, A. V. (1905). *Lectures on the Relation between Law and Public Opinion in England during the Nineteenth Century.* London: Macmillan.

Dickens, Charles ([1838] 2002). *Oliver Twist.* London: Penguin.

Dickens, Charles ([1850] 2004). *David Copperfield.* London: Penguin.

Digby, Anne (1975). "The Labour Market and the Continuity of Social Policy after 1834: The Case of the Eastern Counties." *Economic History Review* 28: 69–83.

Digby, Anne (1978). *Pauper Palaces.* London: Routledge and Kegan Paul, 1978.

Digby, Anne (1994). *Making a Medical Living: Doctors and Patients in the English Market for Medicine, 1720–1911.* Cambridge: Cambridge University Press.

Digby, Anne (2000). "The Local State." In E. J. T. Collins, ed., *The Agrarian History of England and Wales, Volume VII: 1850–1914,* pt. 2. Cambridge: Cambridge University Press. Pp. 1425–64.

Drage, Geoffrey (1895). *The Problem of the Aged Poor.* London: Adam & Charles Black.

Driver, Felix (1989). "The Historical Geography of the Workhouse System, 1834–1883." *Journal of Historical Geography* 15: 269–86.

Dupree, Marguerite (1995). *Family Structure in the Staffordshire Potteries, 1840–1880.* Oxford: Clarendon.

Eastwood, David (1997). *Government and Community in the English Provinces, 1700–1870.* New York: St. Martin's.

Eden, Frederic Morton (1797). *The State of the Poor.* 3 vols. London: J. Davis.

Edsall, Nicholas C. (1971). *The Anti–Poor Law Movement, 1834–44.* Manchester: Manchester University Press.

Eichengreen, Barry (1987). "Unemployment in Interwar Britain: Dole or Doldrums?" *Oxford Economic Papers* 39: 597–623.

Emery, George, and J. C. Herbert Emery (1999). *A Young Man's Benefit: The Independent Order of Odd Fellows and Sickness Insurance in the United States and Canada, 1860–1929*. Montreal: McGill-Queen's University Press.

Emery, Herbert (2008). "Fraternal Sickness Insurance." In Robert Whaples, ed., *EH.Net Encyclopedia*. http://eh.net/encyclopedia/fraternal-sickness-insurance.

Engels, Friedrich ([1845] 1987). *The Condition of the Working Class in England*. Harmondsworth: Penguin.

Engerman, Stanley, and Claudia Goldin (1994). "Seasonality in Nineteenth-Century Labor Markets." In Thomas Weiss and Donald Schaefer, eds., *American Economic Development in Historical Perspective*. Stanford, Calif.: Stanford University Press. Pp. 99–126.

Epstein, Abraham (1933). *Insecurity: A Challenge to America*. New York: Harrison Smith and Robert Haas.

Esping-Andersen, Gøsta (1990). *The Three Worlds of Welfare Capitalism*. Princeton, N.J.: Princeton University Press.

Eveleth, Phyllis B., and J. M. Tanner (1976). *Worldwide Variation in Human Growth*. Cambridge: Cambridge University Press.

Falkingham, Jane, and John Hills (1995). "Redistribution between People or across the Life Cycle?" In Jane Falkingham and John Hills, eds., *The Dynamics of Welfare: The Welfare State and the Life Cycle*. New York: Prentice Hall. Pp. 137–49.

Farnie, D. A. (1979). *The English Cotton Industry and the World Market 1815–1896*. Oxford: Clarendon.

Feinstein, Charles H. (1972). *National Income, Expenditure and Output of the United Kingdom, 1855–1965*. Cambridge: Cambridge University Press.

Feinstein, Charles H. (1990a). "New Estimates of Average Earnings in the United Kingdom, 1880–1913." *Economic History Review* 43: 595–632.

Feinstein, Charles H. (1990b). "What Really Happened to Real Wages? Trends in Wages, Prices, and Productivity in the United Kingdom, 1880–1913." *Economic History Review* 43: 329–55.

Feinstein, Charles H. (1991). "A New Look at the Cost of Living 1870–1914." In J. Foreman-Peck, ed., *New Perspectives on the Late Victorian Economy: Essays in Quantitative Economic History, 1860–1914*. Cambridge: Cambridge University Press. Pp. 151–79.

Feinstein, Charles H. (1995). "Changes in Nominal Wages, the Cost of Living and Real Wages in the United Kingdom over Two Centuries, 1780–1990." In Peter Scholliers and Vera Zamagni, eds., *Labour's Reward: Real Wages and Economic Change in 19th- and 20th-Century Europe*. Aldershot: Edward Elgar. Pp. 3–36, 258–66.

Feinstein, Charles H. (1998). "Pessimism Perpetuated: Real Wages and the Standard of Living in Britain during and after the Industrial Revolution." *Journal of Economic History* 58: 625–58.

Feldstein, Martin S. (1976). "Seven Principles of Social Insurance." *Challenge* 19: 6–11.

Ferrera, Maurizio (1996). "The 'Southern Model' of Welfare in Social Europe." *Journal of European Social Policy* 6: 17–37.

Fishlow, Albert (1961). "The Trustee Savings Banks, 1817–1861." *Journal of Economic History* 21: 26–40.

Flinn, Michael W. (1965). "Introduction." In Edwin Chadwick, *Report on the Sanitary Condition of the Labouring Population of Gt. Britain*. Edinburgh: Edinburgh University Press. Pp. 1–73.

Flora, Peter (1973). "Historical Processes of Social Mobilization: Urbanization and Literacy, 1850–1965." In S. N. Eisenstadt and Stein Rokkan, eds., *Building States and Nations: Models and Data Resources*, vol. 1. London: Sage. Pp. 213–58.

Flora, Peter, and Jens Alber (1981). "Modernization, Democratization, and the Development of Welfare States in Western Europe." In Peter Flora and Arnold Heidenheimer, eds., *The*

Development of Welfare States in Europe and America. New Brunswick, N.J.: Transaction. Pp. 37–80.

Flora, Peter, et al. (1983). *State, Economy, and Society in Western Europe 1815–1975*. Vol. 1. Chicago: St. James Press.

Floud, Roderick (1994). "The Heights of Europeans since 1750: A New Source for European Economic History." In John Komlos, ed., *Stature, Living Standards, and Economic Development: Essays in Anthropometric History*. Chicago: University of Chicago Press. Pp. 9–24.

Floud, Roderick (1997). *The People and the British Economy 1830–1914*. Oxford: Oxford University Press.

Floud, Roderick, and Bernard Harris (1997). "Health, Height, and Welfare: Britain 1700–1980." In Richard H. Steckel and Roderick Floud, eds., *Health and Welfare during Industrialization*. Chicago: University of Chicago Press. Pp. 91–126.

Fogel, Robert W. (2000). *The Fourth Great Awakening and the Future of Egalitarianism*. Chicago: University of Chicago Press.

Ford, Percy (1934). *Work and Wealth in a Modern Port: An Economic Survey of Southampton*. London: George Allen & Unwin.

Fraser, Derek (2003). *The Evolution of the British Welfare State*. 3rd ed. Basingstoke: Palgrave Macmillan.

Freeman, Mark (2000). "Investigating Rural Poverty 1870–1914: Problems of Conceptualisation and Methodology." In Jonathan Bradshaw and Roy Sainsbury, eds., *Getting the Measure of Poverty: The Early Legacy of Seebohm Rowntree*. Aldershot: Ashgate. Pp. 255–74.

Friedman, Milton, and Rose Friedman (1980). *Free to Choose: A Personal Statement*. New York: Harcourt Brace Jovanovich.

Garland, David (2016). *The Welfare State: A Very Short Introduction*. Oxford: Oxford University Press.

Garside, W. R. (1990). *The Measurement of Unemployment: Methods and Sources in Great Britain 1850–1979*. Oxford: Basil Blackwell.

Gayer, Arthur D., W. W. Rostow, and Anna J. Schwartz (1953). *The Growth and Fluctuation of the British Economy, 1790–1850*. Vol. 1. Oxford: Clarendon.

Gazeley, Ian (2003). *Living Standards and Poverty in Britain, 1900–1960*. Basingstoke: Palgrave Macmillan.

Gazeley, Ian, and Andrew Newell (2011). "Poverty in Edwardian Britain." *Economic History Review* 64: 52–71.

George, R. F. (1937). "A New Calculation of the Poverty Line." *Journal of the Royal Statistical Society* 100: 74–95.

George, William (1958). *My Brother and I*. London: Eyre and Spottiswoode.

Gilbert, Bentley B. (1966a). *The Evolution of National Insurance in Great Britain: The Origins of the Welfare State*. London: Joseph.

Gilbert, Bentley B. (1966b). "Winston Churchill versus the Webbs: The Origins of British Unemployment Insurance." *American Historical Review* 71: 846–62.

Gilbert, Bentley B. (1970). *British Social Policy 1914–1939*. Ithaca, N.Y.: Cornell University Press.

Gilbert, Martin (1991). *Churchill: A Life*. London: Heinemann.

Gillie, Alan (2008). "Identifying the Poor in the 1870s and 1880s." *Economic History Review* 61: 302–25.

Glen, W. Cunningham (1866). *Villiers' Union Chargeability Act, 1865*. London: Shaw.

Glennerster, Howard, and Martin Evans (1994). "Beveridge and His Assumptive Worlds: The Incompatibilities of a Flawed Design." In John Hills et al., eds., *Beveridge and Social Security: An International Retrospective*. Oxford: Clarendon. Pp. 56–72.

Goose, Nigel (2005). "Poverty, Old Age and Gender in Nineteenth-Century England: The Case of Hertfordshire." *Continuity and Change* 20: 351–84.

Goose, Nigel (2014). "Accommodating the Elderly Poor: Almshouses and the Mixed Economy of Welfare in England in the Second Millennium." *Scandinavian Economic History Review* 62: 35–57.

Goose, Nigel, and Stuart Basten (2009). "Almshouse Residency in Nineteenth Century England: An Interim Report." *Family & Community History* 12: 65–76.

Gorsky, Martin (1998). "The Growth and Distribution of English Friendly Societies in the Early Nineteenth Century." *Economic History Review* 51: 489–511.

Gosden, P. H. J. H. (1961). *The Friendly Societies in England, 1815–1875*. Manchester: Manchester University Press.

Gosden, P. H. J. H. (1973). *Self-Help: Voluntary Associations in the 19th Century*. London: B. T. Batsford.

Green, David R. (1995). *From Artisans to Paupers: Economic Change and Poverty in London, 1790–1870*. Aldershot: Scolar Press.

Green, David R. (2010). *Pauper Capital: London and the Poor Law, 1790–1870*. Farnham: Ashgate.

Green, John Richard (1903). *Stray Studies*. 2nd ser. London: Macmillan.

Greif, Avner, and Murat Iyigun (2012). "Social Institutions, Violence, and Innovations: Did the Old Poor Law Matter?" Unpublished paper.

Greif, Avner, and Murat Iyigun (2013). "Social Organizations, Violence, and Modern Growth." *American Economic Review: Papers & Proceedings* 103: 534–38.

Griffiths, James (1969). *Pages from Memory*. London: Dent.

Grigg, John (1978). *Lloyd George, the People's Champion, 1902–1911*. London: Eyre Methuen.

Hacker, Jacob S. (2008). *The Great Risk Shift: The New Economic Insecurity and the Decline of the American Dream*. New York: Oxford University Press.

Hacker, Jacob S., et al. (2014). "The Economic Security Index: A New Measure for Research and Policy Analysis." *Review of Income and Wealth* 60: S5–32.

Hallsworth, Joseph (1925). *The Legal Minimum*. London: Labour Publishing.

Harris, Bernard (1988). "Unemployment, Insurance and Health in Interwar Britain." In Barry Eichengreen and T. J. Hatton, eds., *Interwar Unemployment in International Perspective*. Dordrecht: Kluwer. Pp. 149–83.

Harris, Bernard (1994). "The Height of Schoolchildren in Britain 1900–1950." In John Komlos, ed., *Stature, Living Standards and Economic Development: Essays in Anthropometric History*. Chicago: University of Chicago Press. Pp. 25–38.

Harris, Bernard (1995). *The Health of the Schoolchild: A History of the School Medical Service in England and Wales*. Buckingham: Open University Press.

Harris, Henry J. (1920). "British National Health Insurance Act of May 20, 1920." *Monthly Labor Review* 11: 1–11.

Harris, José (1972). *Unemployment and Politics 1886–1914*. Oxford: Clarendon.

Harris, José (1992). "War and Social History: Britain and the Home Front during the Second World War." *Contemporary European History* 1: 17–35.

Harris, José (1997). *William Beveridge: A Biography*. Oxford: Clarendon.

Harrison, J. F. C. (1988). *Early Victorian Britain, 1832–51*. London: Fontana.

Hatton, Timothy J. (1986). "Structural Aspects of Unemployment in Britain between the Wars." *Research in Economic History* 10: 54–92.

Hatton, Timothy J. (1997). "Trade Boards and Minimum Wages, 1909–39." *Economic Affairs* 17: 22–28.

Hatton, Timothy J. (2004). "Unemployment and the Labour Market, 1870–1939." In Roderick Floud and Paul Johnson, eds., *The Cambridge Economic History of Modern Britain*, vol. 2. Cambridge: Cambridge University Press. Pp. 344–73.

Hatton, Timothy J. (2014). "How Have Europeans Grown So Tall?" *Oxford Economic Papers* 66: 349–72.

Hatton, Timothy J., and Roy E. Bailey (1998). "Poverty and the Welfare State in Interwar London." *Oxford Economic Papers* 50: 574–606.

Hatton, Timothy J., and Roy E. Bailey (2000). "Seebohm Rowntree and the Postwar Poverty Puzzle." *Economic History Review* 53: 517–43.

Hatton, Timothy J., and Roy E. Bailey (2002). "Unemployment Incidence in Interwar London." *Economica* 69: 631–54.

Hatton, Timothy J., and George R. Boyer (2005). "Unemployment and the UK Labour Market Before, During and After the Golden Age." *European Review of Economic History* 9: 35–60.

Hatton, Timothy J., and Bernice E. Bray (2010). "Long Run Trends in the Heights of European Men, 19th–20th Centuries." *Economics and Human Biology* 8: 405–13.

Hatton, Timothy J., and Richard M. Martin (2010a). "The Effects on Stature of Poverty, Family Size, and Birth Order: British Children in the 1930s." *Oxford Economic Papers* 62: 157–84.

Hatton, Timothy J., and Richard M. Martin (2010b). "Fertility Decline and the Heights of Children in Britain, 1886–1938." *Explorations in Economic History* 47: 505–19.

Haveman, Robert (1985). "Does the Welfare State Increase Welfare? Reflections on Hidden Negatives and Observed Positives." *De Economist* 133: 445–66.

Hawksley, Thomas (1869). *The Charities of London, and Some Errors of Their Administration.* London: John Churchill.

Hay, J. R. (1978). *The Development of the British Welfare State, 1880–1975.* London: Edward Arnold.

Hayek, Friedrich A. (1976). *Law, Legislation and Liberty. Volume 2. The Miracle of Social Justice.* Chicago: University of Chicago Press.

Heggeness, Misty L., and Charles Hokayem (2013). "Life on the Edge: Living Near Poverty in the United States, 1966–2011." U.S. Census Bureau, SEHSD Working Paper 2013-02.

Henderson, William O. (1934). *The Lancashire Cotton Famine 1861–1865.* Manchester: Manchester University Press.

Hennessy, Peter (1992). *Never Again: Britain 1945–51.* London: Jonathan Cape.

Hennock, E. P. (1973). *Fit and Proper Persons: Ideal and Reality in Nineteenth-Century Urban Government.* London: Edward Arnold.

Hennock, E. P. (1987). *British Social Reform and German Precedents: The Case of Social Insurance, 1880–1914.* Oxford: Clarendon.

Hennock, E. P. (2007). *The Origin of the Welfare State in England and Germany, 1850–1914: Social Policies Compared.* Cambridge: Cambridge University Press.

Hills, John (2004). *Inequality and the State.* Oxford: Oxford University Press.

Hills, John (2017). *Good Times, Bad Times: The Welfare Myth of Them and Us.* Rev. ed. Bristol: Policy Press.

Hilton, John (1923). "Statistics of Unemployment Derived from the Working of the Unemployment Insurance Acts." *Journal of the Royal Statistical Society* 86: 154–93.

Himmelfarb, Gertrude (1991). *Poverty and Compassion: The Moral Imagination of the Late Victorians.* New York: Vintage.

Himmelfarb, Gertrude (1995a). *The De-moralization of Society.* New York: Knopf.

Himmelfarb, Gertrude (1995b). "From Victorian Virtues to Modern Values." Bradley lecture, American Enterprise Institute, February 13.

Hohman, Helen Fisher (1933). *The Development of Social Insurance and Minimum Wage Legislation in Great Britain.* Boston: Houghton Mifflin.

Hollingshead, John (1861). *Ragged London in 1861.* London: Smith, Elder.

Hopkins, Eric (1995). *Working-Class Self-Help in Nineteenth Century England: Responses to Industrialization.* New York: St. Martin's.

Hopkinson, Tom, ed. (1970). *"Picture Post," 1938–50.* London: Allen Lane.

Hoppen, K. Theodore (1998). *The Mid-Victorian Generation 1846–1886*. Oxford: Clarendon.

Howarth, E. G., and M. Wilson (1907). *West Ham: A Study in Social and Industrial Problems*. London: J. M. Dent.

Huberman, Michael (1996). *Escape from the Market: Negotiating Work in Lancashire*. Cambridge: Cambridge University Press.

Huberman, Michael (2012). *Odd Couple: International Trade and Labor Standards in History*. New Haven, Conn.: Yale University Press.

Huberman, Michael, and Wayne Lewchuk (2003). "European Economic Integration and the Labour Compact, 1850–1913." *European Review of Economic History* 7: 3–41.

Hughes, J. R. T. (1969). "Henry Mayhew's London." *Journal of Economic History* 29: 526–36.

Humphreys, Robert (1995). *Sin, Organized Charity and the Poor Law in Victorian England*. New York: St. Martin's.

Humphreys, Robert (2001). *Poor Relief and Charity, 1869–1945: The London Charity Organization Society*. Basingstoke: Palgrave.

Hunt, E. H. (1973). *Regional Wage Variations in Britain, 1850–1914*. Oxford: Clarendon.

Hunt, E. H. (1981). *British Labour History, 1815–1914*. London: Weidenfeld and Nicolson.

Hunt, E. H. (1989). "Paupers and Pensioners, Past and Present." *Ageing and Society* 9: 408–22.

Hurren, Elizabeth T. (2007). *Protesting about Pauperism: Poverty, Politics and Poor Relief in Late-Victorian England, 1870–1900*. London: Royal Historical Society.

Hutt, Allen (1933). *The Condition of the Working Class in Britain*. London: Martin Lawrence.

Jackson, Cyril (1910). *Unemployment and Trade Unions*. London: Longmans, Green.

James, Robert R., ed. (1974). *Winston S. Churchill: His Complete Speeches, 1897–1963. Volume VII, 1943–1949*. New York: Chelsea House Publishers.

Johnson, Lyndon B. (1965). *Public Papers of the Presidents of the United States. Lyndon B. Johnson, 1963–64*. Vol. 1. Washington, D.C.: Government Printing Office.

Johnson, Paul (1985). *Saving and Spending: The Working-Class Economy in Britain 1870–1939*. Oxford: Clarendon.

Johnson, Paul (1993). "Small Debts and Economic Distress in England and Wales, 1857–1913." *Economic History Review* 46: 65–87.

Johnson, Paul (1994). "The Employment and Retirement of Older Men in England and Wales, 1881–1981." *Economic History Review* 47: 106–28.

Jones, D. Caradog (1927). "Pre-war and Post-war Taxation." *Journal of the Royal Statistical Society* 90: 685–728.

Jones, D. Caradog (1931). "The Social Survey of Merseyside: An Analysis of Material Relating to Poverty, Overcrowding, and the Social Services." *Journal of the Royal Statistical Society* 94: 218–66.

Jones, D. Caradog, ed. (1934). *The Social Survey of Merseyside*. Vol. 1. London: Hodder and Stoughton.

Jones, Gareth Stedman (1971). *Outcast London: A Study in the Relationship between Classes in Victorian Society*. Oxford: Clarendon.

Journal of the Statistical Society of London (1864). "The Cost of the Cotton Famine in Relief of the Poor." 27: 596–602.

Kato, Junko (2003). *Regressive Taxation and the Welfare State: Path Dependence and Policy Diffusion*. Cambridge: Cambridge University Press.

Keith-Lucas, Bryan (1952). *The English Local Government Franchise: A Short History*. Oxford: Blackwell.

Kelly, Morgan, and Cormac Ó Gráda (2011). "The Poor Law of Old England: Institutional Innovation and Demographic Regimes." *Journal of Interdisciplinary History* 41: 339–66.

Keynes, John Maynard (1926). *The End of Laissez-Faire*. London: Hogarth Press.

Keynes, John Maynard (1971). *The Collected Writings of John Maynard Keynes. Volume 27. Activities 1940–1946. Shaping the Post-war World: Employment and Commodities.* London: Macmillan.

Kidd, Alan (1984). "Charity Organization and the Unemployed in Manchester c. 1870–1914." *Social History* 9: 45–66.

Kiesling, L. Lynne (1996). "Institutional Choice Matters: The Poor Law and Implicit Labor Contracts in Victorian Lancashire." *Explorations in Economic History* 33: 65–85.

Kiesling, L. Lynne (1997). "The Long Road to Recovery: Post-crisis Coordination of Private Charity and Public Relief in Victorian Lancashire." *Social Science History* 21: 219–44.

King, Steven (2000). *Poverty and Welfare in England, 1700–1850: A Regional Perspective.* Manchester: Manchester University Press.

King, Steven, and Alannah Tomkins (2003). "Conclusion." In Steven King and Alannah Tomkins, eds., *The Poor in England, 1700–1850: An Economy of Makeshifts.* Manchester: Manchester University Press. Pp. 258–79.

Kiniria, Maxwell (2016). "Hardly Worth Chaining Up? The Effect and Cost-Effectiveness of 'Welfare Reform' in Victorian Britain, 1857–1885." Unpublished paper, Cornell University.

Knott, John (1986). *Popular Opposition to the 1834 Poor Law.* New York: St. Martin's.

Knowles, K. G. J. C., and D. J. Robertson (1951). "Differences between the Wages of Skilled and Unskilled Workers, 1880–1950." *Oxford Bulletin of Economics and Statistics* 13: 109–27.

Kuznets, Simon (1952). "Long-Term Changes in the National Income of the United States of America since 1870." In Simon Kuznets, ed., *Income and Wealth of the United States: Trends and Structure.* Cambridge: Bowes and Bowes. Pp. 29–241.

Kynaston, David (2009). *Family Britain, 1951–57.* London: Bloomsbury.

Leaper, Robert (1992). "The Beveridge Report in Its Contemporary Setting." *International Social Security Review* 45: 17–37.

Lee, C. H. (1979). *British Regional Employment Statistics, 1841–1971.* Cambridge: Cambridge University Press.

Lees, Lynn Hollen (1998). *The Solidarities of Strangers: The English Poor Laws and the People, 1700–1948.* Cambridge: Cambridge University Press.

Leighton, Sir Baldwyn (1872). *Letters and Other Writings of the Late Edward Denison.* London: Richard Bentley.

Leivers, Clive (2009). "Housing the Elderly in Nineteenth-Century Derbyshire: A Comparison of Almshouse and Workhouse Provision." *Local Population Studies* 83: 56–65.

Levi, Leone (1867). *Wages and Earnings of the Working Classes.* London: John Murray.

Lindert, Peter H. (1994). "The Rise of Social Spending, 1880–1930." *Explorations in Economic History* 31: 1–37.

Lindert, Peter H. (1998). "Poor Relief before the Welfare State: Britain versus the Continent, 1780–1880." *European Review of Economic History* 2: 101–40.

Lindert, Peter H. (2003). "Voice and Growth: Was Churchill Right?" *Journal of Economic History* 63: 315–60.

Lindert, Peter H. (2004). *Growing Public: Social Spending and Economic Growth since the Eighteenth Century. Volume 1: The Story.* Cambridge: Cambridge University Press.

Lindert, Peter H. (2017). "The Rise and Future of Progressive Redistribution." CEQ Working Paper 73, CEQ Institute, Tulane University.

Lindert, Peter H., and Jeffrey G. Williamson (1982). "Revising England's Social Tables 1688–1812." *Explorations in Economic History* 19: 385–408.

Lindert, Peter H., and Jeffrey G. Williamson (1983a). "English Workers' Living Standards during the Industrial Revolution: A New Look." *Economic History Review* 36: 1–25.

Lindert, Peter H., and Jeffrey G. Williamson (1983b). "Reinterpreting Britain's Social Tables, 1688–1913." *Explorations in Economic History* 20: 94–109.

Lindert, Peter H., and Jeffrey G. Williamson (2016). *Unequal Gains: American Growth and Inequality since 1700*. Princeton, N.J.: Princeton University Press.

Linsley, Colin A., and Christine L. Linsley (1993). "Booth, Rowntree, and Llewellyn Smith: A Reassessment of Interwar Poverty." *Economic History Review* 46: 88–104.

Lloyd George, David (1910). *Better Times: Speeches by the Right Hon. D. Lloyd George*. London: Hodder and Stoughton.

Loch, C. S. (1894). "Mr. Charles Booth on the Aged Poor." *Economic Journal* 4: 468–87.

Loch, C. S. (1902). "Relief and Distress" (Letter to the Editor). *Times* (London), December 22, p. 8.

Loch, C. S. (1910). *Charity and Social Life: A Short Study of Religious and Social Thought in Relation to Charitable Methods and Institutions*. London: Macmillan.

Lowe, Rodney (1990). "The Second World War, Consensus, and the Foundation of the Welfare State." *Twentieth Century British History* 1: 152–82.

Lowe, Rodney (1994). "A Prophet Dishonoured in His Own Country? The Rejection of Beveridge in Britain, 1945-1970." In John Hills et al., eds., *Beveridge and Social Security: An International Retrospective*. Oxford: Clarendon. Pp. 118–33.

Lucas, Robert (2004). "The Industrial Revolution: Past and Future." *Economic Education Bulletin* 44: 1–8.

MacKay, Thomas (1899). *A History of the English Poor Law*. Vol. 3. London: P. S. King.

MacKinnon, Mary E. (1984). "Poverty and Policy: The English Poor Law 1860-1910." D.Phil. thesis, Nuffield College, Oxford University.

MacKinnon, Mary (1986). "Poor Law Policy, Unemployment, and Pauperism." *Explorations in Economic History* 23: 299–336.

MacKinnon, Mary (1987). "English Poor Law Policy and the Crusade Against Outrelief." *Journal of Economic History* 47: 603–25.

MacKinnon, Mary (1988). "The Use and Misuse of Poor Law Statistics, 1857 to 1912." *Historical Methods* 21: 5–19.

Macnicol, John (1980). *The Movement for Family Allowances, 1918–45: A Study in Social Policy Development*. London: Heinemann.

Macnicol, John (1998). *The Politics of Retirement in Britain, 1878–1948*. Cambridge: Cambridge University Press.

Maddison, Angus (2003). *The World Economy: Historical Statistics*. Paris: OECD.

Malthus, Thomas Robert ([1798] 2008). *An Essay on the Principle of Population*. Oxford: Oxford University Press.

Mann, P. H. (1904). "Life in an Agricultural Village in England." *Sociological Papers* 1: 163–93.

Manufacturers Relief Committee (1844). *Report of the Committee . . . for the Relief of the Distressed Manufacturers*. London: R. Clay.

Marshall, T. H. (1950). *Citizenship and Social Class and Other Essays*. Cambridge: Cambridge University Press.

Marx, Ive, Brian Nolan, and Javier Olivera (2015). "The Welfare State and Antipoverty Policy in Rich Countries." In Anthony B. Atkinson and Francois Bourguignon, eds., *Handbook of Income Distribution*, vol. 2b. Amsterdam: Elsevier. Pp. 2063–2139.

Marx, Karl, and Frederick Engels (1953). *On Britain*. Moscow: Foreign Languages Publishing House.

Masterman, C. F. G. (1901). "Realities at Home." In Charles Masterman, ed., *The Heart of the Empire: Discussions of Problems of Modern City Life in England*. London: T. Fisher Unwin. Pp. 1–52.

Masterman, C. F. G. (1902). "The Social Abyss." *Contemporary Review* 81: 23–35.

Masterman, C. F. G. (1909). *The Condition of England*. London: Methuen.

Matthews, R. C. O. (1954). *A Study in Trade-Cycle History: Economic Fluctuations in Great Britain, 1833–1842*. Cambridge: Cambridge University Press.

Matthews, R. C. O. (1968). "Why Has Britain Had Full Employment since the War?" *Economic Journal* 78: 555–69.

Matthews, R. C. O., C. H. Feinstein, and J. C. Odling-Smee (1982). *British Economic Growth, 1856–1973*. Stanford, Calif.: Stanford University Press.

Mayhew, Henry (1861). *London Labour and the London Poor*. 4 vols. London: Griffin, Bohn.

McBriar, A. M. (1987). *An Edwardian Mixed Doubles: The Bosanquets versus the Webbs*. Oxford: Clarendon.

McCord, Norman (1976). "The Poor Law and Philanthropy." In Derek Fraser, ed., *The New Poor Law in the Nineteenth Century*. London: Macmillan. Pp. 87–110.

McKibbin, Ross (1974). *The Evolution of the Labour Party 1910–1924*. Oxford: Oxford University Press.

McKibbin, Ross (1990). *The Ideologies of Class: Social Relations in Britain, 1880–1950*. Oxford: Clarendon.

Meyer, Bruce D., and James X. Sullivan (2012). "Winning the War: Poverty from the Great Society to the Great Recession." *Brookings Papers on Economic Activity* 45: 133–200.

Mill, John Stuart ([1848] 1909). *Principles of Political Economy*. London: Longmans.

Mitchell, Brian R. (1988). *British Historical Statistics*. Cambridge: Cambridge University Press.

Mokyr, Joel (2009). *The Enlightened Economy: An Economic History of Britain 1700–1850*. New Haven, Conn.: Yale University Press.

Money, L. G. Chiozza (1912). *Insurance versus Poverty*. London: Methuen.

Monypenny, William F. (1910). *The Life of Benjamin Disraeli, Earl of Beaconsfield*. New York: Macmillan.

Morgan, Kenneth O. (1984). *Labour in Power: 1945–1951*. Oxford: Clarendon.

Morris, Jenny (1986). *Women Workers and the Sweated Trades: The Origins of Minimum Wage Legislation*. Aldershot: Gower.

Morris, R. J. (1990). *Class, Sect, and Party: The Making of the British Middle Class, Leeds 1820–1850*. Manchester: Manchester University Press.

Mowat, Charles L. (1961). *The Charity Organisation Society, 1869–1913: Its Ideas and Work*. London: Methuen.

Murray, Charles (2006a). *In Our Hands: A Plan to Replace the Welfare State*. Washington, D.C.: AEI Press.

Murray, Charles (2006b). "A Plan to Replace the Welfare State." *Focus* 24: 1–3.

Murray, Charles (2009). *The Happiness of the People*. Washington, D.C.: AEI Press.

Neave, David (1996). "Friendly Societies in Great Britain." In Marcel van der Linden, ed., *Social Security Mutualism: The Comparative History of Mutual Benefit Societies*. Bern: Peter Lang. Pp. 41–64.

Neison, Francis G. P. (1877). "Some Statistics of the Affiliated Orders of Friendly Societies (Odd Fellows and Foresters)." *Journal of the Statistical Society of London* 40: 42–89.

Nordhaus, William D., and James Tobin (1973). "Is Growth Obsolete?" In M. Moss, ed., *The Measurement of Economic and Social Performance*. New York: NBER. Pp. 509–32.

Oddy, Derek J. (1982). "The Health of the People." In T. Barker and M. Drake, eds., *Population and Society in Britain 1850–1980*. New York: New York University Press. Pp. 121–41.

Ormerod, P. A., and G. D. N. Worswick (1982). "Unemployment in Interwar Britain." *Journal of Political Economy* 90: 400–409.

O'Rourke, Kevin H., and Jeffrey G. Williamson (1997). "Around the European Periphery 1870–1913: Globalization, Schooling and Growth." *European Review of Economic History* 1: 153–90.

Osberg, Lars, and Andrew Sharpe (2002). "An Index of Economic Well-Being for Selected OECD Countries." *Review of Income and Wealth* 48: 291–316.

Osberg, Lars, and Andrew Sharpe (2005). "How Should We Measure the 'Economic' Aspects of Well-Being?" *Review of Income and Wealth* 51: 311–36.

Osberg, Lars, and Andrew Sharpe (2014). "Measuring Economic Insecurity in Rich and Poor Nations." *Review of Income and Wealth* 60: S53–76.

Owen, A. D. K. (1933). *A Survey of the Standard of Living in Sheffield*. Sheffield: Sheffield Social Survey Committee.

Owen, David (1964). *English Philanthropy, 1660–1960*. Cambridge, Mass.: Harvard University Press.

Patterson, James T. (1998). "'Reforming' Relief and Welfare: Thoughts on 1834 and 1996." In D. T. Critchlow and C. H. Parker, eds., *With Us Always: A History of Private Charity and Public Welfare*. London: Rowman & Littlefield. Pp. 241–59.

Paul, Ellen Frankel (1980). "Laissez Faire in Nineteenth-Century Britain: Fact or Myth?" *Literature of Liberty* 3: 5–38.

Peacock, Alan T., and Jack Wiseman (1967). *The Growth of Public Expenditure in the United Kingdom*. New ed. London: George Allen & Unwin.

Peden, G. C. (1983). "Sir Richard Hopkins and the 'Keynesian Revolution' in Employment Policy, 1929–1945." *Economic History Review* 36: 281–96.

Peden, G. C. (1985). *British Economic and Social Policy: Lloyd George to Margaret Thatcher*. Deddington: Philip Allan.

Peden, G. C. (1988). *Keynes, the Treasury, and British Economic Policy*. Basingstoke: Macmillan.

Pember Reeves, Maud (1912). "Family Life on a Pound a Week." Fabian Tract No. 162. London: Fabian Society.

Pember Reeves, Maud (1913). *Round about a Pound a Week*. London: G. Bell.

Perkin, Harold (1969). *The Origins of Modern English Society, 1780–1880*. London: Routledge & Kegan Paul.

Pilgrim Trust (1938). *Men without Work*. Cambridge: Cambridge University Press.

Pipkin, Charles W. (1931). *Social Politics and Modern Democracies*. Vol. 1. New York: Macmillan.

Political and Economic Planning (1937). *Report on the British Social Services*. London: PEP.

Pollard, Sidney (1965). "Trade Unions and the Labour Market, 1876–1914." *Yorkshire Bulletin of Economic and Social Research* 17: 98–112.

Pollitt, Harry (1933). "Introduction." In Allen Hutt, *The Condition of the Working Class in Britain*. London: Martin Lawrence. Pp. ix–xvii.

Popplewell, Frank (1912). "The Gas Industry." In Sidney Webb and Arnold Freeman, eds., *Seasonal Trades*. London: Constable. Pp. 148–209.

Porter, J. H. (1970). "Wage Bargaining under Conciliation Agreements, 1860–1914." *Economic History Review* 23: 466–75.

Poynter, J. R. (1969). *Society and Pauperism: English Ideas on Poor Relief, 1795–1834*. London: Routledge and Kegan Paul.

Poyntz, Juliet Stuart (1912). "Introduction: Seasonal Trades." In Sidney Webb and Arnold Freeman, eds., *Seasonal Trades*. London: Constable. Pp. 1–69.

Preston, Samuel H., et al. (1972). *Life Tables for National Populations*. New York: Academic Press.

Priestly, J. B. (1967). *All England Listened: The Wartime Broadcasts of J. B. Priestly*. New York: Chilmark Press.

Purdy, Frederick (1862). "Extent of Pauperism in the Distressed Unions in Lancashire . . . , 1861–62." *Journal of the Statistical Society of London* 25: 377–83.

Rank, Mark R., et al. (2014). *Chasing the American Dream: Understanding What Shapes Our Fortunes*. Oxford: Oxford University Press.

Ransom, Roger L., and Richard Sutch (1986). "The Labor of Older Americans: Retirement of Men On and Off the Job, 1870–1937." *Journal of Economic History* 46: 1–30.

Read, Donald (1959). "Chartism in Manchester." In Asa Briggs, ed., *Chartist Studies*. London: Macmillan. Pp. 29–64.

Read, Donald (1972). *Edwardian Society 1901–15: Society and Politics*. London: Harrap.

Riley, James C. (1994). "Heights, Survival, and Material Comfort: A Comparison of Results." Indiana University Population Institute for Research and Training, Working Paper No. 95-4.

Riley, James C. (1997). *Sick, Not Dead: The Health of British Workingmen during the Mortality Decline*. Baltimore: Johns Hopkins University Press.

Roberts, Robert (1990). *The Classic Slum: Salford Life in the First Quarter of the Century*. London: Penguin.

Robson, William A. (1934). "Unemployment Insurance and Poor Relief: Further Testimony before the Royal Commission on Unemployment Insurance." *Social Service Review* 8: 109–30.

Rodgers, Daniel T. (1998). *Atlantic Crossings: Social Politics in a Progressive Age*. Cambridge, Mass.: Belknap.

Roosevelt, Franklin D. (1950). *The Public Papers and Addresses of Franklin D. Roosevelt. 1944–45 Volume. Victory and the Threshold of Peace*. New York: Harper & Brothers.

Rose, Michael E. (1965). "The Administration of Poor Relief in the West Riding of Yorkshire c. 1820–1855." D.Phil. thesis, Oxford University.

Rose, Michael E. (1966). "The Allowance System under the New Poor Law." *Economic History Review* 19: 607–20.

Rose, Michael E. (1970). "The New Poor Law in an Industrial Area." In R. M. Hartwell, ed., *The Industrial Revolution*. Oxford: Oxford University Press. Pp. 121–43.

Rose, Michael E. (1971). *The English Poor Law 1780–1930*. Newton Abbot: David & Charles.

Rose, Michael E. (1976). "Settlement, Removal and the New Poor Law." In Derek Fraser, ed., *The New Poor Law in the Nineteenth Century*. London: Methuen. Pp. 25–44.

Rose, Michael E. (1977). "Rochdale Man and the Stalybridge Riot: The Relief and Control of the Unemployed during the Lancashire Cotton Famine." In A. P. Donajgrodzki, ed., *Social Control in Nineteenth Century Britain*. London: Croom Helm. Pp. 185–206.

Rose, Michael E. (1981). "The Crisis of Poor Relief in England, 1860–1890." In W. J. Mommsen, ed., *The Emergence of the Welfare State in Britain and Germany, 1850–1950*. London: Croom Helm. Pp. 50–70.

Routh, Guy (1965). *Occupation and Pay in Great Britain, 1906–60*. Cambridge: Cambridge University Press.

Routh, Guy (1980). *Occupation and Pay in Great Britain, 1906–79*. London: Macmillan.

Rowntree, B. S. (1901). *Poverty: A Study of Town Life*. London: Macmillan.

Rowntree, B. S. (1918). *The Human Needs of Labour*. London: T. Nelson.

Rowntree, B. S. (1937). *The Human Needs of Labour*. New ed. London: Longmans, Green.

Rowntree, B. S. (1941). *Poverty and Progress: A Second Social Survey of York*. London: Longmans, Green.

Rowntree, B. S., and Bruno Lasker (1911). *Unemployment: A Social Study*. London: Macmillan.

Rowntree, B. S., and G. R. Lavers (1951). *Poverty and the Welfare State: A Third Social Survey of York Dealing Only with Economic Questions*. London: Longmans, Green.

Ryan, Pat (1985). "Politics and Relief: East London Unions in the Late Nineteenth and Early Twentieth Centuries." In Michael E. Rose, ed., *The Poor and the City: The English Poor Law in Its Urban Context, 1834–1914*. New York: St. Martin's. Pp. 134–72.

Sandberg, Lars G., and Richard H. Steckel (1997). "Was Industrialization Hazardous to Your Health? Not in Sweden!" In Richard H. Steckel and Roderick Floud, eds., *Health and Welfare during Industrialization*. Chicago: University of Chicago Press. Pp. 127–59.

Schmiechen, James A. (1984). *Sweated Industries and Sweated Labor: The London Clothing Trades, 1860–1914.* Urbana: University of Illinois Press.

Searle, G. R. (1992). *The Liberal Party: Triumph and Disintegration, 1886–1929.* New York: St. Martin's.

Searle, G. R. (2004). *A New England?: Peace and War 1886–1918.* Oxford: Clarendon.

Sells, Dorothy M. (1923). *The British Trade Boards System.* London: P. S. King.

Sells, Dorothy M. (1939). *British Wage Boards: A Study in Industrial Democracy.* Washington, D.C.: Brookings Institution.

Sen, Amartya (1979). "Issues in the Measurement of Poverty." *Scandinavian Journal of Economics* 81: 285–307.

Sen, Amartya (1981). *Poverty and Famines: An Essay on Entitlement and Deprivation.* Oxford: Oxford University Press.

Sen, Amartya (1987). *The Standard of Living.* Cambridge: Cambridge University Press.

Sen, Amartya (1997). *On Economic Inequality.* Expanded ed. Oxford: Clarendon.

Sen, Amartya (1999). *Development as Freedom.* New York: Knopf.

Shapely, Peter (2000). *Charity and Power in Victorian Manchester.* Manchester: Chetham Society.

Smiles, Samuel ([1866] 2002). *Self-Help: With Illustrations of Character, Conduct, and Perseverance.* Oxford: Oxford University Press.

Smiles, Samuel (1876). *Thrift.* New York: Harper & Brothers.

Smith, David C. (1986). *H. G. Wells: Desperately Mortal.* New Haven, Conn.: Yale University Press.

Smith, H. Llewellyn (1910). "Economic Security and Unemployment Insurance." *Economic Journal* 20: 513–29.

Smith, H. Llewellyn (1932). "Old Age and Poverty." In H. L. Smith, ed., *The New Survey of London Life and Labour. Volume III. Survey of Social Conditions. (1) The Eastern Area.* London: P. S. King. Pp. 188–215.

Smith, Richard M. (1998). "Ageing and Well-Being in Early Modern England: Pension Trends and Gender Preferences under the English Old Poor Law c. 1650–1800." In Paul Johnson and Pat Thane, eds., *Old Age from Antiquity to Post-modernity.* London: Routledge. Pp. 64–95.

Smout, T. C. (1979). "The Strange Intervention of Edward Twistleton: Paisley in Depression, 1841–3." In T. C. Smout, ed., *The Search for Wealth and Stability.* London: Macmillan. Pp. 218–42.

Solar, Peter (1995). "Poor Relief and English Economic Development before the Industrial Revolution." *Economic History Review* 48: 1–22.

Solow, Robert M. (1998). *Work and Welfare.* Princeton, N.J.: Princeton University Press.

Southall, Humphrey R. (1998). "The Economics of Mutuality: An Analysis of Trade Union Welfare Systems in 19th Century Britain." Unpublished manuscript.

Spender, Harold (1909). "Unemployment Insurance." *Contemporary Review* 95: 24–36.

Spender, J. A. (1892). *The State and Pensions in Old Age.* London: Swan Sonnenschein.

Stead, Francis H. (1909). *How Old Age Pensions Began to Be.* London: Methuen.

Steckel, Richard H., and Roderick Floud (1997). "Conclusions." In Richard H. Steckel and Roderick Floud, eds., *Health and Welfare during Industrialization.* Chicago: University of Chicago Press. Pp. 423–49.

Supple, Barry (1974). "Legislation and Virtue: An Essay on Working Class Self-Help and the State in the Early Nineteenth Century." In Neil McKendrick, ed., *Historical Perspectives: Studies in English Thought and Society.* London: Europa. Pp. 211–54.

Szreter, Simon (1988). "The Importance of Social Intervention in Britain's Mortality Decline c. 1850–1914: A Re-interpretation of the Role of Public Health." *Social History of Medicine* 1: 1–37.

Szreter, Simon (1997). "Economic Growth, Disruption, Deprivation, Disease, and Death: On the Importance of the Politics of Public Health for Development." *Population and Development Review* 23: 693–728.

Tawney, R. H. (1915). *The Establishment of Minimum Rates in the Tailoring Industry under the Trade Boards Act of 1909*. London: G. Bell.

Tawney, R. H. (1920). *The Acquisitive Society*. New York: Harcourt, Brace and Howe.

Tawney, R. H. (1927). "The Trade Boards Systems: The Historical Aspects of the Subject." In League of Nations Union, *Towards Industrial Peace*. London: P. S. King. Pp. 18–29.

Tawney, R. H. (1931). *Equality*. New York: Harcourt, Brace.

Tawney, R. H. (1941). *Why Britain Fights*. London: Macmillan.

Tawney, R. H. (1972). *R. H. Tawney's Commonplace Book*. Cambridge: Cambridge University Press.

Taylor-Gooby, Peter (2013). *The Double Crisis of the Welfare State and What We Can Do about It*. Basingstoke: Palgrave Macmillan.

Thane, Pat (1978). "Non-contributory Versus Insurance Pensions 1878–1908." In Pat Thane, ed., *The Origins of British Social Policy*. London: Croom Helm. Pp. 84–106.

Thane, Pat (1983). "The History of Provisions for the Elderly to 1929." In Dorothy Jerome, ed., *Ageing in Modern Society*. London: Croom Helm. Pp. 191–99.

Thane, Pat (1984). "The Working Class and State 'Welfare' in Britain, 1880–1914." *Historical Journal* 27: 877–900.

Thane, Pat (1996). *Foundations of the Welfare State*. 2nd ed. London: Longman.

Thane, Pat (2000). *Old Age in English History: Past Experiences, Present Issues*. Oxford: Oxford University Press.

Thomas, Mark (1988). "Labour Market Structure and the Nature of Unemployment in Interwar Britain." In Barry Eichengreen and T. J. Hatton, eds., *Interwar Unemployment in International Perspective*. Dordrecht: Kluwer. Pp. 97–148.

Thomas, Mark (1990). "Unemployment in Edwardian Britain: A New Perspective." In Erik Aerts and Barry Eichengreen, eds., *Unemployment and Underemployment in Historical Perspective*. Leuven: Leuven University Press. Pp. 36–50.

Thompson, E. P. (1967). "The Political Education of Henry Mayhew." *Victorian Studies* 11: 41–62.

Thompson, Flora ([1945] 2011). *Lark Rise to Candleford*. Oxford: Oxford University Press.

Thompson, F. M. L. (1988). *The Rise of Respectable Society: A Social History of Victorian Britain, 1830–1900*. Cambridge, Mass.: Harvard University Press.

Thompson, Governor Tommy, and William J. Bennett (1997). "The Good News about Welfare Reform: Wisconsin's Success Story." The Heritage Lectures, no. 593. Washington, D.C.: Heritage Foundation.

Thomson, David (1986). "Welfare and the Historians." In Lloyd Bonfield et al., eds., *The World We Have Gained: Histories of Population and Social Structure*. Oxford: Basil Blackwell. Pp. 355–78.

Timmins, Nicholas (1995). *The Five Giants: A Biography of the Welfare State*. London: Harper-Collins.

Titmuss, Richard M. (1950). *Problems of Social Policy*. London: HMSO.

Titmuss, Richard M. (1956). *The Social Divisions of Welfare: Some Reflections on the Search for Equity*. Liverpool: Liverpool University Press.

Titmuss, Richard M. (1958). *Essays on "The Welfare State."* London: George Allen and Unwin.

Tocqueville, Alexis de ([1835] 1997). *Memoir on Pauperism*. Chicago: Ivan Dee.

Tomlinson, Jim (1987). *Employment Policy: The Crucial Years, 1939–1955*. Oxford: Oxford University Press.

Tout, Herbert (1938). *The Standard of Living in Bristol*. Bristol: Arrowsmith.

Townsend, Peter (1981). "The Structured Dependency of the Elderly: A Creation of Social Policy in the Twentieth Century." *Ageing and Society* 1: 5–28.

Townsend, Peter (2010). *The Peter Townsend Reader.* Bristol: Policy Press.

Trainor, Richard H. (1993). *Black Country Élites: The Exercise of Authority in an Industrialized Area, 1830–1900.* Oxford: Clarendon.

Treble, John G. (1987). "Sliding Scales and Conciliation Boards: Risk-Sharing in the Late 19th Century British Coal Industry." *Oxford Economic Papers* 39: 679–98.

Tressell, Robert ([1955] 2005). *The Ragged Trousered Philanthropists.* Oxford: Oxford University Press.

Trevelyan, Sir Charles (1870). *Three Letters on London Pauperism.* London: Longmans, Green.

Veit-Wilson, John (1992). "Muddle or Mendacity? The Beveridge Committee and the Poverty Line." *Journal of Social Policy* 21: 269–301.

Veit-Wilson, John (1994). "Condemned to Deprivation? Beveridge's Responsibility for the Invisibility of Poverty." In John Hills et al., eds., *Beveridge and Social Security: An International Retrospective.* Oxford: Clarendon. Pp. 97–117.

Watson, Alfred W. (1920). "Unemployment Insurance Bill." *Journal of the Institute of Actuaries* 52: 72–80.

Watts, Harold (1968). "An Economic Definition of Poverty." In Daniel P. Moynihan, ed., *On Understanding Poverty: Perspectives from the Social Sciences.* New York: Basic Books. Pp. 316–29.

Watts, John ([1866] 1968). *The Facts of the Cotton Famine.* London: Frank Cass.

Waugh, Edwin (1867). *Home-Life of the Lancashire Factory Folk during the Cotton Famine.* London: Simpkin, Marshall.

Webb, Augustus D. (1912). "The Building Trade." In Sidney Webb and Arnold Freeman, eds., *Seasonal Trades.* London: Constable. Pp. 312–93.

Webb, Beatrice (1926). *My Apprenticeship.* London: Longmans, Green.

Webb, Beatrice (1948). *Our Partnership.* London: Longmans, Green.

Webb, Josephine (2000). "Social Security." In A. H. Halsey and Josephine Webb, eds., *Twentieth-Century British Social Trends.* New York: St. Martin's. Pp. 548–83.

Webb, Sidney, and Beatrice Webb (1897). *Industrial Democracy.* London: Longmans, Green.

Webb, Sidney, and Beatrice Webb (1909a). *The Minority Report of the Poor Law Commission. Part I: The Break-Up of the Poor Law.* London: Longmans, Green.

Webb, Sidney, and Beatrice Webb (1909b). *The Minority Report of the Poor Law Commission. Part II: The Public Organization of the Labour Market.* London: Longmans, Green.

Webb, Sidney, and Beatrice Webb (1911). *The Prevention of Destitution.* London: Longmans, Green.

Webb, Sidney, and Beatrice Webb (1929). *English Poor Law History. Part II: The Last 100 Years.* Vol. 1. London: Longmans, Green.

Webster, Charles (1982). "Healthy or Hungry Thirties?" *History Workshop* 13: 110–29.

Wells, H. G. ([1905] 1967). *A Modern Utopia.* Lincoln: University of Nebraska Press.

Western, Bruce, et al. (2012). "Economic Insecurity and Social Stratification." *Annual Review of Sociology* 38: 341–59.

Wilkinson, J. Frome (1891). *Mutual Thrift.* London: Methuen.

Williams, Gertrude (1936). *The State and the Standard of Living.* London: P. S. King.

Williams, Karel (1981). *From Pauperism to Poverty.* London: Routledge & Kegan Paul.

Williamson, Jeffrey G. (1984). "British Mortality and the Value of Life, 1781–1931." *Population Studies* 38: 157–72.

Williamson, Jeffrey G. (1990). *Coping with City Growth during the British Industrial Revolution.* Cambridge: Cambridge University Press.

Williamson, Jeffrey G. (1995). "The Evolution of Global Labor Markets since 1830: Background Evidence and Hypotheses." *Explorations in Economic History* 32: 141–96.

Winter, J. M. (1983). "Unemployment, Nutrition and Infant Mortality in Britain, 1920–50." In J. Winter, ed., *The Working Class in Modern British History: Essays in Honour of Henry Pelling*. Cambridge: Cambridge University Press. Pp. 232–56.

Witmer, Helen Leland (1932). "English Health Insurance and the Poor Law: The Health Insurance Acts and the Number of Persons Relieved." *Social Service Review* 6: 83–107.

Wohl, Anthony S. (1968). "The Bitter Cry of Outcast London." *International Review of Social History* 13: 189–245.

Wohl, Anthony S. (1970). "Introduction." In Andrew Mearns, *The Bitter Cry of Outcast London*. New York: Humanities Press, pp. 9–50.

Wood, George H. (1900). "Trade Union Expenditure on Unemployed Benefits since 1860." *Journal of the Royal Statistical Society* 63: 81–92.

Wood, George H. (1901). "Stationary Wage-Rates." *Economic Journal* 11: 151–56.

Wood, George H. (1910). *The History of Wages in the Cotton Trade during the Past Hundred Years*. London: Sherratt and Hughes.

Woodroofe, Kathleen (1977). "The Royal Commission on the Poor Laws, 1905–09." *International Review of Social History* 22: 137–64.

Wright, Thomas (1868). *The Great Unwashed*. London: Tinsley Brothers.

Wrightson, Keith (2000). *Earthly Necessities: Economic Lives in Early Modern Britain*. New Haven, Conn.: Yale University Press.

Wrigley, E. A., and R. S. Schofield (1981). *The Population History of England 1541–1871: A Reconstruction*. Cambridge: Cambridge University Press.

Young, Michael, and Peter Willmott (1957). *Family and Kinship in East London*. London: Routledge and Kegan Paul.

Youngs, Frederic A. (1979; 1991). *Guide to the Local Administrative Units of England*. 2 vols. London: Offices of the Royal Historical Society.

INDEX

The Princeton Economic History of the Western World
Joel Mokyr, Series Editor

A NOTE ON THE TYPE

This book has been composed in Adobe Text and Gotham.
Adobe Text, designed by Robert Slimbach for Adobe,
bridges the gap between fifteenth- and sixteenth-century
calligraphic and eighteenth-century Modern styles.
Gotham, inspired by New York street signs, was designed
by Tobias Frere-Jones for Hoefler & Co.